The Banality
of Indifference

Zionism and the Armenian Genocide

The Banality
of Indifference

Yair Auron

Transaction Publishers
New Brunswick (U.S.A.) and London (U.K.)

Third paperback printing 2007

Copyright © 2000 by Transaction Publishers, New Brunswick, New Jersey.

This volume was made available to the English-reading public through a grant from the Zoryan Institute for Contemporary Armenian Research and Documentation, Cambridge, Massachusetts, Toronto, Ontario.

Library of Congress Catalog Number: 00-021063
ISBN: 978-0-7658-0881-3
Printed in the United States of America

Library of Congress Cataloging-in-Publication Data

Auron, Yair.
  [Banaliyut shel ha-adishut. English]
  The banality of indifference : Zionism and the Armenian genocide / Yair
Auron ; translated by Maggie Bar-Tura.
    p. cm.
  Includes bibliographical references (p.) and index.
  ISBN 0-7658-0881-1 (paper: alk. paper)
  1. Armenian massacres, 1915–1923. 2. Genocide—Armenian—Moral
and ethical aspects. 3. Jews—Palestine—History. 4. Zionism—Palestine—
History 5. Palestine—History—1917–1948. 6. Hebrew literature, Modern—History and criticism. 7. Genocide in literature. 8. Armenian massacres, 1915–1923, in literature. I. Title.

DS195.5 .A9713 2000
956.6'2—dc21   00-021063

Contents

Prologue

This study seeks to examine both the attitudes of the Jewish community (the Yishuv) in Palestine (Eretz Yisrael) and of the Zionist leadership toward the massacres committed by the Turks against the Armenians at the turn of the twentieth century. These atrocities began in the last decade of the nineteenth century and reached their peak in the massive destruction of Armenians during the First World War. This book seeks also to make the reader aware of the genocide of the Armenian People.

At the same time, the book raises theoretical and philosophical questions, particularly in the introduction and final two chapters, which relate directly and indirectly to the specific subject of our research: the debate over the concept of genocide, and the uniqueness of the Holocaust in comparison to other instances of genocide, including the Armenian genocide.

The opening chapter presents a short historical survey of the history of the Armenians and a description of the events connected to their destruction. Part of the body of research discusses the events in Palestine during the First World War which, directly and indirectly, subjectively and objectively, were related to the destruction of the Armenians. The purpose of the discussion is to expose an aspect of the history of the Yishuv during the War from a perspective previously neglected by the historiography.

The central part of the book comprises chapters that discuss "The Reactors" (to the destruction of the Armenians) and "The Indifferent" (to it). The quantitative division between "The Reactors" (the larger part) and "The Indifferent" (the smaller part) should not mislead us. In reality, the vast majority of the Yishuv was indifferent and only a small minority reacted.

This research is the result of an ongoing effort to examine a subject that has been repressed and ignored in the Israeli historical and collective memory, as well as in the collective memory of the world, and thus has disappeared from our historical consciousness. I became involved in the subject in the framework of my activity as a researcher of contemporary Jewish studies and as an educator. I was troubled by a sense of oppressive discomfort and criticism of the evasive behavior, verging on denial, of the various governments of Israel regarding the memory of the Armenian genocide and I wanted to examine both the overt factors and the deeper and more complex factors leading to such behavior which to me seems morally unacceptable, particularly since we Jews were victims of the Holocaust.

After I began to explore the motives for the present behavior regarding the Armenian genocide, I realized that the issues must be examined from the beginning, i.e., from the period in which they occurred. For more than ten years, I have been involved in the subject and my research has carried me to unanticipated places and events. It has revealed to me, I must confess, a reality that I did not expect. I had hoped to find a greater degree of identification with the suffering of the Armenians, more empathy, and more attempts to help, within the scope of our very limited possibilities. Instead I found much indifference and an attitude that stressed the particular rather than the universal.

I have chosen as the motto of the present book a passage from our Jewish sources: "Thus was created a single man, to teach us that every person who loses a single soul, it shall be written about him as if he has lost the entire world, and every person who sustains a single soul it shall be written about him as if he has sustained the entire world." (*Mishna, Sanhedrin,* IV, 5).

This passage was revised in later versions and the phrase "from the People of Israel" was added so that the line no longer reads "every person who sustains" or "loses a single soul," but rather "every person who sustains or loses a single soul from the People of Israel." In editions of the *Mishna* generally available today we usually find the later "amended" version.[1]

In this context, it is worth quoting one sentence from "In Praise of Forgetting," a controversial article by Yehuda Elkana that appeared in the Hebrew daily newspaper, *Ha'aretz*, on March 2, 1988. Elkana wrote, "From Auschwitz came, in symbolic terms, two peoples: a minority which claims 'it will never happen again,' and a frightened and anxious majority which claims 'it will never happen to us again.'"

Between those two versions, in the tension between particularism and universalism, fluctuates Israeli society and the public debate within it. The crime of genocide is an extreme and total case of harm inflicted by human beings on other, innocent human beings. One of the indirect aims of this book is to increase our sensitivity to this aspect of human life—beyond what has happened to us; to raise awareness to the occurrence of genocide or genocidal acts in the past and the present, before our very eyes, and to the danger of its occurrence in the future. In the course of recent years such atrocities took place on a broad scale in the former Yugoslavia and in Rwanda. It is important, I believe, to encourage the individual to think about this phenomenon, to examine his stand, his personal responsibility, and his possibilities to react. Genocide is an evil against which we must struggle in order to minimize its appearance as far as possible.

A necessary, although certainly insufficient, condition for confronting this evil is knowledge and awareness of the existence of evil and the circumstances of its occurrence. Those who stand on the sidelines inevitably give succor to the murderers, never to the victims. Morally, we cannot sit idly in the face of criminal acts of genocide. We cannot accept the argument that "nothing can be done...such things happen." Evil does not cease to be evil when it hurts another.

I wish to express special thanks to two people whose help went far beyond what is generally found among researchers. In moments when I despaired over the slow progress of my research, or when I doubted its relevance and importance, they never failed to encourage and support me. They are Dr. Haim Zeligman, researcher at the Yad Tabenkin Research Institute and member of Kibbutz Givat Brenner, and George Hintilian, historian and member of the Armenian community of east Jerusalem.

My thanks also to my friends Dr. Ariel Horowitz and Orly Zarfati, who joined with me in developing a curriculum for the teaching of "Sensitivity to the World's Suffering: Genocide in the Twentieth Century," and to Avi Antman for his friendship and unflagging support. Thanks also to Ms. Amira Hagani, who edited this book with skill and dedication, and to Ms. Maggie Bar-Tura for her excellent translation.

The people of the Nili Archives in Zichron Yaakov, the Central Zionist Archives, the Nubar Pasha Armenian Archives in Paris, and the staff of the Yad Tabenkin Library at the Efal Seminar Center, have my gratitude for their assistance and their unfailing courtesy.

I am also grateful to the Memorial Foundation for Jewish Culture for its generous grant. I extend my thanks to the Zoryan Institute for Contemporary Armenian Research and Documentation, Cambridge, Massachusetts, and Toronto, Ontario, for its generous support in making this book available to the English-reading public. I would especially like to thank Kourken M. Sarkissian and Dr. Levon Chorbajian for their encouragement, as well as Professor Vahakn N. Dadrian for his remarks on the English translation. The English edition has been revised and updated, making use of additional sources that have become available.

My thanks also to Dr. Irving Louis Horowitz, Ms. Mary E. Curtis, and Laurence Mintz from Transaction Publishers for their professional assistance.

No one is to be held accountable for the book's shortcomings, for which I alone take responsibility.

Dr. Yair Auron
Tel Aviv, 1999

Note

1. See on this subject the important essay by Haim Yehuda Roth, "The Moral Fluctuation in Jewish Ethics," in his book, *Religion and Human Values* (Jerusalem: Magnes Publishers, 1973), pp. 89-91. Haim Yehuda Roth points to the fact that the commentaries almost never address this and writes, "This fact leads one to reflect that our great teachers, who reveal such deep sensitivity to the most minute details of history and philology, are afflicted by amazing obtuseness in everything having to do with morality."

Introduction

Conflicting Interpretations

This book explores the attitudes of the Yishuv, the small Jewish community in Palestine, and of the Zionist movement toward the Armenian People, and the atrocities the Armenians suffered at the hands of the Turks at the beginning of this century, which reached their height during the First World War. The Turkish slaughter of the Armenians during 1915-16 was one of the most horrible deeds of modern time. Henry Morgenthau, Sr., the American ambassador to Turkey at the time, described it as "the greatest crime in modern history...." "Among the blackest pages in modern history this is the blackest of them all." Morgenthau was one of the few people who tried to assist the Armenians, insofar as circumstances allowed, in order to contain the scope of their destruction.

The First World War ended in the victory of the Allied Powers: the United States, England, and France. The Armenians believed that with the war's end these nations would help them attain sovereignty and, indeed, during the course of the war explicit declarations were made to that effect. However, the declarations were not realized and the Armenians remained without a sovereign state of their own. For many years they were forced to make do with an Armenian Republic within the borders of the former Soviet Union.

The Second World War was to bear witness to the Holocaust, making humanity aware of deeds even more evil and widespread than those that had occurred during the First World War. Three years after the war's end, Israel achieved its independence, largely due to the efforts of the Zionist movement. The correlation of "Holocaust-Rebirth" became

5

one of the central motifs in the historical consciousness of the young Jewish state. The Holocaust has become a formative component, not only in the historical memory and in the Jewish-Israeli identity of Israeli Jews, but in the identity of Diaspora Jewish communities as well. The Jewish community of North America, which, for the most part, had no direct experience of the events in Europe, was affected no less deeply, and over the years the Holocaust became a touchstone in the collective memory of Western European and American society. The Holocaust Memorial Day is noted on the American civil calendar. Yet the Armenian genocide has remained the private historic memory of the Armenian People. The triumphant allies, who had ignored the Armenians, chose largely not to recollect the tragedy. The Turks denied—and continue to deny vehemently—the crimes they committed against the Armenians, belittling the scope and significance of deeds intended utterly to destroy a civilian population. The memorial day of the Armenian genocide does not appear on the American calendar; several editions of the *Encyclopedia Britannica* mention it in only one brief sentence; and it is mentioned only in passing in the *Encyclopedia Judaica*.

There were, of course, exceptions. One of those who was deeply shocked was the writer, Franz Werfel, whose opus about the Armenian massacre, *The Forty Days of Musa Dagh*, stirred many. Werfel, a Jew, was born in Prague, lived in Vienna, and served in the German army during the First World War. After the German annexation of Austria in 1938, he fled to France and from there to the United States.

The idea for his book was born in March 1929 during the course of a stay in Damascus. "The miserable sight of some maimed and famished-looking refugee children, working in a carpet factory, gave me the final impulse to snatch from the Hades [the mythological Greek Deity ruling the underworld] of all that was, this incomprehensible destiny of the Armenian nation," wrote Werfel. The book shocked millions throughout the world when it was published in Germany in 1933. Hitler had already come to power and *The Forty Days of Musa Dagh* was burned, together with other forbidden books. It was translated into Hebrew in 1934 and was widely read by young people in Palestine. Moreover, it had a significant impact on the members of the Jewish youth movements who established the Underground in the ghettos in Poland in 1942-43.[1]

Despite the reactions that Werfel's book inspired, the murder of the Armenian People was not incorporated into Western collective memory.

In retrospect, some would view the "forgotten genocide" of the Armenians as a portent. It came to be known as "the crime of silence," and the "prologue to the Holocaust." Hitler was quoted as saying, in August 1939, before the invasion of Poland, "It is a matter of indifference to me what a weak western European civilization will say about me...." He said that he sent the Death Squads to the east to destroy the Polish race without mercy because "only thus shall we gain the living space [Lebensraum] which we need. Who, after all, speaks today of the annihilation of the Armenians?"[2]

It may be an exaggeration to claim that the almost total lack of public debate and the absence of an international tribunal of the Turks for their massacre of the Armenians during the days of the Young Turk government enabled Hitler to believe that history would not hold him accountable for his crimes against humanity. Nonetheless, the fact that Hitler was aware of the Armenian massacre as a "crime without punishment" is significant and thought-provoking.

A connection between the Armenian genocide and the Holocaust is mentioned not only by the murderers. Among the small minority of the surrounding society that tried to help, the memory of the slaughter of the Armenians was part of a conscious and practical attempt to oppose the destruction of the Jews. The efforts of Henry Morgenthau, Jr., are a prime example. The son of the American ambassador in Constantinople during the massacre of the Armenians, Morgenthau, Jr., was Secretary of the Treasury in Roosevelt's wartime government. He was one of the public figures who tried to shake the American government out of its serene indifference to the destruction of the Jews. Morgenthau, Jr., is considered responsible for the change in U.S. government attitude toward the destruction of European Jewry and for the attempts to provide assistance, albeit too little and too late. At Morgenthau's insistence, he met with President Roosevelt on January 16, 1944, to discuss "the problem of the remaining Jews in Europe."[3]

In his conversation with President Roosevelt, Morgenthau warned of the failure of the American State Department to take effective steps to save the remnant of European Jewry. In addition, Morgenthau claimed to have clear proof that not only was the State Department ineffectual in its treatment of the problem, it was "actually taking action to prevent the rescue of the Jews." The protocol of the meeting indicates that the following points were raised during the discussion:

"The Secretary [Secretary of the Treasury Morgenthau] said he was convinced that effective action could be taken, and referred to the results that his father, Henry Morgenthau, Sr., had obtained when he was [United States] Ambassador to Turkey in getting Armenians out of Turkey and saving their lives."

The president stated that "he agrees that some effective action could be taken, and referred particularly to the movement of Jews through Rumania into Bulgaria." Following that meeting, President Roosevelt decided to establish without further delay the War Refugee Board.

Two Minorities

For many years the Jews and the Armenians lived as minorities in the shadow of great peoples and powers, different from them in their ethnic identity and their religious belief. A majority of the Armenians remained in their homeland after Armenia lost its independence and lived as Christians under Muslim Turkish rule for hundreds of years. The Jews were exiled from their country and returned only after many generations. During the last decades of the nineteenth century, a Jewish national liberation movement—the Zionist movement—began to grow, together with other expressions of Jewish nationalism. The same period saw the awakening of an Armenian national movement which sought autonomy, sovereignty, and freedom for the Armenians.

Both the small Jewish settlement in Palestine, which grew with the waves of Zionist immigration in the decades before the First World War, and the Armenian community within the historic borders of Armenia, were subject to the rule of the Ottoman Empire. The Jews, the Armenians, and the Greeks all enjoyed the status of a religious community of autonomous but secondary standing to Islam: a "millet."

The slaughter of the Armenians was carried out in the last decade of the nineteenth century, with additional massacres occurring in 1909. The rise of the Young Turks aroused great hopes among both the Zionists and the Armenians. During the war, both minorities suffered under the oppressive and brutal Turkish regime, but their fates were, in the end, very different. The brutalities of the Turkish rulers toward the Jewish population of Palestine ended with relatively small loss of life and minor damage to property while, on the other hand, the Armenians suffered the massacre of hundreds of thousands as part of a systematic plan of the Turkish government. As we shall see, controversy surrounds the estimate of the number of victims. Some estimate the number at a

Introduction 9

million men, women, and children; others claim that the number is far higher. The Arab population in Syria and Lebanon also suffered more severely than the Jewish population in Palestine.

It is worth noting that the Jewish population in Palestine feared a "similar fate," and was stricken with anxiety about potential disaster similar to the Armenian precedent. This book will not deal directly with the question of what saved the Jews from a "similar fate." The various explanations to this critical question will be explored in the course of discussion of various issues; was it the result of American intervention on behalf of the Jews, the involvement of Germany, a Turkish ally, in the execution of the Armenian genocide, the Jews' enlistment of public opinion and their power (real or imagined) over the international media, or perhaps the obedient behavior of the Jews, in contrast to the rebelliousness of the Armenians? Is it possible that the Turks had no interest in destroying the Jewish community in Palestine because the Jewish problem was less significant to them than other national problems, and when their interests changed, during the later stages of the war, they no longer had sufficient power?

Can the examination of two small and oppressed minorities justifiably raise questions about the importance of the attitude of the small, weak Jewish population in Palestine, barely managing to survive, toward the slaughter of the Armenians? Did the Jews even have the capability to take action?

On the practical level, the answer is clear. The Jewish population in Palestine was not able to offer real assistance, but deeds are only part, only one component of historical events. Attitudes, positions, and public opinion are all meaningful, at least on the ideological, moral, and ethical levels. We can hope that taking a position may sometimes bear direct results and influence events.

Research studies indicate three factors influencing genocide:

1. A powerful "sacrificer" or immolator who believes he has the power and that "suitable" circumstances exist to assist implementing and disguising the genocide.
2. A victim in a position of significantly inferior power vis-à-vis the sacrificer.
3. Everyone else—the others—observers and spectators who can affect the fate of the victim and sometimes even save him.

The "others" can be roughly divided into three categories. (1) The indifferent who do not intervene in the acts of murder. They may be shocked and revulsed. They may demur in elementary humanitarian terms, but no more than that. (2) The accomplices. (3) Those who assist the victims. We ought to examine the claim that those who remain on the sidelines always give comfort to the sacrificers and never to the victims. The great powers did little to prevent the mass murder of the Armenians during the First World War. England and France remained on the sidelines. The United States, and Ambassador Morgenthau in particular, tried to help by diplomatic and monetary means, limited by the fact that the U.S. was neutral during most of the war (until April 1917). In contrast, we find that concentrated pressure by the great powers during a previous Turkish massacre of the Armenians in the 1894-96 period was an important factor in bringing the slaughter to an end.

Germany, an influential ally of Turkey, although able to do much to stop the murders had no interest in doing so and was involved directly and indirectly in the Armenian genocide.[4] Furthermore, it has been claimed that German officers assisted the Turks in planning the destruction—in assembling and transporting the victims, and probably in developing the methods of destruction.[5] The Germans, no doubt, bear some of the responsibility and even some of the guilt for the mass murder of the Armenians in World War I. This view, as we shall see, was shared at the time of the events by Aaron Aaronsohn, a leading figure in Palestine.

Prior to the war and in its early stages, a large part of the Jewish community in Palestine and most of the leadership of the Zionist movement was pro-Turkish and pro-German, and some continued to support them almost to the end of the conflict. Supporters of the Turkish-German alliance believed the fate of the Zionist movement and the future of the Jewish community in Palestine was linked to that of the Ottoman Empire, and thus to that of Germany. The Zionist leaders leaned, for the most part, toward the Centrist powers that had either committed the atrocities against the Armenians or, at best, done nothing to prevent them. In retrospect, most of the leadership of the Zionist community in Palestine supported not only the losing side, but also the "bad" side—the immolators and the murderers.

The Zionists' support of Turkey and Germany had nothing to do, of course, with the murder of the Armenians, but one can nonetheless ask whether their support of the Centrist powers determined the Zionists' attitude and conduct (or lack thereof) toward the atrocities. The unavoidable conclusion is that it apparently did. Regarding the question of whether the atrocities against the Armenians changed Zionist orientation, the answer is no.

Again, we are not talking only about practical, concrete action. Considering the difficult circumstances in which the Zionists found themselves, it may have been impossible or nearly impossible to take action. It appears that, lacking any viable alternatives, the mass murder of the Armenians did not cause the Zionists to reconsider their position and rechart their political course, nor did it cause deep concern or moral outrage at the nature of their alliance.

The internationally oriented activists in the political wing of the Zionist movement understood at an early stage of its development that a patron in the form of a great power was needed to advance the movement's aims. This strategy began with Theodore Herzl, the founder of political Zionism, who tried to operate in Turkey, Germany, and afterwards in England. Herzl, himself, was aware of the Armenian question, which was part of the Ottoman Empire's agenda during the decades surrounding the beginning of the century.

We would be remiss if we did not recall that some of the public figures who supported the British were also remarkably silent about the disaster of the Armenians. To the best of our knowledge, no records can be found describing outrage on the part of leading Zionist supporters of the British, among them Jabotinsky and Joseph Trumpeldor, who knew of the atrocities committed against the Armenians. Jabotinsky's failure to react is surprising. When he mentions the massacre of the Armenians it is from the perspective of realpolitik, in the framework of Zionist policy and its postwar goals.

The pro-British Zionist leadership in London during the war, led by Chaim Weizmann and Nachum Sokolow, maintained connections from 1917 to 1920 with Armenian representatives, and both Weizmann and Sokolow expressed sympathy for the Armenian cause. The prime connection between the Zionists and the Armenians in London and Paris was the British diplomat Mark Sykes. Sykes' vision of a postwar Middle East was based on a Jewish-Arab-Armenian alliance under British influence. We will address this unrealized vision later. Sykes, it should be remembered, was a key figure in the British government and instrumental in bringing about the May 1916 Sykes-Picot Agreement, which drew the post-First World War division of the Middle East between the British and the French Empires, and the November 1917 Balfour Declaration which expressed: "His Majesty's favor [for] the establishment in Palestine of a national home for the Jewish people."

If lack of response is to be condemned, there may be "extenuating circumstances" that explain this lack of sensitivity to the sorrows of others. We must judge the Zionist lack of reaction within the context of the desperate situation of the Jewish community in Palestine, which was, at that time, struggling to survive. Well-grounded concerns, both objective and subjective, placed the future of the Zionist endeavor in doubt. There was grave fear that the efforts of decades, which had finally begun to bear fruit, would have been for naught and that the Yishuv would not survive the war. When the question of the Yishuv's attitudes to the Armenian tragedy is raised, the answer is usually that the Jewish population and its leadership put all of their energy into survival, to ensure that the "Armenian experience" would not be repeated in Palestine. The tiny Yishuv was almost totally self-absorbed.

This study also reveals that there were very few reservations about the Turks and the Germans, and their deeds against the Armenians. It can be argued, not without a great deal of truth, that the Yishuv and the Zionist leadership had no other options and yet it is surprising that we found no evidence of condemnation in journals, internal protocols, and letters. The official Yishuv behaved as if the Armenians were not their affair. The only concern was that what had happened to the Armenians should not happen to them.

The position of the Nili group, a small Jewish underground intelligence organization in Palestine, was unique in its overt sympathy for the Armenian victims. We will discuss at length the significance of the Armenian massacre for Nili. Weizmann and Sokolow in London also condemned the atrocities, and there were additional expressions of outraged identification in writings, newspapers, and literature, at various times by individuals including Itamar Ben Avi, Bernard Lazare, Yaakov Rabinovitch, and Aharon Reuveni. Neither political orientation nor pro-British leanings fully explain why these particular individuals spoke out.

The decision of an individual or a group of individuals to protest and to attempt to act to the extent they are able is complex, involving several levels of one's personality and values. Why do two people react differently in the face of human suffering? Why, as Eitan Belkind describes in his memoirs, does one endanger oneself, writing and reporting about the murder of the Armenians, in an attempt to arouse the world? And why does the recipient of the report, resident in a safe place, return the letter, as his cousin did?[6] How did Avshalom Feinberg dare, even as he was attempting to build the pro-British Nili spy network, to criticize British indifference to the plight of the Armenians?

During the First World War, there were a number of visitors from Palestine to the American Embassy in Constantinople. We can assume that many of them saw the list of donors to the Armenian cause. Why then was Yitzchak (Lyova) Schneerson the only one to remark at the large number of American Jews among the donors: "what unseen sensibility arouses our Jewish brothers to come to the aid of the Armenians?" he asked in his journal in 1916.[7]

Numbers of young Jews from Palestine served in the Turkish army during the First World War. Others tried to avoid conscription, and among those who served, some eventually deserted. We have not found a connection between the decision to desert and the Turkish atrocities against the Armenians. Did the deserters think about such a connection?

There are no clear-cut answers to these questions. We will relate to them through the historical sources at hand. Even if the explanation for the official disregard is to be found in the immediate and compelling concern of the Yishuv for its own survival, the fact remains that the individuals who spoke out against the Armenian genocide were capable of sensitivity to the suffering of others, despite their own desperate personal circumstances.

The Victims—The Particular and the Universal

We have mentioned the fact that the Jews and the Armenians were both minorities subjected for years to the oppressive rule of national-religious majorities. It would be fair to say that both groups were, in their own eyes and in the eyes of others, vulnerable and tempting victims par excellence.

The study of genocide is a relatively new field of research that has flourished in recent decades due to the incidence of acts of genocide in the twentieth century and most particularly the Holocaust. One of the most difficult questions surrounding such research is whether one can construct conceptual frameworks and categorical definitions concerning genocide. Questions also arise concerning the uniqueness of the Holocaust and the possibility of comparing it to other instances of genocide in general and to the Armenian experience in particular.

This study does not intend to draw an analogy between the genocide of the Armenian People and the Holocaust that befell the Jewish People.

We must recognize the unique factors involved in the Holocaust of the Jews that result in a significant difference between the two events. The conflict between the Armenians and the Turks was free of racial dimensions. It was a bloody ethnoreligious conflict, within the larger framework of nationalist struggles for independence, in which a powerful adversary destroyed a large civilian population, yet there does not seem to have been an intention of total eradication to the very last Armenian. Nonetheless, Armenians in most regions were affected, and Armenian women were bought, sold, raped, and forcibly married to Turkish men.

While there is no justification for the Turkish deeds, we must also remember that a small revolutionary segment of the Armenian people was a rebellious, agitating, unsubmissive element in the crumbling Ottoman Empire. Furthermore, the Armenians themselves acted violently upon certain targeted oppressors in several locations. There is an ongoing debate about the significance, meaning, and interpretation of the differences between the destruction of the Armenian People and the Holocaust of the Jews. Armenian historians and Armenians, in general, tend to emphasize the similarities between the two events, sometimes adopting the term "Holocaust" in describing the disaster that befell them. Israeli historians, on the other hand, seek to emphasize the singularity of the Holocaust.

Yehuda Bauer, a preeminent Israeli historian of the Holocaust, distinguishes between "Holocaust," "the policy of the total, sacral Nazi act of mass murder of all Jews they could lay hands on," and "genocide," "which was horrible enough, but did not entail *total* murder if only because the subject people were needed as slaves."[8] Bauer points out that "clearly what was happening to quite a number of people in Nazi Europe was genocide." He goes on to say that "not to see the difference between the concepts, not to realize that the Jewish situation was unique, is to mystify history. On the other hand, to declare that there are no parallels, and that the whole phenomenon is inexplicable, is equally a mystification." Bauer recalls the partial parallel of the Gypsies during the Nazi period and the murder of most of the Armenian population in Anatolia at the hands of Enver Pasha's soldiers during the First World War. After briefly describing the points of difference between the two events, he writes, "The Armenian massacres are indeed the closest parallel to the Holocaust."[9]

Another prominent Israeli historian, Israel Gutman, also compares the Holocaust to mass murders that occurred prior to, or after, the Second World War. Gutman explores the difference between the case of the

Jews and that of the Armenians and the Gypsies. He stresses the totality of the Jewish Holocaust and the fact that "the essence of the Holocaust is murder which was given the imprimatur of ideology."[10] Gutman asserts that the Holocaust cannot be viewed as an example of genocide. He emphasizes,

> In truth, the trend of unification, to stress the similarities and uniform aspects of the historical events mentioned [such as the murder of the Armenians and the slaughter in Biafra] to the Holocaust of the Jews in World War II, is of secondary importance. The difference and the distinction are decisive, indicating the uniqueness of the Holocaust as an historical phenomenon.[11]

Gutman sums up:

> The Holocaust is distinct from similar crimes and is an unprecedented event in the history of the Jews and of humanity....Blurring the uniqueness of the Holocaust, or integrating it into a long list of crimes, even if done out of good intentions, aids in distorting the historical picture and may encourage the rebirth of the murderous ideology. Therefore, understanding its uniqueness demands not only the obligation of remembrance but also the perception of the meaning of the events and the dangers embodied in them.[12]

This approach, which seeks to distinguish between "genocide" and the "holocaust" that befell the Jews in Europe, viewing the Holocaust as a unique event, is expressed in *The Encyclopedia of the Holocaust, whose* chief editor was, again, Israel Gutman. The entry for "genocide" ends thus:

> The experts on the subject all agree that genocide is a component of the Holocaust, but it has been contended that the Nazi crime against the Jewish people was unique and extended far beyond genocide, by virtue of the planning that it entailed, the task forces allocated to it, the killing installations set up for it, and the way the Jews were rounded up and brought to extermination sites by force and by stealth, and above all, because of the stigma and charge of collective guilt with which the Jews as a whole were branded —of being a gang of conspirators and pests whose physical destruction must be carried out for the task of society's rehabilitation and the future of mankind. *All of this creates a unique kind of crime, more comprehensive and widespread than genocide* [My emphasis].[13]

It is worth remembering: the term "genocide" was first used in 1933 by the Jewish legal expert, Raphael Lemkin, at a legal conference in Madrid, and further defined and analyzed in his writings during the Second World War. The concept of genocide was accepted in the international legal system as the comprehensive definition of the destruction of a people. On December 9, 1948, the United Nations General Assembly adopted a convention for "The Prevention and Punishment of the Crime of Genocide."

The term has since been used in various contexts to mean the murder of human beings because of their affiliation with a racial, ethnic, or religious group, regardless of individual guilt, solely with intent to destroy the group in whole or in part.[14]

The convention adopted by the United Nations specifically mentions the commission of the following acts—meant to hurt, fully or partially, national, ethnic, racial, or religious groups—as elements of the crime of genocide:

1. Killing members of the group;
2. Causing serious bodily or mental harm to members of the group;
3. Deliberately inflicting on the group conditions of life calculated to bring about its physical destruction in whole or in part;
4. Imposing measures intended to prevent births within the group;
5. Forcibly transferring children of the group to another group.

In his penetrating essay, "European History as Background to the Holocaust," historian Yaakov Talmon writes about the destruction of European Jewry, "Thus this campaign of destruction is utterly different from all the slaughters, the mass murders, the bloodlettings and destruction of life throughout history." After noting several examples, including the pogroms in Poland in 1648-49, he goes on to state that the Holocaust was different even from the slaughter of the Armenians and the Greeks at the hands of the Turks in various periods.

The Nazis' destruction of European Jewry was exceptional among all mass murders in the detailed and exact planning which preceded it and in its systematic implementation; in its unemotional cold-bloodedness; in the decision—diligently implemented—to wipe out everyone so that not a trace would remain; in the prevention of any possibility that one might avoid one's fate—by surrendering or by joining one's enemies, by conversion or by enslavement.[15]

Other Israeli historians do not compare the two events nor do they analyze and compare the concepts of genocide and holocaust. An exceptional study is Yisrael Ring's book, *Are There Laws in Genocide*, which explores the possibility of categorizing instances of genocide throughout history, including the Holocaust. Ring terms the Armenian genocide "a model for recent history," or a "purifying precedent" which laid the ground for the Holocaust. Thus, that most extreme of tragedies, the Holocaust, is not the first instance of institutionalized mass murder.[16]

Among those who have explored the philosophical and theological aspects of whether the Holocaust was unprecedented are Eliezer Schweid, Emil Fackenheim, and American philosopher, Richard Rubinstein.[17] In contrast to the approach that tends to stress the uniqueness and singularity of the Holocaust, at least some of the researchers outside of Israel, among them Jews, categorize the Holocaust as genocide. While they may or may not note the uniqueness of the Holocaust, they assert that every instance of genocide is unique.

The Jewish historian, Helen Fein, deals with the Holocaust in her book, *Accounting for Genocide*, and the victimization that preceded it.[18] The characteristics of the process were, according to Fein, similar in the case of the Armenians in Turkey and the Jews in Germany. At the same time, Fein indicates the differing political role of the Armenians who could challenge the central political regime and of the Jews in Germany who were most likely to view themselves as "Germans" of the Jewish faith. The prior conditions which led, in her view, to the premeditated genocide of both the Armenians and the Jews were

1. The victims have previously been defined outside the universe of obligation of the dominant group: exclusion of the Jews from the Christian world, exclusion of the Armenians from the Islamic world.
2. The rank of the state has been reduced by defeat in war and or internal strife—in the case of Turkey, the weakening of the Ottoman Empire; in the case of Germany, its defeat in the First World War.
3. The rise to power of an elite which adopts a new political formula to justify a nation's domination and/or expansion, idealizing the singular rights of the dominant group—in the case of the Armenians, the rise of the Young Turks and pan-Turanism; in the case of the Jews, the rise of Nazism.
4. The calculus of costs of exterminating the victim—a group excluded from the circle circumscribed by the political formula—changes as the perpetrators instigate or join a (temporarily) successful coalition at war against antagonists who have earlier protested and/or might conceivably be expected to protest persecution of the victim: Turkey enters the First World War as an ally of Germany.

According to Fein, there are both differences in the background and parallels in the prior conditions that led to the genocide of the Armenians and the Holocaust.

Another researcher, Robert Melson, wrote *Revolution and Genocide*, which he dedicated to his grandparents who perished in Treblinka in 1942.[19] Melson concludes that inasmuch as the genocide of the Armenians and the Holocaust both were total domestic genocides of peoples, they are essentially different from other instances of genocide and mass destruction in the modern era. Analysis of the events indicates, says Melson, that the two instances of genocide were

1. A product of revolutionary transformation in the Ottoman Empire and in imperialistic Germany.
2. The victims were ethnoreligious groups with a traditionally low status that had dramatically improved its socioeconomic situation in modern times.
3. Both instances of genocide occurred during a world war.

Thus, claims Melson, there is a similar etiology.[20] Nonetheless, he recognizes significant differences between the two genocides, including the status of the Armenians in the Ottoman Empire versus the status of the Jews in Europe, and the intentions and methods of the perpetrators. The Jews, historically, were stigmatized pariahs in Europe, different from the status of *dhimmis,* ascribed to the Armenians; messianic German racism and the device of the death camp were significantly different from Turkish nationalist ideology and the process of massacre and starvation which characterized the Armenian genocide.

Melson points out three differences: First, because of the difference in the social and territorial status of the Jews and the Armenians, the reactions to the aspirations of the Jews in Germany were different from the reaction to those of the Armenians in Turkey. An anti-Armenian ideology equivalent to European anti-Semitism never developed in the Ottoman Empire. Second, because the reach of Nazi millenarian racism was wider than the Turkish Committee of Union and Progress's integral nationalism, the scope of the Holocaust was broader than the Armenian genocide. The Young Turks were motivated by nationalism, not by racism. Third, comparison of the methods of extermination reveals that while the death camps were a successful adaptation to the exigencies of mass murder in the Third Reich, less sophisticated methods, including repeated massacres and mass starvation, can be efficient in implementing total domestic genocide.[21]

At the same time, Melson believes that these differences do not substantially weaken the comparison between the two cases. On the contrary, the differences in etiology and methods of destruction enable us to understand how a total domestic genocide proceeded under specific conditions.

Two additional researchers, Frank Chalk and Kurt Jonassohn, published a book in 1990 which deals with the history and sociology of the phenomenon of genocide.[22] In addition to a conceptual framework of genocide, a definition of genocide and its prior conditions, they present a typology of genocide and a historical survey of its occurrence. The book surveys twenty-two cases of genocide and murder with the characteristics of genocide, from ancient times (3000-1000 B.C.), and including the massacre of the Indians in the seventeenth, eighteenth, and nineteenth centuries, the murder of the Hereros in South West Africa at the beginning of this century, the slaughter of the Armenians in Turkey, instances of genocide in Soviet Russia in the middle of this century, and the genocide of the Gypsies and the Holocaust of the Jews at the hands of Nazi Germany. Afterwards, Indonesia (1955-56), Bangladesh (1971), Burundi (1972), Cambodia (1975-78), and the mass murders in Eastern Timor (1975). They also mention the extermination of the Amazonian Indians during the course of the current century.

The sociologist and political scientist, Irving Louis Horowitz, studied the phenomenon of genocide, in general, and the Holocaust and the Armenian genocide, in particular, from the perspective of the social sciences.[23] In a controversial article, Horowitz attacked the tendency to emphasize the singularity of the Holocaust, taking exception to the debate, which he refers to as a "bizarre struggle"[24] among Holocaust survivors about what acts of extermination deserve the name of Holocaust. For Horowitz, the search for exclusivity in death has strange implications.

Horowitz rejects all of the attributes that, according to Fackenheim, make the Holocaust unique, citing examples from the Armenian experience and from the destruction of two million Cambodians—35-40 percent of that nation. He criticizes Fackenheim's theological approach, as well as Elie Wiesel's mystical approach, expressing reservations about the mystery of silence and the silence that surrounds mysterious acts. The role of the social sciences in this regard, as in other issues, says Horowitz, is to rationalize the irrational, obliging us to understand why genocide has occurred.

The Armenian genocide was part of the "historians' debate" which aroused public opinion in Germany and beyond during the years 1986-89. German historians of the first rank attempted, during that period, to revise painful sections of their country's scarred history during the Third Reich by banalization and relativization of the destruction of the Jews. As part of this revision, they compared the Holocaust to other cases of mass destruction, including the Armenian genocide.

Ernst Nolte, one of the outstanding German historians, claimed that Auschwitz was not a unique phenomenon. A similar case of genocide, he claimed, had been committed in 1915 when the Turks brutally murdered one and a half million Armenians. Nolte remarked that one of the founding fathers of Nazism, Max Erwin Von Scheubner-Richter, who was in Armenia at the time, described the massacre as "Asiatic barbarism." Less than a quarter of a century later, said Nolte, the Nazis committed similar crimes.[25] In books and essays, Nolte claimed that one can find many parallels to Auschwitz in the twentieth century, among them the murder of the Armenians, the genocide in Vietnam in the 1960s and 1970s, and in Afghanistan in the 1980s, as well as the murder of millions of Cambodians by the Pol Pot regime.[26] In Nolte's opinion, there have been so many crimes like the destruction of the Jews, in various countries, that it may be viewed as a "normal twentieth-century barbarity."[27] Nolte and other German historians compare Auschwitz to the gulags of Stalin's Soviet Union. Nolte goes on to say that not only were the Nazi atrocities similar to acts committed by other peoples, the Nazi policy of extermination was no more than an imitation of genocidal policies implemented by other nations. Andreas Hillgruber, one of the great experts on contemporary European history, has, through complex and torturous arguments, tried to emphasize the relativity of Auschwitz, presenting it in the context of other acts of genocide— Stalin's mass murders in 1939-40 and the Turkish destruction of the Armenians in 1915.[28] There is no doubt that the aim of Nolte, Hilgruber, Fest, and other neoconservative historians is to blur the distinctions and to ignore the uniqueness of the Holocaust.

The British historian, Evans, who has studied the "historians' debate," rightly rejects the tendentious nearsightedness of the German historians' approach. He negates the equation with the Allied bombing of German cities, the comparison with American policy in Vietnam in the 1960s and early 1970s, or with the Soviet invasion of Afghanistan in the 1980s. One cannot view these acts, severe and brutal as they were, as genocide. Thus he also justly rejects the equation of Auschwitz to the Soviet gulag and the Pol Pot regime in Cambodia. Evans points out the difference between these acts and the awful slaughter of the

Armenians by the Turks while emphasizing their difference from the acts of the Nazis:

> They were more deliberate, on a wider scale, and concentrated into a far shorter time, than the destruction of human life in Vietnam and Afghanistan, and they were not carried out as part of a military campaign, although they did occur in wartime. But these atrocities were committed as part of a brutal policy of expulsion and resettlement; they did not constitute an attempt to exterminate a whole people.[29]

> As the historian Michael Marus has pointed out, many Armenians stayed alive in Turkey during the massacre and the Turks felt no sense of failure when the slaughter ended without the eradication of the entire Armenian people or even most of it. Finally, the murder of the Armenians was the result of real political confrontations, not the fruit of an obsessive and paranoid fantasy.[30]

Evans rejects Helen Fein's charge that he is trying to deny or understate the severity of all instances of genocide, other than that of the Jews at the hands of the Nazis. He contends that there has been inflation in the use of the term, "genocide," "which though certainly less dramatic and more subtle than Nolte's position, arrives at the same result, albeit from a completely different direction."[31]

It is worth noting that Armenian historiography tends to distinguish both the Armenian experience and the Holocaust from all other instances of genocide, casting doubt on the validity of the Jewish approach to the Holocaust as "unique."[32] Armenian researchers frequently use the term "the Armenian Holocaust" to define the tragedy that befell their people.[33] Armenians sometimes quote a headline that appeared in the *New York Times*, September 10, 1895: "Another Armenian Holocaust." The secondary headline was, "Five Villages Burned, Five Thousand Persons Made Homeless."

Pierre Vidal-Naquet, the French-Jewish historian and thinker, also writes about the comparison between the two events, attitudes towards them, and denial of responsibility for murder:

> The Armenian case has always fascinated me...as a Jew I could not but be concerned about the similarities and differences in the fate of these two differing groups of humanity. One, like the other, has been the victim of an enormous historic crime; one, like the other, is torn between a center—real or imagined—and a diaspora; one, like the other, struggles against the most

demented ideologues, sometimes in its own midst; torn between the burden of remembrance of the past and a history which does not always liberate from memory, one, like the other, grapples with the big denial....[34]

In contrast, the American Jewish scholar, Steven T. Katz, claims that the Shoah (the Holocaust) is a "singular event in human history" and that "the Shoah is the only example of true Genocide—a systematic attempt to kill all the members of a group—in history."[35]

It thus seems, after this incomplete survey of interpretations, that a cautious claim can be made that the trend of comparison between cases of genocide, sometimes blurring the uniqueness and singularity of the Holocaust, particularly with regard to the massacre of the Armenians and the Gypsies, is growing in the international literature on the subject. On the other hand, the Jewish-Israeli discussion on the subject shows evidence, especially in recent years, of what may be a growing tendency to emphasize the exclusivity and uniqueness of the Holocaust and of Jewish suffering.

The claims of the Holocaust as exclusive and unique seem reasonable to me in light of their scientific and principled arguments. They certainly carry weight when the Holocaust is examined from the perspectives of European society and humanity as a whole. Various forces in the world, with a variety of motives, have tried and will continue to try to blur the unique nature of the Holocaust and there is no doubt that the stresses and needs of the present affect our view of the past.[36] At the same time, defining the Nazi genocide against the Jews as a crime unique in human history certainly does not mean acceptance or forgiveness of the collective crimes and acts of genocide which have disfigured the face of humanity in the twentieth century.

Totally different aspects come to the fore, I believe, in the Jewish-Israeli context. We must ask how we, as Jews, or perhaps more stringently, how we as Israeli Jews relate to the tragedies of others. While not losing sight of the enormity of the Holocaust, are we not obligated, nonetheless, to examine the similarities, that which is comparable, or analogous? The lines of comparison and of resemblance do not make events identical, but they may help us to describe the differences and the similarities. Furthermore, the claim of singularity has meaning only if we distinguish between what is the same and what is different.

Historical comparisons do not necessitate identical judgments regarding two events, nor obliteration of the differences between them.

On the contrary, historical comparisons locate and isolate the equivalent aspects in order to discern the differences between them. If we do not compare the Holocaust to other acts of genocide we cannot claim that it is unique. Only upon comparison can we see that the Holocaust is not identical to other genocides that have occurred. Israeli society has emphasized the unique, sometimes without comparison and without learning about the genocide perpetrated against other peoples. We must not be confused; similar cases are not identical cases, analogy is not identicalness.

A balanced approach, integrating both tendencies, is given expression in the Holocaust Museum in Washington, D.C. The museum emphasizes the singularity of the Holocaust while relating directly to the other victims of the Nazi regime, particularly the Gypsies. A mention of Hitler's words from August 1939 ("Who today remembers the massacre of the Armenians?") appears on the wall as a permanent exhibit in the museum.

In this context it is worthwhile to mention two important articles which appeared in the anthology, *A Mosaic of Victims, Non-Jews Persecuted and Murdered by the Nazis.*[37] The centerpiece of the anthology is a series of lectures delivered during three days of discussions held in 1987 on the controversial question: Who were the victims of the Holocaust? Can we distinguish between the Final Solution of the Jewish problem and the Nazi policy toward other ethnic and religious groups? If so, what are the distinctions?

One of the articles was written by the anthology's editor, Michael Berenbaum, the former director of the research institute of the Holocaust Museum in Washington, in which he emphasized "The Particularity and the Universality of the Holocaust." In Berenbaum's view, a comparison of the Holocaust to other instances of mass murder does not necessarily weaken the unique nature of the Holocaust, but rather clarifies it. For example, inclusion of the Armenian experience in a discussion about the Holocaust deepens our moral sensitivity and sharpens our perception and indicates generosity of spirit and adherence to moral principles. We must allow our suffering, despite our inability to share it, to unite us in the condemnation of inhumanity, rather than separating us in the arithmetic of catastrophes.[38]

In *Modernity and the Policy of Destruction*, philosopher Richard Rubinstein calls attention to the fact that genocide has become a fundamental characteristic of modern culture as we know it. In Rubinstein's estimate, there is a historical continuity between the random mass murders during the period of European demographic expansion beyond its territorial borders and the planned autocannibalism of our time.[39] I believe that this is the proper approach when examining the uniqueness of the Holocaust and that this approach will be increasingly accepted among students of the Holocaust and genocide in the future.

Israeli society frequently arrives at conclusions, meanings, and lessons of the Holocaust which are essentially Zionist and Jewish. Less frequently, it learns the universal lessons of that terrible experience: the tragedies of others are of more than minor importance. The Holocaust has become a primary component of our collective identity as Jews and Israelis, particularly for non-religious Jews.[40]

Thus the arguments for the singularity of the Holocaust appear in conscious and unconscious contexts, sometimes inappropriately. There are factual bases for both total uniqueness and total distinctiveness but there are, without question, also deeper impulses in some sectors of Israeli society drawn from a sense of "chosenness," isolation, and a belief in "a People that dwells alone," and in the xenophobic notion that "all the world is against us." Indeed, significant parts of Israeli society nurture the feeling of isolation and separation from the world.

From the perspective of the victims it does not matter if they have been condemned to death because of their membership in a particular racial group or because they are part of a national minority or a social class. From this perspective, condemnation of acts of genocide must be total, with no room for relativization, and study of the tragedies of others can highlight the universal significance of the Holocaust. Only a dialectical approach that combines the particular with the universal will enable Israeli society to create the necessary integration between our understanding of our Holocaust and our attitude toward other acts of genocide.

The 1920s and 1930s: The Once and Future Victim

The Jews and the Armenians were not just national-religious minorities who suffered at the hands of the majority and surrounding society. Each people was frequently a victim; their self-perception as victims became an important part of their self-identity when relating to the surrounding society.

The Armenians during the First World War and the Jews during the Second World War became the archetypal Victim. The parallel fate of these two peoples, of a persecuted minority that became a sacrificial victim, was apparent even before the disasters that befell them during the World Wars. The attitude of the Jews toward the slaughter of the Armenians during the First World War therefore raises questions about the relationship between the present and future victim on two levels: First, the Jews were, we shall see, terribly vulnerable at the very same time that the Armenians were being persecuted and this fact was of deep concern to them. Second, the Jews felt that what had happened to the Armenians (and from which they had been spared) during the First World War could happen to them, in one form or another, in the future.

Although this book does not deal with that period, a non-exhaustive, eclectic investigation reveals that the primary attitude of the Jewish community in Palestine toward the Armenian tragedy was one of a lesson to be learned: "Look what happened to the Armenians! We must ensure that such things will not happen to us; that we will not be seriously damaged; that we will not be forgotten by the world. The Armenians and the Assyrians symbolize what must never happen to us." Several reminders may suffice: in June 1937, prior to the publication of the British Royal Commission's report, the Zionist leader and thinker, Berl Katznelson, criticized the weakness of the Zionist leadership in London, "our London," which did not believe that the recent Arab riots against the Yishuv could be used as an argument in a diplomatic campaign to revise the terms of the British mandate: "They [the Zionist leadership in London] did not dare to proclaim that without accelerated large scale immigration of Jews [to Palestine], we will remain in Palestine like the Armenians in Turkey and the Assyrians in Iraq." That is, a persecuted minority.[41]

David Ben Gurion also related several times during the 1930s to the lessons of the Armenians and the massacre of the Assyrians, viewing their fate as a compelling and significant example of broken promises. Ben Gurion touched upon the massacre of the Assyrians, despite its limited scope (in August 1933, hundreds were murdered), apparently also because it was committed by Arabs.[42] He wrote in his journal, on June 17, 1936, that he had prepared questions for friends in the British Parliament, in the event of an attack against us by the Arab lobby. One of the questions was, "What does the massacre of the Assyrians in Iraq teach us?"[43]

At a meeting of the Jewish Agency Executive on May 19, 1936, during a debate on the establishment of a Royal Commission, Ben Gurion stated that the Balfour Declaration by itself is of little comfort and added,

I assume that I am speaking with people with great political understanding. Since the time when the Balfour Declaration was issued and the Mandate was confirmed, the Treaty of Versailles has been torn to shreds, and the covenant of the League of Nations, signed by 34 nations, is in tatters. The Assyrians were deceived; the Armenians were deceived. The Locarno Treaty, guaranteed by three great nations—England, Italy and France—has been nullified.

But, said Ben Gurion,

This is the paradox: It is not so easy to breach a contract with the Jews....The promise of a national home was made to the Armenians, and violated. The Armenians are Christians yet a million of their people were slaughtered during the War, and the promise made to them of a national home was broken. Despite the weakness and poverty of the Jews, it is apparently not so easy to break a promise made to the Jews.[44]

Moreover, during the 1920s and 1930s, a number of articles appeared in the press in Palestine, usually in the form of reportage, dealing with the Armenians and their fate. The articles expressed sympathy and identification with the tragedy and misery of the Armenian refugees in particular, together with criticism of the cynicism and hypocrisy of the community of nations. An article which appeared in *Contras*, a journal of the Jewish labor movement in Palestine, in 1920, is illustrative:

Wretched Armenia did not attain in San Remo even the vague promise that we were given. The rulers of the world, commanding great nations, found a democratic argument: there is no single piece of land in which the Armenians were a majority of the population, and no government is willing to take upon itself the mandate, nor the burden and the worry involved in one.[45]

Contras also quotes the London paper, *The Nation*, reporting that the massacre of the Armenians and the Greeks in Cilicia has resumed. England and France are doing nothing to stop it. "The source of this humiliating defeat is to be found in the competition between France and England," quotes *Contras* from the British paper.

Contras, number 62, from 1921, reports in its "World" section on the Armenian revolt and the establishment of an Armenian Republic in the Soviet Union in similar terms:

While the League of Nations was considering how to provide international aid to Armenia (each government volunteered only moral support to that wretched country for fear that France and England would use any more substantial aid for their own purposes), there has been a revolt in Armenia and that country has joined the community of Soviets.

The paper asserts that "the founding of a Soviet community in Armenia is an important victory for Bolshevik politics in the Near East."[46]

In a similar spirit, Hans Cohen writes in 1927 in *Hapoel Hatzair*, another journal of the Jewish labor movement in Palestine, about the "fate of the Armenian refugees."[47] He mentions the presence of 150,000 Armenian refugees in Syria and Lebanon, and analyzes the Armenian problem whose "humane and historical weight is not limited solely to the borders of Syria." Hans Cohen protests the impotence of the League of Nations and concludes thus:

> The great Armenian refugee camp located near Beirut, whose current sanitary and living conditions recall the awful days of the war, must remain for now to serve as a testimony that even though the need for war propaganda has passed, there is no place for the humanitarian goals of that great conflict, only for its aims of destruction. [48]

Additional expressions of this sort are to be found several times in the Palestine press of the 1920s and 1930s.[49]

After the First World War, Israel Zangwill (1864-1926) wrote several essays about the Armenian problem. Zangwill, an original and nonconformist thinker, assisted Theodore Herzl early in his career. He resigned from the Zionist Federation after the proposal to establish a Jewish Homeland in Uganda was rejected, and founded the Jewish Territorial Association. He wrote, "I bow before this higher majesty of sorrow. I take the crown of thorns from Israel's head and I place it up on Armenians."[50]

At the end of the Great War and during the early 1920s, Zangwill addressed the slaughter of the Armenians when discussing the subject of crime and punishment—punishment of Turkey for its crimes against the Armenians, and questions of justice and power in politics.[51]

In the years prior to the Second World War, an analogy to the Armenians was drawn by another nonconformist who had split from the Zionist mainstream—Abba Achimeir. Achimeir, a proponent of the plan to evacuate the Jews from Europe, wrote in 1936 (under the pseudonym, Abba Sikra) in his article, "The Alphabet of Zionism," "The Jews who oppose the evacuation plan, are the same ostriches who bury their

heads lest they see the approaching hunter.... The opponents of the evacuation plan are unwittingly creating the fate of the Armenians in Turkey
for their own people."[52]

Another significant reference to the fate of the Armenians and the
fear that the Jews may be doomed to a similar fate appears in a memorandum sent by Mordecai Bentov, a leader of the left-wing Hashomer
Hatzair movement, to Justice Louis D. Brandeis on October 21, 1938,
after the Evian Conference and before Kristallnacht. Brandeis offered
to convene a meeting, under the auspices of the American government,
of prominent figures (Brandeis himself, Winston Churchill, Lloyd
George, the Archbishop of Canterbury, Leon Blum, and others) in order to appeal to public opinion in the democratic world. After describing the tasks in organizing the meeting, he emphasized,

> Some of the directions suggested above may appear fantastic, but we are in
> an emergency situation which cannot be compared to anything which the
> Jewish People has faced for hundreds of years. It seems that everything
> hangs in the balance, and if we do not move mountains, we may be con-
> demned to the fate of the Armenians during the World War.[53]

Finally, we look at the writings of the journalist, Dr. S. Gross in
Ha'aretz Almanac, which appeared in the fall of 1943, at the height of
the Holocaust. Among the articles in this respected journal was a column which dealt with Diaspora Jewry. In summing up the situation of
Diaspora Jewry in 1942, Gross wrote,

> The fourth year of the war will be remembered in history as the year of
> violence greater than any other suffered by the Jewish People in recent
> generations. Not since the Chmielnicki Rebellion in Poland and the Ukraine
> in the middle of the seventeenth century have the Jews known such acts of
> mass destruction. The events of the past year exceed even the awful period
> of three hundred years ago. It is obvious that there is no possibility today to
> examine each and every piece of information. Despite the reservations which
> every historian must accept if he is to maintain his professional conscience,
> *it must be determined that the German regime has brought a holocaust
> upon the Jews of the European continent which has no parallel except that
> which befell the Armenian nation in the First World War* [My emphasis].[54]

In the fall of 1943, the unprecedented dimensions of the destruction
of the Jews were not yet known and the comparison to the murder of
the Armenians was not yet perceived as problematic. But the Holocaust
created a new and unprecedented reality and fundamentally changed

"standards of reference." The unique characteristics of the Holocaust, as well as its dimensions, were such that the analogy with the Armenian genocide was to be considered by some as inappropriate. We shall see later that additional national considerations were also brought to bear after the establishment of the State of Israel.

Notes

1. See chapter 7 in this book, "The Forty Days of Musa Dagh: Symbol and Parable."
2. For Hitler's comments on the Armenians, see K. B. Bardakjian, *Hitler and the Armenian Genocide* (Cambridge, MA: Zoryan Institute, 1985).
3. "The Problem of Saving the Remaining Jews in Europe," Memorandum for the Secretary's Files, F.D.R. Library, Hyde Park, NY, *Henry Morgenthau's Diaries*, book 688, part 2, p. 190.
4. For an engaging and valuable analysis of this important issue, see Vahakn N. Dadrian, *German Responsibility in the Armenian Genocide: A Review of the Historical Evidence of German Complicity* (Watertown, MA: Blue Crane Books, 1996).
5. Marjorie Housepian, "The Unremembered Genocide," *Commentary*, September 1976; Ulrich Trumpener, *Germany and the Ottoman Empire 1914-1918* (New York: Caravan Books, Delmar, 1989), pp. 200-70.
6. See the section on Eitan Belkind, "Witness to a Terrible Tragedy."
7. Y. L. Schneerson, *From the Journals of a Nili Member* (Haifa: Renaissance, 1967), p. 24 (Hebrew).
8. See Yehuda Bauer, "Against Mystification—The Holocaust as an Historical Phenomenon," in *The Holocaust in Historical Perspective* (Seattle: University of Washington Press), 1978, pp. 35-36.
9. Ibid., p. 36.
10. See Yisrael Gutman, "The Uniqueness and the Universal Character of the Holocaust," in *Struggles in Darkness* (Tel Aviv: Sifriat Poalim, 1985), p. 62 (Hebrew).
11. Ibid., p. 53.
12. Ibid., p. 68.
13. Genocide, *The Encyclopedia of the Holocaust* (New York: Macmillan Publishing Company, 1990), vol. 2, pp. 553-55 (Written by Marian Moshkat).
14. Ibid.
15. Yaakov Talmon, "European History as Background to the Holocaust," *In the Age of Violence* (Tel Aviv: Am Oved, 1975) (Hebrew).
16. Yisrael Ring, *Are There Laws in Genocide* (Tel Aviv: Sifriat Poalim, 1987), p.49 (Hebrew).
17. Eliezer Schweid, "Is the Holocaust Without Precedent?," *Battle at Dawn* (Tel Aviv: Hakibbutz Hameuchad, 1991) (Hebrew); Emil Fackenheim, "The Holocaust as a Unprecedented Event in History, Philosophy and Theology," *Daat*, no. 15, 1985 (Hebrew); Richard Rubinstein, *The Cun-*

ning of History (New York: Harper and Row, 1975); *The Age of Triage: Fear and Hope in an Overcrowded World* (Boston: Beacon, 1983). Rubinstein deals with the subject in other studies as well.

18. Helen Fein, *Accounting for Genocide: National Responses and Jewish Victimization During the Holocaust* (New York: The Free Press, 1959), pp. 3-18.
19. Robert F. Melson, *Revolution and Genocide: On the Origins of the Armenian Genocide and the Holocaust* (Chicago and London: The University of Chicago Press, 1992).
20. Ibid., p. 256.
21. Ibid., pp. 256-57.
22. Frank Chalk and Kurt Jonassohn, *The History and Sociology of Genocide: Analyses and Case Studies* (New Haven and London: Yale University Press, 1990).
23. Irving Louis Horowitz, *Taking Lives, Genocide and State Power* (New Brunswick, NJ: Transaction Publishers, 1980).
24. Irving Louis Horowitz, "Genocide and the Reconstruction of Social Theory," *Armenian Review* (spring 1984), vol. 37, no. 1, p.2.
25. Richard J. Evans, *In Hitler's Shadow: West German Historians and the Attempt to Escape from the Nazi Past* (New York: Pantheon Books, 1989), p. 27.
26. Ibid., p. 31.
27. Ibid., p. 32.
28. Ibid., pp. 45-65.
29. Ibid., p. 86.
30. Richard J. Evans, *In Hitler's Shadow* (Tel Aviv: Am Oved, 1991), p.104 (Hebrew edition).
31. Ibid., p. 169. "German Revisionism," *Present Tense*, November/December 1989, vol. 17, no. 1, pp. 2-5.
32. Vahakn N. Dadrian, "The Convergent Aspects of the Armenian and Jewish Cases of Genocide, A Reinterpretation of the Concept of Holocaust"; R. Hrair Dejemejin, "Determinates of Genocide: The Armenians and Jews as Case Studies," in *The Armenian Genocide in Perspective*, edited by Richard G. Hovannisian (New Brunswick, NJ: Transaction Publishers, 1987), pp. 85-97.
33. Richard G. Hovannisian, *The Armenian Holocaust: A Bibliography Relating to the Deportations, Massacres and Dispersion of the Armenian People, 1915-1923* (Cambridge, MA: Armenian Heritage Press, 1980).
34. From "And From the Power of the Word..." *Davar*, 27.3.92. The article was sent by Pierre Vidal-Naquet to the Russell Tribunal that convened in April 1984. An updated version appeared in the anthology of articles, Pierre Vidal-Naquet, *Les Juifs, la Memoire et le Present*, II, Paris, 1991.
35. Steven T. Katz, *The Holocaust in Historical Perspective* (New York: Oxford University Press, 1994).
36. The phenomenon of historical revisionism with regard to the Holocaust may yet become more acute, but it appears that the scientific community—and others—have learned to cope with its manifestations. Never-

theless, we must continue to be on guard. On the other hand, the phenomenon is far graver with respect to the Armenians. The Turks have never really recognized their responsibility and their guilt for the destruction of the Armenians.

37. *A Mosaic of Victims, Non-Jews Persecuted and Murdered by the Nazis*, edited by Michael Berenbaum (New York: New York University Press, 1990).
38. Ibid., p. 34.
39. Ibid., p. 9.
40. Yair Auron, *Jewish-Israeli Identity* (Tel Aviv: Sifriat Poalim, 1993), see especially the chapter, "The Holocaust and Me," (Hebrew).
41. *The Letters of Berl Katznelson, (1930-1937)* (Tel Aviv: Am Oved, 1984), pp. 345-46, letter 200, to the Labor Central Committee, London, 15.6.1937 (Hebrew).
42. In 1933, a year after Iraq had promised, at the time of its acceptance to the League of Nations, to protect the minorities within its borders and to treat them with equality and justice, the Iraqi army massacred the Assyrians who had resided in Iraq for generations.
43. David Ben Gurion, *Memoirs*, vol. 3 (Tel Aviv: Am Oved, 1976), pp. 275-76 (Hebrew).
44. Ibid., pp. 220-21. Ben Gurion returned to the same motif in a letter he sent to the Labor Party Central Committee from London, 29.6.1936. Ibid., p. 298.
45. "Armenian Affairs," *Contras*, 1920, vol. 2, no. 38, p. 10.
46. "The Revolt in Armenia," *Contras*, 1921, vol. 3, no. 62, pp. 11-12.
47. Hans Cohen, "The Fate of the Armenian Refugees," *Hapoel Hatzair*, 1927, vol. 20, issue no. 10, pp. 8-10.
48. Ibid., p. 10. "On the Subject of the Armenian Refugees in Syria, Colonel Kish presents information to the Political Committee of the Zionist Federation in London, since, under certain circumstances, it may be useful in negotiation with the Mandatory government, despite the fact that the status of the Armenians in Syria is different from ours in Palestine." Central Zionist Archives, (S25/519), 28.11.1926.
49. See, inter alia, B.M. Ashkenazy, "The Armenians in Syria," *The Near East*, (London and Jerusalem: Kedem Publishers, 1932), pp. 191-98. The essay was written in 1930, and published previously in *Bustanai*; Liza Lindback (a staff person of the Refugee Department of the League of Nations, who described her impressions of a visit) "The Armenian Woman in Exile," *Dvar Hapoelet*, 31.7.1934, vol. 1, no. 5.
50. Israel Zangwill, *The Voice of Jerusalem* (London: W. Heinemann, 1920), p. 353; also quoted by Ronald Storrs, *Memoirs* (Tel Aviv: Mitzpe Publishers, 1938), p. 655.
51. See, inter alia, Zangwill's essays, "The Principle of Nationalities," "The Illusion of the Jewish State," and others.
52. Abba Sikra, "The Alphabet of Zionism," *Hayarden*, 7.10.1936.
53. The Central Zionist Archives, 5/25/5476.
54. S. Gross, "Diaspora Jewry in 1943," *Ha'aretz Almanac* (1943-44), p. 49.

1

The Armenians—The Struggle for Survival[1]

Background: History and Geography

The history of the Armenian People is the history of an ongoing struggle for self-preservation, survival, and the maintenance of a coherent Armenian identity and culture.

The Armenians attribute their origins to the ancient tribes that dwelled in Asia Minor in the prehistoric period. Armenian settlement in the region between the Black Sea and the Caspian Sea (particularly around the Van Peninsula) began around 1000 B.C. The city of Van began to develop at about the same time, followed by the development of Yerevan (the present capital city of Armenia, the former Soviet Socialist Republic of Armenia). Greek and Persian sources from the sixth century B.C. contain clear evidence of sizable Armenian settlement in the plateau of Armenia.

The Armenian Plateau lies between the Black Sea and the Caspian Sea to the east, and between the mountains of the Caucasus, the Taurus Mountains, and Mesopotamia (present day Iraq) to the south. The plateau rises to an average height of over 1,800 meters and is considered, together with the surrounding mountains (3,000-4,000 meters), to be "historic Armenia." Mount Ararat, rising from the plateau to the height of 5,156 meters, has become the symbol of Armenia. The area of historic Armenia is approximately 380,000 square kilometers, 90 percent of which is today empty of Armenian population.

In the second century B.C., an Armenian dynasty, whose official language was Armenian, came to power. During the succeeding two centuries Armenia achieved economic prosperity, territorial expansion, and a developed urban society.

The period between the first and seventh centuries A.D. was characterized by a struggle for domination over the Armenian plateau between Rome (later the Byzantine Empire) and the Persian Empire. The struggle between these two great powers permitted the establishment of Armenian kingdoms as buffer states between the adversaries. The kingdoms even managed at times to achieve complete independence. At other times, they were forced to pay taxes to the neighboring powers in order to preserve internal autonomy, and at other times they were under direct foreign rule.

Christianity became the official religion of Armenia in A.D. 301, making the Armenians the first people to officially adopt Christianity. Acceptance of Christianity and the development of an Armenian alphabet, which led to a literary flowering at the beginning of the fifth century, enabled the Armenians to create a distinct culture. In the century following the loss of their independence, this culture helped the Armenians to identify themselves as a separate ethnic-religious group, and to prevent their assimilation into the neighboring populations and powers.

The relative stability in the region was disturbed at the beginning of the seventh century following the Arab conquests and the founding of the Arab-Islamic Empire. Armenia was under Arab rule from 645 to 850, and the decline of the empire at the end of the ninth century made possible the revival of the Armenian kingdom for a short time. The Byzantine Empire annexed Armenia in 1045. Shortly thereafter, in 1064, central Asia and the Armenian plateau were invaded by Turkish-Seljuki tribes, and for the next three hundred years Armenia was subjected to repeated invasions by the Turks and the Mongols, followed in the fourteenth century by the Tatars.

Despite the circumstances, various attempts were made to reestablish autonomous Armenian political entities. At the end of the eleventh century, a large number of Armenians immigrated to the Cilicia region of southwest Turkey, on the shores of the Mediterranean Sea. In 1080, an Armenian kingdom was established in Cilicia which survived until 1375. The kingdom developed connections with Europe and Asia, and the new center enjoyed a period of cultural prosperity.

In the mid-fifteenth century, the Ottomans became the major power in Asia Minor and captured the last vestiges of the Byzantine Empire, making Constantinople their capital. (Kushta, or Constantinople in

European languages, was first called Byzantine and is known today as Istanbul. It was the capital of the Eastern Roman Empire for more than eleven hundred years. Afterwards, for four hundred years, it was the capital of the Ottoman Empire.) During that period most of historic Armenia was controlled by the Turks, with small sections in the hands of the Persians. As a result of the foreign rule, numbers of Armenians immigrated to other countries and reached positions of influence in commerce and finance. The Ottoman State quickly became the dominant power in the Balkans, most of the Middle East, and North Africa. The Armenians, like the Jews and the Greeks, comprised an ethnic-religious minority within the Ottoman Empire. As non-Islamic communities, these minorities had second-class standing, often subject to official discrimination. They were obligated to pay special taxes, prevented from bearing witness in religious courts of law, and forbidden to carry arms. This administrative system was known as millet (denoting a religious community).

Each of the three major non-Islamic minorities—the Armenians, the Jews, and the Greeks—enjoyed a measure of administrative autonomy in its internal affairs: culture, religion, education, internal adjudication. The Turkish authorities recognized the head of the religious establishment of each community as its leader. Under this arrangement, the Armenians enjoyed considerable cultural autonomy, with the Armenian Church playing an important role. The Patriarch, head of the Armenian Church, was personally responsible for the religious, educational, and legal activities of the Armenian community, as well as for tax collection. The church, the language, and the distinct ethnic identity worked to preserve a unique Armenian identity within the Ottoman Empire.

The Jewish religious leadership, headed by the Chief Rabbi of Turkish Jewry (Hacham Bashi), occupied a position in the Ottoman Empire similar to that of the Patriarch of the Armenian Church, and the Chief Rabbi was considered the representative of all the Jews in the Ottoman Empire. It is fair to note that Ottoman Turkey generally treated its minorities with tolerance. Until the mid-nineteenth century, the Armenians were also treated with tolerance and were considered, like the Jews, a "loyal community."

The Nineteenth Century

In the nineteenth century, historic Armenia was divided between the Ottoman Empire, which controlled most of its territory, and Russia.

The Armenians under Russian rule achieved economic and cultural prosperity. The majority of Armenians in the Ottoman Empire lived as farmers, mostly in the six eastern districts of the empire in the Armenian plateau: Erzurum, Sivas, Bitlis, Harput, Van, and Diyarbakir, which were also known as the "six Armenian provinces." The Armenians comprised a significant percentage of the population in these regions.

Some 250,000 Armenians lived in the capital city, Constantinople, and were prominent as bankers, merchants, public servants, and architects. During the eighteenth and nineteenth centuries, the Armenians, like the Jews, held important positions in the capital as middlemen and translators in international commerce. Beginning in the seventeenth century, an "Armenian diaspora" developed, together with centers of Armenian cultural activity, in Europe.

Nevertheless, in the eighteenth and nineteenth centuries, the Turkish administrative, financial, and military structure began to crumble due to internal corruption and external pressure. By the nineteenth century, the Empire was in danger of economic collapse and the ethnic-religious minorities began to make increasing demands for equality, democracy, and independence. Some of them, like the Greeks, attained their independence at the beginning of the nineteenth century.

The Ottoman rulers felt threatened by what appeared to be the disintegration of the Empire. The European powers followed the events with interest, coveting the territories and spheres of influence in what would become, in their estimation, the former Ottoman Empire. These developments increased intolerance and oppression.

During the second half of the nineteenth century, after generations of relatively peaceful relations, hostility grew between the Christian Armenians and Muslim Turks and Kurds. Armenians were frequently attacked by their Muslim neighbors. Following the Crimean War between Russia and Turkey (1853-56), the European powers demanded that the Sultan improve the conditions of his Christian subjects, including the Armenians, and, in 1863, the Armenians, through a special constitutional decree, were again recognized as a special ethnic-religious community, like the Greeks and the Jews, with much improved legal rights.

National Awakening

The last two decades of the nineteenth century witnessed a national awakening among the Armenian population. In the 1880s, Armenian political activity, based on the ideas and hopes of nationalism and freedom, began to take shape. The weakening Ottoman Empire, "the sick man of Europe," fueled these hopes. The independence of Bulgaria and Serbia in the 1870s, as well as the achievements of other national movements in the Balkans, fired the imagination of the Armenians. But unlike other Balkan peoples, the nationalist activity of the Armenians, located in eastern Anatolia, did not serve the geopolitical interests of the European powers.

In 1877-78, during the Russian-Turkish War, Armenian revolutionaries from Russia joined the Russian military forces, which invaded eastern Anatolia, and established contact with their brethren in the Ottoman Empire, encouraging them to rebel against the Sultan. Most of the Armenian population remained loyal to the Sultan and the war ended relatively quickly. In March 1878, Russia and Turkey signed the San Stefano Treaty which guaranteed protection for the Armenians. The Great Powers, concerned with events on the eastern front, convened in Berlin to draft the Berlin Treaty which guaranteed, in clause 61, among other rights, those of life and property in the Armenian provinces of Anatolia, and promised reforms.

> The Sublime Porte [the formal term for the seat of the Turkish government] undertakes to carry out, without further delay, the improvements and reforms demanded by local requirements in the provinces inhabited by Armenians, and to guarantee their security against the Circassians and Kurds.

> It will periodically make known the steps taken to this effect to the powers, who will superintend their application.

In fact, nothing was done.

Unrest throughout the Empire brought severe reprisals from the authorities, most harshly in April 1876 when the Turks committed mass slaughter in Bulgaria, killing 12,000-15,000 Bulgarians. The massacre aroused horror in Europe.[2]

The Armenians feared the repeat of such atrocities against them as well. At the end of the 1880s, two revolutionary Armenian political organizations were formed, "Hunchak" (Bell), and Dashnak (Association), together with other political organizations. Their centers operated in several European cities and in Tiflis (Tbilisi in the Caucasus). They incited the Armenian population in the eastern provinces against the Ottoman authorities and in August 1894 a "rebellion" broke out near the town of Sassun, causing the Turks to react with great brutality, murdering much of the Armenian community. Reports that spread through Europe on the massacre of twenty thousand people seem to have been exaggerated. Localized conflicts between the Armenians, the Turks, and the Kurds continued from 1894 to 1896. In August and September of 1896 events escalated and reached Constantinople. In September 1895, the Armenians had held a mass demonstration to protest the findings of a governmental investigative commission, appointed to look into the earlier events. The Muslim population of Constantinople attacked the demonstrators, committing yet another massacre, which was accompanied by violent outbursts against the Armenians in numerous cities in Anatolia. These acts of murder and brutality against the Armenians continued throughout the Empire during 1896. Diplomatic representatives of Great Britain, France, and Russia protested vigorously against the situation and the Sultan renewed his promise to institute reforms (October 17, 1895), again, never to be implemented.

In a renewed attempt to bring the Great Powers to their aid, the Armenians instigated a carefully planned program of terror against the Ottoman government. On August 26, 1896, an armed Armenian group took control of the main branch of the Ottoman Bank in Constantinople. The Armenians, who had barricaded themselves in the bank building, demanded implementation of the promised reforms. The Sultan, Abd al-Hamid II, refused to meet the demands. In the days that followed, thousands of Armenians in Constantinople were massacred. In order to ease the situation (i.e., to appease Western public opinion), the Sultan declared mass amnesty and appointed Christian officials in the Armenian provinces. At this point, Britain proposed military intervention to aid the Armenians in eastern Anatolia, but the Russian Czar, fearing a British military presence in the heart of the Ottoman Empire, opposed the idea, as did France. When it became clear that the Great Powers did not intend to come to the aid of the Armenians, the tensions abated and for a while it seemed that life in Anatolia would return to normal. But the relative harmony that had characterized relations between the Armenians and the Muslims for hundreds of years evaporated, and a mutual hostility grew, reaching new heights in 1915, worse than anything that had occurred before.

Armenian estimates of the number of Armenian victims during the period 1894-96 reach 150,000 and even 200,000, with a similar number of refugees. The response of the Great Powers, although divided and ambivalent, was apparently one of the factors which ultimately brought the atrocities to a halt.

The long rule of Sultan Abd al-Hamid II over Turkey (1876-1908) was harsh not only for the Armenians. Criticism of his corrupt and oppressive regime was particularly strong among European and Western-educated Turks in Turkey itself. The Sultan was, in the eyes of his critics, a model of the narrow-minded and autocratic ruler. Small groups from among his critics established the "Committee for Union and Progress."

The group, known also as the "Young Turks," sought to renew the Medhat Pasha's Constitution of 1876 and to establish a centralized parliamentary government which could unite the disparate elements of the Empire. In July 1908, they instigated a military revolt, took power, revived the constitution and held elections for the Parliament.

When the Young Turks overthrew the Sultan's regime, Armenian leaders, including the Dashnak Party, hoped that they would be able to realize their aspirations for autonomy. The rise to power of the Young Turks brought the Armenians equal rights—including the right to serve in the army, which had previously been reserved for Muslims only—and sent Armenian representatives to the new Parliament. Nonetheless, bloody riots against the Armenians broke out in March 1909 in Cilicia, near the sea. Some 20,000 Armenians lost their lives and Armenian neighborhoods and villages were looted and burned. The Armenian expectations quickly faded and after a brief spring of warm relations with the minorities, the Young Turks turned out to be even less amenable to the idea of Armenian autonomy than Sultan Abd al-Hamid II.

The Young Turks found themselves under heavy pressure, domestically from the conservatives and supporters of the Sultan, and externally from foreign forces that hoped to gain from political instability. In the 1912 Balkan War, the Ottoman army was routed. In the 1911-13 period, after losing most of its European and North African territories, the defeated Empire shrank into the boundaries of Asia Minor and the Asian part of the Middle East.

In response to the defeat, nationalist Turks developed the idea of Pan-Turkism—unity with Turkish speakers in the east and expansion into central Asia. Their ideas affected the Young Turks who adopted a policy of discrimination against the minority groups within the disintegrating empire. The pro-Islamic-Turkish ideology, known as Pan-Turanism, envisioned a strong centralized state with purely Turkish components. The Armenian plateau in the east, with its large Armenian population, was an obstacle to realizing this vision. Thus, the Young Turk government degenerated into a regime characterized by a military dictatorship ruled by a small leadership group.

After 1913, Turkey was ruled by a triumvirate of Enver Pasha (Minister of War), Talât Pasha (Minister of the Interior), and Jamal Pasha (Minister of the Navy, who was also the commander of the Fourth Army in the Levant).

The Longest Decade: 1913-1923

The second decade of the twentieth century seemed, at first, to hold promise for the Armenians. The Young Turks and the Union and Progress Party, which had come to power, and established a government which seemed to be more liberal than its predecessor. Furthermore, the Armenians hoped that the Young Turks had learned from their crushing defeat in the Balkan Wars of 1912-13, and from their mishandling of the Empire's nationality problems. Additionally, the tensions and rivalry between the Great Powers seemed to have subsided, making them more disposed, perhaps, to support the Armenian cause.

The assassination of the Serbian crown prince in Sarajevo on June 28, 1914, was the opening shot of the First World War. A month after the assassination, on July 28, 1914, Austro-Hungary declared war on Serbia. Germany, hoping the war would serve its great power interests, attacked Russia, and two days later declared war on England and France.

The war between Russia and Turkey would prove to be disastrous for the Armenians. In the course of the nineteenth century, Russia had extended the borders of its empire at Turkey's expense in the Caucasus and expanded its influence in the Balkans. The Young Turks viewed Russia, because of its control over the Turkish-speaking population of Central Asia, as their sworn enemy, and hoped that a German victory over Russia would enable them to realize their Pan-Turanian dream. In actuality, the war between Turkey and Russia meant that the Armenian plateau turned into the battlefield of the opposing forces, bringing total destruction for the Armenian population.

Turkey entered the war only after three months of formal neutrality, although Enver Pasha, as early as August 2, had signed a secret political and military pact, promising Turkish support for Germany's war against Russia. Armenians outside Turkey supported the Allied Powers, although the Armenians in Turkey declared that they would fulfill their Turkish patriotic duty in the event of war, just as the Armenians in Russia vowed to fight for Russia. At a conference of the Ottoman branch of the Dashnak Party, which took place in August 1914, Armenian nationalists declared their solidarity with Turkey, in the event of war against Russia. But when the war actually broke out, the Armenians were torn between various options and took an ambivalent stand. The wealthy classes in the Armenian community, particularly in Constantinople and other major cities, were mostly loyal supporters of the Empire. On the other hand, much of the lower class, especially the villagers in regions of the border and the Russian front, saw the approaching Russian army as their national liberator.

In November 1914, the Russians published a declaration that promised national liberation to the Armenians on the condition that they oppose their Ottoman masters. Some Armenians answered the call; small numbers of Armenian soldiers deserted from the Turkish army and some in the area of the battles gave assistance to the Russian forces. There are differing versions of the scope of this phenomenon and its significance.

In the winter of 1914-15, the Ottoman army mounted a major attack against the Russians. The Turks still hoped for a speedy realization of the Pan-Turkish dream, but the attack was poorly planned and implemented. Enver Pasha, who had assumed command of the Third Army, made fatal errors which led to the loss of most of his forces and the loss of wide stretches of territory to the Russian army. There are those who point to Enver Pasha's direct responsibility for the military defeat as the motive for his search for a scapegoat; the Armenians were accused of treachery by Enver Pasha and his supporters. It was alleged that Armenian betrayal, according to the Empire's rulers, had caused the defeat. Alleged military needs were presented as explanation for "evacuations" from the battle areas. To this day, the Turkish government claims the treachery of the Armenians as the explanation for what subsequently befell them.

The Genocide

The year 1915 brought no significant developments on the Caucasus front. Military attention was focused in other directions but the smokescreen of an all out war and the evacuation of most of the foreign diplomatic corps from various parts of the Empire—some sixty-five diplomats in all—created comfortable conditions for the concealment of a widespread genocide. At the outbreak of the fighting, some 75,000-100,000 young Armenians were conscripted into the Ottoman army, and, by order of Enver Pasha, were transferred to "work brigades" where they were systematically murdered.

During the night, between April 23 and April 24, 1915, the Constantinople police broke into the homes of the Armenian elite in the city. Two hundred thirty-five Armenian leaders—politicians, writers, educators, lawyers, etc.—were taken to the police station and then deported. Several hundred others were taken in the days that followed.

Elimination of its leadership left the Armenian community confused, fearful, and unable to offer resistance to the Turks. This pattern, eliminating the leadership first, repeated itself in the six eastern provinces where most of the Armenian population was concentrated, and in Cilicia. Thus, April 24 symbolizes for the Armenians the beginning of the genocide, and thereafter has become the annual memorial day of the Armenian genocide.

At the beginning of June 1915, the Turkish government issued an order, which was never ratified by the Parliament, to deport all non-Turkish populations residing near the Turkish military supply lines, which were, in fact, everywhere. The edict was aimed at the Armenians, although they were not explicitly mentioned. At the same time, non-Armenian communities were exempted from the order. But the deportations affected Armenians not only in the area of fighting against the Russians; the Armenians in the Cilicia region, on the shores of the Mediterranean, far from the battle zones, were also deported in the course of 1915 (viz. the story of "Musa Dagh.") and some of them were among the first to be expelled.

The earlier "Van Affair" offered a convenient opportunity for the government to base its alleged claim of Armenian treachery. Kurdish soldiers in the Ottoman army were eager to butcher the Armenian population which jointly inhabited the eastern region of Anatolia. After the atrocities started, survivors fled to the city of Van. The Armenians, the majority in the city, took power, erected fortifications to prevent atrocities by the Turkish army, and established a local government. On May 18, the Armenians welcomed the Russian forces, but due to reversal of events in the battlefield, the Turkish army managed to recapture Van on August 4. Sick and elderly Armenians who remained behind were massacred when the Ottoman forces entered Van and spent their wrath on the Armenian quarter of the city.

The implementation of the "evacuation order" of the Armenians— their expulsion and murder—was assigned to the police and units of the Ch'ette, the Special Organization which was established by the Ministries of the Police and the Interior. The Special Organization was a paramilitary unit created especially for this purpose and manned by criminals and convicts who were released from prison.[3] The evacuation and expulsion of the Armenian population was an important part in the process of genocide. The evacuation was announced in public places in the Armenian villages and towns. The population was usually given several days to prepare for the evacuation necessitated, as it were, by military needs. The evacuees were permitted to take their personal effects with them and were given a promise that their homes and property would be protected until their return.

They were then gathered in convoys and ordered to march south toward the Syrian Desert. The genocide usually comprised several stages. At first, after leaving the village or the city, males over the age of fifteen were separated (it should be remembered that the men between the ages of twenty-five and forty-five, who were serving in the Ottoman army, were murdered), taken to a spot not far away, and executed by shooting or more primitive methods.

Women, children, and the elderly were sentenced to a slower and more drawn-out death. They were forced to march hundreds of kilometers. The convoys traveled through the most difficult terrain, under harsh climatic conditions, and were frequently subjected to attacks by units of the Special Organization, the gendarmes, and the local population, particularly the Kurds. Women and children who managed to survive the journey were kidnapped and handed over to Turkish families as servants (in fact, slaves); many were sold in slave markets. Women and children were raped. Mothers were forced to leave their dying children behind and to continue on. Entire families committed suicide.

Throughout the long and arduous march, the deportees were given only minute quantities of food and water. The starvation and thirst, the cold and the heat, the epidemics that broke out due to the thousands of unburied bodies, all these increased the number of fatalities. The intended direction of the journey was the region around the city of Aleppo in northern Syria. From there, the few who had survived that far were transported to the desert regions of Iraq and Syria. Out in the desert, near Dir a(l)-Zor, many of the survivors were executed. Very few of those who had begun the journey lived to see its end. Estimates place the number of survivors at ten percent and, in certain convoys, even fewer. (The report of the American Consul in Aleppo to the American Secretary of State on October 16, 1915, detailed the tribulations of one of the convoys in which only 150 women and children, out of 18,000 deportees who began the march, reached Aleppo seventy days later.) [4]

It appears that by July of 1915 the Armenians had been expelled from the six eastern provinces and most of them had already been murdered. During the latter half of 1915 the deportations were carried out in the Armenian areas of Cilicia.

Between April and November of that year (or possibly until September) most of the genocide of the Armenians was carried out. According to estimates, between 600,000 and 800,000 Armenians were exterminated during those months. Estimates of the total number of Armenian victims range from 600,000 to two million. The United Nations Subcommission for Human Rights Report in 1985 estimates the number at "at least one million." Armenian sources ascertain that one and a half million of their people were murdered between the years 1915 and 1923. Some researchers use a figure of 800,000 while others reckon that 1,800,000 Armenians were killed between 1894 and 1923, and an additional million were forced to leave their historic homeland. The debate relates also to the estimated size of the Armenian population in Turkey during the period, and whether the period of the genocide should be figured from 1894 to 1923, or only between the years 1915 and 1916.

The estimate, in any case, is that approximately half of the Armenian population in Turkey was annihilated—one-third of the Armenians in the world. Before 1915, there were some 2.5 million Armenians living in Turkey. At the beginning of the 1990s, their number was estimated at 40,000-60,000. Not only was the population murdered, but thousands of churches, monasteries, and other Armenian sites were destroyed. The Turks made noticeable efforts to obliterate all traces of Armenian culture and presence in the Armenian regions—the core of historic Armenia.

Small groups of Armenians managed to save themselves from deportation at the time. Not all Armenians in Constantinople and Izmir were expelled due to several factors, including the presence of foreign representatives in those cities, while others were sometimes permitted to stay because they possessed special skills, usually for military purposes.[5] Others were offered the chance to convert to Islam and a few accepted the offer. And some Armenians survived because there were Turks, Kurds, and Greeks who were willing—at great personal risk—to hide children and even whole Armenian families.

Additionally, some Armenians were saved by flight or by resistance. An example is the Armenians who lived near the border and were able to cross over into Russia. Rarer are the instances of Armenians who managed to defend themselves and to survive, like the famous case of Musa Dagh whose fighters and families were ultimately saved by French ships. To these survivors must be added the numbers who managed to survive the months of the deportation marches and the camps afterward.

Yet the importance in understanding the Armenian tragedy is not the exact number of victims, which will probably never be known. What matters is the fact that more than half of the Armenian population in the Ottoman Empire was systematically murdered, while the remainder was forced to leave its historical homeland in which its forebears had lived for almost three thousand years. Another important fact is that these acts were committed by the sovereign government of Turkey.

The Continuation of the First World War and Its End

The beginning of 1916 brought additional victories to the Russians who conquered territories populated by the Armenians. It seemed that new horizons were opening for the Armenians. The Russians now controlled the areas that were intended for their control or influence, according to the terms of secret agreements signed between England, France, and Russia in 1915-16, regarding the postwar division of spheres of influence in the areas of the former Ottoman Empire. One of the most important of these agreements, the Sykes-Picot Agreement, signed by England and France on May 9, 1916, had great implications for Palestine as well. After the Russians had been informed of the terms of that agreement and accepted them, it was renamed as the Sykes-Picot-Sazanov Agreement (Sazanov was the Russian Foreign Minister at the time).

There were military upsets during 1917. The United States entered the war in April of that year, and in October there was a revolution in Russia, which later became the Soviet Union. The Bolsheviks came to power, encountered complex, intractable problems, and the new government came to the conclusion that it needed to make peace at almost any price. A cease-fire was signed between Russia and Germany shortly after the Revolution, on December 18, 1917, in Brest-Litovsk, and was followed by overtures toward a separate peace.

The fact that Russia—the Soviet Union—was willing to give up its intended spheres of influence in the Asian Turkish regions of the defeated Ottoman Empire was disastrous for the Armenians. By the terms of the agreements between the Allied Powers, Russia was to have controlled the six Armenian provinces.

On March 3, 1918, a peace treaty was signed between Turkey, Germany, and the Soviet Union. In January 1918, U.S. President Woodrow Wilson proclaimed his "Fourteen Points" for peace, stating that the Turkish regions of the Ottoman Empire should become sovereign and that other national groups, namely Kurds and Armenians, formerly under Ottoman rule, had the unconditional right to security and an unencumbered opportunity for autonomous development. Between the end of February and the end of April 1918, the Turks pressed north to the Caucasus and conquered territory beyond the boundaries which had been designated by treaty in Brest-Litovsk.

In April 1918, the Independent Caucasian Republic was established. It was a strange creation, composed of Georgia, Armenia, and Azerbaijan, fragile and doomed to collapse, and it fell apart only a month later. On May 26, Georgia declared its independence, followed two days later, on May 28, by Armenia and Azerbaijan. A peace treaty was signed between Germany, Turkey, and the three republics in June. The young Armenian state, in the region of Yerevan and Lake Sevan, was born under the most difficult circumstances, and its viability was questionable from the outset.

In 1919, a peace conference was convened in Paris, attended by two Armenian delegations—one from the Armenian Republic and the other a delegation of diaspora Armenians that operated in Europe. The two delegations tried to coordinate a joint position, not always successfully. Armenian representatives also participated in the San Remo Conference in April 1920.

In 1919, the idea of a mandate was officially proposed with the encouragement of General Smuts, prime minister of South Africa, and the blessing of President Wilson of the United States. It should be remembered that mandatory rule was also imposed on Palestine after the war and was considered by the Zionist movement to be a significant gain.

The Armenians' hope for a mandatory rule over the Armenian provinces, explicitly mentioned in several decisions of the victorious powers, was never realized. The possibility of an American mandate in the Caucasus was considered and rejected by the American Senate that preferred not to get involved. Another proposal, supported by the Armenian delegation headed by Nubar Pasha, for a French mandate in Cilicia, in southeast Anatolia—or in parts of that region—was also rejected, this time by the French because of imperial considerations. Cilicia was, as noted previously, an independent Armenian monarchy between the eleventh and fourteenth centuries. More than 200,000 Armenian refugees had gathered there after the war, only to flee from the region when the Turks returned.

In 1919 and 1920, peace treaties were signed and the First World War was over. First to be signed were the treaties between the victorious Allied Powers and Germany (the Treaty of Versailles, June 1919), followed by Austria and Bulgaria. In June 1920, an agreement was signed with Hungary; and finally, on August 10, 1920, the Treaty of Sèvres was signed with Turkey. In this latter agreement it was decided to establish an independent Armenian state, although the question of its borders was left open, to be determined later by President Wilson. Wilson allocated 75,000 square kilometers to the Armenian state in part of the eastern provinces (the Armenian districts), but the agreement to divide the Caucasus between Turkey and the Soviet Union effectively torpedoed the idea of a united and independent Armenian Republic. Although the Turkish government signed the treaty with the victors, the actual body in control of Turkey, the Turkish Nationalist Party led by Mustapha Kemal, opposed the creation of an independent Armenia. In September 1920, Turkish forces led by Kemal attacked the weak young Armenian Republic which asked for a cease-fire. The territory of the republic was cut from 60,000 to 20,000 square kilometers, marking the beginning of the end of the Armenian Republic which managed to survive only two and a half years. Mustapha Kemal, an officer in the Ottoman army, took power in Turkey, putting an end to the Ottoman Empire, and on October 29, 1923, founded the Turkish Republic, the "new Turkey." Mustapha Kemal was named "Ataturk," the father of modern Turkey.

In 1921, agreements were signed between Mustapha Kemal's government and Soviet Russia which reinstituted, in effect, the 1878 borders between the two countries, with the exception of the transfer of the city of Batum to the new Georgian Soviet Socialist Republic. For the Armenians this meant that the Turks were once again the masters in the Armenian provinces, which, due to the war and the genocide, were empty of Armenians. There are, to this day, no Armenians living in ninety percent of the area of historic Armenia. In 1921, an agreement was also signed between Turkey and France to determine the border between Turkey and Syria, which was under French mandate. France had reconsidered its position and was now willing to cede Cilicia to Turkey, resulting in another mass exodus of Armenian civilian population fearful of renewed Turkish rule. More than 200,000 refugees fled to Syria and Lebanon, uncertain that they would find safe haven there. The refugee ships were turned back at first, until the French authorities gave an order permitting them to land. A few Armenian refugees also reached Palestine.

In 1922, Turkey also managed to improve its position in its war against Greece. The Turkish military victory over Greece led to a wave of almost a million Greek refugees who fled the area of Izmir. The Armenians who had survived the entire war in Izmir were also forced to flee, following widespread incidences of arson, looting, raping, and killing by the Kemalist forces capturing the port city. Eventually, a brutal transfer of 1.2 million Christians for 350,000 Muslims was carried out between Turkey and Greece.

The year 1923 signaled a new political order in the Near East. The Treaty of Lausanne replaced the agreements which had been reached three years earlier at Sèvres. Signed on July 24, 1923, the Treaty of Lausanne marks the beginning of a new era in the history of the Near East and the end of the history of the Armenians in Turkey. We should remember that in 1915 there were some two and a half million Armenians in Turkey.

Contrary to explicit public promises by the Allied Powers made as early as 1915, the Armenians were ignored by the West. In the face of adamant denials of genocide by the Turks, diplomatic agreements made no mention of the words "Armenia" or "Armenians." The refugees were not given the right of repatriation, and no mention was made of compensation, rehabilitation, or return.

Cooperation between the Russian Bolsheviks and Turkish nationalists also played a role. The deposed leaders of the Young Turks, Enver Pasha and Jamal Pasha, aided the cause of the Soviet Union in Central Asia from 1920 to 1922, hoping that their service to Soviet imperialist interests would be rewarded and that they would return to power and realize their Pan-Turkish dream. Enver Pasha attended the "First Conference of Eastern Peoples," which took place in Baku, the capital of

Muslim Azerbaijan, in September 1920, under the auspices of the Third Communist Internationale. At the same time, the Soviet Union reached agreements with Mustapha Kemal, emphasizing the cynicism of the new regime which had rejected or abandoned its earlier revolutionary ideals in order to preserve the interests of the Russian empire.

The tiny Armenian Republic, a territory of 30,000 square kilometers (its capital city, Yerevan), located within the domain of the Soviet Union, was to become a limited expression of Armenian sovereignty over an area that was less than ten percent of the territory of historic Armenia. Even Mount Ararat, Armenia's emblem, remained under Turkish rule. After the collapse of the Soviet Union in 1991, Armenia became an independent country, and shortly afterward became entangled in a war with neighboring Azerbaijan. Vestiges of the conflicts and controversies of the First World War period, which had lain dormant during seventy years of Soviet domination, reemerged from the ruins. Some three and a half million Armenians live in the Armenian Republic and an additional three and a half million are scattered around the world, including a substantial community of almost 800,000 in the United States. There are large concentrations of Armenians in the Middle East—in Lebanon, Syria, Egypt, and Iran. Approximately 200,000 Armenians live in France.

World Reaction

The Armenian genocide was, without question, committed with the knowledge and presence of the diplomatic representatives of Turkey's allies, the German, and the Austro-Hungarian Empires. They were to be found in the capital as well as in other cities throughout the Ottoman Empire. American diplomats were also stationed in various parts of the Empire until April 1917, when the U.S. abandoned its position of neutrality and joined the war against Germany.

German military representatives were stationed throughout the Empire. Germany was Turkey's military ally, equipping the Turkish army, and involved at the highest levels in training and commanding Turkish troops. German military commanders and soldiers undoubtedly knew, saw, and it is alleged, participated—at least indirectly—in the genocide.

Furthermore, throughout the Empire there were American, German, and other missionaries, as well as teachers, tourists, and travelers who reported what they saw. Journalists wrote and reported as well. As early as spring 1915, reports of the Armenian genocide reached the outside world, prominently featured with frequency in the European and American press. On May 24, 1915, France, England, and Russia issued a joint protest and warning against the acts of murder. In August 1915, in response to accusations of German responsibility, at least as an ally, the German government delivered a protest to the Ottoman imperial authorities.

Germany's role in the Armenian genocide has only recently begun to come to light.[6] Germany was perhaps the only country that could have changed the Turkish policy of genocide at that time. Henry Morgenthau, the American ambassador in Constantinople during the years 1913-16, wrote to the Secretary of State on June 10, 1915, that the German embassy would make do with "giving advice and a formal protest for the record, in order to absolve themselves of responsibility in the future."[7] The letter was one of many, which Morgenthau sent.

Documents that appeared in the West during the war revealed terrible events. Of particular interest are the U.S. State Department documents (later made public) compiled in "The Blue Book" by Toynbee and Bryce, which appeared during the war, and the publications of the German missionary, Dr. Johannes Lepsius, some of which appeared during the war and some only after its end. Each of these publications contains hundreds of documents.

Additionally, there were publications by private persons. A German teacher in Aleppo, Dr. Martin Niepage, published what he and others had seen in *The Horrors of Aleppo*, (published in English in 1917). Dr. Armin T. Wegner, a German medical officer, published photographs and reports of what he had seen. Wegner worked to oppose the Nazis in the 1930s and was accorded the title of "Righteous Gentile" by the Yad Vashem Holocaust Memorial Museum in Jerusalem. By December 1915, more than a hundred articles and items about the Armenian genocide had appeared in the first six pages of the *New York Times* alone. So the world did know, and in real time. Nonetheless, during the course of the war, Turkey consistently denied the accusations of planned mass deportation and murder.

In fact, after 1916 the attempts at protest became, for all practical matters, meaningless. By that time most of the Armenian population of the Plateau and Cilicia had been exterminated and the Armenian Plateau was empty of Armenian inhabitants.

In the framework of this short survey of political and military developments up to the end of the war and the peace agreements that followed, it is worthwhile to note, even briefly, the humanitarian efforts that were made. Beginning in April 1915, American and German missionaries attempted, to the best of their limited abilities, to aid the survivors. Despite attempts of the authorities to stop them, they supplied food, water, and sometimes refuge in monasteries. In September 1915, the American ambassador in Constantinople, Morgenthau, requested emergency aid from his government, and in the same year the American Committee for Armenian and Syrian Relief (ACASR) was established. In 1916, assistance efforts, under the auspices of Congress, were reorganized as the "Near East Relief" (NER). The organization collected substantial sums of money from foundations, private donors, and the government. During the advanced stages of the expulsions, when the deportees who survived the march arrived in Aleppo, workers of the organization, assisted by missionaries, provided first aid, water, food, and clothing. Representatives of the American consulate took part in the assistance efforts. Later on, refugee camps were organized in various places in the Middle East for the survivors; schools were organized and orphanages were established for children. Some of the Armenian children who were found in the homes of Turkish families were returned and rehabilitated.

There is no doubt that tens, perhaps hundreds of thousands, of Armenians were saved due to these assistance efforts. The survivors began their attempts to rebuild their lives, which lasted for years.

Was It Genocide?

Ambassador Morgenthau said about the Turkish atrocities against the Armenians: "I am certain that there is, in all of human history, no episode as terrible as this." The American general, James G. Harbord, who was sent in 1919 to investigate the situation in the areas previously inhabited by the Armenians, wrote, "The mutilation, coercion, torture and death have left a mark which will not be quickly forgotten in hundreds of Armenian valleys. The traveler in this region is only infrequently released from the evidence of the greatest crime of all times."

After the defeat of the Central Powers, the three leaders of the Young Turks fled their country. The new Turkish Prime Minister admitted that the Turks had committed deeds so despicable that the human conscience would forever tremble. The new government in Constantinople arranged military trials of the Young Turk leaders—Enver Pasha, Talât Pasha, and Jamal Pasha—which were conducted between April and July 1919. The three, together with Dr. Nazim, who was one of the leaders responsible for organizing the Ch'ette death squads of the "Special Organization," were condemned *in absentia* to death, but no steps were taken to carry out the verdict. Many of those accused of taking part in the genocide were never tried or even removed from their official positions. The legal procedures ended after several months and prisoners accused of war crimes were released and sent home.

Another significant fact should be recalled: Talât Pasha, the most prominent of the three Young Turk leaders who had escaped abroad, was pro-German and found political asylum in Berlin after the war. He was assassinated on March 15, 1921, by a young Armenian, Soghoman Tehlirian, whose family had been murdered. The assassin was tried in Berlin on June 2-3, 1921, and the trial aroused much interest. To the surprise of many, he was acquitted by the German court. "Why Talât's Assassin was Acquitted" was explained in an article published in the monthly supplement of current history section of the *New York Times* in July 1921. The answer, according to the article, was that the trial raised evidence of the responsibility of the Young Turk leadership for the Armenian genocide, including copies of Enver Pasha's direct orders to implement the massacres. The orders call to "annihilate the various forces which have for centuries been an obstacle in its way, and to this end it is obliged to resort to very bloody methods" (Telegram from March 25, 1915). In another telegram, from September 16, 1915, he says, "However tragic the measures taken may be, no regard must be paid to either age or sex, or to conscientious scruples." In a telegram from March 3, 1915, he states, "To that end we must assume full responsibility."[8] The trial also uncovered the responsibility of German military authorities "who at the least had allowed the massacres to continue without protest....The terrible massacres and the callousness of the German military authorities to the horrors going on under their eyes."[9] In the opinion of the article's author, the documents presented in court "prove, once and for all, that the aim of the Turkish authorities was not deportation but extermination."

Epilogue

Talât Pasha is viewed in Turkey today as a national hero. His bones were repatriated to Turkey by Nazi Germany in 1943 and interred in a national mausoleum in Constaninople. The Turkish state, has denied—with the exception of the short period mentioned—and continues to this day to deny that there was ever a policy of intentional destruction of the Armenians. The Turks have invested considerable effort in erasing the memory of the Armenians and the Armenian history in the Ottoman Empire, as though they had never been part of it. Huge sums have been spent and continue to be spent to deny the guilt. Armenian sites, including churches, have been neglected, looted, destroyed, or requisitioned for other uses, and Armenian place names have been changed.

There is no doubt of the proof, based on different and various sources from the period, that the comprehensive mass extermination of the civilian population in various regions of Turkey (and certainly not just in the battle zones) was carried out at the indisputable order of Turkish authorities in Constantinople. While certain facts and details can be legitimately debated, and some of the Armenian claims about the genocide can be questioned, the historical sources, only a small part of which have been mentioned in this survey, create an unequivocal and unshakable picture. (Unless there has been some fantastic conspiracy to invent thousands of documents and reports from various sources in differing countries, including the United States which was neutral, and Germany and Austria, who were allies of the Turks, and to fabricate hundreds of newspaper items in numerous countries....) The term "genocide" did not exist, we should remember, at the time the atrocities were committed against the Armenians, but what the Young Turks did to the Armenians was indeed genocide. Again, one can argue with some of the facts, details, or circumstances, but there can be no doubt about the fact of the genocide itself. In this sense, the denial of the Armenian genocide is very similar to the denial of the Holocaust of the Jews.

The Armenians talk of the "forgotten genocide" which took place under three regimes—the Sultanate, the Young Turks, and the forces of Mustapha Kemal. The Turks, on the other hand, talk about the "alleged genocide" and charge the Armenians with treachery and subversion. It appears that massive efforts of denial and contemporary political interests are part of the attempt to undermine the certainty of the claim that there was, indeed, a genocide. These efforts have succeeded in creating disagreements among researchers, seemingly historical controversies, and claims of lack of proof. The result of Turkish efforts has been intentional neglect and repression of the subject, and the creation of confusion over the events surrounding it.

The world has, without question, mostly forgotten the destruction of the Armenians. Question marks about the event arise also in the academic and intellectual world. The noted Jewish scholar of the Middle East, Professor Bernard Lewis of Princeton University, in an interview published in *Le Monde* (November 16, 1993), spoke about "the extenuating circumstances" of the Turks in the murder of the Armenians. "Turkey had an Armenian problem, because of the Russian advance and the existence of an anti-Ottoman population in Turkey which sought its independence and openly expressed its support for the Russians who were coming from the Caucasus," he says. "There is serious doubt," claims Lewis, "whether there was an intentional policy of the Ottoman authorities which led to a decision to systematically exterminate the Armenian people." Lewis also refuses to talk about genocide in the context of the murder of the Armenians, and calls the Armenian genocide "the Armenian version of that history." The Armenians claim that the historian has been unduly influenced by the Turkish officially sanctioned effort, particularly since the 1970s and 1980s, which attributes the fate of the Armenians to their alleged betrayal of the Turks. The Armenians reject the betrayal theory. Armenian historians claim that, "from the perspective of the historian, Lewis' position is utterly baseless."[10]

Lewis's comments aroused sharp controversy in France. Thirty intellectuals sent a letter of protest. Among the signatories were several Jewish scholars, including the historian Pierre Vidal-Naquet, author of the essays on "The Murderers of Memory," the deniers of the Holocaust. The Armenians sued Lewis for "denial of the Armenian genocide," on the basis of the same clause in French law which has been used against deniers of the Jewish Holocaust. The defense tried to prevent the case from coming to trial. The court rejected the defense claim, heard the case and decided, on November 18, 1994, to dismiss the charges not on grounds of innocence or of insufficient evidence, but for lack of jurisdiction and legal competence of the court. Armenian organizations in France, together with other organizations and public figures, are currently attempting to have the law changed to include all cases of genocide. An additional stage in the affair ended in June 1995. A French civil court found Lewis guilty of denying the fact that the Armenian genocide had occurred. He was sentenced to a pay the symbolic fine of one franc and ordered to publish the court's decision in *Le Monde*, the newspaper in which the affair had first begun.

Despite the abundance of publications and mass of evidence from the war years and the 1920s, the memory of the Armenian genocide has gradually dimmed over the years. The Armenians were caught up in a struggle to survive and to rebuild their individual and communal life. Some underwent a process of acculturation, assimilating into the five continents to which they dispersed after they were expelled from their homeland. The Western world, slightly embarrassed by its abandonment of the Armenians, preferred to ignore their fate, and within the international real-politik, the Armenians were utterly powerless. The 1920s and 1930s were also decades of struggle against totalitarian and fascist regimes. After the Second World War, the world was stunned and absorbed by the horrors of the Holocaust. There are Armenians who assert that interest in the Holocaust was at the expense of the Armenian tragedy, which became "the forgotten genocide." It should be remembered that at the same time the Turks destroyed the Armenians, they wiped out other minority populations, albeit considerably smaller in size, like the Assyrians. They have been even more forgotten by the world, and their destruction has become "the obliterated genocide."

Since the 1960s and 1970s a certain change has begun in the public awareness of the Armenian genocide. In the 1970s and early 1980s, Armenian organizations have committed terrorist acts against Turkish institutions and diplomats in various parts of the world. The acts of terror, aimed at arousing world opinion, resulted in raising the Armenian issue, and it was during those years that the important scientific research on the subject of the Armenian genocide began. The fruits of this research have had some effect and scholars, intellectuals, educators, and human rights activists have begun to reexamine the issue. The growing awareness of the Holocaust may also have sparked new interest in the Armenian genocide, and the multigenerational Armenian trauma is the subject of a greater understanding and response than in the past. In January 1984, President Francois Mitterand of France gave public recognition to the historical fact of the Armenian genocide; and in 1985, the United Nations, through its Sub-commission on Human Rights, recognized the atrocities committed against the Armenians as genocide. (In 1973, such recognition was denied due to pressure by the Turkish government.) In 1987, the European Parliament in Strasbourg declared that Turkey could not join the European Community unless, among other things, it recognized its responsibility for the genocide. In contrast, in 1989, a motion was defeated in the American Congress, although it was supported at one stage by a majority of the members, which would have declared April 24 as the official memorial day of the Armenian genocide.

The Czech writer, Milan Kundera, once wrote that man's struggle against power is the struggle of memory against forgetting. In this sense, all of the reasons which justify remembrance of the Holocaust are valid for the Armenian genocide as well. Furthermore, it is the Turkish governments that have ruled after the crimes were committed which deny that they ever took place. The Turks have escaped judgment for their crimes and have been partially successful in their denials, with the direct and indirect assistance of some of the world's powers, based on selfish political considerations. Turkey is a country that committed terrible crimes of murder—and a country that continues to deny what it did. It is as if Germany had denied its crimes in the Second World War.

The destruction of the Armenian people in the second and third decades of the twentieth century is an undisputed fact. Forgetfulness and intentional efforts of denial have resulted, several decades later, in questions, most of them tendentious, which did not exist before. This alone raises doubts and questions about historical memory, historical consciousness, and historical research, as well as musings about the morality of the world in which we live. Recognition of the Armenian genocide on the part of the entire international community, including Turkey (or perhaps, first and foremost, by Turkey), is therefore a demand with historical, moral, and educational significance of the first order. Understanding and remembering the tragic past is an essential condition, even if not sufficient in and of itself, to preventing the repetition of such acts in the future.

Notes

1. The survey which follows was written mostly on the basis of the following studies: Essays of Vahakn N. Dadrian, "The Secret Young-Turk Ittihadist Conference and the Decision for the World War I Genocide of the Armenians," *Holocaust and Genocide Studies*, vol. 7, no. 2, fall 1993, pp. 173-201; "The Role of the Special Organization in the Armenian Genocide during the First World War," *Minorities in Wartime*, 1993, pp. 50-82; "The Role of the Turkish Military in the Destruction of the Ottoman Armenians: A Study in Historical Continuities," *Journal of Political and Military Sociology*, vol. 20, no. 2, 1992, pp. 257-88; "Genocide as a Problem of National Law and International Law: World War I, the Armenian Case and Its

Contemporary Legal Ramifications," *The Yale Journal of International Law*, vol. 14, no. 2, summer 1989, pp. 221-334. Since the publication of my book in Hebrew, Vahakn N. Dadrian's important study, *The History of the Armenian Genocide: Ethnic Conflict from the Balkans to Anatolia to the Caucasus*, was published by Berghahn Books in 1995. Richard G. Hovannisian, *The Armenian Holocaust: A Bibliography Relating to the Deportations, Massacres, and Dispersion of the Armenian People, 1915-1923* (Cambridge, MA: Armenian Heritage Press, 1980); James Reid, "The Armenian Massacres in the Ottoman and Turkish Historiography," *Armenian Review*, vol. 37, no. 1, spring 1984; Christopher J. Walker, *Armenia— The Survival of a Nation* (New Jersey: Routledge, revised second edition, 1990); *Journal of Political and Military Sociology*, vol. 22, no. 1, summer 1994, pp. 1-202. The entire issue is dedicated to studies dealing with the Armenian genocide. For documentation from the period which has recently come to light, see, inter al., Rouben Adalian, ed., *The Armenian Genocide in the U.S. Archives, 1915-1918* (Alexandria, VA: Chadwick-Healey, 1991); Ara Sarafian, *United States Official Documents on the Armenian Genocide*, vol. I, *Armenian Review* (Watertown, MA, 1993); Yves Ternon, *Les Arméniens: Histoire d'un Genocide* (Paris: Seuil, 1996).

2. Outstanding in his protest was the British statesman, William Gladstone, in his pamphlet, *The Bulgarian Horrors and the Question of the East*. Gladstone was also one of the prominent defenders of the Armenians during the attacks against them from 1894 to 1896.

3. Vahakn N. Dadrian, "The Role of the Special Organization in the Armenian Genocide during the First World War," *Minorities in Wartime*, Oxford/Providence, 1993, pp. 50-82.

4. *The State Department File,* 867. 4016/225, no. 278: "J.B. Jackson, Aleppo, Syria, 16.10.1915, to the Secretary of State, Washington."

5. See Dadrian, *History of the Armenian Genocide*, p. 227, note 2.

6. Ulrich Trumpener, *Germany and the Ottoman Empire 1914-1918* (New York: Caravan Books, Delmar, 1989). See also Dadrian's important book on this subject, *German Responsibility in the Armenian Genocide* (Cambridge, MA: Blue Crane Books, 1996).

7. *The State Department File*, R.G. 59, 867. 4016/57 no. 278, 10.6.1915.

8. George R. Montgomery, "Why Talât's Assassin was Acquitted," *New York Times*, July 1921.

9. Ibid.

10. "Un entretien avec Anahide Ter-Minassian et Claude Mutafian," *Le Monde*, 16.4.1994. See also, Yoram Bronovsky, "Was There an Armenian Holocaust?" *Ha'aretz*, 15.4.1994.

2

Palestine During the First World War

The Jewish Community in Palestine during WWI[1]

On the eve of the First World War, the Jewish community (the Yishuv) in Palestine (Eretz Yisrael) was in a process of growth and development. Since 1882 it had more than doubled its numbers, and of 700,000 inhabitants in the area of Palestine west of the Jordan River, 85,000 were Jews. Of these, half were part of the "Old Yishuv," concentrated in the four holy cities: Jerusalem, Hebron, Safed, and Tiberias. Half were part of the "New Yishuv," immigrants who had arrived at the end of the nineteenth century and the beginning of the twentieth, and they changed the face of the Jewish community in Palestine.

Forty-four agricultural villages had been established between 1881 and 1914, with a combined population of 12,000. An urban Jewish settlement had developed in Jaffa and its environs, where Tel Aviv was founded in 1909. By the eve of the war, Tel Aviv's population had grown to 10,500, and Haifa had three thousand Jewish residents. The coming of the New Yishuv turned Jerusalem into a vibrant city with a Jewish majority (45,000 Jews). At the same time, small communities with tens of inhabitants were established in Acre, Gaza, Beersheba, Nablus, and Bet Shean, all of which were overwhelmingly Arab cities during this period.

Contrary to the Jews of the Old Yishuv who survived mostly on philanthropy from Jewish communities abroad, the New Yishuv created the foundations of a modern economy in the country: agriculture—based mostly on orchards and groves—artisanship, emerging industry, commerce and services, together with an infrastructure of public institutions, including primary and secondary schools, academic institutions of higher learning, such as the Technion Institute in Haifa, the Bezalel School of Art in Jerusalem, and teachers' seminaries in Jerusalem and Tel Aviv. They established other institutions as well: medical services, farmers' associations, a teachers' association, and the first political parties: "Hapoel Hatzair" ("The Young Worker") and "Poalei Zion" ("Workers of Palestine"). The Jewish community had graduated from the initial stages of settlement and laid the foundations for continued development on its course toward becoming a "National Home" for the Jewish People.

The First World War split Jewish support between the opposing forces, the Central Powers (Germany, Austro-Hungary, and Turkey) and the Allied Powers (England, Russia, and France). Most of the Jews throughout the world, with the exception of the Jews in Russia, saw no choice but to support the country in which they resided and its allies (albeit with varying degrees of enthusiasm). International Jewish organizations, which suddenly found themselves torn by a war that was not theirs, usually declared their "neutrality," hoping thus to "bypass" the war and to continue their activity.

The Zionist movement also chose a path of neutrality but its situation was more problematic, since the focus of its activities was in a region of utmost strategic importance to both sides: Palestine. It was almost impossible for the Zionists in Berlin, London, and New York to reach agreement over a desirable policy. The Russian Zionists were mostly hostile to the anti-Semitic regime of the Czar, as were the Zionists in the United States (which entered the war only in 1917). They hoped to gain the support of Germany and Turkey for the Zionist cause. Opposing them were the Zionists of Western Europe who looked for their salvation to Britain, with its many interests in the Middle East.

The problem became even more complex due to the nature of the Jewish settlement in Palestine, where many of the inhabitants were citizens of the Allied Powers. Most of the Jews who had immigrated in the early years of the twentieth century were citizens of Russia—Turkey's enemy in the war. In view of these complexities, the Zionist leadership, both in Palestine and abroad, preferred to maintain a low profile, adopting a policy of persuasion and reconciliation in an attempt to attain a safe status until the end of the war. The prevailing attitude in the Zionist establishment was that taking a gamble on possible winners might destroy all that had been achieved by the movement to date. And despite debate within the Yishuv about support for one of the sides, it was clear that the Turks were the rulers of the land. According to this school of thought, the Turkish regime, although corrupt, ineffective, and unsympathetic to the Zionist cause, had—at least until that time—refrained from actively persecuting the Jews. The potential danger to the continued existence of the Yishuv, should it be perceived as disloyal to Turkey—particularly in light of Turkish suspicions and sensitivities on this subject, was clear.

The Yishuv maintained economic ties mostly with the Diaspora Jews in Eastern and Western Europe. The members of the Old Yishuv survived almost entirely on donations from abroad—from Russia in particular. This assistance was severely curtailed by the fact that Russia, Britain, and France were in the enemy camp as far as the Turks were concerned.

The New Yishuv was also affected; financing of credit and investments came mostly from the Zionists in Eastern Europe and Britain. One of the major sources of funding for the agricultural villages and the purchase of land was connected to the French Barons: Rothschild and Hirsch, and this pipeline of investment also dried up during the war.

The fledgling Jewish economy was gravely affected by the contraction of investment and financing, both in its day-to-day affairs and in its long-term development plans. Commercial ships ceased to dock in Palestinian ports, and the Russian and Austrian ships which had provided a connection between the Jews in Palestine and the lands of their birth no longer appeared in Jaffa, the country's major port. The stream of letters and money from the Diaspora became a trickle. People and institutions that had depended on this support were left destitute and in need of public assistance. Since these were previously the well-to-do in the community, their penury resulted in sudden economic collapse, especially in the urban population. Workers and artisans were left without work, and shopkeepers and merchants were left without a livelihood.

The agricultural sector was also hurt by the general crisis. Although the farmers who worked unirrigated fields were not hurt, the communities based on orchards, whose existence depended on their ability to market their oranges, almonds, and wine in Europe, were severely affected. Especially hard was the situation of day laborers due to layoffs in the orchards and vineyards. Panic continued to grow when the authorities declared a moratorium and all banks were closed. Credit was cut off, the prices of imported foodstuffs and basic commodities sky-rocketed, and a shortage of bread was already felt in the first days of the war.

The situation further deteriorated after Turkey entered the war at the end of 1914 and Palestine turned into a military base from which Turkey and its allies planned to stage their attack on the Suez Canal and Egypt. Syria and Palestine were obliged to supply the food and materiel needs of the Turkish Fourth Army. A war tax, assessed by public committees, was levied on the residents. The majority of the committee members were Arabs and the sums levied from the allegedly wealthy Jews were high.

Even more burdensome than the tax payments were the numerous confiscations and requisitioning of means of transport, food, and other materiel for the army which promised compensation after the war. Confiscation of the wheat harvest, straw, and other field crops affected mostly the Arab villages, but the Turkish army also needed horses, wagons, pipes, engines, barbed wire—all of which it sought out in the Jewish villages. Both the general confusion and bribery were sometimes able to soften the harshness of the decrees. In early 1915, for example, the Jewish agricultural villages were ordered to turn over all of the water pumps and piping in their possession. The farmers feared that their orchards would be damaged, but after intercession at headquarters in Jerusalem, the Turks agreed to be satisfied with fifteen pumps and 3,000 meters of iron piping. Forced labor quotas, known as "suhkra," also imposed a heavy burden on the Jewish villages. Tens of people were called up to build roads, lay railway lines, and carry out other tasks for the army. For the most part, the village councils were required to supply both the horses and the wagons to transport the people to their labor sites. And the economic situation became even more desperate as the Turkish currency dropped in value.

To the calamities of war was added a plague of locusts in early March 1915. A swarm of locusts migrated from the desert and descended upon the fields and vineyards of the country. After eating their fill, the insects began to lay their eggs while new swarms, thicker than the first, spread their destruction throughout the spring. Within ten days, when the eggs began to hatch, the hungry locusts covered every patch of green in the country. In their battle against the locusts, the Turkish authorities continued to prove their ineffectiveness. The army headquarters ordered all of the country's inhabitants to collect the locust eggs, and to deliver a daily quota of one rotelle (approximately three kilograms) of eggs per inhabitant to the local leaders in the villages and towns. But only a small number of residents obeyed the order, while most people either ignored it or paid off the authorities with a small "bakshish" ("tip"). Only in June 1915, did the locusts take wing and abandon the country. Although the damage was severe and the year's crop was lost, the farmers' worst fears were not realized: the damaged trees and vines bore fruit.

A year passed and the war continued. The Turkish army had returned in February 1915 from a defeat at the Suez Canal; a second year passed, and, in August 1916, the Turks set out on a new campaign at Suez and were again beaten. The country was exhausted by its efforts to support the huge army camps year after year, and army conscriptions weighed heavily on the whole population. Hunger became more widespread. The Turkish army brought with it severe contagious diseases, especially typhus and typhoid fever, which claimed numerous victims during the war years.

The policy of the Turkish authorities toward the Jewish settlement in Palestine was a mixture of hostility and indifference, ameliorated by bribes and pressure by representatives of the Great Powers, protectors of the Jews. Since preferential status of "capitulations" was attached to foreign citizenship, most of the Jews in the country preferred to retain their foreign citizenship.[2]

On September 8, 1914, Turkey, through an Imperial Order, nullified the capitulations that were a thorn in its side. Most of the Yishuv had, for tens of years, been accustomed to consular protection and when this was removed their anxiety was great. Nullification of the capitulations also affected relations between Jews and Arabs in Palestine since the Arabs viewed the Turkish decree as a vindication of their position.

When the war broke out, the Turkish authorities issued an order for the expulsion of all enemy nationals. The Yishuv was stunned; some 50,000 Russian nationals were ordered to leave immediately on neutral ships. Although some of them obeyed the order, the overwhelming majority requested permission to stay. Thanks to the efforts of Henry Morgenthau, the American ambassador in Constantinople and himself a Jew, and others, enemy nationals were given a choice: to leave the country or to become Ottoman. A movement to encourage "Ottomanization" was created with the encouragement of the leadership of the Yishuv but encountered difficulties when it was discovered that the naturalization tax was forbiddingly high. After further intercession, the tax was reduced and when army conscription began, the government decided to defer the enlistment of the new "Ottomans" for one year.

However, given the state of communications throughout the Empire, implementation of decisions made by the upper echelons was dependent upon local commanders, among them the unsympathetic military commander of Yaffa, Hassan-Bey, and the civilian governor of the region, Bahaeddin. They were both strongly identified with Jamal Pasha, commander of the Fourth Turkish Army and of Syria, Palestine, and Transjordan, who sought to undermine the strength of the Zionist movement and to exploit the talents of the Jews to benefit the war effort. Thus Jamal Pasha's subordinates were quick to implement the expulsion order, and on December 17, 1914, more than 500 Jews were expelled from Jaffa. The event left a deep impression. Bahaeddin, responsible for the expulsion of hundreds of Jews, instigated searches for weapons and illegal documents in the homes of Jewish leaders, ordered the Hebrew-language signs to be removed from shops and replaced by signs in Turkish, and ordered the postal offices to refuse to accept letters in Hebrew or Yiddish. Furthermore, he ordered the girls' school in Jaffa and the local Jewish court to be closed. When protest was made against his actions, Bahaeddin was removed from his post, due in part to Morgenthau's intervention and the advice of the German government. Jamal Pasha then appointed Bahaeddin as his secretary, in which position he continued to fight all activities which he viewed as a Zionist attempt to establish an autonomous authority. The Jewish National Fund (which raised money from Diaspora Jewry to support the Zionist development efforts in Palestine) was prohibited from issuing stamps. Banknotes, which had been printed when coinage became scarce, were forbidden in Tel Aviv. Bahaeddin also confiscated the arms of the Jewish guards in Tel Aviv and demanded they be replaced by Arab guards.

On January 25, 1915, the authorities released a declaration about Zionism which they ordered *Haherut*, a Hebrew-language newspaper in Jerusalem, to print:

> The Exalted Government, in its resistance to the dangerous element known as Zionism, which is struggling to create a Jewish government in the Palestinian area of the Ottoman Kingdom and thus placing its own people in jeopardy, has ordered the confiscation of all postal stamps, Zionist flags, paper money, banknotes, etc., and has declared the dissolution of the Zion-

ist organizations and associations, which were secretly established. It has now become known to us that other mischief makers are maliciously engaged in libelous attempts to assert that our measures are directed against all Jews. These have no application to all of those Jews who uphold our covenant....We hope and pray that they will be forever safe, as in the past....It is only the Zionists and Zionism, that corrupt incendiary and rebellious element, together with other groups with such delusionary aspirations, which we must vanquish.

And indeed, the activities of the Turkish authorities during the war period distinguished between the Jews whom they protected and the Zionists whom they persecuted. In order to stamp out the Zionist aspirations and to weaken the status of the Jews in Palestine, the local authorities sought to disarm the new Jewish settlements. Representatives of the Jewish settlements in the Judean region tried vainly to show that the few weapons in their possession were intended for defense against bandits. The rulers were incensed by this claim, threatening heavy punishment if the Zionists should continue their rebellion. The leaders of the settlements, fearful of leaving their inhabitants at the mercy of the Turkish authorities and the hostile Arab inhabitants, were caught in a dilemma. The younger leaders were especially opposed to handing over their weapons.

Weapons confiscated from the Jews were sometimes given to the Arabs. The Jewish settlers saw this as both a burning insult and a grave danger. The confiscation of Jewish arms began in February 1915 in the southeastern Judean region and ended in Zichron Yaakov near the Mediterranean. Not all of the weapons were given up; the Jewish defense group, "Hashomer," refused to relinquish its arms and its leader, Yisrael Shochat, was sharply criticized by other Zionist leaders. In order to undermine the political capability of the Yishuv, Jamal Pasha and his associates decided to expel the Zionist leadership, whether by administrative fiat or after a perfunctory trial.

The size of the Jewish community shrank significantly during the war years, from 86,000 to 55,000, as a result of expulsions, desertions, emigration, and the high mortality rate. Most of those who were expelled or who left were part of the young new population.

Although the situation of the Yishuv was very difficult during this period, it was not unbearable. All of the inhabitants of Palestine, including the Arab population, suffered from the deprivations of war and the inefficient Turkish war machine; the pressures on the Arab population in Syria and Palestine were heavy, thousands of Arabs were expelled from Gaza, and when the British army advanced toward the Levant, the Turks publicly executed leaders of the Arab nationalist movement in Damascus and Beirut. Moreover, the influence of world Jewry on Turkish policy was evident and the American, German, and Austrian Jewish communities succeeded in restraining some of its harsher aspects. Decrees were softened; overly zealous Turkish commanders were replaced and periods of calm followed the times of distress. The persecution and suffering inflicted on the Syrians and the Lebanese were much greater—and they had no one to come to their aid.

The voluntary enlistment in 1915 and 1916 of tens of Jewish secondary school students into the Turkish officer corps can be understood in light of this situation and a desire to demonstrate the loyalty of the Jewish population, as well as an attempt to acquire military experience which could benefit the Yishuv in the future. Jewish officers and NCOs in the Turkish army were scattered from the Macedonian front to the battle zones in Iraq. Though serving under a foreign flag, these Palestinian soldiers usually demonstrated military professionalism, dedication, and loyalty despite the hardships.

The Jewish leadership in the country believed that explicit loyalty to the Turkish regime was essential to the continued well-being of the Yishuv, and the Zionists in Germany lobbied for a public German-Turkish declaration of support for the Jewish settlement in Palestine, along the lines of the British Balfour Declaration.

Important studies have appeared in recent years which deal with the Jewish settlement in Palestine during the First World War (see note 1 to this chapter). The above survey has attempted to give a brief description of the background to the central issues of this book. Among all of the events in Palestine during the period, we will concentrate on the aspects which relate to our subject from a perspective which has been given little attention before: the attitude of the Yishuv to the massacre of the Armenians.

This chapter comprises three sections: the first section examines the information found in testimony from the period of the Armenian massacre. Afterwards, we shall explore two events in which the dangers of a "similar fate" to that of the Armenians became a significant fear among the Jews of the Yishuv at the time: the expulsion of the Jews of Tel Aviv in April 1917, and the discovery of the "Nili" spy network toward the end of the war.

Reports of the Armenian Massacre and Reaction to It

Reports on the atrocities against the Armenians during the First World War reached the public in Western countries in real time. Accounts appeared in the press while the massacres were being committed. In this respect, there is no doubt that both governments and the general public could have been aware of the events when steps could still have been taken to stop them. The means employed by the Turks made the mass murders difficult to hide. Consuls, missionaries, and others in the regions of the atrocities reported them, and their reports reached the newspapers as early as spring, 1915. The *New York Times* had published more than 100 articles by December 1915, most of them on the first pages of the paper. Similar reports were published in Britain, Australia, and other countries. Detailed reports of the acts of destruction were given wide coverage.[3] During the course of the war itself, a number of reports on the genocide were published, among them from the German missionary Lepsius, the Britons Bryce and Toynbee, and the former American ambassador in Constantinople, Henry Morgenthau, Sr. At least some of the reports were apparently known to Aaron Aaronsohn, a prominent member of the Yishuv in Palestine, a high official in the local Ottoman administration and the leader of the Nili spy network, as we shall see.

Examination of various sources from the period indicates that the Yishuv was made aware of the Armenian genocide at an early stage despite Turkish efforts at strict censorship of letters and newspapers from abroad. Furthermore, the authorities forbade publication of all Hebrew-language newspapers in Palestine, with the exception of the officially supervised journal, *Haherut*, which was, in effect, a government organ. In light of the corruption and ineptness of the Turkish regime, we can, nevertheless, assume that ways were found to circumvent the censorship and, indeed, we find considerable evidence to that effect.

Mordecai Ben-Hillel Hacohen was one of the reliable and knowledgeable sources of information about the life of the Jews in Palestine during the period of the First World War. In his journal entry, entitled "Everything is Concealed," on March 20, 1916, he complains that the public in Palestine is unaware of the chain of events during the war:

> According to reports in foreign newspapers, it has been more than five weeks since the Turkish forces were defeated by the Russians in the

Caucasus, and the fortress in Erezrum and in other cities such as Van and Mush were conquered. It may be that the Russian force has already reached Musselle, and we, resident here, know nothing. The whole affair is being concealed from us, and the local commander [Hassan Bey] has ordered the reading room in the city to remove the German newspapers and it is also being said that he has ordered the Poste not to deliver German newspapers to the reading room without his prior censorship.[4]

A day earlier he writes, "Yesterday, at Dr. Tahon's, I saw copies of *Hazefira* which has resumed publication in Warsaw, for the first time since war was declared. I was very happy to see them."

In his journal, Hacohen relates to the Russian attack which began in November 1915, perhaps intending to join up with the British forces in Mesopotamia. In January 1916, they launched another attack in Armenia, winning quick victories, and occupied the cities of Armenia— Erezrum, Van, Mush, Trebizond, and others—which had been held by the Turkish army and whose population had been slaughtered.

On February 2, 1917, in a journal entry entitled "The Armenian Refugees," Hacohen states,

A great number of Armenians have been exiled to Syria and Palestine, a surviving remnant of the thousands and tens of thousands whom the Turks evilly robbed, destroyed and annihilated in the cities of Armenia at the beginning of the war, before the Russians entered Armenia. In their naked- ness and complete deprivation these wretched creatures have arrived here. Last winter in Damascus I already saw these pitiful women and children, starving in the streets. They told horrible stories of the grief and loss which have afflicted the Armenians, how parents sold their sons and daughters as slaves for one majida rather than see them die of hunger....The Armenians have also been brought to Haifa. The well-to-do in their community are trying to establish a public association that will care for the poor. This ex- iled people has learned from the Jews, the eternally exiled people, and they have also established an assistance committee and grocery shops and other public institutions to aid the weak and wretched until the storm of these awful events shall pass.[5]

Hacohen's reaction is one of shock and pity: "the wretched," "grief," "loss," "awful events" are the words he uses to describe the situation of the Armenian refugees whom he describes as a "surviving remnant." He also compares "this exiled people" to the Jews," the eternally exiled people."

The Jewish community in Palestine shrank during the war years, as did the Christian and Muslim communities. The number of Armenians, on the other hand, grew significantly with the arrival of the refugees from the genocide during the war and after it. Thus, the Armenians (Gregorians) more than doubled their numbers from 1,173 in 1914 to 2,528 in 1922, in the Jerusalem region alone.[6]

The memoirs of Moshe Smilansky, a leader of the Jewish agricultural settlements and a writer, also serve as an important reference source of the history of the Yishuv during the war period. His memoirs of the first year of the war were written as the events occurred and his impressions of the subsequent war years were written after the war ended. His writings include explicit reference to the Armenian genocide in the context of the already grave situation of the Jewish settlement in Palestine "in the first year of the war." Smilansky describes the Ottomanization, the problems relating to it, the departures, and prohibitions against leaving the country. He writes,

> Will the villages empty out? And what will the Arabs say? 'An expulsion decree against the Jews'...and they will descend upon the Jews to loot their property. For a moment it seemed to us that there was an evil and brutal intention here, which only the Turkish mind is capable of inventing....Does not the smell of blood rise from this intention? Is this not a preparation for massacre, like the massacre of the Armenians? The confused mind envisions terrible scenes.[7]

In Smilansky's memoirs of the second year of the war we find, among others, entries like "Jamal Pasha's Attitude Toward the Germans," "Fear of Death" (which descended upon the Jewish community in the country), and "The Massacre of the Armenians." He writes,

> And from the corner of the earth, from Armenia, shocking rumors have reached us. The government and the Kurds have committed a terrible massacre of all of the Armenian inhabitants. They slaughtered every man and left only the elderly, the women and the children alive. And these they scattered to the edges of the country. They dispersed the Armenian exiles to Syria, to Transjordan, and to the Druse Mountains. And they sold the young girls in every marketplace. And the local peasants bought them for concubines and maidservants. People from Jaffa, who traveled to Syrian cities on matters of business, saw the encampments of these wretched people in every railway station. They were like herds of starving animals. Beaten, wounded, naked and barefoot. Their faces and eyes filled with horror and deathly fear...and in their eyes one could see how the young virgins were sold in the market for pennies...and a crowd of the "faithful" who gathered to look at the exiles, would point at them: these are to the slaughter.

> The testimony of eye witnesses aroused fear and panic in the audience. Who knows what would have been our fate, were it not for Morgenthau, the American representative in Constantinople, and the fear of the world press which is 'controlled' by the Jews.[8]

We don't know exactly when this excerpt was written by Smilansky. We can only estimate from its place in the memoirs, which he finished writing in late 1918, and from the chronology of events.[9] It appears that the excerpt relates to the period of autumn 1915, or the winter of 1915-16, at the latest.

In addition to his deep shock at what had happened to the Armenians, Smilansky expresses anxiety about a similar fate, together with hope for rescue and deliverance. The fear of a similar fate is a motif that recurs in reactions at the time.

Meir Dizengoff played a central role in the leadership of the Yishuv during the First World War. His role and importance grew after September 1916 when other leaders and other public figures were deported. He carried much of the burden of resistance to the Turkish authorities and survival efforts of the Yishuv, and was, in effect, its spokesman at the end of the war.

In 1931, Dizengoff wrote "Recollections from the Recent Past," emphasizing that this is not a history or a diary. Nonetheless, his document, *With Tel Aviv in Exile*, is an important source for the history of the Yishuv, as seen through the eyes of one of its leaders. Dizengoff recalls the Armenian experience more than once. During the entire war period, Dizengoff worked in close cooperation with the Zionist delegation in Constantinople, which was pro-German and pro-Turkish. According to him, there were also excellent relations with the German consul in Palestine, "with whom I was acquainted." The consul served as a conduit for transferring funds to the Yishuv, on orders from the German ambassador in Constantinople.

In his memoirs, written years later, Dizengoff also relates that the figures who assisted, and perhaps saved the Yishuv were "the Germans who apparently postponed the affair" [the trial of the leaders of the Yishuv]. In his estimate, the fact that Jamal Pasha became more sympathetic to the Jews was due to Germany: "Indeed, the German influence certainly helped in effecting this change of attitude" and the attitude of the regime became more balanced.[10] It should be remembered that Smilansky attributed more importance to Morgenthau's efforts to save the Yishuv.

Dizengoff mentions the Armenian genocide in his memoirs only in the context of threats by Jamal Pasha and Enver Pasha during their visit to the country: "Zionists beware! If you oppose us we will do to you what we have done to the Armenians."[11] He mentions fear of "the fate of the Armenians" again, with regard to the discovery of the Nili pro-British spy network, not as a threat on the part of the authorities but as an expression of his own concern: "Fear of death and total ruin enveloped us....Now the restraints would be loosened, and we would be doomed like the Armenians to massacre and annihilation."[12]

Arthur Ruppin, director of the Palestine Development Association's office in Jaffa from 1908, played a very important role in the defense and preservation of the Yishuv during the war, thanks to his efforts within in the country and, after his expulsion in September 1916, in Constantinople.

Since he was a German citizen with close ties to the German delegation in the country and to the consuls in Jaffa and Jerusalem, as well as to the German ambassador in Constantinople, Ruppin knew that the Turks would not dare to harm him. Nonetheless, Jamal Pasha could not tolerate the Zionist activities carried out under Ruppin's leadership which the Turk viewed as an attempt to create a state within a state. Jamal Pasha, who was consistent in his policy of 'benevolence toward the Jews, no mercy toward the Zionists," wanted Ruppin out of the way. He threatened to harm the Yishuv if Ruppin did not leave. Ruppin proposed to Jamal Pasha that he leave his position in the Palestine office in Jaffa, move to Jerusalem, and dedicate his time to writing a book on the national economy of Syria. Jamal Pasha accepted the idea and Ruppin moved to Jerusalem where he spent the next nine months writing his book, *The Economy of Syria*, which was highly acclaimed in professional journals.

In order to research his book, Ruppin went to Syria (Beirut, Damascus, Aleppo, Homs, Hama), equipped with letters from Jamal Pasha to the authorities in each city requesting that they give Ruppin their full cooperation. The trip to Syria was made in late 1915 or early 1916. Ruppin remarks in his memoirs, "In my journeys I saw many Armenians who wandered half starved throughout the land, and traces of the terrible massacres of the Armenians were evident everywhere."[13]

This is the only reference which deals with the Armenian tragedy in Ruppin's memoirs, *My Life*. The book combines excerpts from the diary he kept at the time with memoirs written in later periods, up to

1941.[14] Surprising? Perhaps not. In any event, it is noteworthy that a figure like Ruppin, a liberal and a humanist in his world view, made do with only two lines to deal with the "terrible massacres of the Armenians," the traces of which "were evident everywhere." Ruppin remarks in the introduction to his autobiography that his memories were naturally more vivid regarding the events in which he was directly involved and that the subjects treated in his book were determined by personal considerations.

Unlike Ruppin, Levi Yitzchak Schneerson, a member of the Nili network, was deeply affected by the fate of the Armenians. Schneerson accompanied Aaron Aaronsohn on his trip to Constantinople in July 1916 for the purpose of establishing connections with the British. Aaronsohn continued on from Constantinople to Germany, Denmark, and England. Schneerson returned to Palestine and served as the contact for the Nili members who had remained in the country to gather intelligence for the headquarters of the British forces in Cairo. While in Constantinople, he wrote in his journal, on August 12, 1916:

> I have been to the American embassy. I saw Montgomery (the secretary). A pleasant fellow but a 'Syrian.' Nothing yet from Mr. Aaronsohn [who had already left Constantinople by then]. In the beautiful hall I saw a plaque with names of donors to the Armenian victims. The Jewish names are very prominent and the sums of their donations are very fat. There is some hidden sensibility, which arouses our Israelite brethren to come to the aid of the Armenians. Will not the fate of the Jews in Palestine be like that of the Armenians? Would that my dark prophecies be proved baseless.[15]

Not only Armenian refugees reached Palestine during the war. Stolen Armenian property also reached the country in roundabout ways. "The Shepherds," a group of Zionist pioneers who sought to promote the involvement of Jews in animal husbandry, was, in the winter of 1915-16, tending a herd of 400 goats in an isolated spot in the Galilee. A Jew by the name of Pace from Tiberias had purchased the herd from the Turkish army which had stolen it from the Armenians. Pace had made an agreement with "The Shepherds" similar to the agreements usual among Arab shepherds, but the herd was in poor condition, having suffered from extended neglect and malnutrition. Intensive efforts of "The Shepherds" to care for the herd were to no avail.[16]

We will examine the reaction of the members of the Nili organization to the Armenian genocide at a later point. It is reasonable to assume that what was known to the members of Nili was known, or could at least be known, to additional people in the Yishuv and we can surmise that there exists additional testimony from the period. In any event, from the excerpts that have been cited—important sources for the study of the Yishuv during the period of the First World War — we can conclude with certainty that the terrible Turkish massacre of the Armenians was known at the time. The knowledge was accompanied by fear and anxiety lest the Jewish settlement in Palestine suffer the same fate as the Armenians. That fear increased significantly during two events to which we now turn our attention: expulsion of the Jews from Tel Aviv and the discovery of the Nili spy network.

The Expulsion of the Jews from Tel Aviv

In the spring of 1917, the small Jewish community in Palestine was stunned by an order issued by the Turkish authorities for the deportation of the 5,000 Jews from Tel Aviv to the small farming villages in the Sharon Plain and the Galilee. This may have been the beginning of a plan to deport the Jews in the villages and in the Jerusalem region as an emergency war measure, and the decree aroused grave concern about the future of the Jewish settlement in the country. When the deportation order became known to the Nili organization, its members publicized the plan in the world press. American Jewry was shocked, and the nations fighting against Turkey released reports on Turkish intentions to exterminate the Jews in Palestine, as they had already done to the Armenians. Public opinion in the neutral countries, as well as in Germany and the Austro-Hungarian Empire, was outraged and Jamal Pasha was forced to reconsider his plan of action. He promised food and medical assistance to the refugees from Tel Aviv and cancelled the other deportation plans.

The events surrounding the deportation of the Jews from Tel Aviv were perceived at the time as one of the hardest periods for the Yishuv during the entire course of the war. The suffering, the fears, and the panic were especially great, and engendered a palpable concern that what had happened to the Armenians would happen to the Jews in Palestine. The reaction to the Tel Aviv deportations in April 1917 was a tangible example of cooperation between Aaron Aaronsohn and Mark Sykes, which we will examine at length later. Aaronsohn's reaction to the expulsion order was illustrative of his political approach and methods which differed from those of the prevailing leadership in the country and from much of the Zionist leadership abroad. The Zionist leadership tried to achieve its goals through intercession of the Turkish rulers, while Nili, led by Aaron Aaronsohn, fought the Turks primarily by means of public opinion.

Arthur Ruppin, who was in exile in Constantinople at the time, received the news of Tel Aviv deportations after the fact, together with rumors of the imminent evacuation of Jerusalem. He wrote in his journal on April 25, 1917, "I am in despair. Has it been decreed that within a few days everything we have nurtured and built for years and tens of years will be destroyed?"[17] His assistant, Yaakov Tahon, who ran the office in his absence, wrote in 1919 when summing up the period of the war: "This order [to expel the Jews from Tel Aviv and the surrounding area] stirred amazement and fear. Everyone viewed it as the beginning of the same acts which were committed against the Armenians."[18]

Mordecai Ben-Hillel Hacohen was, we have said, one of the most reliable and observant sources about the history of the Jews in Palestine during the war. In his journal, *The War of the Nations*, he describes in great detail, over tens of pages, Jamal Pasha's expulsion order, the reaction of the Jews, the deportation itself and what Hacohen terms "the exile," and the efforts which were ultimately successful in softening the decree. On the other hand, the information which appears in Aaronsohn's diary on this subject is brief and fragmented. The differences in approach reflected in the two diaries are both fascinating and meaningful.

On March 30, 1917, Mordecai Ben-Hillel Hacohen wrote in his diary: "The noise of wagons on the paving stones was heard throughout the night in Tel Aviv...tumult and the uproar of flight, the sound of the bell of exile...." Jamal Pasha's original order called for immediate evacuation of the Jewish residents of Tel Aviv on the grounds of developments connected with the war against the British forces and fear of impending battles in the area. Indeed, in April 1917, there were two assaults by the British army based in Egypt in the direction of Palestine (the first and second battles of Gaza) which ended in disastrous British defeats. Hacohen describes a petition submitted to the Pasha of Jaffa, requesting that he cancel the deportation order, in the following words:

"Firstly, lest there be discrimination between us and the Germans and the Austrians and Bulgarians, and just as they have been granted permission to remain in the country on their own responsibility, so should we too (Jewish immigrants of Russian origin) be permitted to remain on our own recognizance." Secondly, that time be granted, of at least two weeks, to organize the exodus.

Thirdly, that the poor be permitted also to remain in the Galilee, lower and upper, in the environs of Tiberias and Safed, and not to wander to far-off Hama, desolate of Jews, and to where the long journey, of many days and weeks, will take a killing toll upon them, and their fate will be as the fate of the exiled Armenians of whom tens of thousands perished during the journey. Fourthly, that guards from among us, persons who have fulfilled their military duty, be allowed to remain in our neighborhoods and to protect our houses and property.[19]

Hacohen adds a comment which is significant in our context:

I proposed that we write explicitly in the petition the argument that our poor should not be forced to Hama lest they perish like the Armenians. I attach value to the fact that the Turkish government has been stained in the eyes of the whole country because of its crime against the Armenians, and perhaps the government will reconsider its thoughts of doing thus to the Jews as well, but our politicians said that we must not write this lest it arouse ire against the petitioners.

Fear of the Turkish actions was bound up with alarm that the Turks might do to the Jewish community in Palestine, or at least to the Zionist elements within it, what they had done to the Armenians. This concern was expressed in additional evidence from the early days of the war, from which we can conclude that the Armenian tragedy was known in the Yishuv.[20]

The proposal to publicly warn about possible parallels between the fate of the Armenians and that of the Jews in Palestine as a deterrent was rejected by "our politicians" in Hacohen's words. It is worth noting that Aaron Aaronsohn, who introduced the analogy, did not "invent" it and did not "invent" the fears of a similar fate.

Hacohen says that the Pasha of Jaffa rejected the entire petition and all of its clauses. "He has no power or authority to change any part of the order," and has been sent by Jamal Pasha only to delay the implementation of the deportation. Hacohen goes on to say:

In Neve Shalom, in one of the houses of prayer, a small Yom Kippur day of repentance was held, and they prayed for the cancellation of the expulsion decree. It is said that they opened the Holy Ark, and the elders who were gathered took a vow not to go, not to leave their places and not to abandon the city. There is also logic in this, since there is no doubt that all of the poor and the elderly and the weak that are going are going to their death.

They will die along the way, under the open sky, and is it not better to die here, in one's own bed, to die in the city. It is interesting that our politicians don't even dare to ask or to speak strong words to the governor while the elderly say we should simply rebel and ignore the order.[21]

In the end, the deportation order was postponed several times, and the fear that "all the travelers from Jerusalem say that very soon Jerusalem will suffer the fate of Jaffa" was never realized.[22]

The leadership of the Yishuv sought help from the foreign consuls, among them the German consul.[23] Hacohen's comments contain more than a trace of criticism of the politicians who don't dare to act and he has harsh words for corrupt Turkey: "Their acts of violence and robbery do not end, and they invent libelous charges, sucking the last drop of blood, and anyone can see that our situation in Eretz Yisrael has no solution but a different ruler, whoever that may be."[24] He fears for the safety of his son who is serving in the Turkish army, and talks about the great tragedy of our lives: "And in this frame of thought we have sent the best of our sons to the battlefields to protect Turkey whose downfall we seek, even as a slave seeks shade, salvation....How deep is our sorrow, how enormous the tragedy in our hearts!"

At the same time, upon hearing the rumors about the Turkish victory in the second battle for Gaza, on April 17-19, 1917, which turned out to be accurate, he hopes, "Would that the English would be gone, and their armies return to Egypt, so that the victors would let us alone and would not deport us from our cities, our homes, and our villages!"[25]

Aaron Aaronsohn, who was in Egypt at the time, was extremely worried about the condition of the Jewish community in Palestine and wanted to take action. He shared his concerns and plans with Mark Sykes. They were in agreement that there was grave danger to the Yishuv—the analogy to the fate of the Armenians was obvious—and that Jewish and general public opinion must be enlisted to prevent harsh measures. Aaronsohn believed there was an urgent need to send telegrams to England and the United States informing them of the situation in Palestine, for two reasons: "To appeal for money, and especially to make the world fully aware, before the Turks and the Boche can spread their false version of events."[26] He agreed with the British, after discussion, that "I will present the facts of the events which they will deliver to London, and there they will issue a press release."

The next day, on April 28, Aaronsohn and Sykes met again: "Sir Sykes does not anticipate any objection to my attempt to inform the

Jewish public about the developments in Palestine, and that I urge them to publicly express their support." They agreed that Aaronsohn would send, through Sykes and the Foreign Office, a telegram to Nahum Sokolow in England and to Julius Rosenwald in the U.S. Aaronsohn relates that immediately after the conversation he wrote to Sokolow and Rosenwald. And, indeed, Sykes passed the message that same day to Sir Ronald Graham, in the British Foreign Office, requesting that it be delivered to Chaim Weizmann or Sokolow:

> Aaron Aaronsohn asks me to inform you that Tel Aviv has been sacked. 10,000 Jews in Palestine are now without home or food. Whole of Yischub [sic] is threatened with destruction. Jemal has publicly stated Armenian policy will now be applied to Jews. Pray inform centres [the Jewish communities], without mentioning Aaron Aaronsohn or source of information. Aaron Aaronsohn corresponding with [Julius] Rosenvald by another channel pending [groups omitted]. Aaron Aaronsohn advises and I agree in present crisis Weizman's presence here is essential.[27]

In Aaronsohn's diary for May 9, we find: "Reuters' [press agency] this evening relates, word for word, my memorandum 'The Evacuation of Tel Aviv.'"[28] The press release stated that on April 1 an order was given to deport all the Jews from Tel Aviv, including citizens of the Central Powers, within forty-eight hours. A week before, three hundred Jews were expelled from Jerusalem: Jamal Pasha declared that their fate would be that of the Armenians; the eight thousand deportees from Tel Aviv were not allowed to take any provisions with them, and after the expulsion their houses were looted by Bedouin mobs; two Yemenite Jews who tried to oppose the looting were hung at the entrance to Tel Aviv so that all might see, and other Jews were found dead in the dunes around Tel Aviv. Some of this information turned out later to be inaccurate. Yet it should be pointed out that despite Aaronsohn's tendency to portray the situation in stark, acute terms, he did not purposely falsify it.

His diary from this period is full of worry and fear for the Jews in Palestine, and contains partial and fragmentary reports. For example, the report of two Jews who were hanged, which was not true, appears first in his diary.[29] In retrospect we shall see that the report distributed by Reuters aroused the fury of Jamal Pasha as well as his reaction and, thus, may have achieved its purpose.

From Aaronsohn's diary we learn that he tried to enlist the Jews in Russia, the refugees from Palestine in Egypt, and the Jewish community in the United States, as well as in England. With the help of Sykes,

Aaronsohn sent telegrams to several prominent Jews in the U.S.: to his brother, Alexander, who was there at the time, to Professor Felix Frankfurter, to Judge Meyer Sulzberger and to Justice Louis D. Brandeis of the U.S. Supreme Court. Aaronsohn thought that the information might be useful in organizing a campaign to create Jewish brigades in the United States which would fight the Turks in Palestine. The possibility is mentioned in the telegrams, in various wordings, that "not a trace nor a soul will remain," and then there will be no further excuse for the Jews to refrain from outright war against the Turks.

He talks about the Turkish atrocities against the Jewish population in Palestine and writes to his brother, Alexander: "Jaffa has been evacuated, and reliable sources have reported on atrocities. I am awaiting new and horrible reports." He also emphasizes that the proposals to make efforts to organize Jewish brigades "are mine alone, and are in no way official."[30] There were reservations in some British circles regarding the delivery of the telegrams, "the amazing expenditure of public monies," at the expense of His Majesty's government, and there were those who demanded that Aaronsohn send the telegrams at his own expense. They accused Sir Mark Sykes of exceeding his authority and demanded that he desist. The telegrams were indeed held back and were sent only on June 2, 1917.[31]

There is no doubt that Aaronsohn's activities created shock and led to a reaction. On May 22, he met in Cairo with General Archibald Maurry, the high commander of the Egyptian Expeditionary Forces, who was the highest ranking British officer in Egypt.[32] In a face-to-face meeting with Aaronsohn he said,

> I wish to tell you how upset I am, personally and privately, by the incidents in Palestine. [The idea] to bring upon the Jews the hapless lot of the Armenians makes my soul tremble and arouses sorrow that we are so powerless.[33]

At the same time, Maurry makes it clear to Aaronsohn that "a Jewish division will be of no benefit to me."[34]

Chaim Weizmann also made wide use of the information he received from Aaronsohn through Sykes. He passed the letters on to Jewish and Zionist figures: Chlenov, Sokolow, the Baron Rothschild, Jacobus H. Kann in the Hague, and De Haas and the Zionist office in Copenhagen.

> Jamal Pasha openly declared that the joy of Jews at the approach of British troops would be short lived as he would make them share the fate of the

Armenians....Jamal Pasha is too cunning to order cold-blooded massacres. His method is to drive the population to starvation and death by thirst, epidemics etc., etc., which according to him are merely calamities sent by God. Those who know his methods will not be surprised if after a short time severe punishment is dealt on those who have plundered and pillaged under his orders, or at least with his connivance. This will be in accordance with his established policy of exciting one part of the population against the other and exterminating all those who are not Turanians. Please give it greatest publicity.[35]

It is difficult to determine with certainty what factors caused Jamal Pasha to modify his attitude toward the Jews in April 1917, and why the suffering and destruction were relatively moderate. In his diary, Mordecai Ben-Hillel Hacohen relates that Jamal Pasha met with Dr. Dizengoff, Mr. Krause, and the leaders of the Jewish villages near Jerusalem, and afterwards with Mr. Kalvarisky from Rosh Pina.

They were very upset and anxious lest they hear from the chief commander new decrees, but this was not the case. They arrived and Jamal Pasha put before them a foreign newspaper which contained a harsh description of the actions of Jamal Pasha who expelled only the Jews from Jaffa, looted their property and also hanged two Jews from Jaffa.[36]

These are clearly the reports which were drafted by Aaronsohn and published by Reuters.[37] Jamal Pasha demands that they deny the truth of the reports, and "of course," writes Mordecai Ben-Hillel Hacohen, "the guests expressed their desire to send a protest denying the foreign press reports, which had invented the charges against Jamal Pasha. Of course Kalvarisky also sent telegrams of the sort demanded to several places abroad."[38]

And Hacohen sums up the incident: "Well, the walls have ears, and the fear of public opinion in Europe and America is still very strong in the ruling circles in Turkey. Our tears are more than falling pools of water. This is also for the best."[39] Hacohen also indicates: "There is no doubt that all of the expulsion from Jaffa and the villages around Jerusalem has done awful damage to the Jews and to the Jewish settlement there." The fears of expulsion also raised questions about the future of the Jewish settlement in Palestine. In Hacohen's words, "This has given sustenance to the new problem of the presence of the Jews in Palestine, and the acts of Jamal Pasha have aroused them in full force." According to him, the issue at hand was the proposal to give Palestine to the Jews, as a protectorate of the United States. "We cannot depend nor count upon the protection of the Germans since these same Germans, unwilling and unable, did not save us from the Turks during the time of the expulsions."

It appears that the Germans did try to ameliorate the Turkish actions, and the German consul, Schabinger, won the appreciation and the gratitude of the Zionist leadership in the country. Yet it is not clear whether these efforts had an effect on Jamal Pasha, who had little love for the Germans.[40]

Arthur Ruppin, who was in Constantinople at the time and continued his intensive efforts to help the Jewish community in Palestine, reports in his diary on May 26, 1917:

> The German ambassador [in Constantinople], Richard Kühlmann, called me in to see him today and told me that the Allied press had published false reports on riots against the Jews during the deportations from Jaffa. He asked me to refute these reports. I replied that a seal of antisemitism was stamped upon the expulsion but that no acts of abomination were committed. I will demand a telegram from the Executive Committee in Berlin, I added, which will refute these false reports. The ambassador was satisfied with my reply.[41]

Ruppin went to the meeting with the German ambassador to discuss the latter's demand for a denial of the press reports about the brutality of the deportations. Ruppin complained to the ambassador that his right to receive reliable information about the events in Palestine through the secret codes of the German delegation in Constantinople (which representatives of the Zionist leadership also enjoyed) had been rescinded. Therefore he would be unable to investigate the matter in Palestine. Permission to use the embassy codes was given, and Ruppin delivered a denial to the legation. "But according to him this was not a whitewash of the real state of affairs." Ruppin continues, "Since Jamal Pasha knew that the Jews were regularly informing the German legation of his actions toward the Jews in Palestine, he apparently refrained from implementing some of his plans. He [Jamal Pasha] was, it is true, sympathetic to the French and hostile to the Germans, but feared the Germans nonetheless and was careful not to create trouble with them."[42] Ruppin indicates that one of his tasks in Constantinople was to frustrate, as much as possible, Jamal Pasha's plans, with the help of the German legation which sought the support of world Jewry.

There are varying opinions among historians as to the relative weight of the parties—particularly the United States and Germany—who aided the Jews in Palestine during this period.[43] In contrast, some historians emphasize the influence of Jewish public opinion in the world, since Jamal Pasha—who believed that the Jews had great political strength internationally—feared its alleged power.[44] Without taking a position on the question, the following points should be remembered:

- Aaronsohn's efforts, with Sykes' assistance, indeed aroused public opinion among the Jews and in general, as well as among elements in the governments of France and Britain, regarding the grave danger posed to the Jews in Palestine by the Turks.
- The fear of a repeat of the "Armenian experience" which truly concerned Aaronsohn, was shared by additional people, who were anxious that what had happened to the Armenians was happening or about to happen to the Jews.

Aaronsohn sought to take advantage of the shock inspired by the expulsion from Tel Aviv as a lever for Zionist efforts with the assistance of Sykes, the Frenchman Picot, and others. During this period he worked feverishly and initiated a fundraising appeal to Jews in the Diaspora, especially in Russia and the United States, to aid the deportees, began a campaign for donations among the Jews in Egypt, and tried to encourage Jews to enlist in the Jewish regiments which were to be sent to the front in Palestine.

Following the press reports, Oskar Cohen, a Jewish socialist member of the German Parliament, presented a question to the Chancellor asking if he would be willing to press the Turkish government "to vigorously prevent the recurrence in Palestine of atrocities such as those committed against the Armenians."

On June 8, 1917, Aaronsohn was able to record in his diary, with a bit of satisfaction:

Radcliffe has given me an item from the *Forwards* of May 16, which describes the parliamentary question of the Socialist delegate Cohen in the Reichstag. We should remember that Cohen was insistent about the statement of the German commander of the Fourth Ottoman Corps which claimed that Jamal Pasha's assertion of a military pretext for the evacuation of Jaffa was groundless. All of the German denials, all of their interpolations, the staged interview with Chaim Nachum [the Hacham Bashi, the Chief Rabbi in Constantinople] are corrupt and cowardly.[45] The denial, which was extracted by force from the leaders of the Jewish community in Jerusalem, proves one thing: the cry we raised was effective. The Turks and the Germans were quick to realize that one cannot get away with slaughtering the

Jews like the Armenians. German financing of the war might have suffered because of the Jews. Therefore they ceased the new deportations.[46]

Nevertheless, historian Joseph Nedava's claim, that "the threatened slaughter of the Jews in Palestine was prevented" by efforts of the Nili members, seems exaggerated. Nedava says, "Thanks to the actions of Nili, world opinion was enlisted to moderate the brutality of the Turks during the time of the murders." Nedava further claims that the efforts of Aaron Aaronsohn after the deportation of the Jews from Tel Aviv, in the spring of 1917, prevented additional deportations planned by Jamal Pasha.[47] Aaronsohn's actions, which were intended to sound a warning and to arouse public opinion, succeeded also because the British, at least Sykes, were sensitive to the possible harm to the Jews and Arabs at the time. Germany's position was also a factor in moderating the Turkish attitude toward the Zionists. Within the context of all of these factors, Aaronsohn's contribution was significant.

The position of *Palestine*, the journal of the British Zionist movement, is also of interest in this context. The journal reflected the position of Weizmann and Sokolow with whom Aaronsohn was in contact, through Sykes. *Palestine* suggests taking Jamal Pasha at his word when he declares that the fate of the Jews will be that of the Armenians, and adds that Jamal Pasha will have no need for claims of military necessity in order to implement his threats to do to the Jews what his partners have done to the Armenians. According to *Palestine*, four factors can prevent this disaster:

- The caution of the Turkish authorities who know that the Jews in the world will never forget nor forgive them for such acts. Crimes of this nature will not go unpunished.
- The German government will be perceived by public opinion in general, and by Jewish public opinion in particular, as responsible for such acts. It is true, says the paper, that this fact did not save the Armenians. But the German government knows that the Jews do not compare to the Armenians in terms of their world power, and that the weight of the Jews in Germany is therefore different from that of the Armenians. The Zionists in Germany tried throughout the war to preserve the Jewish national efforts in Palestine.
- Neutral public opinion, both Jewish and general. The fact that the United States had become a combatant in the war made no difference in this context.
- The advance of the British army. The most effective form of security for the Jews would be achieved by Britain's speedy conquest of Palestine. It is possible, according to the paper, to break the current military deadlock, and there is value in a British threat to hold the military and civilian Turkish

authorities directly responsible for a policy of slaughter and destruction of the Jews.

The Discovery of the Nili Affair–Fear of "Armenian Fate" Revisited

The historiography dealing with the Nili affair is divided in its assessment of the actions of this group. Was this handful of young people, most of them from Jewish agricultural villages, who worked from 1915 to 1917 in the service of the British government's intelligence gathering effort and in opposition to the Turkish regime in the country, "lowly spies or national heroes?"[48] The first underground in the country? Traitors or people of distinguished valor? Visionaries or adventurers? Or perhaps all of the above combined?

The group known as "Nili" (an acronym of the passage in the First Book of Samuel, 15:29, "the Glory of Israel will not lie"), comprised fewer than forty members in all. When the network was exposed, at the end of the First World War, the members of Nili and their actions became the subject of hot controversy. Much of the small Jewish community in Palestine at the time condemned the network's actions, and for years afterward there were reservations, rejection and, to some degree, ostracism of the surviving members of the group (the leading figures in Nili were killed). The activities of the group during the war were frequently presented subjectively, in keeping with the outlook of the writer. Nili had enthusiastic supporters and admirers, but it also had opponents, and more than a few bitter enemies.

The enmity which existed between the workers' movement and Nili resulted in the later identification of the political right with Nili, and thereby affected attitudes toward it. Subsequent identification of the revisionist right with the group does not, in my opinion, reflect the political, historical, and social circumstances of the period in which it operated. A more neutral, semi-official definition of the group is "the first Jewish intelligence network."[49]

The decisive stage in the deterioration of relations between the Nili and other parts of the Yishuv was, without question, the discovery of the spy ring in October 1917: "treachery," "separatism," and "betrayal" were some of the terms frequently used regarding the affair.

Historians of the Nili chronicles and its members are usually sympathetic, and sometimes admiring, toward the group, and reject the claim that the spy ring and its discovery could have had disastrous results for the Jewish community in Palestine. According to them, the members of Nili showed dedication to an ideal, extraordinary courage and willingness to endanger their lives and the lives of their families, and willingness to sacrifice themselves for the good of the public. They were aware of the dangers and the chances they took upon themselves, and consciously chose to do what they could to save the Yishuv from the terrible threat it faced. In contrast to its supporters, the opponents and critics of Nili, both at the time of its exposure and years later (the Nili affair continues to be a controversial issue), accuse Nili of gravely endangering the Yishuv. For example, *The History of the Hagana*, in its examination of the role of Nili in the history of the Yishuv, objects to its "special methods," i.e., spying, which Nili used to implement its pro-British orientation, and says,

> The Nili, in its desire to save the Yishuv from the fate of the Armenians, provided the Turkish authorities with the opportunity to exterminate it, and only the utmost efforts, together with complex political circumstances, the rottenness of the regime, and especially the military defeat of Turkey which was already in sight were what saved the Yishuv in those days.[50]

From Turkish sources we can also infer that the fears of the Yishuv about extermination following the discovery of the Nili affair were apparently exaggerated.[51]

We will refrain from broad examination of the Nili affair, which has been widely studied and discussed, and focus on the affair from the perspective of this book: the relationship to the Armenian genocide and possible analogies. The exposure of the Nili network certainly aroused such sharp reactions because it was seen as a threat to the Yishuv, which could result in an "Armenian situation." We will investigate the affair primarily through contemporary sources of the period.

Discovery of the spy network in October 1917 led to deep apprehension in the tiny Jewish community in Palestine of a possible Turkish reaction, and a great fear, not for the first time, that the Armenian experience be repeated in Palestine. In those dramatic days, comments regarding the Armenian genocide appear from two different directions. On one hand, the members of Nili who have been condemned to death describe their motives, and on the other hand, the fearful residents of the Yishuv, most of whom had no previous knowledge of Nili's activities, blame its members, in various ways, for causing, or potentially causing, a recurrence of the Armenian experience in Palestine.

The difference between the two approaches should not be ignored: the members of the Nili organization were strongly affected by the Armenian tragedy and it became an important motive for their pro-British activity—quick action needed to be taken to spare the Jewish community in Palestine from what had happened to the Armenians. The most effective means to this end would be assistance to the British, and even espionage, which might endanger the group and the entire Yishuv.

In contrast, the residents of the Yishuv were hostile and accusatory toward Nili because they believed that its activity had jeopardized the entire community and might indeed have resulted in a recurrence of what had happened to the Armenians in Palestine. Thus, Nili had to be isolated, ostracized, and even to be turned in to the Turkish authorities.

Most of the Yishuv and its leadership was acutely anxious after the spy ring was discovered and distanced itself from Nili, emphasizing that the organization was separatist and marginal, and did not represent the wider community. Thus, they hoped to placate the fury of the Turkish rulers and soften the expected repercussions. There was even an assassination attempt on the life of Lishansky who was considered, (together with Sarah Aaronsohn), to be a key activist of Nili, by members of the mainstream "Hashomer" paramilitary organization. The Armenian massacre was mentioned again, in the context of the Nili affair, by several people, both in their comments at the time and in later recollections, stressing that the activities of Nili could have brought down on the Yishuv a terrible disaster, like that which had befallen the Armenians.

Dr. Hillel Yaffe resided in the village of Zichron Yaakov between 1907 and 1919. His relations with his neighbors, the Aaronsohn family, were strained, and he was sharply critical in his diaries and letters and in the memoirs which he published later, of "the ambitious Aaronsohn brothers." The following description of events in Zichron Yaakov appears in his diary on October 6, 1917:

On the 4th of October the Governor [of Haifa] convened the committee and the leaders of the village and lectured them in French. He said that there is in Zichron an anti-government spy network, headed by 'Tovin' [Yosef Lishansky's underground code-name], and it is essential to deport him. If not, he [the governor] will use any means necessary, and is ready to punish a hundred innocent people in order to find the guilty party....And he will not be thwarted. He recalled his actions against the Armenians — he barehandedly killed several Armenians, and his soldiers killed thousands of them! He will not leave a single house standing in Zichron if the residents persist in their stubbornness. Not a trace will remain of the village if they do not reveal Lishansky's hiding place to him.[52]

Mordecai Ben-Hillel Hacohen expresses in his diary a position close to that of the leadership of the Yishuv at the time, albeit somewhat more critical because he was less pro-Turkish and pro-German. His diary includes comments on the Nili group in 1917, when the leaders of the Yishuv learned of the activities of Nili, in March 1917, and when the network was uncovered by the Turks, in October 1917. Hacohen views the Zionist efforts in Palestine as a king on the chessboard of the Jewish nationalist movement, to be protected at all costs, because it is not a "pawn" which can be sacrificed. He stresses,

In any event, we Jews will always remain loyal and remember our mission in this land: to preserve the existence of the Jewish community, because we have been entrusted as its protectors here by the nationalist movement. And our role demands sacrifices from us, which we must make willingly. Our political understanding will not allow us to be a ball in someone's game. In the current chess game of our national movement, the existing Jewish settlements in Palestine cannot be considered a mere pawn which may sometimes be sacrificed. It is of central value, like that of the king which stands at the center and must be protected at all cost. Never will what happened to the Armenians happen again.[53]

In his last sentence, Hacohen hints at the Nili group. As far as we know, at least some of the leaders of the Yishuv, among them prominent figures in Tel Aviv, were aware of the activities of Nili in March 1917, apparently due to efforts of Nili to enlist new members and as a result of negotiations between the Nili leadership and leaders of the Yishuv regarding transfer of aid through Nili.[54] On March 14, 1917, Hacohen writes "Regarding the Guests of Rechav the Prostitute" [i.e., the spies]:

Following a particular event which the heart cannot reveal to the pen, the executive committee of the workers' organization, "The Young Worker," adopted the following declarations which will be binding on all the members: (1) We recognize that our participation today in the general effort to achieve our national goal can be expressed only if the existing Yishuv is preserved; (2) Our realpolitik in the current situation is complete civic loyalty; (3) In the event of possible changes in the future, we will maintain our position of complete neutrality; (4) Any action which takes the Yishuv beyond the above limits will be considered an attack upon the existence of the Yishuv.

Hacohen concludes his quote from the decisions of "The Young Worker" from March 3, 1917, which define the actions of Nili as "an attack upon the existence of the Yishuv," and adds, "These decisions, and particularly the event which was worse than unfortunate and led to the decisions, were the subject of a special meeting of the leaders of the Yishuv." The latter were fearful that the activity of Nili would prove disastrous for the Yishuv. Closed meetings were held in Jerusalem and Jaffa at which the espionage was strongly condemned, and demands were made that the affair be made public in order to save the Jewish community from present catastrophe and future disgrace, but the mouse was not found who would bell the cat, and the matter was silenced."[55]

In the end, the danger was averted for several months and the network was discovered only in early October 1917. On October 18, 1917, after a break of almost three weeks in his diary, Hacohen writes,

I stopped my journal for a time because I could not keep in the house writings and articles like this, which could bring suspicion on their author. The espionage affair based in Aaronsohn's laboratory at Atlit has created great fear in all of us. The government has apparently decided to turn the matter into a general Jewish affair in the country. It has placed the suspicion of espionage on all of the Jewish public in Palestine, and now no one can be certain that his house will not be searched, that he will not be arrested and then tortured in the prison cells of the Turkish investigators, and that he will not be remanded to a military trial. Not a man among us is safe.[56]

Afterwards, the writer describes at length the arrests and punishments in the Jewish settlements around the country: "There is not a village or Jewish site in all of the lower Galilee and Samaria where people were not arrested and brought to Nazareth, and they were charged with involvement in the spy activities, and a military trial awaits them all....And this calamity has reached Judea as well." In subsequent days, Hacohen repeats his description of "this terrible catastrophe brought down on the village [Zichron Yaakov] and the Yishuv by the Aaronsohns. Awful, the situation is awful."[57] The author rejects Jamal Pasha's intention to lay suspicion and blame for the actions of Nili "on our heads, on the head of every Jew just because he is a Jew. This formula is known to us from Russia at the beginning of the war."[58] In Hacohen's opinion, if anyone is to be blamed it is Jamal Pasha himself. "It was he who brought Aaronsohn close to him and made him an official, and gave him licenses and also permission to leave the country...[as well as] excellent, exceptional treatment."[59] Ultimately, Jamal Pasha stopped the persecutions and threats against the Jews. The leadership of the Yishuv convinced him that the spying was the act of isolated individuals. Jamal Pasha hoped to prevent a repeat of the international public opinion campaign against him that followed the deportations from Tel Aviv. The efforts of the leadership of the Yishuv vis-à-vis the foreign consulates, and especially the German legation, also helped. Moreover, it is doubtful whether Jamal Pasha actually intended to instigate riots against the Jews as severe as those of the Turks against the Armenians. And even if he had wanted to, it is doubtful that he was able, in the last stages of the war, when the English were close to the borders of Palestine.

In fact, the death throes and the impending final days of Turkish rule in the region were an additional source of anxiety for the leadership of the Yishuv. In his diary, on November 15, 1917, Hacohen writes about a meeting of the local council of the Jewish village of Petach Tikva which had taken place the day before:

> The meeting was called to discuss the new situation which is developing in light of the advancing British forces. First of all, we must prevent the masses and the young people from making any demonstration or manifestation against the new army. Heaven forbid that we forget the lesson learned by the residents of Galicia and especially the terrible massacre in Armenia after the previous rulers returned and recaptured the places which they had conquered before and lost....We must be very moderate, cautious in our actions, and always restrain our emotions.[60]

In his memoirs written in 1931, Meir Dizengoff also deals with the Nili affair. He was fortunate to be in Damascus when the affair exploded. "And who knows how the events would have affected me if I had been in the Haifa area that night?...Two hours after my departure the soldiers came to Zichron Yaakov to arrest me, at the orders of the Kaymakam, because I was a friend of Lishansky."[61] He mentions the arrest of suspects in Zichron Yaakov, and Hadera, who "were subjected to an inquisition."

> The terrible torture endured by Sarah Aaronsohn, Aaron's sister, and their aged father....These are days more terrible than any known heretofore by

this agonized community — days of brutal reprisal. We are surrounded by fear of death and total annihilation....Because if until now the Germans have prevented the Turks, for well known reasons, from doing to us what they want, and Jamal Pasha, who had numerous Arab dignitaries hanged in Syria, refrained from executions in our communities and showed us 'mercy,' clearly the restraints will now be removed, and we shall be massacred and annihilated like the Armenians.[62]

From Damascus, where some of the deportees from Palestine were living, Dizengoff sent a telegram to Jamal Pasha in Contantinople, requesting aid for the Yishuv and the deportees. In response to Dizengoff's message, Jamal Pasha immediately sent a telegram to the governor of Jerusalem saying, "He requests that the Pasha of Jerusalem summon Dizengoff to him and to warn him that his frequent requests for aid may cause danger. In the past, he assisted him and responded to his requests." (This was indeed the case regarding the deportation from Tel Aviv in April 1917.) "Now, when most of the Jews of Palestine are engaged in espionage against me, I give his demands a different interpretation. Advise him that by this behavior he endangers himself and all of those under his supervision."

Hacohen, who claims to have seen the telegram (probably a copy of it) at a meeting of the Immigration Council in Petach Tikva, describes it thus: "It cannot be stated what was most prominent in this telegram: irrationality, stupidity or malice, but it certainly combined of all three."[63] According to Hacohen, the message said that "some of the Jews of Palestine are engaged in espionage," rather than "most of the Jews of Palestine," as Dizengoff had reported.

Dizengoff interprets the danger to which Jamal Pasha alludes: "The meaning of this danger was already explained to me by Enver Pasha himself during his visit to Jaffa, when I was presented to him as a Zionist by Jamal Pasha. He said to me then, 'Zionists beware! If you oppose us we will do to you what we have done to the Armenians.'"[64] After intensive efforts, Dizengoff manages to be received by the angry Jamal Pasha, and succeeds in placating him. Dizengoff describes at length his version of what was considered at the time to be a fateful meeting with Jamal Pasha:[65]

When he saw me approaching his desk, Jamal Pasha sprang angrily from his chair, glared at me and growled like an ancient lion: What?! What have you to tell me about espionage?! Who is to say that the man who stands before me is not another Aaronsohn?! Are not all the Jews....

'If so then arrest me! Arrest me!' My cry of anguished despair spilled out suddenly and I stepped back as if bitten by a serpent....

My outburst interrupted his words, and I, unaware at the moment of where I was and who was speaking to me, was filled only with deep and torturous pain, and heartbreaking sorrow. All of the contempt and insult, the agonies and tortures which these days have inflicted upon us suddenly burst out from my heart in a cry of bitter despair.

'Arrest me if I am a spy in your eyes! Arrest me together with all of the other innocents! You have found two or three spies—would you accuse us all?! Are there no spies among the Turks? And why has your fury been unleashed only at the Jews?! Why do you mistreat us so?! Your officers together with the civilian officials, in order to justify their own failure and defeat, have put all of my people together into a band of spies and traitors! We have taken Ottoman nationality and we know our obligation: We have neither betrayed nor done anything against Turkey! Sincere—I shout—we are sincere!'

At my cry, from an anguished soul, the tyrant stood and looked at me, and his anger seemed to dissolve. He pointed to a chair for me to sit, resumed his own seat, and replied, 'If I thought you were a traitor, I would not have received you in my office. But consider the great disappointment you have caused me. All of my friends warned me saying, do not trust the Jews. But I drew you near to me. Kaiser Wilhelm wished to send me experts and technical advisors from Germany but I refused and said, the Jews will be my experts and advisors in Palestine. And this is the way Aaronsohn demonstrates his honesty and loyalty! I allowed him to go to Berlin for his so-called scientific purposes—and he ran off to the English and organized this sort of spy ring against me! In Constantinople I was in favor of the Ottomanization of the Jews, I trusted you and accepted you, I saw your villages and favored them, I met with you and Antabi for the good of Zionism. And now, *Nous sommes trahis!*, we have been deceived!'

In my reply I stressed only the following: Individual traitors can be found in any people at times like this, and when they are caught they should be tried without mercy; but to humiliate and mistreat an entire people so cruelly is something that no enlightened government should do!

When I saw that his anger had passed and that we could enter into negotiation, I asked him to allow my two colleagues, Brill and Kalvarisky (who had accompanied me and were anxiously waiting in the corridor) to enter into his presence.

But as soon as they entered, the tyrant's ire returned and he shouted at Kalvarisky, 'I know that you are the one who has informed the Jewish Colonization Association office in Paris of all that occurs here! And therefore know this, if the investigation of the spies and the actions of the authorities become known publicly in Europe, you will be hung in your Rosh Pina!'

The tyrant continued to complain and to vent his anger on us and on all the Jews. And I could see that his anger was intended now to inspire terror. I sensed that for some reason the Turks were not able to do to us what they had done to the Armenians; it was convenient for Jamal Pasha to be placated so that he would appear to be merciful of his own volition.

We finally took our leave of him cordially, although we did not shake hands, and the next day I received from the offices of the Fourth Camp money and food for the emigres as I had requested!

'Victory,' said my friends, Brill and Kalvarisky, who were with me at the time, 'You tried and you prevailed!'

Nevertheless, the interrogation in the military court continues even after this victory. I have also learned that all of the prisoners have been questioned particularly about me, and some of the accused have been promised clemency by Jamal Pasha if they reveal to him where Dizengoff gets his funds.[66]

From Damascus, Dizengoff went to Constantinople at the request of Dr. Arthur Ruppin. The Balfour Declaration had already been issued by the British Government, Allenby had taken Jerusalem, and the Turks still ruled the northern part of Palestine. Turkey and Germany issued a joint declaration in support of the Jews and Zionism. Dizengoff relates,

By the way, I discovered there the following detail: the largest newspaper in Constantinople, *Tanin*, published an article justifying the government's actions against the Armenians. The article says that the Armenians brought the calamity upon themselves by their behavior toward the government, and that the Zionists in Palestine remained safe only because of the wise and cautious leadership of Dizengoff and Kalvarisky. I am doubtful whether our wisdom was the reason, but the caution was, in any case, not at all superfluous.[67]

It was only natural that each of the three men present at the meeting, Dizengoff, Brill, and Kalvarisky, would enhance his own role at what Kalvarisky defined as the "historic discussion." Chaim Margalit-Kalvarisky, one of the central figures in the struggle of the nascent Jewish settlement in the Galilee during the First World War, remembers the decisive meeting slightly differently.

Chaim Margalit-Kalvarisky was, at the time, the representative of the Jewish Colonization Association in the Galilee and resided in Rosh Pina. His close connections with "Hashomer," and to groups that he helped the workers' movements to establish did not prevent him from admiring Aaronsohn, although he did not condone the acts of espionage. Born in 1868, Kalvarisky went to Palestine in 1895 and was the secretary of the Bnai Moshe Society in Jaffa. In his later years, he dedicated most of his energies and activities to reapprochement between Jews and Arabs. He was critical of the policy of the Zionist movement which put much of its efforts into relations with Turkey, and later with England, while neglecting relations with the local population. In the 1930s, Kalvarisky wrote his memoirs which included comments about the subject at hand:

> During the war, the Jews and Arabs became brothers-in-sorrow, and suffered together. Not many people know that after the matter of espionage in Zichron Yaakov became known, there was a real danger that all the Jews would be deported from Palestine. A year earlier, the Turkish authorities were already aware that Jews were passing secrets to the enemy. Because of their suspicions, they decided, then, to expel the Jews from Tel Aviv, but when they discovered with certainty that all along the seacoast, from Rishon to Zichron, prominent Jews were involved in espionage, the rage of the Turks and the Germans became murderous. This was at the end of 1917 and the beginning of 1918. In order to put an end to the matter, *the high command decided to expel all of the Jews from the coastal plain and to deport them to Asia Minor, in other words to treat them like the Armenians* [emphasis mine]. They rounded up many men suspected of evading their military duty, whom they had previously ignored. There were over 300 Jewish prisoners in the jail in Nazareth, former watchmen, and an even greater number of prisoners in Damascus. The situation was awful. Only a handful of the leadership was left in the country.

> I have said that loyalty to the government and good relations with the neighbors, which I had stressed in all of my actions since the beginning of the war, were what saved the situation. This is the place to say it. *The order to treat the Jews like the Armenians was already prepared*, but friendly Arab government officials revealed the secret to me, and I decided to speak with Jamal and warn him that such a step would endanger the Ottoman Empire. This was in the presence of Dizengoff and the late Brill. Both of them trembled with fear. Jamal threatened to have me hanged from a tree in the center of Rosh Pina if I continued to interfere in politics and to incite Eu-

rope against Turkey, but in the end he retreated when I told him that I had never incited the Europeans against Turkey, and that my loyalty to the homeland was not weaker than that of the most loyal Turks.[68]

Kalvarisky was called to Damascus and held meetings in preparation for the decisive meeting with Jamal Pasha, commander of the Fourth Army. In unpublished sections of his memoirs, he describes the meetings in great detail:

> In the meantime I received word from a fairly dependable source that the high command was very angry at the Jewish settlement, and they were consulting about the possibility of a general deportation of all the Jews of Palestine to the furthest provinces of the Empire (Eastern Anatolia), and that the high officers were demanding to treat them like they had treated the "treacherous" Armenians. That not everyone was agreed on this, and that the German and Austrian consuls had no objection to repressions of acts of treason like those that had been uncovered among the Jews. Obviously this information depressed and disturbed me very much. Jamal Pasha's delay in receiving me seemed to me to indicate that the information was indeed accurate. I revealed this to Dizengoff and he said to me, 'From Jamal Pasha one can expect anything. It is difficult to make him angry but once his ire has been aroused he is merciless. To hang a man is for him a petty matter.' 'All of this,' I said to Dizengoff, 'is not very encouraging but I want you to tell me what to do in this situation." I have no advice for you, but from what Brill said after he was present at your meeting with Kutchuk Jamal, I conclude that you are the only one among the Jews whom both of the Jamals trust. Ali Fuad Bey also trusts you. Try to talk to him and influence him. Regarding the big Jamal, there is no way of knowing how he will receive us and what he will say. We will say to him whatever God puts in our mouth.'
>
> On the appointed day, at the appointed hour, the three of us, Dizengoff, Brill, and I, arrived at the headquarters. The sentry let us into the anteroom of the Pasha's office and requested that we wait for several minutes. Dizengoff asked to go in first, in order to talk to the Pasha first about matters relating to Tel Aviv and the refugees.
>
> I agreed, and he went in first. I didn't have time to exchange more than two or three words with Brill when we heard a great shout in the Pasha's office, and immediately afterwards the door opened and Dizengoff, agitated and trembling all over, rushed over to me, asking and pushing me into the Pasha's office. I went in and saw before me the following scene: the Pasha stood on the other side of his desk, his visage was terrible and infuriated, and after my greeting, Bonjour Excellence, he opened his mouth and said, 'I cannot give you my hand or shake yours as usual this time. I gave my hand to the so-called scholar Aaronsohn, who bragged about being a friend of the Turks.

What irony! The friend of the Turks who works as a spy in the headquarters of General Allenby in Egypt. Is it possible to trust any of your co-religionists after such deeds? I ask you, Mr. Kalvarisky!' To which I replied, 'Since you have asked me, I will answer you in the affirmative: yes, Your Highness, it is certainly possible to trust them. One must only be honest and not to torture everyone because of the crime of one individual. This is a great calamity for us, and we Jews, more than others, are sorry that such traitors to the homeland could have been discovered among us, but one must not conclude from this that all the Jews of Palestine are traitors — that would be far from the truth,' and I continued, 'There have been rumors that in the highest echelons of the headquarters a long list of decrees and laws against the Jews is being prepared. Among them, deportation of all the Jews from Palestine to the farmost districts of the Ottoman Empire, to Eastern Anatolia, and to treat them like the traitorous Armenians. I beg you and plead with you not to allow this thing to happen, for two reasons: (a) because the Jews of Palestine are not traitors. If several guilty ones have been found among them, they should be punished according to the law, but the guiltless and innocent should not be made to suffer, lest the righteous be swept away with the wicked; (b) as a friend of the Turks, I would not wish such a terrible thing (mass deportation in the height of winter) to be done. Such a deed can do harm to Turkey in Europe and America.' While I spoke the Pasha listened silently, but at my final words he could no longer contain himself and as he glared at me he said, in a hoarse, angry voice, or rather, he shouted, 'Mr. Kalvarisky, you have already tried once to incite all of Europe against us at the time of the evacuation of Tel Aviv. I warn you, if you try again to interfere in our affairs, I will have you hanged in the center of Rosh Pina.' And he added, 'You see, Mr. Kalvarisky, I am frank and I say what is in my heart.'

I protested vigorously against the accusation that I am not loyal to the Ottoman government and added, 'If you were truly frank, Your Majesty, you would have to say that you have suspicions about me.' And to this he replied, 'You are right, Mr. Kalvarisky, and indeed I asked Mr. Dizengoff to inform you that I have suspicions about you, and I waited for explanations from you, and since you did not come to me and did not refute the suspicion, I concluded that it was true. If someone has not been forthcoming about this matter and has not fulfilled his mission faithfully, it was Mr. Dizengoff and not me.' With this, the interview came to an end.[69]

Upon his return from a previous meeting with Jamal Pasha, Kalvarisky stopped off in the village of Metulla and told Yisrael Giladi, the leader of "Hashomer," about the meeting:

'I know,' began Jamal Pasha, 'that there is an organized spy ring operating in the country. I am not yet certain if they are Arabs or Jews, but I want you to know—and to inform your colleagues—that heaven help the people whose sons are these cursed spies. We taught the Armenian people a lesson about such deeds, and we will not hesitate to take the same steps in this case.'[70]

Kalvarisky's detailed descriptions of the events surrounding the discovery of the spy ring are testimony that a harsh Turkish reaction to the espionage was possible and, indeed, was given serious consideration. In any event, fear of a fate similar to that of the Armenians was real and aroused deep apprehension among the leaders of the Yishuv.

A Disclaimer with an Historical Perspective

The question of the extent of an existential danger to the Jewish community in Palestine is both a difficult and a delicate one. We could accept the subjective feelings within the Jewish community and among individuals, but in retrospective, Palestine—and the Jewish community within it—fared much better than any other Asian region under Turkish control.

After the reforms of 1856, the district (Sanjak) of Jerusalem was separated from the province (Wilayet) of Damascus and made the autonomous division (Mutazaraflik) of Jerusalem, headed by a governor of Wali rank (as that of a province). From 1873, the Mutazaraflik of Jerusalem was controlled directly by the government in Constantinople. More importantly, the consuls of the European powers were given special authority to manage and protect the affairs of their nationals in the Mutazaraflik of Jerusalem, which was roughly the equivalent of Palestine. In no other region did foreign consuls have such extensive powers and effective means of protection of the local inhabitants. Their power was reduced but never eliminated altogether even during the war period.

During the war years, the Jewish community suffered much from reduced assistance from overseas. And yet, that assistance was never fully cut off, and in extreme cases that meager support made the difference between survival and mass starvation and death, which were the horrible fate of the inhabitants of Lebanon.

We have no evidence to show that the tiny Jewish community in Palestine was regarded as a threat. Jews of Russian origin were probably seen as a nuisance. However, no other community, certainly not in the Levant, was as orderly and submissive as the Jewish community in Palestine. At a time of a wide-scale Arab revolt, which was launched in 1916 and engulfed Arabia, Transjordan, and Syria, and destroyed thousands of Turkish soldiers, numerous fortifications, and dozens of supply lines, there is no record of a single attack by a Jewish settler on a Turkish soldier.

The brutal, often murderous abuse of the Armenian, Arab, and Maronite communities by the Turkish authorities during the war years is well documented. It had its impact, no doubt, on the Jewish inhabitants of Palestine. Whether this is a sufficient explanation or an excuse for Jewish timidity and indifference to the suffering of the Armenians is beyond our sources to reveal.

Notes

1. The purpose of the following survey is to briefly provide background to our discussion of the central issues of this book. For more comprehensive information about the Jewish community (the Yishuv) in Eretz Yisrael during this period, see Mordechai Eliav, ed., *Siege and Distress, Eretz Yisrael During the First World War* (Jerusalem: Yad Izhak Ben-Zvi, 1990); Nathan Efrati, *From Crisis to Hope, The Jewish Community in Eretz Yisrael During World War I* (Jerusalem: Yad Itzhak Ben-Zvi, 1991). This survey is based partly on the monograph, *Nili, 1915-1917: The First Hebrew Intelligence Network* (Tel Aviv: IDF Chief Education Officer, 1980).
2. Capitulations—a system of rights which bestowed special status on foreign nationals in the Ottoman Empire: immunity from obligations imposed on Ottoman citizens, such as military conscription, forced labor, and taxation, as well as immunity in Ottoman courts. The consuls of foreign powers with capitulation rights protected their citizens in countries throughout the Ottoman Empire.
3. Richard D. Kloian, ed., *The Armenian Genocide: News Accounts from the American Press, 1915-1922* (Berkeley, CA: AAC Books, 1985).
4. Mordechai Ben-Hillel Hacohen, *War of the Nation* (Jerusalem: Yad Itzhak Ben-Zvi, 1985), p. 262. (Henceforth: *War of the Nations.*)
5. Ibid., pp. 475-76.
6. See Uziel Schmeltz, "Population Characteristics of the Jerusalem and Hebron Regions at the Beginning of the Twentieth Century," *Cathedra*, no. 36, Jerusalem, 1986.
7. Moshe Smilansky, *Memoirs*, vol. 3, 1921, p. 31.
8. Ibid., pp. 125-26.
9. Smilansky's memoirs which appear under the title, "The First Year of the War," were written as a diary.
10. Meir Dizengoff, *With Tel Aviv in Exile*, Tel Aviv, 1931, pp. 24, 45, 126-27. (Henceforth: Dizengoff.)
11. Ibid., p. 100. See also p. 80. Even if Dizengoff does not quote Enver Pasha exactly, the quote is certainly representative of the spirit of his message and its meaning as understood by the Jewish community in Eretz Yisrael.

12. Ibid., pp. 84-85.
13. Arthur Ruppin, *Excerpts from My Life* (Tel Aviv: Am Oved, 1968), pp. 257-58. (Henceforth: *My Life.*)
14. There may be additional references in his personal archives.
15. Lyova Yitzchak Schneerson, *From the Journals of a Nili Agent* (Haifa: Renaissance, 1967), p. 24.
16. Yaakov Goldstein, *"The Shepherds Fraternity," The Idea of Pioneering Jewish Animal Husbandry during the Second Aliya (1907-1917) and Its Realization* (Tel Aviv: Israel Defense Ministry Publications, 1994), pp. 30, 138-41.
17. Arthur Ruppin, *My Life, Part II*, p. 298.
18. Y. Tahun, "Eretz Yisrael During the World War," (Report), first printing, Jaffa, 1919 (typewritten), p. 32.
19. *War of the Nations*, pp. 533-34.
20. See the section, "Reports of the Armenian Massacre and Reactions to It."
21. *War of the Nations*, p. 536. He also reports that Dr. Krieger figured the medicinal aid we need to prepare. "And according to his estimate, there will be a great many weak and ill on the way, and he invoked a figure shocking and horrible to us. According to him, disease will take a toll in the refugee camps of some 25 percent of the exiles!"
22. Ibid., April 4, 1917, p. 591.
23. Ibid., pp. 537, 547, 571.
24. Ibid., p. 584. He continues, "The Turkish stomach is not capable of absorbing foreign peoples—they either rise up and jumble around, and then it must vomit them out, or they rot and spoil within it and around it. The Greeks and all the Balkan peoples rose up against Turkey and gained their independence proudly, while Turkey brings down the Armenians, killing them left and right, and slaughtered the Syrians and the Lebanese in body and soul. The end will be one of two choices: either they will choose the Balkan peoples or they will be witnesses of desolation."
25. Ibid., p. 592, (April 30, 1917).
26. Yoram Efrati, ed., *The Aaronsohn Diaries, 1916-1919*, Karni, 1970, p. 252 (April 27, 1917). (Henceforth: *Aaronsohn Diaries.*)
27. *Sledmere Papers*. R. Graham noted on the document that "Weizmann plans to leave on May 11 for Egypt. He and the other Zionists here were well aware of the dangers which threaten the Jews—which will increase once the actions of the Zionists become known to Turkey, but they found them important enough to take the risk." Matters were also brought to the attention of high officials in the British Foreign Office. See *Aaronsohn Diaries*, p. 255, footnotes.
28. Ibid., p. 265.
29. *Aaronsohn Diaries*, April 19, 1917, p. 243: "I have learned of the riots against Jews in Jaffa. Two Yemenites were hung from trees. They are all that is left of the Jews in the city. Robbery and looting of all that belongs to the Jews, under the loving eyes of the Turkish police. Jamal Pasha promises, cynically, that he is expelling the Jews for their own good." See also pp. 244-46, 257, 269, 270.

30. Ibid., pp. 275-77.
31. Ibid., according to F.O. 371/3101 65760.
32. He was replaced in June 1917 by General Allenby, following the British defeat in the second Gaza campaign in April 1917.
33. Ibid., p. 278. The parentheses appear in Aaronsohn's diary.
34. Ibid. In Maurry's opinion, the Jewish units will be able to serve at the front only in another year, at the earliest. "And I would like you to have no illusions, we want to be open and frank."
35. *The Letters and Papers of Chaim Weizmann* (Jerusalem: Israel Universities Press, 1975), series A, vol. 7, no. 373, to Jacobus H. Kann, May 5, 1917. (Herein Weizmann Letters).
36. *War of the Nations*, June 1, 1917, pp. 618-19.
37. Although Mordechai Ben-Hillel Hacohen writes in his journal that Jamal Pasha mentioned the French Havas press service, apparently because Jamal Pasha knew French.
38. Ibid., pp. 619, 621. (The wording of one of these telegrams can be found in the Central Zionist Archives). See also *Aaronsohn Diaries*, pp. 321-22, footnote 22.
39. *War of the Nations*, p. 623. The United States apparently had influence over Turkey even after relations between the countries were cut off on April 20, 1917. After verifying the reports of Jamal Pasha's threats to massacre the Jews in Palestine, the American Secretary of State, Robert Lansing, called upon the representatives of the neutral nations, on May 22, 1917, to protest the persecutions.
40. Ibid., p. 623, footnote 2.
41. Ruppin, *Excerpts from My Life, Vol. II*, p. 289.
42. Ibid., p. 272.
43. Isaiah Friedman, for example, attributes great importance to the German assistance to the Jewish community in Eretz Yisrael during the war. See Isaiah Friedman, *Germany, Turkey and Zionism*, (Oxford: Oxford University Press, 1977); Isaiah Friedman, "Germany and Zionism, 1897-1918," *Cathedra for the History of Eretz Yisrael and Its Yishuv*, no. 16, 1980, pp. 30-31.
44. See Livneh, p. 248.
45. *Aaronsohn Diaries*, p. 292.
46. Criticism of his attitude toward the Zionist endeavor in Palestine and his failure to help the young people from Palestine who were in Constantinople appear in additional sources. See also, *War of the Nations*, pp. 411-12.
47. Joseph Nedava, Introduction to *Yosef Lishansky, Papers and Letters* (Tel Aviv: Hadar, 1977), p. 19. (Henceforth, *Lishansky*.)
48. Taken from the title of the book by Yehuda Yaari-Polskin, which was first published in 1931.
49. *Nili 1915-1917: The First Jewish Intelligence Network* (Tel Aviv: I.D.F. Chief Education Officer, 1980).
50. *The History of the Hagana, Vol. I* (Tel Aviv: Maarachot, 1964), p. 383.

51. Aziz Bek, *Intelligence and Espionage* (In Syria, Lebanon, and Palestine During the World War, 1913-1918). Translated and annotated by Eliezer Tauber (Ramat Gan: Bar Ilan University Press, 1991).
52. See Hillel Yaffe, et al., *The Generation of the Brave, Memoirs, Letters and Diaries*, (Tel Aviv: Dvir, 1939), pp. 531, 616-18.
53. *War of the Nations*, p. 498, March 6, 1917.
54. Kalvarisky knew about the activities in early March 1917, and reported them to the heads of "Hashomer." See also *Lishansky*, p. 36.
55. *War of the Nations*, p. 504; Smilansky, pp. 270-71.
56. See *War of the Nations*, pp. 719-20.
57. Ibid., pp. 724-25, 730.
58. Ibid., p. 135.
59. Ibid.
60. Ibid., pp. 745-46.
61. Meir Dizengoff, *Memoirs*, p. 84.
62. Ibid., p. 85.
63. *War of the Nations*, p. 734, November 6, 1917.
64. Dizengoff, p. 100.
65. Ibid., pp. 101-104.
66. "However, even Lishansky, the spy, who sent me a request for financial assistance in order to prepare an escape from prison—and I refused to give it to him—was cautious when interrogated about me and my work during this emergency." [footnote in the original]
67. Ibid., p. 114.
68. C.M. Kalvarisky, "Relations Between the Jews and the Arabs During the War," *Our Aspirations*, vol. 2, no. 3, spring 1931. In our opinion, Kalvarisky was not given his due respect by Zionist historiography. A reader of Moshe Smilansky's memoirs from the same period, describing the situation in Judea, finds that the phenomenon of Arabs informing on the Jews to the Turks, and the weakened status of the Jews in the eyes of the Arabs because of the Turkish authorities' treatment of the Jews were important factors in the deterioration of the situation of the Yishuv in Judea. Smilansky also says, "During the difficult days in Judea, the Galilee was serene." "In the Jewish settlements in the Galilee there are no cries nor screams, no grief nor despair." See, Smilansky, *Memoirs*, vol. 3, p. 51, etc.
69. See the Central Zionist Archives, A113/1.
70. According to the recollections of Moshe Levitt, a member of "Hashomer." See Shaul Dagan, *From Tel Adashim to Hamara* (The Memoirs of Moshe Levitt, member of "Hashomer"), The Society for the Preservation of Nature in Israel, p. 108.

3

The Reactors

This chapter presents the reactions to the Armenian genocide of individuals and groups within the Yishuv and the Zionist Movement who did more than note its occurrence or express sympathy for the pain and suffering of the Armenians. The reactions took the form of a moral sensibility, an attempt to arouse public interest in the tragedy and to spark others to action. The people who reacted were, for the most part, unable themselves to act directly, and expressed their pain at their helplessness, both as Jews and as human beings.

Among the individuals we will encounter are some who reacted and acted during the war itself: the members of the Nili group in Eretz Yisrael, and members of the Zionist delegation—particularly Chaim Weizmann and Nachum Sokolow—in London. The circumstances in which they operated were, of course, different: Nili operated under the threatening military authority of the Turks while the Zionist delegation was able to act more freely in London.

Additionally, we will explore reactions from other periods, including the controversy between Theodor Herzl and Bernard Lazare regarding attitudes toward the Armenians and the Turkish rulers at the turn of the present century. The sections on Itamar Ben Avi focus on the Turkish massacre of the Armenians in 1909 and its ramifications. The treatment of the Armenian genocide in the literature of Eretz Yisrael, mostly in the 1920s, is explored at length in a separate chapter. "The Forty Days of Musa Dagh: Symbol and Parable" examines the significance of Musa Dagh for the Jewish public in Eretz Yisrael and in the ghettos of Europe in the 1930s and 1940s.

Herzl, Bernard Lazare, and the Armenians

The question which stands at the center of this study—why does one person care while another remains indifferent; why does one individual react while another refrains from reaction or even condemns it—has numerous psychological, philosophical, moral, and ethical facets which are outside of the scope of this work. Nonetheless, we hope that this research will raise questions and contribute to the public debate on these issues.

There are at least two precedents for the reactions in the Yishuv to the horrible atrocities committed against the Armenians during the First World War. The first is in reference to actions taken by Theodor Herzl, the founder of political Zionism and "prophet" of the modern Jewish State.

The well-known Jewish thinker, Hannah Arendt, published an article in July 1942, entitled "Herzl and Lazare,"[1] which describes the impact of the Dreyfus Affair on both men, and their turn toward Jewish affairs as a reaction to anti-Semitism. As assimilated Jews, both of them understood that a normal life would be possible only if the aims of the emancipation were truly achieved. In fact, what they saw was that the Jew was becoming the pariah of modern society.[2] Both men were disengaged from Jewish religious tradition. As intellectuals, they did not identify with what Arendt calls narrow and parochial Jewish cliques which had somehow grown up within the framework of gentile society.

For both Herzl and Lazare, Jewish identity had political and national implications and both men found themselves in confrontation with the prevailing forces in the politics of the Jewish world—mostly philanthropists. It was this confrontation, according to Arendt, which led them to believe that the dangers threatening the Jewish People were not only external anti-Semitism, but also the existing internal reality. With this, says Arendt, the similarity between Herzl and Lazare ends and the differences, which ultimately led to a break between them, begin.

As a result of the Dreyfus Affair, Herzl viewed the entire non-Jewish world as hostile; his universe was divided between Jews and anti-Semites. His solution was to be an escape to a homeland or salvation by means of a Jewish State. For Lazare, on the other hand, the territorial question was secondary. The primary question in his eyes was the need of the Jews for national liberation. More significant than escape from anti-Semitism was engagement of a people in the struggle against its enemies. This fundamental position was clearly expressed in his defense of Dreyfus and his essay on anti-Semitism in Rumania. He sought not a defense—in one form or another—against anti-Semitism, but true partners in the struggle, whom he hoped to find among the oppressed minorities in Europe at the time.

Arendt points out that both men encountered great resistance among their own people, but Herzl, with the help of Austrian and German Jewry, managed to succeed where Lazare failed. Lazare's courageous, outspoken defense of Dreyfus brought the wrath of most of French Jewry upon him. His failure was so complete that his contemporaries ignored him until he was "discovered" by Catholic writers. "Better than we, those men knew that Lazare was a great Jewish patriot as well as a great writer."[3]

Herzl and Lazare admired each other greatly and later became adversaries. In his diary from 1896, Herzl writes about Lazare, with admiration and affection, as an "excellent type of a fine clever French Jew." The following day Herzl writes, "the agreeable Lazare has brought Mr. Meyerson from the Havas Agency and the local [Parisian] Zionist groups to see me." Herzl, the intellectual, adds with satisfaction, "Afterwards, Nordau and the sculptor Beer came by. In having these men of cultural eminence in my own room and on my own ground I left with renewed assurance of the vast progress my idea has made."[4]

It seems that the differences between Herzl and Lazare of which Arendt speaks—while revealing overt enthusiasm for the latter—were strongest and most interesting in relation to the Armenians. It should be pointed out that the considerable historiography, which deals with Herzl, pays very little attention to Herzl's initiatives regarding the Armenian question, although they are described in detail in his diaries.[5]

Herzl was involved in a number of ways in Armenian affairs because of his contacts with the Turkish Sultan. The immediate cause of dissension between Lazare and Herzl on the Armenian question was the appearance of a public expression of admiration for the Turkish Sultan issued by the Fifth Zionist Congress, held in Basle in the final days of December 1901. Herzl reported to the Congress on his meeting with the Sultan several months earlier:

In May of this year I had the honor to be received in a rather lengthy audience by His Majesty, the Sultan Abd al-Hamid II. The kindliness and cordiality of the reception were such as to justify the highest hopes. The attitude and language of His Majesty gave me the feeling that the Jewish people has a friend and protector in the ruling Khalif. The Sultan has authorised me to make this statement. Let the Jews of the world hear it, let them understand what prospects this fact opens for them, and may they finally be ready for action which will mean self-help for them and a contribution to the new blossoming of the Turkish Empire.[6]

At Herzl's initiative, the Fifth Zionist Congress sent public greetings of admiration to the Sultan in order to create sympathy for Turkey. The telegram contains an "expression of dedication and gratitude which all of the Jews feel regarding the benevolence which His Highness the Sultan has always shown them." Earlier, as mentioned, Herzl had praised the Sultan in his opening address to the Congress.

The Sultan's note of thanks, sent the following day, was a relief to Herzl. "Until the Sultan's reply was received, on the second day of the Congress, I had been trembling," Herzl said.[7] "Up to that time he could have still denied even the beginning of a relationship between us, as well, but he fulfilled all of my expectations. With this wire, issued by the Basle telegraph office, my situation is certified and regularized. Again I have escaped from danger and since then I am calm." Herzl goes on to complain about the members of the Congress: "Incidentally, my Congress bunch did not rate the wire at its full value. They understand nothing. They overestimate small things and value big things lightly. But it's enough that I know it." And he adds a significant comment: "The political value of the congratulatory note of the Basle Government is lesser, but its moral value is greater."

Bernard Lazare was incensed at these matters. Lazare (1865-1903) participated in the Second Zionist Congress, which was held in 1898, and was received with adulation as a courageous proponent of Dreyfus.[8] Herzl was both pleased and honored by his participation. Lazare was a member of the Zionist Executive Committee but resigned after only a few months. In a letter to Herzl on March 24, 1898, he writes that the leadership of the Zionist movement "tries to direct the Jewish masses as if they were an ignorant child...that is a conception radically opposed to all of my political and social opinions, and I cannot, therefore, assume responsibility for it."[9]

"The Armenian context" appears in Lazare's writings in his article "The Jewish Nationalism," written in 1897 and published in his book *Job's Dungheap*. Anti-Semitism, in his estimate, is a reality which will continue. As long as Christianity exists and Jews are scattered among the nations, they will incur hatred and anger. They will be considered inferior, both materially and morally. What is the solution to this, asks

Lazare. "I am well aware that for the Christian peoples an Armenian solution is available, but their sensibilities cannot allow them to envisage that." (The editor of Lazare's collection of essays indicates that the reference was to the massacres of the Armenians by the Turks in 1895 and 1896 which were perpetrated before the eyes of the European powers.)[10]

Lazare published "The Zionist Congress and the Sultan," an article critical of Herzl, in the Armenian journal, *Pro Armenia*, which appeared in Paris from 1901 to 1908.[11] Among the members of its editorial board were Georges Clemenceau, Jean Jaures, and Anatole France. Clemenceau, who was considered by some to be pro-Armenian, nevertheless abandoned the Armenian cause and broke his explicit promises to them, when he was head of the French government at the end of the First World War. Lazare's decision to publish his article in an Armenian journal was a way of expressing his support and identification with their struggle:

The Zionist Congress which gathered in Basle paid honor to the Sultan Abd al-Hamid II. The delegates, or those who present themselves as such, of the most ancient of all oppressed peoples whose history has been written in blood, have sent their blessing to the worst of murderers. They are part of a people, six million of whose brethren groan under the boot of the Czar, not to mention those who are treated like beasts in Rumania, in Galicia, in Persia, in Algier, and even in those countries which consider themselves civilized. They are pariahs, and in great numbers wasted away by hunger and pain. Every day they are slaughtered and sacrificed [in the original: *en holocauste*] to some Moloch. They are inundated by mud, curses, and venom.

Their understanding of the true and living image of the fabled Jesus is as forgiveness for the sacrificers instead of rebellion against them. And this people, wounded and bloody, is cast at the feet of a Sultan covered with the blood of others. Not a single protest was heard at this conference [the Congress]. Not a man could be found who would say to the leaders, blinded like a herd, 'You have not the right to shame your people.' Not a man will take responsibility for this mistake, for this miserable error, which the members of the Congress in Basle have taken upon themselves and their emissaries.

Those who live in the darkness of the Russian territories, in the crypt of Vilna, in the wretched shanties of Berdichev and Odessa, without electricity, heat or air, do not know the Red Sultan [a term for the Sultan because of the blood he had spilled], nor the murdered Armenians and all of the oppressed peoples of the Ottoman Empire.

The promised land has been held up before those who are dying of hunger. They have been shown the land of date palms and grape vines, of easy living under free skies, and their pitiful heart has melted at the thought of possible happiness. In the Middle Ages, their fathers, as wretched as they, streamed toward the sea, following a new prophet, and drowned, believing that their arms raised up above the waves were about to clutch the fruits of Canaan.

And today their heirs follow their leader, heedless of the paths he chooses. But this man is a modern prophet who convenes parliaments and conducts the diplomacy of light opera, like the grand ruler of Gerolstein [a vacation town in Germany].

Such is he, and such are the leaders of the Zionist movement who share responsibility with him. Yesterday the Jews were sent to bow to the Kaiser Guillaume [Wilhelm, the German Kaiser] and today they bow before the Sultan. Tomorrow they will prostrate themselves at the feet of the Czar, and then we shall witness the great and beautiful vision of the slave who licks his master's boots.

This is what the members of the Zionist Steering Committee of Vienna call practical politics, realpolitik. In fact, this is the politics of the ghetto, the politics of the enslaved, suitable for those who march hand in hand with the most zealous rabbis of Galicia, Russia and Poland.

This is also the politics of falsehood, because for the price of a bribe one can meet with Abd al-Hamid II; for the price of a gratuity one can be received at the Sultan's palace, Yildiz Kiosk, be 'awarded' a medal, and—if one pays enough—to be awarded a diamond pin.[12] But you will not receive a scrap of land in Syria, because the Sultan himself, even if he wanted to grant Eretz Yisrael to the Jews—and he does not want to—could not do so. This is the politics of lies, because even if the land of their ancient homeland were given to the Jews tomorrow, they would perish in that land. Because the grand endeavor for which we must strive is the intellectual and moral revitalization of the Jewish People. Toward this aim we must strip this people of its superstitions and ignorance. We must wrest it from economic slavery. Only on the day of its liberation can [the Jewish People] realize its goals in freedom. On that day its rotten bourgeoisie will be allowed to attack the oppressed, but the people will raise its hand against all the oppressors and will not join with them.

In addition to his political and moral criticism of the actions of Herzl and the Zionist Congress and their relations with the Sultan, Lazare presents a lucid and penetrating social critique. The Socialist-Anarchist Lazare stresses the necessity of self-liberation of the Jewish People, its rejection of superstition, ignorance, and social and economic decadence. He also condemns the fanatical rabbis with whom Herzl cooperates.

Herzl writes in his diary on January 23, 1902, "In the Paris propaganda sheet *Pro Armenia* Bernard Lazare has published a mean, malicious article against me, on the occasion of the exchange of Congress telegrams with the Sultan. This is probably far from unwelcome to the J.C.A. [The Jewish Colonization Association], whose director Meyerson is an intimate friend of his." He adds, in French, "What interest can he possibly have, apart from the nice gesture in defending the Armenians?"[13]

Herzl does not reply to the substance of the criticism. In any event, we do not know if he responded and how, beyond what appears in his diary.

Criticism of the Congress' decision was heard in other quarters as well. The editorial board of *Pro Armenia*, which published Lazare's article, commented on Lazare's timely protest against the Zionist Congress which had sent a disgraceful telegram of admiration to the Sultan and received the Sultan's thanks. The paper also published the protest of Armenian students, together with all of the other foreign students in Geneva, who had expressed their protest at the Zionist Congress, while taking care not to hold the oppressed Israelites [a common French term for the Jews at the time] responsible for crimes against humanity committed by others: "The Association of Armenian Students of Geneva, in its meeting today, decided: Together with warm expressions of sympathy for the oppressed Israelite People, we must express our deep outrage at the Zionist Congress over the letter of solidarity which it sent to the Red Sultan—of which we learned from the press."

A total of approximately one hundred Bulgarian, Georgian, Israelite, Macedonian, Polish, and Russian students who gathered in the Café Bonaparte on December 31, 1901, decided to voice their deep contempt and protest against the Zionist Congress for the greetings it had sent to the arch-murderer, Abd al-Hamid II.[14]

This protest drew a response from Herzl. In summing up the Congress he writes in his diary:

Oh yes, another thing, something that distressed and vexed me a great deal. When the Sultan's answering telegram became known through the papers, I received wires from Geneva and Lausanne from meetings of students of all nationalities, particularly Armenians, Bulgarians, Macedonians, Russians, Poles, etc. who express their contempt and indignation on account of my telegram to the 'Red Sultan.'

It is not clear from Herzl's words what saddened him and what angered him. He adds one cynical sentence with practical implications: "However, this [the protest of the students] will probably do me good with the Sultan."[15]

Chaim Weizmann, then a young man living in Geneva, was genuinely troubled by Lazare's article and the students' protest. In 1899, at the age of twenty-five, he received his doctorate in chemistry. Weizmann was active at the time in the framework of the "Democratic Faction," and was, in effect, its leader. This group functioned as the loyal opposition in the World Zionist Organization. The Faction not only defended the principles of the Basle Platform, it also supported Herzl's leadership.[16] It sought to attract young people and Jewish students from liberal circles who were unaffiliated with the Zionist movement, which they viewed as conservative and bourgeois. Weizmann and his comrades fought hard in Geneva and other places against the "Jewish assimilationists, who exist here in various guises and who use revolutionary phraseology as a cover, are always ready to calumniate Zionism...the generation of the desert."[17]

Upon their return from Basle to Geneva, where they held a congress for educated Jewish youth and afterwards participated in the Fifth Zionist Congress, Weizmann and his friends heard about the student protest against Herzl. Weizmann wrote anxiously about it to Motzkin (January 20, 1902) and then to Ahad Haam (February 15, 1902), and even sent a letter to Theodor Herzl himself on February 3, 1902: "I hope you will forgive me for troubling you with a local Zionist matter. I refer to the unpleasant business of the protest which was started by the students." The students' decision was, in Weizmann's opinion, "not lacking, of course, in distortions of facts and calumnies of every kind."

In January and February 1902, Weizmann and his colleagues in the "Democratic Faction" organized three meetings in Geneva in defense of Herzl. They persuaded non-Jewish students from Russia and Poland to take public exception to the protest against Herzl. On the first and fifteenth of January they convened student meetings; over ninety people participated in the first and seventy-five in the second meeting. It was decided to condemn Herzl's opponents. The Jews who participated in the protest meetings against Herzl were accused of rash behavior and of dishonoring the Jewish People.

On January 21, Lazare's article (which had already appeared in *Pro Armenia* in Paris) was published in *Genveaux*, the influential journal of the Radical Party in Geneva.

On January 28, there was another meeting of Herzl's critics and another resolution was adopted condemning the Zionist Congress while expressing support for the aspirations of the Jewish People for liberation from oppression.

Another conference of nationalist Jewish students accused the non-Jewish students who had protested against Herzl's telegram of tactlessness and hypocrisy. The Jews who had protested were accused of indifference to the fate of their people, dishonoring it, falsifying facts and causing harm to the Zionist Congress which represented the movement for the revival of the Jewish People. It was also claimed that among the ninety-eight participants in the protest rally against Herzl, eighty had abstained and only eighteen had voted in favor of the condemnation. Weizmann was very active in these meetings and apparently drafted the wording of the resolutions.

Weizmann's letter to Herzl was written after the second publication of Lazare's article and after the second protest rally against Herzl: "We cannot now, I think, ignore the matter. We are, of course, in a position to make the motives of the meeting abundantly clear: those present were mainly anti-nationalists and anti-Semites (Greeks and Rumanians), people who, on principle, consider any and every national movement objectionable; the Jews are out-and-out assimilationists; they can also be branded for their flirtation with the anti-Semites."[18]

But the sharp attacks aside, it appears that Weizmann was embarrassed. He turns to Herzl respectfully and cautiously to ask for advice and direction which contains no trace of criticism:

> But should we answer by giving them the facts of the case? Should we explain that the toadyism we are accused of is based on a malicious distortion of the facts, that the telegram to the Sultan is to be taken as an act of diplomatic courtesy? Frankly, I am afraid of embarking on this sort of thing lest I should make an awkward slip somewhere. If you are in favour of our entering into explanations here, might I ask you if you would be good enough to draft the relevant passage of the resolution for me? We shall then include it in our resol[ution]. Should some reply, perhaps, be made to B.-L.? There is need of one.
>
> In the Jewish press we shall, of course, tell these gentlemen the plain truth, but for non-Jewish public opinion the shortest, sharpest answer possible is enough. This is a responsible step, as I am sure you will agree, and I therefore beg you not to refuse us your support in this matter. These pieces of impertinence cannot be allowed to go entirely unanswered.
>
> I shall await your reply with impatience. We must make haste.

Herzl's reply is not available. The declaration of the nationalist students supporting Herzl was adopted on February 12, along the lines suggested by Weizmann. The Democratic Faction published a statement on the issue in the *Frankfurter Zeitung*, and the newspaper, *Hamelitz*, also published articles on the subject.

Weizmann writes forcefully against the protesting students, and particularly against the Jews among them. It is clear that he fears their influence and power, and perhaps expresses a sense of frustration. Zionism was in its early stages. Among the Jewish students in the West there were signs of awakening, in contrast to previous years. "There are already some Zionists," he writes to Ahad Haam, but there are also many who are always ready to denounce Zionism. "Much effort is wasted on this generation of the desert and, O God, the things that are done by other nations without a word of protest demand the most intense efforts from our entire nervous system. One needs a whole arsenal of logical arguments to make these callous people understand that the death of Jewry is a bad thing."[19]

Weizmann, (whose positions were liberal and critical of the more conservative Herzl) was, like others in radical Zionist circles, apprehensive of the influence of the revolutionary movements and their universal and generalist tendencies, and of the Jewish "Bund" which attracted many young Jews at the time. They were vexed by the Jews who rallied to the causes and suffering of other peoples instead of struggling against the suffering of their own people. Weizmann was also disappointed by Lazare's attitude. In May 1901, Lazare had promised Weizmann to lecture at the young people's conference on the economic situation of the Jewish People. Lazare, who was highly respected in radical circles, was Weizmann's preferred speaker. A month later Lazare wrote to Weizmann that he could by no means take part in a conference of the young Zionists. "The Congress has accepted the Basle Platform; I do not accept it."[20]

Lazare believed that the Basle Platform was not suited to the needs of the Jewish People which needed to be released from the chains of tradition and internal enslavement, and to be educated in the spirit of rationalism before it could acquire its own land. Weizmann was now concerned about the possible influence of Lazare's essay.

In that same year, in August 1902, Weizmann wrote to Vera Khatzman, his future wife, about a long conversation he had had in Berlin with Edward Bernstein ("The famous one!") and his daughter. "I took him to task for taking up the cause of the Armenians and not taking up the Jewish cause. He declared, 'If I had any Jewish feeling, I should be a Zionist. Perhaps this will come about.' Together with him we cursed the assimilationists. Bernstein will write in our journal in the future against the assimilationists; he is on the road to Zionism and his daughter made a donation."[21]

From 1917 to 1919, Weizmann took positions sympathetic to the Armenian tragedy and the Armenian struggle. The tone of his words in 1902 strongly recalls the reactions which appeared to Franz Werfel's book, *The Forty Days of Musa Dagh*: why should a Jew be involved with the suffering of other peoples instead of with the tribulations of his own people? There is a hint here of the tensions and possible competition which may characterize fledgling national movements.

Lazare continued his efforts to strengthen the identification and joint struggle of all oppressed peoples. He participated in the Brussels Congress, held on July 7-8, 1902, which was attended by supporters of the Armenians from various countries. He took part in the debates and in the formulation of the resolutions which were adopted.

Bernard Lazare's life, like that of Herzl, was brief. In September 1903, at the age of 38, he died. A memorial essay in his honor was published in *Pro Armenia* which praised his enormous contribution as a talented writer with the courage to defy convention, his brave struggle in defense of Dreyfus, and the sacrifices he was forced to make. The essay recalled his defense of the Jews of Eastern Europe whose heart-rending misery he learned about in his extensive travels. Lazare was a man of many parts and many ideals.

Throughout his life he endeavored to realize his ideal of justice. He condemned those who talked about universal justice but were sensitive only to their own pain, or to the pain of their family, their tribe, or their own country. This, said Lazare, led to "public and universal disaster." He died, the paper wrote, while he still had much to contribute to the cause of justice and humanity.[22]

Lazare, a figure who was ignored or blurred by his contemporaries and is almost unknown in Israel, has been the subject of renewed interest in recent years. Two major biographies have been written about him, including a study by Jean-Denis Bredin, author of *The Affair* which deals with the Dreyfus Affair. Bredin entitled his biography *Bernard Lazare, From Anarchist to Prophet*.[23] Lazare was described by the French Socialist (and Jewish) leader, Leon Blum, as a righteous man. The Catholic writer, Charles Peguy, who has played an important role in preserving Lazare's memory, called him a saint. Bredin's title reminds us, consciously or unconsciously, of another figure, the visionary of the Jewish State who was called a prophet in his own lifetime: Theodor Herzl. We shall return to Herzl and his attitude toward the Armenians.

There is no doubt that Herzl knew of the Armenian problem, which occupied public opinion and European diplomacy in the last decade of the nineteenth century. Did Herzl wish (and if so, to what extent) to make use of the Armenian problem which burdened the Turkish Sultan, in order to promote his Zionist goals? It appears that Herzl did indeed try to make use of it, as a proponent of the Sultan rather than the Armenians, whether as an intermediary or helping the Sultan in his battle over public opinion.

In May 1896, Herzl's attention was focused on creating ties with the Sultan at the earliest possible opportunity.[24] Herzl had two political advisors at the time, neither of them Jewish. One of them, Hechler, identified with the Zionist cause and remained loyal to the Zionist movement until after Herzl's death. The other, Philip Michael, a knight of the House of Nevlinsky, was courted by Herzl who paid him handsomely and was never sure whether his advisor was a true supporter or a boastful charlatan.[25]

Nevlinsky, a diplomatic agent and journalist with widespread connections in the ruling circles of Constantinople, was allegedly sent by the Sultan on a secret mission to the Armenian committees in Brussels, Paris, and London, to persuade them to submit to the Sultan, after which the Sultan would implement, "voluntarily," the reforms which he refused to implement under pressure from the foreign powers. Nevlinsky proposed that Herzl enlist the aid of the Jews in negotiation with the Armenians. "In return, he will tell the Sultan that the Jewish influence had rendered him this service. The Sultan would show his appreciation of this."[26] Nevlinsky told Herzl that money was not important to the Sultan. "He had absolutely no understanding of its value—something that may frequently be observed among Rulers. But there was another way of winning the Sultan over: through supporting him in the Armenian situation." Herzl's reaction to the proposal: "The idea immediately struck me as excellent, but I told him that we shall not give our aid away free, i.e., give it only in return for positive counter-services to the Jewish cause." The connection between efforts to mediate with the Armenians and the Zionist cause was clear.

Nevlinsky suggested that a cease-fire be demanded of the Armenians. The Armenian committees are preparing for battle in July. They must be persuaded to delay this for a month. We will use this interim for negotiation with the Sultan. Nevlinsky himself wishes, because of his interest in the Jewish cause, to continue with the Armenian affair, so that the one matter may benefit the progress of the other.

Herzl writes to Max Nordau about the planned mediation efforts regarding the Armenians, and asks for his quick response. Nordau (1849-1923), a noted doctor and Jewish writer in Paris, was one of Herzl's earliest and closest colleagues and the spokesman of the Zionist movement at its congresses. He cabled his response to Herzl: "No!" Herzl adds in his diary, "This means that he does not want to get involved in Armenian affairs, and I do not know if he is not fed up already; but I await his next letter anxiously."

In his reply to Herzl, Nordau writes that he has no acquaintances or influence among the Armenians in Paris, and in London he also has no connections with the Armenians. Nordau asks Herzl to remember that he is a private individual. Nevertheless, he recommends that Herzl be very cautious in his ties with the Turks and the Armenians, who seem to be very cunning. More realistic than Herzl, Nordau warns that the Sultan may want to use the good offices of the Jews in his dealings with the Armenians, but will give nothing in return; these are promises which cannot be depended upon.[27]

Nordau was a close friend and a loyal colleague to Herzl and Herzl revealed to him the details of his plan: "If we help him in this he will be very grateful. This is a matter of survival for him. In order to keep the reins in our hands, we must obtain a cease-fire from the Armenian people rather than immediate peace. During the cease-fire we will negotiate with the Sultan."[28]

Herzl assumed that the English could benefit from his efforts and he, in return, would benefit from the English.

I have quick, good access to Salisbury [Lord Robert Salisbury, British Prime Minister at the time]. He can effortlessly achieve a respectable diplomatic success if he supports the principle of compromise, or, one might say, if he pushes the Armenians to it. It is possible that the relations between England and Turkey may thus be improved. Salisbury will play *le beau role* in the eyes of Europe, while the Sultan will nevertheless not be seen as one who has given in to pressure.

This, writes Herzl to Nordau, is one aspect of the issue. Moreover, "We must also try to influence the newspapers, especially the English and French. We must prepare public opinion for the surrender of the Armenians, and afterwards, for the magnanimity of the Sultan." Herzl says that the Armenian committees in Paris, London, and Brussels must be convinced to go along. He asks Nordau to consult with his advisors in Paris regarding the best way to accomplish this.

> In particular, the committees must be advised that we, the Jews, are interested in this. In any event, it must not become known that we wish to use them in order to establish an independent State of the Jews, lest they also try to use this opportunity to do the same thing, thus adding to our difficulties. At most they should be allowed to know that we wish to have the prohibition against entry into Palestine cancelled, if (at worst) it is necessary to give them a reason for our intervention.

Herzl suggests a more "convincing" explanation for the Armenians:

> But a better and more reasonable argument is this: a loan will be necessary to pay for the damages of the Armenian disturbances (this will be, it can be assumed, one of the demands or a request of the Armenians). A group of financiers wishes to arrange the loan, but on the condition that the Armenians now sign a cease-fire (until August) and afterwards a peace agreement.

Herzl asks Nordau if he is willing and able to support him on this special matter. He asks for a prompt reply:

> Cable me immediately if you have received this letter, yea or nay. One word is sufficient, because if not — I shall have to try to turn somewhere else in Paris.... We must act quickly, because the Sultan's secret agent [the reference is to Herzl's political advisor, Nevlinsky] has already left early this morning for Brussels.

Herzl adds that Dr. Alfred Nussig, "a loyal and dependable Zionist in Paris, will ask to speak with you today and to put himself at your disposal, since he has wired me that he can act on the Armenian matter. Judge for yourself whether he should be involved in the matter, and how much he should be told."[29]

Herzl asks Nordau if he will be able to act in England as well, even though he himself is operating directly there. "But if you are able, do so as well, and do so at once; we must bring all of our forces to bear on this point now. I am very hopeful." He urges action on the Armenian issue and sends a letter to Joseph Solomon (1860-1927), a Jewish painter in London and one of the founders of the Maccabee Club in England). He explains his intention and his method of action, and stresses that the matter must be kept secret. "The Armenians do not need to know that we are seeking to bring about a reconciliation because of our own national interests. If there is no way to intervene directly, is it not possible to generate opinion in the English press favorable to an Armenian surrender?"[30]

Herzl asks Solomon to speak with Lucien Wolf: "Mr. L. Wolf will easily understand the great significance of this affair, and I hope he will help as best he is able." Lucien Wolf (1857-1930), journalist, researcher, and Jewish public activist, was initially supportive of Herzl, but later became a strong opponent of Zionism. He interviewed Herzl in July 1896 (see below), in an interview which was intended to gather support for Herzl in English public opinion. Herzl's comments in that interview regarding the Armenians should be seen in that light.

Herzl also corresponds with Nevlinsky and reports to him on the progress of his activities: "I have made efforts on your behalf, and I am hopeful that they will become apparent to you." Herzl reports on efforts vis-à-vis the English government, which seem in retrospect to have been meaningless. "And regarding my co-religionists," writes Herzl,

> I have already pushed them forward between London and Paris. But among my friends there are some with a fairly serious complaint. They claim that we are in danger *"de travailler pour le roi de Prusse"* and even if peace is achieved, we will be quickly forgotten. One of our friends, a person of considerable influence, is opposed to any intervention of this sort, because he believes that the disintegration of this great body [the Ottoman Empire] would be of most benefit to us. Whereas I, as I told you at the beginning, believe it is in our interest, if we understand it correctly, to move in the direction you yourself proposed. I wish to preserve our existing power and to strengthen it since, as it will shortly become clear, we are dealing here with friends.

Herzl was convinced that "as the first proofs of a sympathetic attitude to our cause become evident the opponents will come over to my side."[31]

In the course of the following months, Herzl reported to Nevlinsky several times on his activity on the Armenian matter. He spent twelve days in Constantinople at the end of June 1896, meeting with high-ranking officials, including the Grand Vizier, but did not meet with the Sultan himself during this sojourn. The question of the Armenians came up in his discussions, and Herzl was asked to show his "good will," and demonstrate his authority, by agreeing to soften the critical attitude of the European press toward Abd al-Hamid II because of his treatment of the Armenians. He was also asked to persuade the Armenian leaders in exile to accept the Sultan's authority, in return for unspecified concessions.[32]

In his journal entry for June 22, 1896, Herzl describes his conversation with Nevlinsky who had told him about the latter's discussion with the Sultan the day before, regarding the Sultan's refusal to receive Herzl:

> He could not and would not receive me as a journalist after this experience he had had with Bacher and the N.F.Pr. [the *Neue Freie Presse*, the Viennese, Austrian newspaper for which Herzl worked]. A few months after Bacher's interview our paper had published the most malicious attack on his person that had ever appeared in the Press—including the English and Armenian press. The Sultan complained about this to the Austrian ambassador, Calice, and expressly regretted that the latter had introduced Bacher to him.
>
> On the other hand, he is willing to receive me for an audience as a friend—after I do him a favor. And this is the service he demands of me: that I prevail upon the newspapers of Europe (in London, Paris, Berlin and Vienna), to present the Armenian question in a fashion friendly to Turkey, and that I convince the Armenian leaders themselves to surrender to him, whereupon he will be willing to meet all sorts of their demands.
>
> In his discussion with Nevlinsky, the Sultan spoke figuratively....He said: 'For me, all of my peoples are like children who were born to me by different wives. The sons are my sons, and even if they have conflicts among themselves, there are no conflicts between them and me.'
>
> I told Nevlinsky at once that I am ready to take action. I must be given a practical explication of the Armenian question: which Armenian leaders must be convinced, which newspapers must be brought around, etc. Of course I shall be better able to succeed in my efforts if the Sultan will receive me for an interview.
>
> Nevlinsky said: 'He will receive him and grant him an important medal.' I replied: 'I have no need of a medal. I need only an interview now. Our only task today is to plant the seed.'
>
> We held our conversation in the garden of a cafe in Bebek on the Bosphorus. We sat in the shade of a tree, in the heavy noonday heat.[33]

And Nevlinsky nurtured Herzl's hopes. According to Herzl's diary, written the day after the visit, Nevlinsky told him, "if you succeed in pacifying the Armenians, to arrange a loan of two million pounds for the lighthouses and if we obtain a letter from Bismarck [which supports the transfer of Palestine to the Jews] — we will bring the matter to a conclusion within eight days."[34]

After a short stay in Vienna, Herzl went from Turkey to London with the intention of trying to establish an "Association of the Jews" there. On the way he was received in Sophia with great enthusiasm. In contrast, his reception in London was chilly, reserved, and sometimes almost hostile. His connection with the Armenian problem had already been exposed in the media, after Herzl gave an interview to the Jewish journalist and activist, Lucien Wolf, which appeared in the *Daily Graphic* on July 6, 1896.[35]

In the interview, Herzl expressed support for the liberal nationalist ideas current in Europe during this period, which had resulted in the unification of Germany and Italy and the liberation of the Balkans. He took exception to the criticism of the Chief Rabbi of England who had termed his plan "fantastic" and had warned English Jewry to keep a distance from it. "I do not appeal to the bourgeois spirit. I turn my sights to the sort of people who, in our time, created the unification in Germany and in Italy, who liberated the Greeks, and made the Balkans free peoples." The interview ends thus:

> Upon taking my leave, I asked the Doctor if there was any truth in the rumour, that the Turkish Government supports the program in order to obtain Jewish support against the Armenians. Certainly not, he answered vigorously, 'Can you imagine the Jews condoning any sort of atrocity? Have they themselves not suffered enough from such things?' Nonetheless, I did not visit Constantinople without investigating the question of the subject peoples of the Turkish Empire, and I truly believe that people in England have not been entirely fair toward the Sultan. He personally abhors brutality, and he honestly yearns to live in peace with all of his subjects. In a recent discussion of this question, he made a particularly apt comment. 'My subjects,' he said, 'are like the children of different wives. They argue amongst themselves but they can have no quarrel with me because I am their father.'

The fact that Herzl had first tried to enlist Lucien Wolf, his interviewer, in the Armenian matter, puts Herzl's comments into their proper context. His statements are aimed at public opinion and at the Sultan, with intent of supporting the Sultan while minimizing the criticism at his support. Herzl condemns all acts of atrocity, but feels that the English have not been entirely fair toward the Sultan and tries to improve his public image.

In various entries in Herzl's diary during May, June, July, and August 1896, we find evidence of his attempts to establish contact with the Armenian committees in Europe so that he might serve as a mediator. It is clear that his offer to mediate is not sincere. In view of his desire for a political achievement at almost any price, he wants to use the role of mediator for his own political needs. He exploits his connections, makes contacts and holds a number of meetings with Armenian leaders in various places in Europe. In his diary, Herzl admits that the Armenians were hesitant about his offer to mediate. Describing his meeting in Vienna with the Russian Armenian leader, Allahverdof, he says that the latter was not candid with him, because he is Russian and therefore afraid of his government. Herzl adds, "It seems that he also did not trust me. In the end it was agreed between us that he will speak about me as a friend of the Armenians in London, and will calm the atmosphere in his circle."[36]

Herzl also worked through Lucien Wolf, "to initiate certain efforts in the press to calm the controversy over the Armenian issue" — in other words, to defuse criticism of Turkey in the press.[37] Herzl shoots in all directions on the Armenian question. He hopes that his mediation efforts will serve the interests of the English (who will appreciate his efforts) and enable England to reestablish its influence in Turkey.[38]

He also wants to meet with Avedis Nazarbikian, leader of the Hunchaks, a revolutionary Armenian party which was strongly influenced by the Russian "Narodnya Volya." "I want to explain to this revolutionary that it is best for the Armenians to reconcile now with the Sultan, a step which will not prevent them from presenting their demands again later, when Turkey is partitioned." When the two met in London, the atmosphere was full of distrust and the meeting led to nothing.[39] Herzl writes contemptuously of the Armenian revolutionary leader that "his political ideas are confused, his acquaintance with the European situation downright childish." Furthermore, "And as it seems, his word is obeyed by the poor people in Armenia who are being massacred. He lives in London, not uncomfortably."

Herzl also describes the wife of the Armenian revolutionary who speaks incessantly in Armenian, "evidently against me. She has a wicked look; and who knows how much she is to blame for the bloodshed. Or is it the evil look of the frightened, the persecuted?"[40]

From Herzl's point of view it was felicitous that Turkey was in trouble. The worse Turkey's situation became, the better it would be for the Zionist cause. Turkey would need assistance, and would therefore agree to Herzl's requests, in return for the help it so desperately needed. Herzl, who has not made quick strides, consoles himself in his diary with the hope that it may be best to wait until the situation deteriorates.

The deterioration occurred at the end of August 1896. In a letter which Herzl marks "top secret," he writes to Zadok Cohen, the Chief Rabbi of Paris, that "he has received some sensational and decisive news from Constantinople. People there are inclined to enter into negotiations with us immediately....The financial distress has reached a climax." Now the knife is at their throats. "It is now or never that we shall get Palestine."[41]

But several days later "terrible news has come from Constantinople. The building of the Ottoman Bank was stormed by Armenians. Murders, killings, bombs, street-fights. Order appears to have been restored, but the impression on the world is deplorable."[42] As a result of the disturbances and increasing severity of the attacks against the Armenians, which had continued with ups and downs for the better part of two years, since 1894, there was real concern for the future of the Sultan. "From London comes the news that the Powers are giving some thought to deposing Abd al-Hamid II. If this comes about, the Zionist idea will be dead for a long time to come. A new Sultan will find money and won't need this combination."[43]

Herzl feared that replacement of the Sultan would skewer his plans. The status of a new Sultan in world opinion would be different from that of the present "Red Sultan," who was identified with the murder of Armenians. He would be able to find sources of aid. Herzl attempted to rouse public action to support the Sultan despite the worsening of the atrocities against the Armenians. He turned to Jacob de Haas (1872-1937), the editor of the weekly *Jewish World* from 1892 to 1900, one of Herzl's first supporters in England, and later one of the organizers of the Zionist Organization in the United States: "This will be a disaster for us if the Sultan is deposed now. Could you therefore write something in the *World*?"[44]

And, indeed, it appears that de Haas made an effort so that the British press would not give wide coverage of the Armenian massacre. The atrocities strengthened the English and general Jewish opposition to negotiation with the Sultan. The Sephardic Chief Rabbi of London, Dr. Gaster (with whom Mark Sykes had made contact when he first began to establish connections with the Zionists in Britain in 1916, as we shall see later), promised de Haas that he would write a personal letter to the Sultan, "so that the Sultan should not think that a significant part of the Jews oppose him." Herzl wrote to de Haas, "Dr. Gaster's letter to the Sultan will make a good impression. Of course he must not condone the massacres of the Armenians, since praise of such abominations may excite hatred against us."[45]

Herzl suggests that Gaster write merely a declaration of support, without going into the matter of the Armenians. "Please be so good as to say especially that after my speech in London (in the Maccabee Club on July 6, 1896) in which I praised the Sultan as a friend of the Jews, the Jews everywhere in the world can be counted as his friends who wish the Sultan well."

Herzl knows that the Sultan's actions are an "abomination," but is ready to whitewash them if this will benefit his cause. Because of the increasingly severe persecutions of the Armenians, Sir Samuel Montagu, a Jewish banker and public figure and a Liberal member of the British Parliament, refused to participate in the respectable Jewish delegation which Herzl wanted to organize at the time in order to negotiate with the Sultan in Constantinople.[46] The idea of the delegation never bore fruit. Pressure from the press and from the major powers (particularly England) was apparently one of the factors in the cessation of the slaughter of the Armenians at the end of 1896. But the great powers did not go so far as to replace the ruler in Constantinople. Such a step was not in Germany's interest.

Other great powers, for their own reasons, and because of the rivalry between them, preferred a weak ruler in Turkey who could be manipulated. Herzl was in favor of preserving the wholeness of the Ottoman Empire, in which framework he hoped the Zionist movement could achieve its goals. The Sultan's weakness was an advantage for Herzl: "The financial situation of Turkey is so dire that it can be improved only by the wealth of the Jews."[47] But Herzl, who was very anxious to assist the Sultan, was not able to obtain the funds which he had promised the Turks. In fact, he was not even able to arrange a small loan, not in 1896 nor later.[48] The slaughter of the Armenians had aroused public opinion in Europe against the Sultan. Herzl was therefore unable to make any progress in his relations with the Turks.

Herzl's contacts and attempts to reach an agreement with the Turks continued throughout his career. In the beginning of 1898, he met twice with the Turkish ambassador in Berlin, Ahmed Tewfik.

> He is not ill-disposed to our cause but he has chosen a course which is of no help to us. He would like to draw the Jews to Turkey but without an independent territory and without autonomy. We are supposed to bring funding sources to Turkey and as remuneration they will receive us 'in friendship.' I told him that this was no solution and has no lasting value. It would be the settlement of new Armenians in Turkey.[49]

This is a recurring theme for Herzl: "Not to become the new Armenians." In a speech before the Austrian Jewish Association on November 7, 1896, he said, "Large-scale settlement which we believe to be desirable can only be described as settlement which is based on a self-defense capability and has autonomous rights. Otherwise we shall simply be transplanting latter-day Armenians."[50] What is good for the Armenians—and what they must settle for, according to his words and deeds—is not good enough for the Jews.

The controversy between Lazare and Herzl at the end of 1901 and the beginning of 1902 is an expression of the differences of opinion over the means, permissible or impermissible, to achieve their goals. Herzl, who sought political success at almost any price, was not particular about his means. It ought to be mentioned that his efforts, attempts and intercessions with the Turks were in vain and did not achieve their goal. It is possible that they were doomed from the beginning.

Itamar Ben Avi's Editorial "We" and the Armenians

As early as 1909, a fascinating controversy raged in the Jewish and Eretz Yisrael press around one small article, "We," written by Itamar Ben Avi, "the first Hebrew child." The dissension over this editorial article will lead us to additional treatments of the Armenian issue in the press in the years from 1894 to 1909. It should be emphasized that this section does not exhaust the coverage of the Armenian question and the public debate surrounding it in the Jewish and Eretz Yisrael press during these years. Our examination is eclectic: one item leads to another. A more systematic investigation would certainly uncover additional material. Nonetheless, there is no doubt that the attitudes were significant and expose a thought-provoking mosaic of varied reactions to the Armenian tragedy.

The Attitude Toward the Massacre of the Armenians in the Jewish and Eretz Yisrael Press, 1894-1909

The slaughter of the Armenians occurred in 1909, following atrocities against the Armenians during the years 1894-1896 in various parts of the Ottoman Empire, including in Constantinople, the capital city. Estimates vary regarding the number of victims in those years. Some put the number of Armenian dead at 300,000 while others estimate the number at 150,000 dead and a similar number forced to become refugees. In 1909, after the failed attempt to roll back the revolution of the "Young Turks," which had taken place the year before, additional atrocities were committed against the Armenians. These events, in the context of the counterrevolution, took place during the two weeks between April 13 and April 27.

Hatzvi, Eliezer Ben-Yehuda's newspaper, which was edited at the time by Itamar Ben Avi (Ben-Yehuda's son), appeared daily in Jerusalem. In effect, *Hatzvi* was the only Hebrew daily during this period. In Issue 173, from May 16, 1909, in the section of "Latest News" under the headline, "The Slaughter of the Armenians," we read:

> The slaughter of the Armenians has not ceased. Every single day the Muslims are killing hundreds of Armenians. The four thousand soldiers who are in the province are also taking part in this terrible massacre. In Adana alone six thousand and five hundred people have been murdered, and in the rest of the country another thirty thousand, approximately. The gentiles have also suffered terribly from this massacre. Two French schools in Adana were utterly destroyed; the American school is in danger, and on the first of May [1909] the French monastery was burned.

Two days later, on May 18, again under the headline "The Slaughter of the Armenians,"

> According to the latest reports which have reached us, we can give a fairly clear picture of the new and terrible slaughter of the Armenians. The massacre began in Adana on April 14, and there were two days of horrifying murders. Fifteen thousand people have been left homeless, thousands have been killed, and three hundred wounded. For two days there was a respite and the residents were able to catch their breath, but, on April 18, the military forces known as 'Bashi-Bouzouk' attacked the Armenian school in which thousands of Armenians sought shelter and opened fire upon these poor people. The school was set afire, most of the refugees were burned, and those who tried to escape the flames were shot by the soldiers. The fire

in the school spread to the surroundings, destroying four churches, five schools and hundreds of homes.

The fire raged for two days. Thousands of people were burned to death, and those who were saved were set upon by thieves. On the evening of April 20, some twenty thousand Armenians gathered in two of the largest factories in the city. They were jammed inside, without food or water, without hope, and at night when these wretched people tried to get some sleep and to forget their sorrows, the awful sound of shots was heard outside. The poor people thought that their end had come, and their joy was boundless when it became known that the shooting was in celebration of the victory of the Turkish Parliament.

At the same time that relative peace was being restored in Adana, and bread and rice were being distributed to the wretched who only yesterday were rich and well-to-do, the slaughter was spreading in the Adana province. Within several days twenty thousand people were slaughtered and killed, and the government is helpless to stop the massacre.[51]

The following day, in Issue 176, in the same section, under the headline "Massacre in Adana" the account was, "according to latest reports, some two thousand Muslims were killed. And more than five thousand were wounded. The number of Armenian victims has risen to more than thirty thousand."

Twelve days earlier, in Issue 163, Tuesday, May 4, Itamar Ben Avi published an unsigned editorial entitled "We." The editorial begins thus: "We are a peculiar people. Yes, we!" The editorial is written in two parts. The first part relates to the alleged attempt of Sultan Abd al-Hamid II, two weeks previously, to reestablish control over the Turkish capital, Constantinople, and to wipe out the achievements of the "Young Turks." The counterrevolution failed. Itamar Ben Avi terms the counterrevolution, "a terrible act, an act which has outraged all the lovers of freedom in wretched Turkey and in the entire world. In one moment, with stunning suddenness, the shadow of the former regime has covered the face of the common homeland. Oh how damnable, how accursed was that shadow." But this section of the editorial deals mainly with the fact that the Jews stood on the sidelines, "watching from the side and waiting," and did nothing.

But while in all of the countries of Turkey peoples were shaken by a strong national sense; while the 'Young Turks' organized as a courageous band; while the Christians, like the Greeks and the Bulgarians, were quick to raise their voices and speak out, by the thousands, to strengthen the Armenian and Parliamentary camps, as a united people, announcing to Young Turkey that they will act as one to oppose the arrogant insurgents, at that time what did we do, we the Jews? Yes, we! Alas, nothing.

Even the six hundred Jews from Saloniki who joined forces with the "Young Turks" against the enemy did not do so as Jews.

Not only was the number small, very small, too small, compared to the numbers of the sons of other peoples in the Macedonian camp, moreover these Jews did not take part as members of one nation together with their comrades, the Christians and the Muslims; each of these six hundred heroes went to battle as a private individual who felt that his homeland was endangered, and a natural impulse pushed him to save it. But the Jewish People as a whole, five hundred thousand Jewish citizens in greater Turkey, this entire people stood aside coldly and fearfully; one could almost say, with deep indifference. As is always the case with the Jews.

Ben Avi continues his attack:

This is an ancient Jewish characteristic. Only that which directly affects him: pogroms against his brethren in Russia or Rumania, poverty among the 'Israelites' in Persia or Morocco, the oppression of the Jews in Arabia or the Falashas in Abyssinia can rouse the Jew to give financial or spiritual aid. But a war for freedom, waged by his neighbors, who are for the time being his masters, participation in the general effort, in the state which belongs to him and to the rest of the peoples around him—do not, do not ever demand that of him; he will not do it!

Once, during the early days of the latest and accursed revolution, we thought that the Jews in our cities, in our country of Eretz Yisrael, would be sparked upon hearing of the Ottoman troubles; we thought that the Jews would move together in one motion to the Jerusalem office of the Committee, and offer their plentiful assistance: money, people, whatever you ask! We thought that the Jews would come to the Turks and tell them: Listen! We, the Ottoman Jews, have come to you, and offer you our hands, loyal hands. Your war is our war, your defeat is our defeat, and your victory is our victory. But when the day of triumph arrives, when the Turkish Parliament is restored to its rightful place, when you Young Turks have established your benevolent regime, remember us, the Jews. Remember that among all the peoples in the land, we too are a people, like all others, and we shall demand from you our rights. We have no wish for a special state, for a special king, for a special army.

But we wish for you to recognize our language as an Ottoman language; we want you to respect our community, just as you respect the communities of the Armenians, the Greeks and the Arabs. And in particular we want you to cancel, immediately and without delay, all of the restrictions which the former regime put on us and which you have left in place, despite your Parliament. These are our demands!

Had we come to them in this manner; would that we were true pioneers, free and courageous, who knows whether the military commander would then have dealt harshly with us? Who knows if he would not have agreed with us, especially in these moments of danger, when everyone thought the Turkish Parliament had been lost forever and that Abd al-Hamid II had returned to his tyranny? Then, perhaps, we might have saved our situation and our honor.... But we....Yes, we!

We did nothing, because we were timid, because the matter did not affect us directly, utterly. Unfortunately these Turks where not Jews. Unfortunately we had covert sympathy for the enemy of the Turkish Parliament, Abd al-Hamid II. Sympathy because we believed that Abd al-Hamid would always be our friend, our generous and merciful supporter. That is why we stood aside; that is why we chose to be, in the words of the wise commander, the rearguard; that is why we continue today, two weeks after the revolution and a week after the victory of the 'Young Turks' to be indifferent. We are watching from the side and waiting. We are a peculiar people.

Yes, we!

In the second part of the editorial, Itamar Ben Avi blames the Jews for indifference to the atrocities which the Turks are committing against the Armenians. In blunt and provocative language, apparently intentional, he condemns the egocentricity and ethnocentricity of the Jews. He also takes exception to the "monopoly of suffering" which the Jews have appropriated to themselves, ignoring the fact that "there is another people in the world which suffers like the Jews."

Another minor comment: we have been told that the Armenian community in Jerusalem turned to Rabbi Salant requesting that he encourage the members of his community to contribute a bit of money for the pitiful relatives of the Armenians who were slaughtered by the Muslims in Adana and its environs. Fifteen thousand Armenians were massacred, murdered, put to death. Fifteen thousand—and this horrifying number means nothing to us! As always with the Jews! Go tell the Jews that there are pogroms in Russia, against the Jews of course; go tell them that a couple of hundred of their coreligionists have been killed, and you shall see what fearsome effect your words have upon them: Jews have been killed! The poor Jews! Once again they have been the victims of zealotry and barbarism! The pitiful Jews! And at once they will shove their hand into their pocket and give generously to aid the survivors.

But go tell them that there is another people in the world which suffers like the Jews. Go describe to them the sorrows of that people, years and years ago, when that very Abd al-Hamid II gave the order and three hundred thousand of them were exterminated—an entire nation! Go, tell them moreover that only two weeks ago another fifteen thousand Armenians were taken to the slaughter, wretched Armenians.

A slight grimace on their lips, a short heartfelt sigh, and nothing more. The Armenians are not Jews, and according to folk tradition the Armenians are nothing more than Amaleks!

Amaleks? We would give them help? To whom? To Amaleks? Heaven forbid! What Rabbi Salant replied we do not know. But he did not say much, of that we can be sure. And the proof? We today, at *Hatzvi*, are initiating a collection for the benefit of the devastated Armenians. We ourselves will give to this effort 10 francs to the wretched who are left, to the widows and orphans, the bereaved, the blind, the lame and the sick. And we call upon all of the Jews in our country to deliver to our editorial offices their donation for the Armenians, the donation of the oppressed to the oppressed, the donation of a people without a country to a people without a country—will the Jews hear us? Will they rise to our call? We shall see!

The Controversy

The editorial staff of *Hatzvi* contributed ten francs to aid the Armenians, and the workers of *Hatzvi* one franc. The editorial aroused fierce reaction in the Jewish and Eretz Yisrael press and it was attacked for its style, sharpness, and bluntness. But most of the critics attacked *Hatzvi* for slandering the Jews "as the worst enemies of Israel," and for "spreading libel about us." With regard to the content, the critics take exception to the charge that the Jews care only about themselves: the Jews are taking part in the struggle for freedom and liberation in the world. An additional charge was that the paper had taken anti-Turkish stands which might endanger the Yishuv; in this case, taking a stand on the side of the Armenians who were in a conflict with the Turks. *Hatzvi*'s position was "baseless persecution, which could only lead to strife and contention between peoples." It is interesting that some of the sharpest reactions were in regard to the Armenians.

Three days after the editorial appeared, the storm burst. On Friday, May 7, *Hatzvi* published as its lead story on the front page an open letter to the editor from Dr. A. Mazie. The writer was Dr. Aharon Meyer

Mazie who had come to the country in 1887 to serve as a doctor in the agricultural villages established by the Baron Rothschild, and, in 1902, had moved to Jerusalem to serve as chief of staff at Bikur Holim Hospital. Mazie was active in public affairs in Jerusalem, including during the period of the First World War, and was considered a man with wide horizons and broad knowledge in a number of fields.[52] Dr. Mazie rejected the claims of *Hatzvi* that the Jews had refrained from helping the Armenians because the latter were considered Amaleks by the Jews.

As a Jew in general, and an Ottoman Jew in particular, I hereby protest vigorously against these comments of the editor, which may lead to feelings of enmity, animosity, and needless hatred between the grieving, bitter Armenians and their neighbors, the innocent Jews who have lived with them in peace and tranquility in our land and others from ancient days.

And if the masses nevertheless do not show their generosity in bringing donations to *Hatzvi*, this is merely because of the terrible hostility which currently prevails among the Jews who subsist here on haluka [donations from abroad] which is diminishing and not sufficient for them. And in truth they have not been very generous toward their own brethren—coreligionists—who suffered so greatly during the pogroms in Russia; but no one accused them so harshly then because it would have been unthinkable to suspect them in this matter. Only with regard to the Armenians does the editor lay suspicion upon the blameless

And the enlightened and educated Jews? Who among them would harden his heart and not speed to the assistance of innocent unfortunates? And particularly for the sake of the Armenians who have suffered so terribly; many still remember the sacrifices made by some of their finest young people in defense of the Jews during the pogroms in Russia. Had *Hatzvi* called for donations in the regular way and in the language which ordinary people use to call for donations and arouse compassion, everyone would surely have taken part willingly, to the best of their ability — as is always the case in these situations. But unfortunately the editor of *Hatzvi* chose a different method, to spread libel about us that we had cast off all pity from the Armenians-Amaleks, and only "a slight grimace on our lips" touches us at the rumour that fifteen thousand of them have been slaughtered. And in his great mercy, the editor will also show us the way to repentance, by giving him our charitable contributions, ransom money for our sinners' souls. My heart may be broken by the need to refute this spurious charge as mere wanton libel which will only cause strife, contention and conflict between the two peoples. Yet in days such as these when 'cold' winds blow in the world and in our own villages, I consider it a holy duty, 'in the name of truth and peace', to say to the young editor so that all may hear: Desist from your ways, which will bring you no glory! And I must point out that *Hatzvi*'s story that the Armenian community in Jerusalem approached Rabbi Salant etc., does not fit with the truth, and the real fact is this: In Beirut a committee to aid the Armenians was established under the leadership of the American consul there, and this committee comprised members from several cities, one of whom was the American consul in Jerusalem, and it was he who sent the petition of the Beirut committee to the esteemed Rabbi Salant. And according to what I have heard, the petition was distributed to the committee of all of the yeshivas; and perhaps additional other institutions participated in it as well. And now individuals can also send their contributions to the American consul in Jerusalem who is a member of the Central Committee.

In any event, even if there are not many donations to his fund, this will not be proof for the editor of *Hatzvi* that 'heaven forbid that the Jews help the Amaleks.' It is possible that many Jews will send their donations directly to one of the members of the Central Committee. In the hope that in the future the honorable editor will be more moderate in his judgment of the Jews in general and of the Jews in our country in particular, I sign this with best wishes! Dr. A. Mazie.

It should be noted that Dr. Mazie's mention of the assistance proffered by the Armenians to the Jews during the pogroms against the Jews in Russia, recurs in other letters. Other reactions were received by the newspaper in the days that followed and were also given a prominent place in *Hatzvi*. In Issue 168, a large headline appears on the second page: "New Protests," and under it a secondary headline: "Rishon Lezion Boycotts *Hatzvi*. Subscribers Sent Us A Strong Protest, Our Agent Cannot Sell Latest Editions. *Hatzvi* Was Sent Back To Us." Among the reactions was a letter to the editor from M. Meyerovitch, a leader of the village of Rishon Lezion, strongly rejecting the thesis of the article which is, in his opinion, very succinct:

It levels at the Jews the terrible charge that they have stood utterly aside in the whole war for freedom, and that we come to life only when the matter affects our own cause, Jewish causes, and even then only when others have laid the foundations with their blood and soul. I find no reason to respond here to other claims of 'We' which are truly horrifying, and I think it will be sufficient if I relate only to the general impression which 'We' made upon its readers.

This accusation which 'We' makes against us does not refer only to the Jews of Eretz Yisrael. It is leveled against the Jews of the entire Diaspora. Are not the claims of the article similar to the charges used by the greatest enemies of Israel to besmirch our name throughout the world? Are these not the words of the Russian oppressor Severin? Are they not the words of Shtecker, Druman and their comrades? And just when the finest people in the world and righteous gentiles are trying to remove from us this unbearable injustice.

The claim against Ben Avi that his words repeated "the charges used by the greatest enemies of Israel" also appears in other letters. The writer calls upon the editor of *Hatzvi* to quickly clarify his remarks, "to remove from us the disgrace which his words have brought upon him."

In this same issue, "in the very same language!," appears an open letter signed by twelve subscribers to the paper, who write in the name of all of the subscribers in Rishon Lezion. In the letter, which is a bitter attack on the editor, Itamar Ben Avi, they write: "Woe to you that editors such as this are your standard bearers! Woe to you as a newspaper whose editor is a mere lad!" "How can a peculiar people such as ours produce an editor of a Hebrew daily, national newspaper in Eretz Yisrael, for whom the history of his people and its bravery in the field of freedom and liberty from its earliest days until the present are a closed, incomprehensible book." The letter continues,

And so let us make clear to you that so long as *Hatzvi* is in the hands of such an editor who does not understand what his people and the times demand of him, we shall keep our distance from this newspaper, and in vigorous protest at his article, which is based on ignorance, and perhaps on hatred for his own people, we hereby return all of the copies of today's issue. In the name of all of the subscribers in Rishon, we request that the honorable editorial board save itself the effort of sending us its newspaper anymore.

The present editor *en chef* has ired us more than sufficiently in recent days and we, indeed a peculiar people, lacking to date another Hebrew organ in Eretz Yisrael have therefore kept our silence for the sake of the language in whose defense Ben Avi presumes to do battle....However, the latter has gone too far and we say to him: 'Stop! You have gone this far but we shall let you go no farther....'And the lack now truly felt in Eretz Yisrael, we shall take steps to fill as soon as possible. We shall succeed for the time has certainly come!

Below their signatures, the writers added,

One more small comment! To the wretched and persecuted Armenians, who in the Scriptures, according to the editor (Does he know what the Scriptures are?), we have been informed are Amaleks, we express our support. We herein also protest against the acts of violence against them, and express our condolences for their great sorrow, regardless of the fact that the Armenians have never shown either particular affection or material or spiritual support for us, as one people without a country to another, in the course of all of our troubles which surely did not affect them. And we had decided, even before Ben Avi's superfluous proposal, to offer them our scant assistance, in the name of humanitarianism and in the name of a people without a country, of course, as a token of our benevolent feelings toward them. May the Lord console them in their grief and bereavement.

It is worth noting the reservations of the writers toward the Armenians: "[T]he Armenians have never shown either particular affection or material or spiritual support for us, as one people without a country to another, in the course of all our troubles which surely did not affect them." It will be recalled that others emphasized the assistance of the Armenians to the Jews during the Russian pogroms. The editor also adds, "the things that were hastily written to us by our agent Segal in Rishon Lezion":

Your lead article "We" in *Hatzvi*, Issue no. 163, aroused terrible ire in Rishon. Almost all of the subscribers have boycotted *Hatzvi*. They do not wish to accept their issues and will also not permit the sale of *Hatzvi* to others. On Wednesday evening, when the post arrived from Jaffa, many of the subscribers gathered near the postal shed and would not let me distribute *Hatzvi*.[3] One of the subscribers who did yet not know about the boycott and who received his paper from me, aroused the fury of the boycotters and one of them angrily grabbed the paper and tore it up in front of the large crowd which stood there. Now they are sending back the issues from yesterday and the day before, and have written a letter of protest which you shall receive shortly.

In Issue 171, three days later, the paper reports that the boycott of the paper in Rishon Lezion has ended, "and as of today *Hatzvi* will resume its shipment to its subscribers without hindrance." On the same day, the editorial board also announces its decision to cease publication of the letters of protest:

We have yesterday received from our agent, Segal, in Rishon Lezion, a letter in which he enquires why we have ceased to send our newspaper to that village. There was indeed a boycott against us in Rishon Lezion, but the boycott was only for one day and no more. Currently—these are more or less the words of our agent—everything has been forgotten, and our subscribers have asked to resume reading our newspaper daily. The agent also requested the previous issues for his subscribers. Pursuant to this letter, yesterday we sent all that was requested and as of today *Hatzvi* will resume shipment to its subscribers without hindrance.

On the same day we received a sharp protest from Gedera. The readers of *Hatzvi* can be certain, from recent events, that we would not refrain from publishing the protest from Gedera, signed by eight signatories, but we cannot fill our paper everyday with protests, especially when they are unacceptably vulgar, in which case *Hatzvi* has the right not to print them. It should be sufficient for the correspondents from Gedera if we announce that their letter of protest against the wicked editorial, "We," was far stronger than that of their colleagues from Rishon Lezion.

This morning we also received a letter of protest from Haifa, signed by ten people. We will refrain from publishing it for the reason stated above.[54] Many personal letters, from men and women, also reached us. Most of them are written in anger at us and at our editorial. We hope to be forgiven if we do not publish them and are satisfied with saving them at our office. *Hatzvi* has fulfilled its duty and will now move on to other matters at hand.

It should be added that the campaign against *Hatzvi* was also waged in the context of a "press war" and the competition between newspapers. *Havazelet*, the most veteran among the newspapers, which then appeared three times a week, was reported to be gathering signatures of people who would promise not to buy *Hatzvi* in the future, because it weakened the spirit of the people. The hope was that if it could gather two hundred signatures (in addition to the three hundred which had already been collected), *Havazelet* would become a daily and *Hatzvi* would ultimately cease to appear. *Hatzvi* proposed "more dignified means of competition: healthy competition, constructive competition."[55]

The zealousness of the Hebrew press was over the limited readership, but there were also ideological differences of opinion. Various circles in the Yishuv were critical of *Hatzvi*'s independent and original positions, and the ideas which its young editor introduced from Paris and Berlin. *Hatzvi* called for Ottomanization, and on the masthead occasionally appeared the call: "Jews, Become Ottomans." The paper believed that as Ottomans, the Jews of the new Yishuv would be able to fight more effectively for their rights in Eretz Yisrael. At the same time, the paper was highly critical of the actions of the Turkish Government and the Turkish police force in the country which caused the authorities to bring charges against the paper and temporarily suspend its publication.

Other sectors of the Yishuv, including the workers' movement, preferred a more moderate, conciliatory stance—some would say obsequious and submissive—toward the authorities. The controversy over the editorial went beyond the columns of *Hatzvi*. *Hapoel Hatzair,* a "vehicle of expression for the Association of Hebrew Workers in Eretz Yisrael, published twice a month by the Central Committee," was one of the most vicious attackers. The association of "Hapoel Hatzair" was the smaller of the two important workers' associations in that period. The other was "Poalei Zion."

Readers' responses also appeared in *Hapoel Hatzair*. One of them, signed by thirty-one residents of Haifa, carries the headline "The Time Has Come," and also appeared in the journal of the Zionist Organization, *Haolam.*[56]

> The time has come to publish a Hebrew journal of substance in our country. A substantive daily Hebrew paper which will not spew abuse and disgrace upon our people, on one hand, and will not imitate the fashions of Berlin and Paris, with all of their shortcomings, and obscenities in general, on the other hand.

> The time has come. The behavior of the only daily newspaper we have in the country in recent days, in general, and its editorial, "We," (*Hatzvi*, No. 163), in particular, has shown us that this newspaper is not able to meet our demands.

Issue 13 of *Hapoel Hatzair* from May 2, 1909, under the headline "From Political Affairs," reports on "the second campaign" of the Turkish revolution which was taking place. The paper praises, in moderate tones, the revolution which characterizes the victory of the province over the center (Constantinople).

> Albeit the second campaign of the Turkish revolution has ended, but we are not entirely sure that the victory of the 'Young Turks' ensures a new regime and that Turkey will begin to live a serene life under the auspices of constitutional institutions. The counterrevolution, although short-lived, managed to leave in its wake terrible tracks of blood. The scapegoat this time was again the unfortunate Armenian people, which here has filled the role of the Jewish people in Russia. In the Adana Province and in Northern Syria there were horrific killings, truly a general massacre by the Kurds and the Turks (the Arabs had no part in this) against the Armenians. Reports estimate the number of dead at ten or fifteen thousand people, but the numbers are, of course, imprecise, and the disturbances have not yet ended in the interior of the country.

Armenian refugees in the thousands are filling the nearby Syrian beaches. Warships of all nations are patrolling Turkish waters, and English troops have landed ashore from Mersina and Alexandretta to create order.

The shock at what was happening to the Armenians is humanitarian anguish and sorrow for the victim. There is no treatment of aspects beyond that. We shall also find similar reactions among inhabitants of Eretz Yisrael to the genocide of the Armenians during the First World War. The newspaper praises the Arabs and the Arab press:

Because at the height of the situation they continued to persist in the goal of 'Union and Progress,' despite the various differences of opinion between them. The Arab provinces were especially outstanding this time; the cities of Syria and Eretz Yisrael were among the first to protest, through their local branches of the Committee, against the counter-revolution, and enlisted their well-known influence to assist the Saloniki victory. The Arab press (we refer to the Egyptian press, not to the Syrian press, most of which waited for several days to see how matters would develop in Constantinople....) rose up as one against the reactionary revolution, released flyers to the Arab and Syrian peoples to stand with the Constitutionalists, and protested sharply against the killings of the Armenians.

The writer ends his article thus:

Feelings of contempt in the whole world for the old Turkey gave way to sentiments of sympathy and affection for the new Turkey. They recall the mass killings of the Armenians, the Greeks and others, which took place under the leadership of Abd al-Hamid II, and Abd al-Hamid II's downfall as the Lord's vengeance and historical justice. And we Jews of Eretz Yisrael, although we cannot take part in this revolution since we are strangers in the land, can nonetheless rejoice in the victory of the 'Young Turks' which will benefit all the peoples of Turkey, including us.

This passage also reveals moderation and caution. In this same issue we find an additional article signed by "Domesticus," who writes in the domestic affairs section. While he lauds the establishment of a Hebrew national militia following the establishment of a militia by the Arabs, he points out that "our militia in Jaffa will be exceedingly praiseworthy even if it deals only with defense of our interests, the smallest and most humble interests."

According to "Domesticus," the editor of *Hatzvi* is not comfortable with such behavior and "in his excessive enthusiasm reached a level which even the worst anti-semites had not reached."[57] The writer ridicules the editor of *Hatzvi* and his idea for a charitable appeal to aid the Armenians. "Domesticus" concludes,

> The tone of the editorial, the attitude of "We" is so insulting as to be the most dreadful disgrace in the history of journalism in our country....And the public in Eretz Yisrael, it must be confessed, understood this and showed the appropriate contempt for this worthless editorial. The public in Rishon Lezion, for example, punished the editor of *Hatzvi* by deciding to return their copies of his paper. But if he will know enough to recant from his ways of sensationalism and surprise, only time will tell.

In the following issue, *Hapoel Hatzair*, No. 14, May 21, 1909, there are additional items and an article about our subject. One, in the "Chronicle" section, reports: "A committee has been founded to aid the victims of the disturbances in Adana (Armenians). Many Jews have made pledges."[58] "Domesticus," in his "Domestic Affairs" column, reports,

> A critical attitude has recently been evident on the part of the public in Eretz Yisrael toward the local press. We find admirable the attitude expressed in the debate which centered around the well-known editorial, "We," which appeared in *Hatzvi*. Protests have arisen from all sides, entire villages took part in them, and little was lacking for the affair to blossom into a total and complete boycott, were not *Hatzvi* the only daily newspaper in the country at the present, for which there is currently no substitute.[59]

The editor, Yosef Aharonovitch, returns to the subject in the same issue in his editorial, "Letters from Eretz Yisrael," which he writes to a friend abroad. He ridicules the idea of the public good:

> This is the great excuse of our generation, a pretext used by those who for some reason are afraid to reveal their true form. In the name of the people and for the sake of the public good, one of the editors of *Hatzvi* heaps abuse on his people, and with unparalleled gall lays an indictment on the Jews which even Druman and his band would sign wholeheartedly.

He ridicules Ben Avi's remarks that the Jews have refrained from actions and deeds for the good of the public:

> State: Cowardly deed! State: The Jews are the first to join every freedom movement, every national revolution! State: Our greatest national tragedy has always been that we worked for the good of the whole, we spilled our blood for the good of the whole to the point of forgetting ourselves! Please

do not anger the editor of *Hatzvi* lest he shortly accuse you of sins which you would never hear even from your greatest enemies!

You know, my friend, who the main supporters are in all of the general institutions, where Jews are forbidden to enter! Who are the first to respond to every groan, in every place, even when it is heard from our tormentors! And you know how fully the Jews participate in the joys of others, and how indifferent they are to the troubles of their own people!

But do not speak, my friend! Do not argue! There stands before you a lover of his people, a seeker of the public good, and when the public good speaks, everything is permissible, everything, including even calumny! And it is unthinkable calumny to open a campaign for donations and to force the Jews of Jerusalem, who themselves live on charity, to make donations from their own charitable allotment! He forgets, this honorable lover of Israel, that when 'some of their coreligionists were killed' namely when three hundred Jewish communities were destroyed in Russia and thousands of Jews were killed and tortured with a brutality previously unheard of, no newspaper reported on 'warships' sent by some government to protect them!

He forgets that even the more enlightened governments made do with an expression of dissatisfaction, and even this was a result of persuasion by the great Jewish financiers. But if the same thing were to happen to another 'people without a country' all of Europe would be astir and come to its defense!

Europe, which was unmoved by the terrible murders of the Jews, is horrified by the spilling of the blood of the poor Armenians, who are certainly no less worthy than some of the trouble-makers killed in the Far East, whom Europe defended. But why go on, the boundless love of the editor of *Hatzvi* for his people has become deviant, and from a lover he has simply turned into a slanderous enemy.

It should be noted that Itamar Ben Avi claimed that the Jews were indifferent to the Armenian massacre. Yosef Aharonovitch makes a different, almost opposite claim: the Armenians are given aid but when Jews are slaughtered, the world is indifferent. Europe, which was unmoved by the terrible murders of the Jews in Russia in the years between 1903 and 1906, is horrified by the murder of the Armenians and seeks to avenge them.

The final reaction to "We," which we will examine here, is that of the author, Yaakov Rabinovitch in *Hed Hazman*.[60] Rabinovitch actually accepts Ben Avi's approach, and takes exception to his attackers. He writes that he has not read the editorial in *Hatzvi*. "I am familiar only with excerpts from it which were published by his opponents. In these excerpts I find complaints about the paucity of our participation in the Turkish revolution, and about our indifference to the tragedy of the Armenians. All of Eretz Yisrael is angry, protesting, and Ben Yehuda [Ben Avi] has already been awarded the honorary title of traitor."

Yaakov Rabinovitch, author and journalist, published short stories, novels, articles and essays. His opinions were frequently rejected by the Zionist frameworks in which he was active.[61] Rabinovitch admits that he was not a follower of Ben Yehuda and openly distanced himself when the latter supported the idea of Territorialism. He states that, "I also refrained from expressing my opinion to him, to his face, about his shortcomings and those of his newspaper." Yet, Rabinovitch continues, "From the days of the Constitution [the 'Young Turk' revolution in 1908], *Hatzvi* has greatly improved, and it may be that the authors in Eretz Yisrael who continue to nurse their old hatred of him are doing him a great injustice in that they will not help him with their participation. There are also parts of the editorial, "We," as presented in the comments of his opponents, with which I find no fault."

Rabinovitch says that he does not know if "we were correct in taking part in the Russian movement...perhaps it is better to stand on the side and let the ruling people solve its cardinal issues with its own resources."[62]

Still, in his opinion, one must distinguish between the Diaspora and Palestine.

This is our country, the land of our future, and we cannot be indifferent to its regime. In defense of the Sephardic Jews we note that of 400 thousand people, most of whom reside in the large cities of the country—half of them in Constantinople, Saloniki, Adrianople and its environs, no more than a few hundred volunteered [during the battle to contain the counter-revolution in April 1909]. In defense of the Sephardis of Eretz Yisrael, it is possible to understand that the recipients of charity are bound to despise liberty. It is possible to oppose the participation of foreign nationals in a domestic war. Everything is possible. But it is also possible to think differently, to be indignant, to become embittered and to chastise.

The Hebrew chastiser is not a traitor. It is a loyal friend who criticises his comrade to his face. If Y.L. Gordon, Smolenskin, Mazeh—who had written 'those accusations,' Ahad Haam and Bialik were traitors, then the writer of 'We' is also a traitor. And it is disgraceful that the writers in Eretz Yisrael and the protesters do not understand this.

With regard to the Armenians, here we must remember the past. The defunct *Hamelitz*, in its day, lauded the participation of Sephardic Jews together with the Turks in the massacre of the Armenians in Constantinople in 1895. And then there were the pogroms in Odessa and cities in the south, and among the names of the sainted defenders we find Armenian students who were killed while defending us. Let us not forget! Few were the Russians and Poles who defended us, but according to estimates, among those who especially came to our aid were the Armenians and their cousins, the Georgians. Let us not forget how they treated us and how we treat their misfortune.

And I remember how every single day I opened our newspaper and was shamed because I found not even a hint of participation in the sorrow of a people whose fate is so close to ours.

But now, by your reckoning, Ben-Yehuda has sinned by reminding you of all this, and for his sins he is Kruscheban [traitor]—because he calls for solidarity among peoples, not for the enslavement of a submissive people, but rather for the solidarity of free peoples.

I have not, as I said, read 'We,' but I have read *Hapoel Hatzair* and I find things which must be treated with respect. And I can advise the writers and the protesters only this: to read these excerpts again and to understand them. Then they may realize that Ben-Yehuda should not be termed Kruscheban.

Itamar Ben Avi—In the Wake of the Controversy

In his memoirs, *At the Dawn of Our Independence*, Itamar Ben Avi refers to the debate over his editorial, "We." He writes that "my greatest dream upon my return to the country the second time was to conduct in our newspaper what the great French journalist, Clemenceau, called 'the grand journalistic wars.' I did not then understand that our country was not yet ready for battles like 'the Dreyfus Affair,' which led to the publication of 'J'accuse' by Emile Zola in Clemenceau's *L'Aurore*."[63]

His moving article, the first of its kind, passed almost totally without the kind of reaction for which he had hoped. But "the conflict between me and the Young Workers' Movement was surprising, difficult and even shattering."

As though it happened today, I remember the cause and the immediate results. In Jerusalem the Armenians conducted a charitable appeal and came to our people. Apparently for fear of the Turkish authorities, the Jews did not take the appeal with the appropriate seriousness and sympathy, and in the Christian communities in the country murmurs began against us. I was moved to correct the impression and I wrote an article with the brief title, "We," in which I warned about the indifference of our people to an unfortunate people like the Armenians. In looking back over the many years since that incident, I admit that even if my comments in the article were justified—and rebuke has been permissible by all of our greatest prophets, from Amos and Isaiah to Jeremiah and Ezekial and Malachi—my newspaper was not the place and the time was not suitable for such an attack.

Nevertheless, I believe that my attackers—foremost among them Zerubavel, the leader of 'Poalei Zion' in our country in those days—greatly exaggerated in calling me 'a traitor to his people,' and in ensuring by their articles in *Ha'achdut*, that the editorial 'We' would remain a dreadful disgrace.

His assertion that the attacks against him were written in *Ha'achdut* was erroneous. *Ha'achdut*, the journal of "Poalei Zion," began to appear only in mid-1910 as a monthly, and from 1911 as a weekly. Zerubavel, to whom Ben Avi attributes the sharp attacks against him, came to Eretz Yisrael only in 1910. On the other hand, the sentences attributed to *Ha'achdut*, like the claim that the editorial, "We," would remain a dreadful disgrace, were, it will be remembered, from *Hapoel Hatzair*.

In his memoirs, Itamar Ben Avi describes at length the delegation of "Poalei Zion," composed of Zerubavel, Brenner, and Zeev Ashur, which came to him late at night and threatened him lest he "continue to turn your newspaper into a vehicle for filth." According to him, Zeev Ashur "opened his black jacket and pointed to the pistol stuck in his belt." Brenner calmed the atmosphere. Ben Avi presents the story as an example of the local-public warfare in those days, which came dangerously close to bloodshed. Ben Avi ties the story, incorrectly in our estimation, to "We." It occurred, if it occurred, later.[64] This argument illustrates the controversy between Itamar Ben Avi and the Labor movement over his alleged oversensitivity and openness to the distress of the Armenians, "to the sorrows of the public," as Aharonovitch puts it. The controversy is also, and perhaps primarily, over attitudes toward the ruling authorities and the degree to which criticism is permissible and desirable regarding the Turkish government. In this sense, the controversy may have been more sociological than ideological, between native born residents and the immigrants who had subsequently achieved positions of leadership in the Yishuv's community. The immigrants, some claimed, perpetuated a "Diaspora" attitude toward the rulers. In contrast to the immigrants, the native-born Jews reveal a bolder and more critical position toward the authorities. These differences of attitude will be seen again in the future: the Nili group was composed mostly of native-born members or people who had come to the country as children. Its leader, Aaron Aaronsohn, was, according to Itamar Ben Avi, "the leader of the native-born community." The immigrants, members of the Second Aliyah wave of immigration, focused primarily on the battle for survival and realization of the Zionist idea. Among the native-born Jews, who were familiar with the Arabs and had been influenced by Western European culture—especially French culture, were people who were more open and able to relate to the sorrows of others. The fact is that Itamar Ben Avi was among the few who wrote and related to the distress of the Armenians. He also participated in the "Conference of Oppressed Peoples" held in Philadelphia from October to December 1918, and chaired by Tomas Masaryk.[65]

Among the twelve participating peoples, in addition to a Jewish representative and an Armenian representative, were representatives from Czechoslovakia, Greece, Albania, Yugoslavia, Lithuania, and Lebanon. Ben Avi reports that the Armenians, the Greeks, and the Lebanese supported the Jews "with extraordinary devotion."[66] He remarks that "thanks to my recommendation, a delegate was invited from poor Armenia, which had been totally forgotten by Masaryk." In 1920, Itamar Ben Avi published in *Doar Hayom*, his newspaper at the time,[67] an article entitled, "And Armenia?" He was critical of the neglect of Armenia during the conclusion of the Treaty of Berlin in 1878, and again after the First World War, "when out of the general destruction some twenty new countries were born."

Not only delegates of the Great Powers, the allied nations, attended the Conference of Paris. Also present were "representatives of countries the strange names of which were previously unknown to many."

Ben Avi develops a theory which will be examined at greater length with a description of Sykes' contacts with the Zionist delegation in London, before and after the Balfour Declaration, and with a survey of Aaronsohn's activities: "An Arab, Judean, Armenian Alliance." Among the delegates and proxies in Paris were according to Ben Avi:

Of course, there were, also, the delegates of the three peoples who are so spiritually close to one another: the Arabs, the Armenians, and the Zionist

Jews. For the first time, after hundreds of years, the delegates of these peoples met as brothers in Paris, and only those who saw them sitting together—the Arab Emir Feisal in his golden kaffiya, Nubar Pasha the Armenian with his white beard, and Chaim Weizmann with his dark and piercing Jewish eyes—as they weighed and discussed the future of their countries, to the great Euphrates, only someone who has seen these three together has known the meaning of a miracle and the finger of God.

Of the three, two are the happiest today: the Emir Feisal and Chaim Weizmann. Only the third, Nubar Pasha the Armenian, is still worried and tearful. Can it be that the expectations of Armenia will be disappointed yet again? Is it possible that yet again new states will be created and the Armenian state will remain a dream? Shall Armenia die for lack of a saviour?

There are whispers to Armenia that she must make additional sacrifices. Dear Lord! Has she sacrificed so little thus far? Have not a million and a half of her residents not died or been killed or disappeared already?[68]

The Armenians also sacrificed the dream of "Greater Armenia" and conceded extensive territories, writes Ben Avi. They had only one hope: "a free Armenia, be it small, hilly and stony, poor and sparse, but free." On a flowery note, he concludes, "and if there is justice in this world, and justice shall reign in western Asia—then we shall be witness to the great day which we have all awaited, and shall see the new tripart alliance, the alliance of the Near East—Jew and Arab, and beyond the Euphrates—Armenia!"

The Newspaper Hed Hazman *and the Armenians, 1908-1909*

The positions expressed in Yaakov Rabinovitch's article are not exceptional among the articles and items which appear in the newspaper, *Hed Hazman* (Echo of the Time), during the years 1908-1909. Subsequent to Rabinovitch's article, we examined issues of *Hed Hazman* during the stormy years in Constantinople, at the time of the Young Turks' revolution, and afterwards during the failed counterrevolution. *Hed Hazman* was a Hebrew-language Zionist daily, published in Vilna. The newspaper occasionally aired criticism of the direction of the "Western Zionists," and political Zionism.[69]

During the attempted counterrevolution and afterwards, the newspaper reported extensively on the events in Constantinople. It also reported details and related the massacre committed against the Armenians at the time, in Adana and other places—"the slaughter of the

Armenians," in the language of that period. The position of the paper was unequivocal:

- Supportive of the Young Turks and the Constitutional victory, and opposed to the Sultan, it also demanded a solution to the national issues in the Ottoman Empire.
- Critical of the ambivalence of the Jewish and Zionist press.
- Supportive of the Armenians and identified with their grief and tragedy, including support of their demands to resolve their national question.

When tensions rose among the opposing forces in Turkey, the paper reported on the Armenian protest against their exclusion from the Turkish army. Formally, they were informed of a one-year delay in the implementation of the decision. The Armenians viewed this as a breach of the Constitution guaranteeing equality between citizens.

Despite their reservations about the actions of the committee of the Young Turks, the Armenians were explicit in their defense of the Constitution. The revolutionary Armenian committees, the Hunchaks and the Dashnaks, "decided to protect the Constitution by all means of terror at their disposal," reports the paper. Armenian women also volunteered to fight for the Constitution.[70] During the riots in Constantinople, even before events were clear, *Hed Hazman* took a firm stand in support of the Young Turks.[71] The Sultan, Abd al-Hamid, is depicted in the article as "a treacherous fox known for his brutality, whose hands are stained with the blood of the Armenians."

The paper is hopeful that the Sultan will be deposed: "The victory of the Young Turks is not only a victory for humanity, justice and integrity, it is a victory for Zionism as well." The article concludes, "Only with the victory of freedom will the Zionist victory come. And all those who place their hopes in the court of the Sultan are mistaken and misleading." The paper sharply condemns the position of the Western Zionists—the Berlin Zionists—as expressed in their journal, *Yiddishe Rundschau*, which takes a neutral stand regarding the events in Turkey. As far as they are concerned, charges *Hed Hazman*, it does not matter who triumphs in Turkey:[72] "This is the politics of slavery," "this is the politics of cowering to the Sultan's palace," "this is a foolish decision."[73]

Throughout the month of April, the paper relates "terrible and horrifying reports of the massacre" of the Armenians. Under the cynical headline, "The Compassionate Sultan," the paper reports that the Sultan wept bitterly upon hearing of the ferocious attacks against the Armenians, but it became clear that they had been instigated at his order. "Indeed the Sultans of Turkey are compassionate people, it should be said."[74] In other articles, the Sultan is described as an "intriguer" and a "murderer."[75]

The newspaper does not withhold its criticism of the Great Powers: "At the time of the slaughter of the Armenians, Abd al-Hamid II was determined to send to one of the monarchies rare pearls and sapphires worth 200,000 francs, and it did not occur to them to reject with a sharp kick of the shoe this blood soaked gift." The paper adds, "what could have stopped him was the intervention of the monarchies. But he knew that because of the jealousy between them, nothing would come of it."[76] The newspaper also rejects the claims of the Turks, including that of the Minister of the Interior, that the attacks against the Armenians were a reaction to alleged assaults of the Armenians against the Muslims: "They threw bombs and burned houses." According to this claim, the Muslims were "forced to respond with acts of violence to the violence of the Armenians."[77] The newspaper brings the testimony of an eyewitness to the "slaughter of the Armenians," who describes how the residents had prepared earlier for these frightful doings. The Muslims, says the paper, threatened "anyone who would dare to defend the Armenians, 'those dogs,' will feel our vengeance. The American mission [in Adana] which gave shelter to the Armenian refugees was set afire, and the missionaries were murdered without mercy in the flames."

Yaakov Rabinovitch relates to the Armenian massacre once more in his article, "Notes."[78] In his opinion, "Freedom for the Armenians will come, even though it would be delayed." The Turks comprise only a quarter of the inhabitants of their kingdom.[29] At the same time, Rabinovitch is also critical of the behavior and shortsightedness of the Armenians.

> One who is short sighted should not engage in politics. One can be drawn by the moment but should never sacrifice all for the moment! And this is what the Zohrabs [the Armenian leaders in Turkey] have done and that is their sin. A weak people must first attend to its forces and to fortify its positions. In dangerous politics only strong peoples can afford to play. They have sufficient power. A weak people should never engage in such matters. A weak people must engage in construction and not in destruction. Destructions have always brought upon weak peoples only pogroms, blood and disgrace. And we Jews should be mindful of this as well.[80]

Rabinovitch believed that the Armenians had erred in their struggle against the Turks. They should not have used acts of violence, force, and sometimes even terror against their Turkish oppressors. The conclusion he reaches from this regarding the Jews: We must beware of using such methods.

Following the revolution of the Young Turks in 1908, the newspaper addressed the issue of "the Turkish Constitution and the Armenians," which was apparently exceptional in the Jewish press of the period: "The question of how the Armenians ought to deal with the renewal of the Turkish Constitution is of great value with regard to the small Asian provinces and the entire kingdom." Because of the importance of the issue, the paper presents excerpts from an article published in another newspaper, *The Poste Zeit*, sympathetic to the distress and struggle of the Armenians. The article condemns the "terrible acts of violence committed against the Armenians in the early and middle 70's of the preceding century," the policy of dispersal and expulsion of the Armenian population, and the "great bloody slaughters in 1895-6."[81]

In the section, "Little Feuilleton," appears an article entitled, "The Workers in Turkey," which is, in fact, an article about the Armenian workers in Constantinople. The paper asks rhetorically, "Is there a man in Europe who knows anything about them? Has anyone heard a thing about their life, their organization and political views? Many false charges have been spread in Europe against this poor people."[82] The writer speaks warmly of the Armenian workers. For example, all of the daily laborers who work at loading and unloading the ships in Constantinople are Armenians brutally exploited and oppressed by the Turks, sometimes in cooperation with their own brethren. "These are honest and loyal people, and I can promise you that all of the charges against the Armenian workers are nothing but a most despicable lie."

Hamelitz and the Armenians, 1895-1896

A reference by Yaakov Rabinovitch in *Hed Hazman* to the attitude of *Hamelitz* toward the Armenians brings us to a somewhat eclectic examination of the treatment by *Hamelitz* of the Armenian question during 1895-1896. In *Hamelitz* of those years we find a different attitude.

Rabinovitch's criticism of *Hamelitz* in those years, which appeared in *Hed Hazman* in 1909, was not unfounded. From 1894 to 1896, there were widespread massacres of the Armenian population, mostly in the interior regions of the Ottoman Empire. Twice in that period the Armenian population was attacked in Constantinople itself, inhabited at the time by some 200,000 Armenians—once in late September-early October of 1895, and again in August-September of 1896, after members of the Armenian revolutionary organization, Dashnaktsutium, occupied the Ottoman Bank in Constantinople. European nations, including France, England, and Russia, tried to intervene for the Armenians, attempting to achieve a solution of the problem in general and a cessation of the massacres in particular. Their action was of some help to the Armenians and appears to have limited the scope of the murders.

Hamelitz was a Hebrew-language daily, published in Petersburg until 1904. Under the banner appeared the following, "A periodical reporting to Jacob everything regarding the Jews in particular and political and scientific matters in general. Published in Petersburg six times a week. Founded by Alexander Halevi Zadarbaum and Doctor Aharon Yitzhak Goldblum." 1895 was "the thirty-fifth year of its publication." The position of *Hamelitz* on the events in Constantinople in 1895 was clearly pro-Turkish. In Issue 210, September 26, 1895, an article appeared in the "Ways of the World" section dealing, among other matters, with the riots in Constantinople.

> How damaging impatience can be to a people can be seen in the Armenian disturbances in Constantinople. The great peoples of Europe have recently begun to intercede for the Armenians, and if the Sultan has not acceded to all of the desires of these nations with regard to corrections in Armenia, it would have been proper to meet most of their demands. But the Armenians would come and undermine the actions of those who seek their welfare.[83]

The anonymous writer (apparently one of the editorial staff) blames the Armenians who should have "sat quietly and waited for the results of the negotiations between the delegates of the three nations who sought to save them and the Turkish government, which would not have sent the delegates away empty-handed." Instead,

> Armenians were found, and, as they say, with the priests at their head, who incited their brethren to create a tumult in the capital city, in order to force the Government to come out against them in great anger. They said that this would be their great salvation, by offering an opportunity for the nations of Europe to separate Armenia from Turkey.

> But this was the mistake of the Armenians, for only the English are perhaps desirous of such a separation but not the other two nations who seek a true peace.

The newspaper describes the events:

The acts of the Armenians who heard the incitement to riot and went to the palace of the Grand Vizier, demonstrating there with cries of 'Long live Armenia,' 'We want a king of our own,' etc., and wished to break into the palace and destroy its gates. Until the soldiers from the army and Turkish residents of the city came to stop the Armenians in their actions, many were injured and killed from both sides. By this action, the Armenians have caused damage to themselves, since by raising a cry for a king of their own, to separate from Turkey, the Turkish government will be justified in its actions in Armenia, and in any event no one will blame the Turkish government for not allowing the Armenians to carry out their plans. Even the government of France, a government of the people, would do the same, for example, were the Italians of Savoy to do in Paris what the Armenians have done in Constantinople.

The writer also blames England: "And the English force made mischief in doing great deeds for the good of the Armenians...by such actions England will not be acclaimed by its allies [France and Russia] for implementing its will through steel and fire, for as it is said, for the sake of peace all their ways shall be peaceful."

Several days later (in Issue 214, October 4, 1895), in the "Overseas" section, the paper deals with the Jews in Turkey.[84] The writer praises the attitude of the Turks toward the Jews and the loyalty of the Turkish Jews to their government.

More power and strength to the Jews, since the High Authority has always shown them abundant mercy because they have not become involved with others and conspiratorial thoughts of rebellion and treason have not entered their hearts. The hands of the government of Turkey have always been filled with the work of quieting the uproar of the many nations which inhabit the country and putting a ring in the nose of insurgents and conspirators who will ever rise up from the masses and strive for renown, to act against the Turkish state and to create a memorial for themselves in the country. And among the Jews there is no outburst nor outcry; the Jews are serene and quiet, praying for the wellbeing of the state and recoiling from nationalist quarrels. The High Authority in Turkey has taken note of this and will always extend to the Jews its covenant of peace; it has given them protection and refuge from the wrath of the Greeks and many other Christian peoples who were hostile to the Jews and full of murderous thoughts of death and destruction. But Turkey has preserved its covenant and its mercy toward the Jews to this very day.

The writer sings a paean of praise to "the signs of love and mercy which the Sultan has always shown to the Jews, and opened his full and broad hand to every act of charity and mercy toward the Children of Israel in Turkey and beyond." The same article deals with the riots in Constantinople several days earlier:

> The Jews are grateful to the Sultan and his government and to his Mohammedan people, ever faithful to their covenant with them, their hands will be forever joined together. When the Armenians conspired to rise up several days ago in riots in the streets of Constantinople, the Sephardic Jews stood together with the Mohammedans and the policemen and their assistance helped them to carry the day against those who had risen up against them. The Armenians who seek greatness and freedom for themselves have shown that they are no longer worthy of this honor, since they almost allowed themselves to raise the banner of rebellion, to spill the blood of innocent people including several Jews whom they had injured and would have murdered. Therefore, the heart of many Jews has been embittered against the bandits that day and, together with the Mohammedans, whose souls are bitter against the murderous conspiracy, they pursued them to the end.

According to the writer, it was the Armenians who conspired and rioted in the streets of Constantinople. The Jews, according to *Hamelitz*, stood alongside the Mohammedans and the policemen and "their assistance helped them to carry the day against those who had risen up against them." According to the paper, many Jews joined with the Mohammedans to strike against the Armenians and "pursued them to the end." The writer praises the actions of the Jews in Constantinople and in fact gives total credence to the Turkish version of events.[85]

In an additional article, published three weeks later, in the "Overseas" section of Issue 231, October 24, 1895, the anonymous writer takes pride in "the miraculous act of observance of the commandment of the prayer shawl of our brethren in the Turkish capital."[86] "Who would believe the rumor that the fringes of a prayer shawl could be a shield against the riots? Who could have prayed and hoped for such things?" The following is the story as it appeared:

> In the Turkish capital disturbance consternation and defeat. The Armenians have arisen in riots, every peaceloving man has been filled with fear and trembling, and the police rush in and the hand of the Mohammedans joins with them to avenge the spilled blood of their brothers. 'Jews, our good and faithful brothers!' cry the Mohammedans, 'Wait a moment, close the doors of your shops, wherefore should the House of Israel join in the crime of the rioters, why should your property be looted and your wealth be plundered?' 'Our faithful brothers, children of our father Abraham!' they call out, 'Rush to our aid, this ungrateful people, the conspiring Armenians, has assembled

against us; give us your hand for you are always loyal to your covenant with us and we shall trust you and fear not!' The shops and houses of commerce are closed at once, and the Jews rush, some to their homes and their wives and children, and some to battle, to save the souls of their brothers and acquaintances who have fallen into the hands of the Armenians, so numerous that they did not recognize them, or since the destroyer was afoot, he no longer distinguished between Jew and Turk and smote them both. Many were the Jews attacked by the Armenians in these days of uproar, whether in malice or in error, but a not inconsiderable number of our brothers fell into the hands of the police and the Mohammedans who did not know they were Jews and whose countenance 'was not proof for them.' Those who were captured called out, 'Stay your hand against us for we are Jews!' and were quickly released from danger. But when the Armenians who were also captured saw that the words 'we are Jews' were as magic to free the prisoners, they joined in at the moment and their cunning enabled some of them to escape like a bird from a trap. But their deception was soon discovered, and their captors ceased to believe them, stopped them, murdered them or threw them into the prisoners' pit. Thus the charm was removed from the cry, ' I am a Hebrew!' and the Jews saw they were in danger because not in every place could they find acquaintances among the police and the Mohammedans who could attest to their identity, nor did their appearance always help them on that day. Then they remembered the fringes on the prayer shawl under their clothes and pulled the fringes out that all might see as if to say, 'This is a sign for us and for you, that we are Jews and not your enemies.' And the fringes of the prayer shawl were as magic threads to pull at the hearts of their captors and to release them unscathed from imprisonment and blows of evil hands. Had the Armenians known of this before, they would have also come with such charms. But the Armenians had never heard of the cure for ills known as the prayer shawl fringes, perhaps because even the Jews had never thought of this before. In this hour of emergency, the fringe became a shield for the Jews against disaster at the erring hands of their captors, and who could have told the Armenians of such signs beforehand? The salvation of the fringe came to the Jews in a flash, truly as a miracle, and how could the Armenians hope and prepare for such a miracle?

It seems that the article can be read in only one way: rejoicing and ridicule of the tragedy of the Armenian victims. The writer is proud that "while this was happening to our brethren in the Turkish capital, there was a miracle apart from the miracle of the prayer shawl fringe." Now they will be able to take the place of the Armenians in economic and commercial activity:

We are used to seeing the House of Jacob crushed under the feet of the two great powers fighting one another. During every catastrophe the Jew will be put on a bloody altar as a sacrificial lamb. Before the powers seek their vengeance from one another, they will join together to spill their wrath and destruction on the Jews. Although war between giants sometimes results in benefit to the Jews, this is only after the Jews have suffered greatly from violence and calamity. Such was not Jacob's portion in the riots in Turkey. Few were the Jews in the capital city who were damaged by the disturbances, while unimagined and unhoped for prosperity and relief came to them, without delay as sometimes happens but rather on that very day, at that very moment. The Armenians had almost managed to raise the banner of rebellion when the Turkish rulers of the land could not longer stand aside. The Armenians are famous for commerce in the capital city in particular and for trade in all of the land of Turkey; the offices of the civil service and the government are filled with them and until now they were among the high ministers. Now, when the heart of the Turks is set against the Armenians, the former seek to prevent the latter from enjoying the fruits of their crime and from taking part in the benefits of office and authority. With regard to all matters of bargaining and commerce the Turks have already found the Jewish merchants who have long been the competitors of the Armenians in commerce. In the capital city a flyer calls: 'Do not buy from the Armenians! Buy only from the Jews! Their wares are of high quality like that of the Armenians! Buy from the Jews and receive good prices!' This flyer did not come from the Jews who have never learned from the ways of their enemies to mix matters of nationality and religion with affairs of livelihood and commerce. The flyer was distributed by the Turks who will tell their brethren of the Jews' renown and loyalty, having never mixed with their enemies and remaining true to the Turks. Thus it is a blessing to treat with the Jews and bring them close. And these times of Armenian riots have truly shown the good works of the Jewish merchants in Turkey, especially in the capital city. The Jewish merchant has come upon good times and he will no longer live in want. Also in matters of officialdom and the government, the eyes of the Turkish ministers are now turned to the Jews, for the latter will in time come to fill the place of the Armenians who have been tainted in the eyes of the Turks and will not longer find the gates of high position and power open to them as before.

In this matter too will the heart of the authorities turn to the Jews who heretofore did not learn the language of the state necessary for high positions, although they have already discovered that every Jew who knows the Turkish language did not find the gates closed and locked before him. And although for tens of years the Turkish government has welcomed with open arms every Jew who wishes to make use of his learning and is worthy of the position, now the Jews would be able to come in great numbers to the gates of position and power, except that the Turkish language is not their tongue and they have not learned to speak the language of the country fluently.

One of the great Turkish ministers expressed his feeling to several Jews saying: 'In light of the current situation, the Armenian officials will no longer be able to remain in their positions of authority. This is clear, but who will come in their stead? They are numerous and who will fill their place? Would that you Jews could take their place! Because of your loyalty and good will, because of your great talents and good qualities, you could be suitable and worthy of such positions, but we are very sorry.'

The minister did not finish his remarks, and the faces of the Jews were covered in shame, because they knew in their hearts that they had erred by remaining apart among themselves and not responding to the entreaties of the authorities to learn the official language and become part of the public.[87]

The Armenians were in no way the enemies of the Jews, but even the injunction to "take no joy in your enemy's downfall" cannot be found in these articles.

The "events of the Ottoman Bank" in August 1896 received no special treatment in *Hamelitz*, although the paper reports on the events in Constantinople in the "Telegrams" section which brings items from Constantinople. Thus, for example, in Issue 190, August 22, 1896, the paper dryly reports on the attacks against the Armenians following the Armenian takeover of the Ottoman Bank:[88] "At the building of the Ottoman Bank a mob, assisted by demobilized sailors, attacked the house of one of the Armenians and destroyed it. They killed the men and threw the women and children out of the window. The soldiers and policemen did not intervene."

Due to the flight of many Armenians to sections of the city inhabited by people of other faiths, the residents are endangered. They are fearful that the mob will attack them as well. Pursuit of the Armenians was very forceful in the Hezkia Quarter, where the number of victims is said to be several hundred. The Sephardic Jews are being blamed for taking part in the murder of the Armenians. There is great fear in the large Armenian communities on the Bosphorus. The army has been fortified with four battalions. Foreign diplomats have demanded that the Guard be send to Tiraffia, Levoy and Kaziri [areas in Constantinople] and their demand has been met.

We have not found an expression of opinion by the newspaper on the information reported. Yaakov Rabinovitch commented on these articles, and especially on the material from 1895. "The defunct *Hamelitz* rejoiced, at the time, over the participation of the Sephardic Jews, together with the Turks, in the slaughter of the Armenians in Constantinople in 1895....I remember how I opened the paper every day and my face would flush with shame because I found not even a hint of sympathy for this nation whose fate is so similar to our own."

Did the Jews of Constantinople Take Part in the Slaughter of the Armenians in 1895 and 1896?

Both the Jews and the Armenians were religious-ethnic minorities in the Ottoman Empire. This fact sometimes caused a certain tension between them. Among the Armenians, a nationalist movement had developed which sometimes used militant and even violent means. In contrast, the half-million Jews living throughout the Ottoman Empire lacked a modern Jewish-nationalist consciousness. They viewed themselves as citizens of the Ottoman Empire, and tried to be loyal to it. The Turkish Jewish leadership and rabbis were ambivalent and sometimes hostile to Zionism. Although the Zionist movement had, as a political movement, a Turkish orientation, they were apprehensive of its damaging effects on their status. The Jews of Turkey preferred relations of cooperation and agreement with the regime and generally tried to placate the authorities.

Between the Jews and the Armenians tensions were also liable to develop over questions of economic competition. The Armenians (except in the rural eastern provinces) and the Jews in the cities filled certain economic roles in commerce, artisanship, administration, and the free professions. Both the Armenians and the Jews were minorities that had developed during the process of modernization which characterized the Empire in the nineteenth century.[89] Tension was also possible on religious grounds between Jews and Christians, including Armenians. At least one case is known of accusations over ritual practices. In 1887, two Jews were accused of kidnapping an Armenian girl during the days before the Passover holiday. The police investigated the incident, and reports of the investigation appeared in the press and created tension between the Jews and the Armenians and Greeks in Constantinople.[90] The fact that Jews were involved in the acts of murder of Armenians in 1895 and 1896 is confirmed by internal Jewish archival documentation. This fact also created a degree of tension between the Jews and the Armenians in Constantinople.

Rabbi Chaim Nachum, the Chief Rabbi of Turkish Jewry for many years and a supporter of the Sultan, reported in 1908 to the president of the "Kol Yisrael Chaverim" Association (the French-Jewish association, Alliance Israélite Universelle) about "an important visit," in his words, which he made to the former Armenian Patriarch, who had lived in exile for twelve years and had recently returned to Constantinople.

He had occupied this position at the time of the massacre of the Armenians, when marginal elements among the Jews in Haskoy [a Jewish Quarter in Constantinople where many Armenians also lived] played a shameful part (which cannot be acknowledged) in helping the Kurds to search out the hiding places of victims. This has left hatred in the hearts of the Armenians toward the Jews. I wished to make this visit in order to repair the past and to promise the sentiments of solidarity of the Jewish community toward the Armenian community. He was very touched by this.[91]

The involvement of the Jews in the massacre aroused harsh feelings within the Jewish community as early as 1896. In a letter on September 21, 1896, a man named V. Gerson writes to the president of "Kol Yisrael Chaverim" in Paris, about an idea floated by a number of Jewish leaders in Constantinople regarding the behavior of the Jews during the slaughter of the Armenians.[92] The idea, according to the letter, was to ask the institutions of "Kol Yisrael Chaverim" to publish an article in the European press which would prove beyond doubt that the Jews in Constantinople had behaved decently and bravely during the recent slaughter of the poor Armenians of Haskoÿ by the Turks and Kurds. The proposed article would show that a number of Jews had endangered their own lives in order to save many Armenians who hid in Jewish homes and were thus saved from certain death.

The writer praises the humanitarian intentions of the proposal but expresses reservations about it: "In their attempt to vindicate our brethren in the capital city, and in their desire to disarm the Antisemites of potential ammunition against us in the future, they may cause damage." In his opinion, publicity is to be avoided, and they must act cautiously and wisely and allow the truth to come to light. The writer admits, "A number of negative elements—allow me to use the expression: some hooligans from Haskoÿ—took part in acts of looting. This is, indeed, the case. But if dishonest Germans or English were to behave thus, ought all of these two nations to be blamed?" The writer is apologetic in explaining the actions of those Jews. The Jews led the Turks and Kurds to the homes of the Armenians so that only the Armenians would be hurt, "and not our brethren." The looting slowed down the search for additional Armenians. Gerson further claims that "the Jews saved Armenians who ran in the streets, fearful and hopeless, their arms upraised to the sky for assistance and mercy. Many were, indeed, helped by the Jews and hidden, and these are the Armenians who blame our brothers for looting." In his opinion, "These poor people should not be

blamed for their lack of gratitude. Their suffering has embittered them."
After the emotions which have shocked them so deeply have passed,
they will understand that the Jews wished to help them and to save their
lives, and sometimes their homes.

> On the other hand, it would be reckless to publicise that the Jews had helped
> the Armenians whom the Ottomans view, perhaps justifiably, as traitors,
> dishonest, anarchists. To assist such traitors and rebels is not patriotic and
> may incur the anger or even the vengeance of the Ottomans. If the Jews
> publish a defense of acts we are accused of but did not commit, who knows
> what may happen to us during the new massacres.

> Therefore no self justification and certainly no publicity. The Armenians in
> the capital city apparently want us to emphasize our good deeds, in order to
> take part in their fate in the event of a new catastrophe, I was told by a wise
> man. Because, if truth be told, the Jews and the Armenians of the Empire
> harbor a traditional hatred of each other, although no one knows why. The
> events which we have witnessed prove that the Jews do not hate the Arme-
> nians except as a reaction. Despite what may be said about them, they be-
> haved with mercy and compassion.

We do not know how the president of Alliance replied to the letter.
We may assume that these are not all of the facts and not even all of the
documentation concerning the role of the Jews — their participation in
one way or another—in the massacre of the Armenians. A more comprehensive examination of the archives of Alliance in Paris may shed
additional light. Nonetheless, I believe that there can be no doubt that
the involvement of Jews in Constantinople in the massacre was shameful.

Notes

1. Hannah Arendt, "Herzl and Lazare," in *The Jew as Pariah* (New York: Grove Press, 1978), pp. 125-30. (Henceforth: Arendt).
2. Pariah: a member of no caste in India, outcast and ostracized, human refuse without rights. The term "pariah" is a central concept in Arendt's percep-tion of the Jewish condition in modern times, as the title of her book testifies.
3. Ibid., p. 30. Arendt refers, first and foremost, to Charles Peguy who lauds Lazare in his book, *Notre Jeunesse*, and in his article, "Le Portrait de Bernard Lazare." Thanks to Peguy, Lazare was able to publish his study of Rumanian Jewry.
4. *The Complete Diaries of Theodor Herzl* (New York and London: Herzl Press and Thomas Yoseloff, 1960), July 18, 1896.

5. An interesting and balanced article on this subject appeared in the *Journal of Palestine Studies*. See Aarwan R. Buheiry, "Theodor Herzl and the Armenian Question," *The Journal of Palestine Studies*, vol. 7, no. 1 (25), autumn 1977.

6. Alex Bein, *Herzl: A Biography* (Philadelphia: The Jewish Publication Society of America, 1941), pp. 370-73. (Henceforth: Bein.) Previously, in London, in a conversation with the editor of the London *Daily Mail*, he praised the Sultan and his positive attitude toward the Jews, in the hope that his words would be read in Constantinople: "I am fully aware that the Jews have no better friend than the Sultan and that our movement is on the right path." Ibid., p. 296. See also Herzl, opening address to the Fifth Zionist Congress, *Before the Nation and the World*, vol.2, p. 117.

7. Herzl, *Diaries*, January 5, 1902.

8. Bein, p. 268.

9. Arendt, p. 129, Ibid., quoting from Baruch Hagani's biography of Bernard Lazare which appeared in Paris in 1919.

10. Bernard Lazare, *Job's Dungheap* (New York: Schocken Books, 1948), p. 68.

11. Bernard Lazare, "Le Congress Sioniste et le Sultan," *Pro Armenia*, no. 4, January 1902, pp. 29-30.

12. A reference to the medals and gifts which the Sultan gave to Herzl during the contacts between them. The bestowal of Turkish medals during the reign of Abd al-Hamid II was so common as to be worthless in the eyes of decent people.

13. Herzl, *Diaries*, January 23, 1902.

14. *Pro Armenia*, no. 4, January 1902. The editorial staff commented that the attitude of the Steering Committee of Vienna was unforgivable since Abd al-Hamid had only recently forbidden Israelites who were not born in Eretz Yisrael to reside in the country for more than three months. Some claimed that the decision was a reaction to Herzl's efforts, and the matter concerned Herzl greatly. ("Israelite": the common term in France, from the time of the Emancipation until the 1960s, for a Jew. Even today use is made of the word "Israelite" instead of "Juif.")

15. Herzl, *Diaries*, vol. 3, pp. 72-73, January 5, 1902.

16. Jehuda Reinharz, *Chaim Weizmann: The Making of a Zionist Leader* (New York: Oxford University Press, 1985), pp. 87-89. (Henceforth: Reinharz.)

17. Chaim Weizmann to Ahad Ha'am, February 2, 1902, in a letter also dealing with the protest against Herzl's letter to the Sultan. *The Letters and Papers of Chaim Weizmann*, series A, vol. 1, Oxford University Press, 1968. (Henceforth: *Weizmann Letters*.)

18. Chaim Weizmann to Theodor Herzl, February 3, 1902. *Weizmann Letters*.

19. Chaim Weizmann to Ahad Ha'am, February 5, 1902. *Weizmann Letters*.

20. Bernard Lazare to Chaim Weizmann, June 26, 1901, from the Weizmann archives. See Reinharz, p. 432 (footnotes).

21. Chaim Weizmann to Vera Khatzman, August 9, 1902. *Weizmann Letters*.

22. *Pro Armenia*, no. 69, September 15, 1903. pp. 357-58.

23. Nelly Wilson, *Bernard Lazare*, (Cambridge: Cambridge University Press, 1978); Jean-Denis Bredin, *Bernard Lazare, De l'Anarchiste au Prophete* (Paris: Fallois, 1992).
24. Bein, p. 198.
25. Ibid., pp. 192-95.
26. Herzl, *Diaries*, May 7, 1896; Bein, p. 198; David Vital, *The Origins of Zionism* (New York: Oxford University Press, 1975), pp. 288-89. (Henceforth: Vital.)
27. Herzl, *Diaries*, May 11, 1896, May 13, 1896. Nordau's reply to Herzl, May 13, 1896, The Central Zionist Archives.
28. Herzl, *Letters*, vol. 1, The Zionist Library, Jerusalem, 1961, pp. 95-97, May 11, 1896.
29. Dr. Alfred Nussig (1864-1944), writer and sculptor, was for some time a member of the Zionist Organization and one of the leaders of the internal opposition in it.
30. Herzl, *Letters*, vol. 1, pp. 98-100, May 12, 1895.
31. Ibid., pp. 100-101, May 13, 1896.
32. Vital, pp. 300-301.
33. Herzl, *Diaries*, June 22, 1896.
34. Ibid., July 1, 1896.
35. Theodor Herzl, "For A Jewish State," *Zionist Writings*, vol. 1 (New York: Herezl Press, 1973), pp. 34-44.
36. Herzl, *Diaries*, July 2, 1896.
37. Ibid., July 8, 1896; *Letters*, p. 119, July 10, 1896.
38. Herzl, *Diaries*, vol. 1, p. 303, July 9, 1896.
39. Herzl writes that several minutes before he went to the home of Nazarbikian, he accompanied Georg Brandes to the railway station. Georg Brandes, an influential Danish-Jewish thinker and literary critic, supported the Armenians and published several essays on the subject. For a period at the end of the First World War he also expressed support for Zionism.
40. Herzl, *Diaries*, July 13, 1896.
41. Ibid., August 25, 1896.
42. Ibid., August 29, 1896.
43. Ibid., September 12, 1896; *Letters*, vol. 1, p. 143, September 12, 1896.
44. *Letters*, vol. 1, p. 143, September 12, 1896.
45. Ibid., pp. 151-52, October 11, 1896.
46. Ibid., pp. 156-57, October 26, 1896.
47. Ibid., p. 154, October 19, 1896.
48. In the spring of 1897, Herzl tried to collect donations for the Turkish wounded in the Turkish-Greek War. "The result was embarrassingly small." Bein, p. 204.
49. Herzl, *Diaries*, February 4, 1898.
50. Herzl, *Zionist Writings*, vol. 1, p. 55.
51. *Hatzvi*, Issue 175, May 18, 1909, p. 2. But most of the article deals with the Jews who stood by, "watching from the side and waiting," doing nothing.

52. Mordecai Ben-Hillel Hacohen expresses his regret, several times in his diary, that Mazie does not know how to put into use his knowledge and talents, and that he does not publish more in the scientific fields in which he works. See *The War of the Nations*, pp. 396-98, (November 18, 1916).
53. The editorial, "We," appeared on Tuesday, the day before.
54. A letter signed by thirty-one residents of Haifa appeared in *Hapoel Hatzair* and in *Haolam*.
55. "The report we have received is of interest: the editorial board of the Jerusalem newspaper, *Havazelet*, is collecting signatures of people who will promise not to buy *Hatzvi* in the future because it weakens the spirit of the people. According to what we have been told, the number of signatures has already reached three hundred. If this number increases by two hundred, then *Havazelet* will become a daily and *Hatzvi* will finally expire. We do not wish to consider the thought of such a terrible possibility. Although we are not great friends of the black lily ["Havazelet" is the Hebrew word for lily], it would never occur to us to fight against it in such a manner. There are more dignified means of competition in the world of journalism: healthy competition, constructive competition. If *Havazelet* makes the effort to be a better paper than *Hatzvi*, the *Hatzvi* itself will bid farewell to its readers. In Mea Shearim, in Zichron Moshe, in Rehovot, the Jews conspired to boycott *Hatzvi*. Some of the boycotters grabbed newspapers from our sellers and tore them to pieces. Others forbade their friends to read the newspaper, and various institutions were warned that if they continued to receive *Hatzvi* they would also be boycotted. And what was all this for? Violent public opinion is not only improper, and unacceptable, it is also damaging: not to us but to the public itself. The boycotters should believe us."
56. See *Hapoel Hatzair*, Issue 14, May 21, 1909, p. 15, and *Haolam*, Issue 18, May 24, 1909.
57. The editors comment: "This is not the place to go into the matter at length. We shall, perhaps, discuss it again in the next issue."
58. *Hapoel Hatzair*, Issue 14, May 21, 1909, p. 16.
59. Ibid., pp. 15-16. The letter to the editor which we have already discussed also appeared in the same issue.
60. The article was reprinted in *Hatzvi* on September 9, 1909.
61. Yaakov Rabinovitch was born in 1875 in the Grodny District. He received a traditional religious education and afterwards studied the general sciences in Switzerland. At the beginning of the century, he was active in the "Hibat Zion" Zionist movement. He visited Eretz Yisrael between 1905 and 1908 and, in 1910, he returned to make his permanent home in the country. He was a regular contributor to *Hed Hazman* during 1908-09. After coming to live in the country he began to write for *Hapoel Hatzair*. An opponent of political Zionism, he was a supporter of practical Zionism as formulated by 'Hibat Zion.' A supporter of partition of Eretz Yisrael and solidarity of the Jewish people, and an opponent of class warfare, he was an unconventional thinker in the Labor movement. During the trial of

Chaim Arlozorov's murderer, he called for reconciliation between the Left and the Right. Even in the years immediately following his arrival in the country, although he was close to "Hapoel Hatzair" circles, he did not automatically support all of the actions of the Labor movement. In later years, he became estranged from the Labor movement and worked outside of it. See Yosef Shapiro, "Yaakov Rabinovitch the Publicist," from Yaakov Rabinovitch, *Paths of Literature*, vol. 1, M Neuman Publishers, 1971 (Introduction).

62. But he adds a footnote: "Nevertheless, I am certain that the best of the Russians and the assimilated Jews will be grateful for the participation of the Jews."

63. Itamar Ben Avi, *At the Dawn of Our Independence* (Tel Aviv: The Public Committee for the Publication of the Works of Itamar Ben Avi, 1961), pp. 208-10.

64. I have found no additional references to Ben Avi's story. Ben Avi states in his memoirs, written forty-four years after publishing the article, that his position and that of his former adversaries on workers' issues were not far apart. Ibid., p. 209. I see no reason not to accept his version of the relationships within the Yishuv.

65. See the Central Zionist Archives, L8/1003, Itamar Ben Avi's report to Nachum Sokolow. Ben Avi reports on the proceedings of the conference and describes his strong emotions when he signed the declaration of independence of the twelve oppressed peoples, in the name of his own people. He wrote about it in detail in an article entitled "With Masaryk in Philadelphia," which appeared in *Doar Hayom*, April 21, 1927, during Masaryk's visit in the country.

66. *Avec une devotion extraordinaire.*

67. *Doar Hayom,* May 5, 1920.

68. Itamar Ben Avi writes: "The riots organized against them by the Turks and the Kurds, even before the riots of Abd al-Hamid in 1894-96, and the massacre during the World War, 'only the Jews perhaps had known the like of.'"

69. *Hed Hazman* appeared in 1903-04 in Saint Petersburg. The paper was founded by Benzion Katz. Starting in 1905, it appeared in Vilna. The editor and publisher during the years in question (1908-09) was P. Margolin.

70. *Hed Hazman,* 77, April 8, 1909, and 78, April 9, 1909, and 88, April 23, 1909.

71. "The Turkish Constitution and Zionism," *Hed Hazman*, 78, April 9, 1909, signed by M. The article appeared as an editorial.

72. The paper indicates that even the non-Zionists better understand the situation.

73. The paper is sharply critical of the *Yiddishe Rundschau* in the previous issue, no. 77, April 8, 1909, and in Issue 83, in a section entitled "In the Israeli Press," quoting : "We place our confidence not only in the new Turkey, since we also trusted the old Turkey, and so we will continue to

trust Turkey as it was, is, and will be." "For us Zionists, Palestina is the mount to which we all turn. Palestina is Turkey, and we hope shall remain such forever."

74. Issue 78, April 9, 1909, signed by N.G.
75. Issue 85, April 20, 1909.
76. Issue 87, April 22, 1909, "From the Days of Power of Abd al-Hamid," signed by B.
77. Issue 85, April 20, 1909; Issue 88, April 23, 1909; Issue 94, April 30, 1909.
78. Issue 100, May 6, 1909.
79. In a different article, in Issue 82, April 15, 1909, it is stated: " To solve the national question properly is the more important issue now facing the Young Turks."
80. Rabinovitch therefore does not place great hopes in the Armenian demand for an investigation, "interpolation" in his terms. The Parliament accepted the government's suggestion to send a "High Commission to Adana to investigate the bloody riots," composed of Armenians and Turks. It was suspected that the Armenian representative in the investigative committee was murdered.
81. "The Turkish Constitution and the Armenians," *Hed Hazman*, 172, 6 (19) August 1908, unsigned. Apparently written by a member of the editorial staff.
82. "The Workers in Turkey," *Hed Hazman*, 166, July 30, 1908.
83. "Ways of the World," *Hamelitz*, 210, September 26, 1895. Another section of the article deals with the appointment of the "new Prime Minister in Austria."
84. "Overseas," *Hamelitz*, 214, 4 (16) October 1895, unsigned (apparently one of the editorial staff).
85. "Overseas," *Hamelitz*, 231, October 24, 1895.
86. In Issue 212 from October 2, the paper reports in the "Telegrams" section: The Turkish government in its reply to the messengers of the foreign governments says that there is no foundation to the charges leveled at the high officials and the Mohammedans, and that only the Armenians are guilty in the riots."
87. The article goes on to level criticism at the Jews of Constantinople for their ignorance of the state language and for not exploiting the possibilities when "all the gates were open to them and knowledge of the Turkish language would have been sufficient to rescue them from their distress and raise them up to power and authority." Criticism is also aired about the "Kol Yisrael Haverim" Association for teaching French, as well as a slightly patronizing comment about the Jews of Turkey, who "were willing to sit in the depths, incapable of action, if assistance did not come from outside to open the windows of their miserable homes to a breeze of fresh air which would disperse the vapors of rot and mold."
88. *Hamelitz*, 190, August 22, 1896, brings a telegram from August 19 (31).
89. See, inter al., Aron Rodrigue, *French Jew Turkish Jew* (Indiana University Press, 1991, pp. 25-88; Stanford J. Shaw, *The Jews of the Ottoman Em-*

pire and the Turkish Republic (New York: New York University Press, 1991).

90. Archives Alliance Israélite Universelle, Paris, IC7, No. 9479, Constantinople, 12.4.1887.
91. Archives Alliance Israélite Universelle, Paris, IC1, 618712, Constantinople, 15.9.1908.
92. Archives Alliance Israélite Universelle, Paris, IC7, 4710 Constantinople, 22.9.1896.

4

The Nili Group and the Armenians

The activities of the Nili Group have been documented by its members and by its survivors who saw themselves as the Nili's disciples and inheritors. The group's adversaries in the Yishuv and the Zionist movement—and they were numerous—also paid great attention to this small group which numbered no more than forty active members. The historiography of Nili, its activities and members, is extensive. While this chapter does not seek to add to it, the body of research written about the members of Nili has not paid sufficient attention to the influence of the Armenian experience and its importance in Nili's activities. This chapter will explore these issues, presenting sources and documents which are published here for the first time.

An empathetic identification with the tragedy of the Armenians appears among a number of the central figures in Nili. We shall examine several of them, including a deeper look at the development of the attitude of Aaron Aaronsohn, the central figure in the group, to the Armenian question.

Avshalom Feinberg: "Silence is a Crime"

Avshalom Feinberg was born in 1889 to a pioneering family. It has been said that he was "born in Gedera, raised in Hadera, and his heart is in Zichron Yaakov." He was Aaron Aaronsohn's assistant in the agricultural laboratory in Atlit and became close to the Aaronsohn family.

Even before the First World War, Avshalom developed a hatred of the Turks because of their cultural backwardness, their moral obtuseness and their opposition to the renaissance of the Jewish People in their land. The weakness and corruption of the dying Ottoman regime seemed diametrically opposed to the Jewish national renewal which he envisioned.

Avshalom received a multilingual education in Palestine and France, and was fluent in Hebrew, Arabic, and French. He was an excitable, imaginative, and romantic poet. On January 20, 1917, during a journey with Yosef Lishansky to reestablish contact with the British, he was killed near the southern city of Gaza.

From a young age, he dreamed of expelling the Turks from Palestine and establishing a Jewish government under the aegis of friendly Great Powers. He saw in the First World War an opportunity to remove the Turks, and viewed the British as the Great Power which would provide the auspices for the national Jewish renaissance.

The Hour of the Oppressed People?

Avshalom was sharply critical of the Turks prior to the First World War. During the first decade of the century, when the orientation of virtually the entire Zionist leadership was pro-Turkish, Avshalom looked forward to the fall of the Ottoman Empire which would, he believed, solve the problem of "the small oppressed peoples." In 1907, he wrote to his father, Yisrael Feinberg, a pioneer from the village of Gedera:

Dearest Father....Do we stand at the opening of a joyous era in which law will prevail over power, in which the small and weary, the sick and hungry will be allowed to live, to breathe, to be sated and content and perhaps even to taste the taste of happiness. The time has come in which the small, oppressed peoples can take their place at the table, in the dining room of the nations, to nourish their physical body, and perhaps even enter the hall where all of the satiated may consider matters of faith, intellect and spirit!

Can you imagine with what interest I follow the events in Turkey and the neighboring countries?[1] I congratulate little Bulgaria on winning its independence....I am pleased and envious of them [the Bulgarians]. And I congratulate little Serbia and microscopic Montenegro for their courageous stand against Austria's greedy aspirations. Who knows whether brute force will triumph over justice this time....The strength of armies is great these days, but perhaps there is greater strength in a people which declares: we want a life of freedom and dignity, a life without shame, fear or enslavement, and we would rather die as heroes than live like this. We would rather drown in the blood of our enemies and die full of strength and dignity.

In any event, Avshalom is convinced that "even if the dream is too rosy and too far off, one thing is indubitable: in the East we stand at the dawn of a completely new era!" The struggle of the Bulgarians will, in his opinion, bear fruit in any case:

> Turkey is weary and a chain reaction has begun. The Armenians whisper to themselves: if it is good to be Constitutional Turks, it is better to be independent Armenians, like Egypt. Their spirit is not that of dogs. And then— if we are in Syria and in Palestine, we too will be able to state our case. We are more numerous than the Bulgarians, the Serbians and the Armenians together. We are paralyzed by the sight of their disaster. But we must gather up 'the dry bones' [Avshalom continues to quote from Ezekial, chapter 37, the vision of the dry bones] of the old skeleton, we must cover it with flesh, weave muscles, inject it with blood and carry it home, where it will find its soul.[2]

He felt hostility towards Turkey, identification with the small nations, and believed that the East stood at the dawn of a completely new era, in which fundamental change would also be possible in the life of the Jews, even before the war. The war created a new reality, full of dangers and opportunities.

At the end of August 1915, Avshalom Feinberg left Palestine. Several days later, on September 6, after a roundabout sea journey via Beirut, he arrived in Alexandria. From there he made his way to Cairo in order to establish contact with the British High Command in Egypt, and with the British intelligence service. Alexander Aaronsohn and his sister, Rivka, had made the same journey three months earlier. Their attempts to make contact with the British continued throughout the month of August without success. These were the first efforts by the Nili group to connect with the British and the beginning of the activities of the intelligence ring.

In October 1915, Avshalom Feinberg sent a comprehensive 150-page report to Henrietta Szold in New York. Szold was the secretary of the Board of Directors of the Atlit laboratory. Avshalom invested much time in writing the detailed report. The byline of the report was "Alexandria, October 1915," from which we understand that it was completed in the latter half of that month.

Feinberg's report to Henrietta Szold appears to be the first written account from Palestine (although it was actually written in Alexandria) of the destruction of the Armenians in 1915. Under the title "Facts and Worrisome Rumors," Avshalom relates:

And now new disasters have come about. The Armenians are being murdered *en masse*. In Van alone, 35,000 were slaughtered at one time. Large numbers of their people in the work brigades are being shot. They are being starved and tortured, due, it is asserted, to premeditated incitement, which was instigated to take vengeance on the rebels! Soldiers, take fire! And the piles of bodies are food for the crows. In the air the question circulates among those who welcome it and those who fear it: when will our turn arrive?[3]

In this early document we can already discern, in addition to the shock at the facts and worrisome rumors, the fear that characterized the Yishuv throughout the war: "When will our turn arrive?"

Approximately a month later, on November 22, 1915, Avshalom Feinberg sent a report from Atlit to Lieutenant Leonard Woolley, an English intelligence officer in Cairo, who had been appointed by the British to oversee the activity of the nascent Hebrew intelligence ring. During the two months he was in Egypt (from September 16 to November 5), Avshalom succeeded in establishing contact with official British elements. In his report to Woolley, Avshalom reports in detail on his activities and the information he has gathered since "Friday, November 5, when I had the honor to receive a farewell blessing from you," and to return to Palestine.

This intelligence report, written originally in French, did not achieve its purpose and the contact with the British was cut off. In vain, Avshalom waited every evening on the beach for the expected British communications ship.[4] The report included a section entitled "Pro Armenia."

It should be emphasized that both of Feinberg's reports were written before Sarah Aaronsohn returned from Constantinople to Palestine on December 16, 1915, with stories about the horrors of the Armenian massacre, some of which she witnessed first-hand during a long and arduous four-week journey.[5]

Although the reports were sent to different people for differing purposes, in light of the mood and the opinions expressed in both reports, and the dates they were written, they appear to express identical positions of the writer regarding the "problem of the Armenians."

"When Will Our Turn Arrive?" The Report to Henrietta Szold

The question, "when will our turn arrive?," preoccupied Avshalom. He says, "Therefore, I ask myself only this: when will our turn arrive?" and "I cannot think about all of this [about our turn which will come] without apprehension and shivering in my bones."

He repeats this in his report to Woolley, in a briefer version: "My teeth are ground down from worry about whose turn is next."[6]

In response to this question and what has saved the Yishuv thus far —with an emphasis on "thus far," Avshalom points out two factors:

- The relations between the Turks and the Arabs: "To our good fortune, the Turks and the Arabs despise and mistrust each other. Otherwise, our fate would have already been sealed for their solidarity would be certain disaster for us."
- The American assistance: After the hangings of Christians and Muslims, Jamal Pasha wanted to hang a number of Jews. "A dybbuk entered Jamal Pasha's heart—in Avshalom's words.

The fact that no Jews have yet been tortured or hung (Manya Shochat and Peretz Pascal from Petach Tikva were ultimately saved from hanging, recalls Avshalom),

> does not in any way calm our spirit. I, myself, am certain that what prevented the execution of these horrifying acts [torture and hangings] was the shred of respect which the Turks still held for the United States of America, and the knowledge that His Honor the Ambassador Morgenthau, in Constantinople, and Dr. Otis Glazebook [the U.S. Consul General in Jerusalem] would spare no efforts to prevent such atrocities.

But it is the nature of things that the respect in today's Turkey is weakening. In order for the Legate Morgenthau to come here, he must make a month's journey. The telegraph service is not available to those condemned to die on the hangman's rope. And what can Dr. Glazebook, known by all to be an honest and charming man, do. Despite his courage, which is admirable for an American citizen, he himself is old, weak, and alone.[7]

Avshalom was full of admiration for the efforts of Morgenthau and Glazebook, and for the American intercession on behalf of the Yishuv in Palestine:

> It is impossible to describe briefly or in passing what the United States has done for us during this gloomy year. America was for us a guardian angel. This plentiful assistance, with all of its good deeds, is worthy of serious examination. I am especially amazed by the personal efforts, the on-going good will, the unflagging, heartfelt courtesy of all who have been here with us, both the permanent representatives of the United States and those who have come from time to time.

Dr. Otis Glazebook, the Consul General of the United States in Jerusalem, is the most outstanding of them whom I mention here out of deep respect. This elderly gentleman has a boundless good heart, and his courage can be compared only to the courage of 'Jesus' disciples." Despite his advancing years, he has not refrained from every possible effort on our behalf.[8]

In the following pages, we will look at additional excerpts from Avshalom's writings concerning Morgenthau and his efforts on behalf of the Armenians. We shall see that Avshalom was aware of the role of the individual and his influence on the flow of history. This seems to be an impetus for his actions on behalf of his own people and on behalf of the Armenians. Avshalom's conclusion is that the fate of the Yishuv depends, in effect, on the arbitrariness of Jamal Pasha. Under the existing circumstances, little can be done:

> Our turn will come one fine morning, when a moment of ill-will, or a fluttering butterfly, or a sunbeam, or any other poetic reason pushes the great commander to implement his cherished plan. And so I mostly ask myself upon whom fate will descend, on that day when the Pasha says that he wants to have his wish for 'breakfast.'

Avshalom goes on to report that between late July and mid-August 1915, disquieting rumors have circulated with regard to conscription of all non-Muslim men between the ages of 18 and 50. However, "Here is the best of the rumors: it has apparently been decided to transfer all of the non-Muslim residents of the coastal plain to the interior of the country, to house them in tents, within all-Muslim settlements." The meaning of this, according to Avshalom, is that:

> Since they don't dare to slaughter us all at once, they will execute us in stages, until we have silently delivered up our souls in the mud. Because the meaning of our deportation to the interior of the country and our dispersion in small groups among the villages of the Arabs is something of which I dare not speak, and you will surely understand this by yourself. All of this would take place without even the bark of a dog, because the coast would be emptied of friends and put under heavy guard so that no one would report about it to foreign countries.

Avshalom emphasizes again and again, "Nothing is certain, but anything is possible!" Nonetheless, such acts can be prevented "only if...beginning right now, by unconventional methods, which will allow quick and timely action."[9] He is filled with a deep sense of powerlessness. The sense of powerlessness which, despite everything, is not total, pushes him and his comrades to act: the sense of powerlessness of what he calls a "young Jew" relates to the fate of the Jews and also, as we shall see later, to the fate of the Armenians.

How awful the expectation and how sweet the hope in the feeling that you are a young Jew, that you were born on the land (the only land which was blessed, the only one which was promised to us with an oath, the only one possible), so that you might see with clarity, and observe what is to come, and to be powerless to act. And a verse from Psalms is frequently on my lips: 'I will lift up my eyes unto the mountains: from whence shall my help come?'[10]

And it is in these circumstances that Avshalom fears:

A mountain of unique responsibility has descended upon us, in this great hour which calls us at last. And then the anxious question arises: Will we rise to this great hour? The bell tolls and will it ring in our ears? Is this a prologue to the trumpet call of the great redeeming renaissance calling to this nation, a nation whose detractors claim is dead. Shall it rise on its feet amid its graves and torment? Or are these perhaps the bells of destruction tolling: Death! Death!

And can one deny it any longer!?

We find additional elements in his report to Henrietta Szold: reservation, criticism, deep fear and even hatred toward the Turks: "I have said, the Turks will do everything possible—and in matters of destruction and devastation, there is no limit to the possibilities of the Turks in order to leave behind them a wasteland....These people, these Turks are simply a plague, and we must remember: this too shall pass, this too shall pass." The question, though, is, "when will I have the privilege of eulogizing the Ottoman Empire?"

And in contrast, great admiration, even adoration, toward the English:

Here [in Alexandria] we have a common interest with the English.

I emphasize this and add that I, myself, say this with full and deep esteem and with great hope...in Egypt, we have a common interest with the representatives of His Majesty, George V, the emperor of Great Britain, the greatest of Britains, which I hope and believe, has not ceased to expand. This is the only empire which has justified its existence for generations, whose integrity in this dark hour of its history engenders deep appreciation in every heart, and love and dedication among all. *And hundreds of millions, citizens of all countries and all peoples, and all religions, are sacrificing their lives for her* [emphasis in the original].

There is no doubt that this paean is overblown. Britain did not meet the expectations, certainly not in full. The members of Nili would come to realize that over time.[11] An indication of this would also be found in Britain's lukewarm attitude toward the Armenian genocide.

In Avshalom's memorandum to Woolley several weeks later, a more critical reaction can be discerned— cautious but penetrating—to the inaction of the English to stop the massacre of the Armenians.

Avshalom Feinberg's "Pro Armenia"

The "Pro Armenia" section of Avshalom's report to Woolley has several components:

- A description of facts and details of the acts of slaughter against the Armenians: the Turks' reconquest of the city of Van, which had been in the hands of the Russians; a description of the convoys of refugees and those deported to forced labor; a description of the sale of Armenian girls and young women. In the beginning of the passage, Avshalom asks his contact, his English operator, "Mr. Lieutenant, I turn to you as a young Englishman. Please turn a receptive ear to my words." Later on he asks, "Do not take consolation in the thought that what I am telling you is based on rumor... this information comes from eyewitnesses, and is confirmed, proven, official."
- Expressions of emotions, the feelings of his stormy soul, and reflections on the massacre of the Armenians. In these sections his strong feelings as a Jew stand out, together with sharp criticism of the Christian (and Western) world which stands on the sidelines when help and rescue were within reach.

My teeth have been ground down with worry. Whose turn is next? When I walked on the blessed and holy ground on my way up to Jerusalem, and asked myself if we are living in the modern era, in 1915, or in the days of Titus or Nebuchadnezzer? And I, a Jew, forgot that I am a Jew (and it is very difficult to forget this 'privilege'); I also asked myself if I have the right to weep 'over the tragedy of the daughter of my people' only, and whether Jeremiah did not shed tears of blood for the Armenians as well?!

Because after all, inasmuch as the Christians—of whom not a few sometimes boast that they have a monopoly over the commandments of love, mercy and brotherhood—have been silent, it is imperative that a son of that ancient race which has laughed at pain, overcome torture and refused to give in to death for the last two thousand years, should stand up....It is imperative that a drop of the blood of our forefathers, of Moses, of the Maccabeans who rose up in the scorched land of Judea, of Jesus who prophesied on the banks of the blue Sea of Galilee, and the blood of Bar Kochba...that a drop of the blood which was saved from annihilation should rise up and cry: look and see, you whose eyes refuse to open; listen, you whose ears will not hear, what have you done with the treasures of love and mercy which were placed in your hands? What good have rivers of our spilled blood done? How have you realized your high ideals in your lives?

Later on, Avshalom requests: "[P]lease forgive me for the tone of my words, Lieutenant, for in this land I have roots in the past, and dreams for the future, and I have graves here, and a home; I have a mother and a sister, and a new generation in my sister's daughter, a dear small child eight years old (the same age as the Armenian children who were sold.) Here does my heart bleed, and scream. Forgive me."

● A request, essentially a demand, to take action on behalf of the Armenians, as an expression of his own suffering and the fact that he is "powerless and weaponless":

And while only a night's journey from here sit idle thousands and thousands of Englishmen, Canadians, and Australians, all of whom volunteered and came to fight, a handful of Arab dogs and Turkish hyenas roll around in the pile of bodies which they diligently build. Consider that a few whiplashes would suffice to disperse this band of cowards. Good heavens, what torture to be powerless and weaponless!

But the brave soldiers who were to have aroused a hallelujah of liberation and rejoicing, do not come.

And while the bloody Germans fill the world with their printed lies and slander, which have been elevated to the level of a 'manifesto,' while the agencies of their *Nachrichten Bureau* [a German news service] defile our cities with photographs of their 'heroes,' descriptions of their 'glorious victories' and maps of their 'conquests'— why do you remain silent? Repugnance and silent contempt are indeed noble, but has not Ecclesiastes said, 'There is a time to remain silent and a time to speak out'? Would it not be worthy to oblige every soldier, or at the very least, every English-French officer, to carry in his pocket a reminder of the heroic deeds of the Turks and Teutons?

Is it not a duty to distribute such reminders in millions of copies among the poor Americans, uplifted in their innocence, to pull them out of their wicked neutrality which has become so harmful at this time? But first of all, is it not the duty of righteous people to speak up, or is it once again a bitter young Hebrew who must do this?!

It should be remembered, that in November 1915, the contacts of the Nili group with the British were just beginning and were not yet fully functioning. Avshalom had just managed to establish contact, after Alexander Aaronsohn had previously failed. Avshalom turned to his operator, his contact, whose trust he still has to earn.

Whatever one's opinion of the actions of the Nili group may be, and no matter what one's position is about espionage as a means to achieve political ends, one cannot deny the existence of a deep moral component—universal, Jewish, and Zionist—in the attitude of Avshalom and the other Nili members toward the massacre of the Armenians and its significance for them.

Résumé

To the long report he wrote to Henrietta Szold, Avshalom added a *résumé*, a twenty-one page summary that includes fascinating comments with great significance for our study. The summary has never been published and it appears here for the first time.

After describing the difficult situation, the struggles, and the suffering which the Yishuv endured as a result of the war, the drought, the locust plague, and the Turkish regime, Avshalom points out the manner of assistance to the Yishuv in its difficult hour. He is appreciative of the aid of the United States and the American Jewish community to the Jewish community in Palestine. And he is full of praise for Morgenthau's efforts on behalf of the Armenians.

Allow me at this point to pay honor to your country. I must say that without American Jewry we would not have been able now to survive in Palestine. Both the United States and our people were represented in these dark days —decisive days, I would say—in the most glorious and valuable manner by Ambassador Morgenthau. Does it not seem that Divine Providence has helped us, this time, by placing this man in this position at this moment? He knew brilliantly how to bring honor to his country and to his origins, and it goes without saying that he will forever deserve the thanks of his people. It is fair to say that this man has entered human history through the front door, by virtue of his approach to the defense of the Armenians. In his defense of the Armenians he acted not only as a brave American and the valuable Ambassador of a great nation. He also gave of himself.

Avshalom relates that the Egyptian newspapers announced Morgenthau's commitment of two million dollars, out of a total of five million dollars, intended to aid the emigration of the wretched Armenians, persecuted by the Turks. He adds,

This constitutes a rousing rebuttal of the petty aphorism that 'charity begins at home.' No! We can only support and applaud these millions, which will ease the suffering of the Armenian victims whose plight may become ours tomorrow. When considering the troubles which have befallen our people in various countries during this year, it is a touching and uplifting sight, that the son of such an impoverished people should be the first to offer aid to another wretched people, with whom we have no ties of blood, faith or tradition?! Is not the nobility here even greater? Oh yes! We can indeed say that the United States and the Jews of America identify with the approach and the grand actions of this great ambassador, whom circumstances have granted the crown of the champion of justice who has become the defender of the weak and oppressed. This is a consolation and a joy. Indeed, in fact one can hope that everyone in this country and all people will see this man as their representative. We can hope that if we can first find what is necessary for others, then afterwards we shall even find what is necessary for ourselves![12]

The Future

In conclusion, Avshalom suggests a number of urgent steps which ought to be taken. Afterwards, under the title, "The Future," he relates to future perspectives and says, "Fate has been sealed. Every day our fate becomes more tied to the Allied countries."

Avshalom deals with the fate of the Jews in the countries fighting in Europe. He points out that the situation of the Jews of Russia may become unbearably difficult, should Russia be defeated. The Jews will become the scapegoat. He ends by saying,

But this is not my affair. My interest does not focus on one part or another of the Jewish People, but on the duty of every Jew to secure for his people the possibilities of a life of value and independent existence, which will include it in the catalogue of nations. Such a possibility will be created once again in history. Many times in the past we have ignored the warnings of fate. With apprehension, I wonder if this may not be the last opportunity.[13]

Since for me the only place in which this renaissance is possible is the *Holy Land, I am therefore duty-bound to describe* how we see matters from here, now: in the battlefields two camps now stand facing each other, the Islamo-Germans and the Anglo-French. Regarding the first camp, one should mention the sacrifice of Alsace-Lorraine, the poisoning of the Danish Barons of Schleswig-Holstein, the seizure of Polish lands, and the racial 'cleansing,' the slaughter of the Greeks at every opportunity, and the ongoing massacre of the poor Armenian nation which is on the brink of death as a victim.

Regarding the second camp, you can simply say: them, Great Britain and France. But for memory's sake I must mention here the Berlin Treaty (1878), and what it said to Serbia, Montenegro, Greece and Bulgaria... I do not have to say what happened to those nations when, *forty* years ago (no more) they were under *Turkish subjugation* [emphasis in the original].

Avshalom indicates the essential difference, moral in his view, between the two camps, and describes what may happen:

Let us have no doubt: to the extent that hapless fate will permit injustice to triumph, the lives of nations will be determined, and those who will suffer the most will be us—always us—from the new agonies which will be added to the existing agonies of thousands of years. Especially in Palestine will we meet our end: *our property will be confiscated, we will be expelled and will be forbidden to return.* This is what awaits us there when Germany "organizes" the East: quick and total death... if they are victorious we are lost; the issue has already been decided.

But they will not triumph. No! Victory will belong to those who knew how to guarantee freedom to hundreds of millions of people belonging to a hundred nations; to those who 125 years ago [the French Revolution] sacrificed millions of people in order to proclaim throughout the world *the rights of Man* and not *the rights of the Frenchman.* They shall be the victors, and there will be a second Berlin Treaty (a better one this time!) which will write the next chapter of what was begun in 1878. This time there will be three claimants: *the Jews, the Armenians, and the Poles* [emphasis in the original].

His informative report, full of myriad details on the activities and budget of the laboratory in Atlit, also deals with the current events of the war. Avshalom reveals his feelings, his sensibilities, and his hopes and fears about the situation in Palestine and the future of the Jews in the country and around the world. Together with his stormy feelings, he presents his political assessments and predictions, sober tactics and strategy, sometimes overlaid with a romantic tone. Avshalom formulates moral positions, and a vision in which the resolution of the problems of nations in general, and of small peoples in particular, plays an important part.

The place of the Armenians is not absent in this vision and appears a number of times. His treatment of the Armenian national question and the tragedy afflicting the Armenians is not merely instrumental; he makes no attempt to justify or explain the pro-British bias of the Nili group.

There is no attempt here to "use" the Armenian problem in order to justify the Nili's actions, as has sometimes been charged. The attitude toward the Armenians and their tragedy is part of his broader, multidimensional general approach to questions of the war, nationalism, the future of small peoples, including the Jewish People, and the chances for bringing the Zionist endeavor to fruition in Palestine. The Jewish People stand in wartime, in Avshalom's opinion, before the only—and perhaps the last—opportunity for renewal and liberation. The fate of the Jewish People depends, in very large measure, on the actions of the Jews. But the chances of the small nations to achieve liberation clearly depend on the victory of the Allied countries, and their fates are intertwined.

Alexander Aaronsohn: "Armenians, My Brothers!"

Alexander Aaronsohn, Aaron's younger brother, was very close with Aaron and Avshalom when they decided, in the course of 1915, to embark on pro-British intelligence activities. Alexander Aaronsohn was entrusted with the job of trying to establish the initial contact with the British in Egypt. Within the framework of the planned intelligence activity, he was to reach Egypt via Beirut, on one of the neutral ships, which continued to connect Eretz Yisrael and Syria with the outside world. There he was to make contact with British military authorities. He was accompanied by his younger sister, Rivka, who had been kept at a distance from the circle of danger when part of the family had begun to engage in covert activity.

The two sailed from Beirut on July 9, 1915, on an American ship, reaching Alexandria only on August 9. Alexander's contacts with the office of the central British Intelligence were not promising. He was not able to acquire their trust, and they were suspicious of a group from Eretz Yisrael which offered its services without asking for any tangible reward. Alexander Aaronsohn was declared *persona non grata* and expelled from Egypt.

On September 3, 1915, he sailed with his sister, Rivka, to the United States where he remained for most of the war—until July 1917—and took part in propaganda and diplomatic activity.

Alexander Aaronsohn was horrified by the massacre of the Armenians. Like Aaron and Avshalom, who had not discussed the matter among themselves, he wrote a short but stirring document entitled "Armenia," in which he called the Armenians to join with the Jews in a joint struggle against the Ottoman Empire. The complete document, in English, can be found in the Nili Archives and is published here for the first time.[14] We do not know to whom the document was sent or whether it was publicized at the time.

Armenia!

The fields are deserted, around the well of the hamlets no Armenian maidens are filling their jars. The Turks have passed there! And can you picture in your imagination what that means, can you understand the horror, the nightmare these words convey? The Turks have passed there.

It means a sudden attack of thousands of armed Kurds and Bedouins and regular Turkish troops on peaceful unarmed villages where the Armenians have been living a life of toil and aspiration for centuries. The young Armenians have been disarmed; they have no weapons to defend the honor of their sisters, mothers and sweethearts. Before their very eyes beastly Turks are outraging the fair Armenian virgins. Babies are killed and smashed on the rocks; men are tortured and outraged.

A million Armenians killed in less than a year! Unarmed, having committed no crime, a million people killed, because they have the heroism of their convictions, because they cannot sell their soul for the sake of their body, because they prefer to die rather than to embrace the religion of hatred, of bestiality, of rape.

And because for almost two thousand years the Armenians have been the bearers of the Christian banner among barbarians. Because they have carried the ideals and aspirations of higher civilization, the Armenians have paid with their blood and soul.

Yet, the Christian nations are looking on the martyrdom of a race and they cowardly turn their eyes away. In vain does the blood of their brethren cry from earth, they close their ears and say: we are not our brothers' keepers.

Armenians, my brothers, a Jew is talking to you. A son of a race persecuted, outraged, wronged, as your race is. You are suffering because you won't abandon the faith that Jesus has given the Christians, and we suffer because we have given Jesus to the nations that call themselves Christians.

Armenians, my brothers, we can expect nothing from the nations, we have only our souls to offer and that is of no marked value. The Turks have an army and that counts. Let us give up hope of a salvation brought by others. Let us get up and defy the world that calls itself progressive and just. Let us join hands and stand up for our rights and not beg for mercy. And if it is God's will that we die, if it is written in the book of our destiny that no redemption is possible for us, let us at least die with the sweet feeling that our virgins, our old men, our babies, our youths have been avenged.

(New York, November 1915)

After Aaron Aaronsohn's arrival in London in October 1916, he sent a letter to his brother, Alexander, full of surprise at his doings. Aaron asks Alexander to explain what he calls "your lack of action," to explain the reason for his failure in Egypt and his extended sojourn to the United States since he left Eretz Yisrael in July 1915.

Aaron adds, "And another clarification I am waiting to receive from you, Lel [Alexander's nickname]: what realistic purpose did you wish to achieve with your publication? I have had no news from home [Eretz Yisrael] but the articles in the *Atlantic Monthly* may greatly incite Jamal Pasha against me, and let us hope it stops with me."

Aaron adds another interesting and significant point: "We have said frankly that fear of not pleasing our oppressors should not conquer us. I say it again, but the end must be of equal value to the danger. Are you sure that you have not sacrificed too much for the sake of a noisy headline?"[15]

Because of difficulties in the postal service, Alexander received his brother's letter after a long delay, and only on May 3, 1917, does he reply to his brother's questions regarding the anti-Turkish propaganda he was conducting, which included his public references to the massacre of the Armenians. He points out:

My article and my book were not written out of ambition for personal honor or fame. If you remember accurately, you encouraged me when I left the country to raise as much of a ruckus as I could. When I arrived here all of our friends put pressure on me to be silent — which I did for six months, despite the cries of internal anti-Zionist protest, and I was understanding. Lately, after considering the general conditions, I decided to come out in the open. We had to publish our opinions. Our English friends did not trust us. To our sorrow, the Jews in America were known as pro-German, and our public in Eretz Yisrael was also seen in this light, so that I had to prove our loyalty [to the Allied Powers]. Even though I knew what price we would pay for our stance, I gave it thought and found that it paid to take the risk. It is too early for you or me to decide if I was right, but God is my witness that it was extremely hard for me to weigh, evaluate and decide.[16]

In his book, *Sarah: The Flame of Nili*, which was written in the early 1940s, Alexander describes in the third person, in strong and blunt language, his doings in the United States after September 1916. He relates that upon arriving in America,

> He found, to his wonder and sorrow, that public opinion tended toward the Germans due to their intensive propaganda, and even the influential figures among the Jews were mostly pro-German, since they were of German extraction.
>
> The Zionist 'leaders,' thanks to their 'acute' political sense, also felt they ought to pray for a German victory. Dr. Schmarya Levin, Dr. Ben Zion Mossinsohn, and Lewin-Epstein [Zionist leaders from Eretz Yisrael] were visiting in America at the time, and they all tended to the German side....Even Ussishkin himself [another Zionist leader], even after the Balfour Declaration, made an enthusiastic speech in Odessa on behalf of the Turks.
>
> In addition to all of these, Dr. [Yehuda] Magnes, whose influence over the rich Jews was very great at the time, preached 'neutrality', since he was a declared pacifist.[17]

Alexander Aaronsohn tried to shake the neutral, not to mention pro-German, mood among American Jews. In his book, articles, speeches, and interviews he tried to arouse anti-German public opinion among the Jews and the broader public. His book, *With the Turks in Palestine*, based on a series of articles which he had published in the influential *Atlantic Monthly* under the title, "Sifcha Achmar, Ya Sultan" ("Your Sword Is Red, Sultan"), made a great impression. The British Foreign Office requested that he forego his copyrights, in order to use the book for propaganda purposes. Alexander agreed, and the book was published in England as well, was translated into six languages, including German, and distributed in neutral countries and in the areas occupied by the enemy.[18] Alexander relates that in speeches he gave throughout America, in conversations and meetings with influential people, whether

Christian or Jew, he managed to arouse public opinion because he did not restrict his activity to Jewish circles. According to him, "he shocked his listeners on behalf of the Armenians, on behalf of the Maronites who were dying of hunger at the order of Jamal Pasha…on behalf of the Jews in Eretz Yisrael who stood on the brink of annihilation."[19]

Alexander Aaronsohn's book was published in the U.S. in October 1916. It is noteworthy that the fear that what had happened to the Armenians might happen to the Jews already found public expression at this early date. Alexander describes the Turks' demand that the Jews surrender their weapons. The demand to disarm had great impact on the Jewish Yishuv, in particular on the more activist circles such as Nili and "Hashomer," especially since some of the weapons taken from the Jews were turned over to the Arabs. The confiscation of weapons from the Jews began in the region of Judea and by February 1915 had spread north to Zichron Yaakov. Alexander relates,

> There is great consternation among us following the recent order of the Turkish authorities to hand over the weapons in our possession….We knew that the order to disarm bode evil….We knew that similar methods were used before the terrible massacre of the Armenians. And we felt, and feared, that they were intending this sort of fate for our people as well. The leaders of our village know that after the weapons have been confiscated, we will have lost our last advantage over the Arabs, our last chance to defend ourselves against sudden attack, and they therefore refused to turn them over.[20]

The refusal to hand over their weapons did not last for long. A number of residents of the village, among them Alexander, were imprisoned and tortured, but the village stood fast in its refusal. But when the Turks threatened to round up the young girls of the village and deliver them to Turkish officers until the weapons were turned over, there was no choice but to obey. "We knew that they were capable of doing this, and we knew what it would mean." The prisoners, including Alexander, were released. Alexander points out that "personally, I felt much happier on the day I was put in prison than on the day of my release…now I knew that our suffering had been useless. Whenever the Turkish authorities desire, the horrors of the Armenian massacres would live again, in Zichron Yaakov, and we should be powerless to raise a hand to protect ourselves."[21]

Aaronsohn's book of 1916 gives expression to the very real fear of a fate similar to that of the Armenians. In the chapter entitled, "A Rash Adventure," which deals, among other things, with methods of leaving the country during the war, he writes, "These American cruisers have already done wonderful rescue work for the Russian Jews in Palestine who, when war was declared, were to have been sent to the Mesopotamian town of Urfa – there to suffer massacre and outrage like the Armenians. This was prevented by Mr. Morgenthau's strenuous representations."[22]

It is worth pointing out that the linkage between the Armenian massacres and the context of events in Eretz Yisrael in late 1914 or early 1915 were made retrospectively; at that time the full extent of the great destruction of the Armenians had not yet taken place.

Even if we discount the propagandist, anti-Turkish aspect of Alexander Aaronsohn's writing, nonetheless, there was in the Yishuv a real fear of acts of severe brutality not unlike what had been inflicted upon the Armenians. There is no doubt that such fear was very tangible among the members of Nili and it has also been revealed in the journals and memoirs of the leaders of the Yishuv and other personalities.

Sarah Aaronsohn: A Shocking Eyewitness Testimony

Sarah Aaronsohn returned to Eretz Yisrael from Constantinople at the end of December 1915, to become another central figure in the underground Nili group.

She was born in Zichron Yaakov in January 1890, and finished her schooling in the village. Under the supervision of her brother, Aaron, she began to assist him in his scientific work. She was very close to her family and involved in the affairs of the village. When her parents sent her to Switzerland to continue her schooling, homesickness brought her back to Zichron Yaakov. In the spring of 1914, she married a well-to-do Bulgarian Jew who resided in Constantinople. The marriage apparently did not work out and the time in Constantinople was the gloomiest period of her life.[23]

In mid-August 1915, while her husband was in Vienna and Berlin on business, Sarah was already deep into her preparations to return to Palestine. Her return surprised her family in Zichron Yaakov. The first notice of her expected arrival was a telegram sent from Aleppo, Syria. Aaron writes in his journal on Tuesday, December 13, 1915, in Zichron Yaakov: "We have received a telegram from Sarah announcing that since Chaim plans to return to Germany on business, she will be coming to spend the winter with us. The telegram was sent from Aleppo and took four days to reach me."[24]

Three days later, Aaron welcomed his sister (during the intervening three days, there are hints in his diary of espionage activity); he records in his diary:

> Most remarkably, the train arrived no more than an hour and a half late. At five o'clock my Sarah arrives at the Zelkind Hotel. Today, just as before, she is the trooper that we knew. Her trip took exactly three weeks, and what sights her eyes have seen! She has known exhaustion, suffered from want, and in front of her very eyes has seen the Armenians tortured by the Turks. She saw hundreds of corpses of Armenians, thrown aside without a decent burial, while dogs feed upon them. She saw how dysentery and typhus ravaged the soldiers around her. There is no reason to repeat all of this here, since my Sarah has promised me that she will write a full account of her journey.[25]

Sarah's "winter visit" became permanent and, until her death and until the end of the story of Nili, she assumed a central role in this drama. The historiography of Nili attaches great importance to Sarah's membership in the group, to the stories of her journey, and to the sights of the Armenian massacre which she witnessed.[26] These were, without question, traumatic for her, and through her testimony, for others as well.

The reports were received at an important stage in the increasingly anti-Ottoman tendencies of the group, and Aaron Aaronsohn would later, on several occasions, repeat his sister's testimony (see below). It should be emphasized that at least for Avshalom, as we have seen, the massacre of the Armenians was a pivotal factor in his feelings and positions even before Sarah returned with her reports. Aaron Aaronsohn also reacts in his diary to the reports of the Armenian massacre, on several occasions prior to his sister's arrival. Nevertheless, the eyewitness reports she brought made the events shockingly real.

In Aaronsohn's journal entry for the day of Sarah's arrival (December 16, 1915), we find: "There is no reason to repeat all of this...[the atrocities which she witnessed on her journey] since my Sarah has promised me that she will write a full account of her journey." Her account of events has never been found, and we do not know whether Sarah never wrote the story of her trip or whether it was written and later lost. In any event, it has not survived in written records.

When Aaron Aaronsohn reached London, in November 1916, he brought his sister's testimony as part of "Pro Armenia":

> A sister of the writer traveled from Constantinople to Haifa in the month of December 1915. She was never hysterical before, but since that trip when-

ever any allusions to Armenians are made in her presence she gets into a fit of hysteria. A few of the things she had actually seen: hundreds of bodies of men, women and babes on both sides of the track and dogs feeding on these human corpses. Turkish women rummaging in the clothing of the corpses in hope of some hidden treasure.

At one station (in Gulek or Osmanieh, the writer can remember no longer where it was), thousands of starving, typhus-stricken Armenians were waiting for days for a train to carry them southwards. They were lying on the ground near the main track and on the sidings. When the train arrived, the engineer, on seeing Armenians on the rails, purposely pushed his locomotive into the mass of Armenians and overran and hurt about fifteen of them. He then triumphantly jumped off his engine, rubbed his hands in joy, and called out to a friend of his, "Did you see how I smashed maybe 50 of these Armenian swines?"

The same witness has seen trains arriving packed with 60-80 Armenians in each car when 40 would have over crowded the car, and at the station 10 or 20 dead (of hunger or typhus). Armenians used to be thrown out of the car and a respective number of alive Armenians packed in their stead. Needless to say, not even a symbolic effort was made at disinfection.[27]

Another point worth noting is that in addition to arranging the documents needed for the journey from Constantinople to Eretz Yisrael, and the various permits for her trip, Sarah required a chaperone, since a woman would find it very difficult to make her way alone given the circumstances of the time. Yitzchak Haus, a member of "Hashomer," had recently been sent to Constantinople by his organization in order to effect the release of Yisrael and Manya Shochat, leaders of "Hashomer," from exile in Boursa, in the Anatolian region of Turkey. His mission failed, and Sarah joined him on his journey back to Eretz Yisrael. They traveled together for three weeks in railway cars full of soldiers, and in peasants' carts on the dirt roads of Anatolia, during the days of massive Turkish troop movements and at the time of the mass expulsions of the Armenians.

Yitzchak Haus kept a sketchy diary during that period. After their return to Eretz Yisrael, Yitzchak spent some time at the Aaronsohn family home in Zichron Yaakov. There is no mention in his diary of their joint trip or of the impact of the Armenian massacre upon him.[28]

Further testimony of the shock which the journey caused Sarah can be found in the diary of another Nili member, Levi Yitzchak Schneerson.[29] He was recruited to Nili because of his friendship with Avshalom Feinberg. The formal reason for his recruitment was the "treason" affair in Hadera—the spurious charge that the Jews of Hadera had allegedly made contact with British warships, in January and February 1915.[30]

In his diary for January 1916, he describes a meeting with Sarah, after they had not met for quite a while: "I was in Zichron Yaakov. Sarah was glad to see me. Remembered me well. Has not changed much despite her life in Constantinople. The conversation was mostly about the Armenians. On her way here she saw things at first hand: how awful those Turks are. If we do not succeed in liberating ourselves from them in time, they may yet do to us what they have done to the Armenians."[31]

After Aaron Aaronsohn left for Europe and Egypt on a mission for the underground, Sarah became, in effect, the leader of the group in Palestine (together with Yosef Lishansky, whose position in the group was complex and problematic and aroused reservations). Sarah Aaronsohn, a young woman in her mid-twenties, displayed admirable courage, resourcefulness, and skill in intelligence work, especially in light of the fact that she had received no training for it. When the espionage ring was uncovered, the Turks besieged Zichron Yaakov. Sarah was captured and tortured. Fearful that she would reveal the secrets of the ring and unwilling to accept the life in prison which awaited her, Sarah committed suicide. She tricked her Turkish guards and managed to make use of the pistol that Aaron had hidden in the house.

The Jewish-Armenian context continued to be very significant for Alexander Aaronsohn as late as the early 1940s, during the Holocaust, when he wrote with overflowing feelings the final chapter of the book he dedicated to Sarah.[32] Alexander describes the last three days of Sarah's life, as she lay dying from her self-inflicted gunshot wounds (October 2-5, 1917). He presents a would-be quote from Sarah:

> The cry of the Armenians sliced through my ears. My eyes saw the agonies and I prayed that I might be blind so as to see no more...you are murderers, bloodthirsty predators, bastards, and I, a weak woman, stood alone to defend my people, lest you inflict upon it what you have done to the Armenians....By myself, with my own hands, I have dug your grave....It is too late for you! You will not survive....You have tortured me in vain....In vain shall you torture the innocent....You are lost....The redeemers are coming....I have saved my people, I have avenged the blood of the Armenians and my curse will pursue you to the end of generations.[33]

And the old man [the father, Ephraim Fishel Aaronsohn] who did not cease, all through his terrible agonies, to cry: 'Hear oh Israel, the Lord our God, the Lord is One!' and his daughter, whose lovely body was blackened from torture, lifted her arms, her hands burned by white hot irons, her fingernails crushed, lifted her arms to her Father in heaven in supplication: 'Our blood is the blood of the Armenians, the blood of all the persecuted!'

Obviously the description of events presented above as Sarah's words should not be viewed as an exact quote or as a factual historical source. There can be no doubt, however, that the description expresses the manner in which the members of Nili, or at least some of them, wished to immortalize their activities. There may also be an expression of Sarah's outcry and of her feelings. But first and foremost this document is an expression of what Alexander estimated his sister's thoughts and feelings to be before her death. This excerpt has become part of the ethos, or even the myth of Nili, which its members shaped and continue to shape. And a key component of this ethos is the Armenian massacre.[34]

Sarah bore her torture heroically, and even the opponents of the Nili remark on her courage and endurance: she revealed nothing, and her agonies only grew worse because her aged father was tortured in front of her. Ivria Lishansky, the daughter of Yosef and Rivka, who was held in the torture rooms together with her brother, Tovia, was witness to this horror and describes it in her memoirs. Because she was a young child, she was allowed to wander between the rooms. Ivria relates that Sarah's voice would rise and fall, but when her elderly father screamed and wept, she let go not even a groan. She cursed her tormentors in French, Yiddish, and Arabic. Sarah would repeat certain phrases over and over during the long hours of torture: they would get nothing from her; don't think that because she is a woman she will ask her torturers for mercy or beg; she had no partners in her activity. And Sarah mentioned, a number of times, the murder of the Armenians.[35]

It should be added that, according to various reliable testimonies, Yosef Lishansky, who was hanged by the Turks, also mentioned the Turkish massacre of the Armenians during his final days, even as he stood on the gallows.[36]

The elements of the Nili ethos which derived from the Armenian context were: horror at the massacres, identification with the Armenians, hatred and loathing for the Turks, protest, a demand for vengeance, struggle: "Lest they do to my people what they have done to the Armenians."

Eitan Belkind: An Eyewitness to a Terrible Tragedy

Eitan Belkind (1887-1979), the son of early pioneering founders of Rishon Lezion, went to Constantinople on his own initiative at the age of fifteen, to study at the military high school. When the war broke out, he was conscripted into the Turkish army as an officer and assigned to the headquarters of Jamal Pasha. In March 1915, he was assigned to assist Aaron Aaronsohn in the battle against the locust plague and became one of the founders of Nili. As an officer, he enjoyed the trust of his commanders and moved freely between the cities and villages, enabling him to pass intelligence information to Nili. He spent time among the Druse in southern Syria and with the Armenians in northern Syria.

In his book of memoirs, *So It Was*, which he wrote sixty years after the events, Eitan Belkind presents his eyewitness testimony of the massacre of the Armenians, which he saw during his service as an officer in the Turkish army. Belkind was assigned to the Fourth Army in order to organize the war against the locusts in the region of Mesopotamia and northern Syria, together with two others: Yaakov Bachar, and an Armenian agronomist by the name of Shirinian, who was a reserve officer. He was summoned from leave in Palestine, and had to return to Damascus. From there he was sent to Aleppo where he sojourned for a week at the end of 1916 or the beginning of 1917.

In his memoirs, Belkind relates that he had written a report on the Armenian massacre at the time it occurred, but the report has not been found. Even if his testimony should be received with caution because of the lapse of time, no one can reject it for this reason. Moreover, his testimony fits with what is known from other sources. Belkind's shock at the massacre of the Armenians should be contrasted to the reactions of the Chief Rabbi of Turkey and his cousin, who rejected any involvement or contact with the issue, even though the degree of their personal risk was considerably less than Belkind's. The following are excerpts of his report dealing with the massacre of the Armenians:

In Aleppo we received instructions that Yaakov Bachar was to be in charge of the Musul region, Mr. Shirinian—an Armenian agronomist who was an officer in the reserves—would be in charge of the Baghdad and Basra regions, and I would attend to Mesopotamia along the river, Nahr al-Khabur, which begins in the Taurus Mountains in southern Anatolia and flows south to the Euphrates, close to the central city Dir a(l)-Zor, and continues south to the region of Tadmor, or Palmyra.

After a week's stay in Aleppo, we were given a carriage harnessed to three horses. We departed Aleppo, turned northeast and reached Ras al-Ayn, where we viewed the construction of the Djerablus Bridge over the Euphrates, which the Germans were building for the Berlin-Baghdad rail line. From there we continued southeast, along the banks of the Euphrates.

On the second day of our journey we saw a corpse floating in the Euphrates River. We were astounded but the soldiers who accompanied us assured us saying that it was only the corpse of an Armenian. We learned that nearby, on the other side of the Euphrates, there was a camp of Armenians who had been exiled there from Armenia. The face of our comrade, Shirinian, went pale when he heard this, and he beseeched us to cross the river and go to the Armenian camp.

We found an encampment of several hundred people, living in small huts made of grasses around them. The area was clean and the huts were built in straight rows. We walked pass the huts and looked in. Inside we saw women and children. When we peeked into one of the huts, Shirinian recognized one of his aunts, who told him that all of the men had been murdered and only the women and children were left.

Shirinian had not known what was happening to his Armenian people. He was deeply shocked, burst out weeping on his aunt's shoulder, but Yaakov Bachar and I comforted him and we told him that we must continue in the duty which had been assigned us. We continued on our way, and as we progressed we saw many more corpses of Armenians floating on the water, feed for the fish.

After six days of traveling we reached Dir a(l)-Zor, the main city of the region, where we presented ourselves to the military commander of the city, a Circassian with the rank of lieutenant colonel by the name of Ahmad Bey. We presented him with our documents and reported on the purpose of our arrival. My friend Yaakov Bachar was given lodgings, but my friend Shirinian and I were arrested. Yaakov Bachar, who came to see us later, explained to us that we were under arrest because we were Armenians. It turned out that the commander suspected that I was an Armenian because he read the name 'Eitan,' which was written in Turkish letters, in which the letter 'Y' is written with two dots underneath and the letter 'T' is written in the same way with two dots above—as 'Eitian,' a name with a clearly Armenian ring to it.

"The more I tried to explain this to the commander," said Mr. Bachar, "I did not succeed in convincing him. I therefore sent a telegram to the headquarters in Damascus." I was incarcerated for two days, until a telegram was received from Damascus to release me. What became of our friend Shirinian I do not know to this day.

In Dir a(l)-Zor, which was a military center, there was also a military hospital, headed by a Jewish doctor name Bettor and a Jewish pharmacist named Adatto. There we learned that Ahmad Bey was the leader of the Circassian brigades which had been called up to destroy the Armenians. The doctor and the pharmacist, who put us up in their spacious house, told us that all of the Armenian men had been murdered on their way here from their cities in Anatolia, and that the attractive women and girls were prey for the Bedouins.

After we received our riding horses and an escort of soldiers, Yaakov Bachar continued on to Musul in his assigned region and I went on to my region, along the Khabur River. The night before we left on our journey, we heard bitter, heartrending cries of women. The Armenian encampment was a kilometer from the house in which we were staying, and the cries continued all through the night. When we asked what was happening, we were told that the children were being taken from their mothers, to be sent to boarding schools in order to continue their studies. But in the morning, when I started on my way and crossed the bridge over the Euphrates, I was astounded to see the waters of the river red with the blood and the decapitated corpses of children floating on the water. The sight was horrifying—and we were powerless to help.

We reached the Khabur River, at the place where it meets the Euphrates. We proceeded north and arrived at a tribe of destitute Bedouins, farmers raising wheat....I continued north, and all along the way I came upon corpses of Armenians—especially children, who had not survived the wanderings and had been left by their parents to die by the roadside.

After a three day ride I reached the heart of Mesopotamia where I was witness to a terrible tragedy. There were in that place two camps—that of the Armenians and, next to it, a camp of Circassians, who were occupied in the destruction of the Armenians. In the Circassian camp, Arab sheikhs had also gathered who were choosing for themselves the prettiest girls and women. While I was there, two Armenian women came up to me, gave me their pictures and asked that if I should sometime get to Aleppo and find their families—whom it is doubtful were still alive—that I give them greetings.

A Circassian officer who saw me conversing with the two Armenian women, ordered me to leave the site—but I remained to see what would become of the Armenians. *The Circassian soldiers ordered the Armenians to gather thorns and thistles and to pile them into a tall pyramid; afterward they tied all of the Armenians who were there, almost five thousand souls, hand to hand, encircled them like a ring around the pile of thistles and thorns and set it afire in a blaze which rose up to the heavens together with the screams of the wretched people who were burned to death by the fire. I fled from the place, because I could not stand to see this horrifying sight. I whipped my horse to gallop with all his strength, and after a mad run of two hours I could still hear the piteous screams, until they were silent. Two days later I returned to this place and saw the charred bodies of thousands of human beings.*

I got as far as the Sanjer Mountains, inhabited by the pagan Yassidi. At the foot of the mountains, on my way to the city of Urfa in the north, I witnessed the slaughter of additional Armenians. The people were miserable, despairing unto madness. In one place I saw an Armenian woman cooking her son in a pot for food. All of the roads were covered with corpses of Armenians.[32]

A Jewess in the Sheikh's Tent

Belkind visited Urfa and its environs, but was then forced to leave.

I therefore turned east, toward the Shumar tribe (the Guards) in the Musul region. The people of this tribe, who raise horses and camels, are handsome Bedouins, and their white faces are covered by a black beard. I searched for the tent of the chief of the tribe, and there, to my joy, I met my colleague Yaakov Bachar. We were served an enormous dinner which included the special dish of this tribe: lamb simmered in milk. I remembered what is written in the Bible—"thou shalt not cook a lamb in its mother's milk." The prohibition comes, apparently, from compassion—but I must say that the dish was most tasty.

At midnight, when the meal was finished, the sheikh went to his tent and we remained in the company of a young child, who stayed to guard the fire which warmed us. Yaakov Bachar and I conversed in French. I told him of what I had done in Urfa, about the murder of the Armenians which I had seen, and he told me about his work in the Musul region. Thus we sat and chatted until the early hours—and then the child, whom we had thought a Bedouin, turned to us and told us in French that he and his mother were Armenians, whom the tribal chief had saved from the massacre. His mother served the chief as a wife, and he assisted in entertaining guests. The child continued to tell us that the chief had a second wife, a Jewess, who had been taken with her family from the city of Keyseri in Anatolia. Her husband and her son had been killed and the chief took her for himself.

We were astonished to hear this, and asked him whether we could meet her. Despite the danger to his own life, the child sneaked into the tent where the Jewess was to be found. All of the inhabitants of the tent were asleep, and the woman managed to come out to us without being observed. She was a young woman of about 25, and very beautiful. She told us that her family's name was Biram, which is a typical Turkish name. Her family lived in the Turkish quarter of the city, and when the Armenians were taken away, she and her husband and son were taken with them, despite all of their protests. Her husband and son were murdered, and she was saved by the chief who took her as his wife. We promised to look after her and returned to our tent.

The following day we parted: Yaakov continued on to Musul and I returned south along the Khabur River.

Eight days later I returned to Dir a(l)-Zor, where I received an order from headquarters to attend also to the Baghdad region, which was supposed to have been the duty of our friend Shirinian who had disappeared. I turned east along the Euphrates River and arrived at the town of Rakka. Near the town I met up with a tribe of Bedouins who claim a relationship with the People of Israel: according to their sheikh, they had arrived there with the Babylonian Exile. But apart from the fact that they considered themselves Jews, they had no tradition of Judaism.

I related to the sheikh the tale of the Jewess who had been brought by mistake with the Armenians from Keyseri, her husband murdered and she married to one of the sheikhs of the Shumar, thus saving her life and that of her son who was with her. He promised to go up to the Shumar tribe and make every effort to save her and take her out of there. I do not know if he kept his promise because I left the place and rode toward Baghdad, which lies on the banks of the Tigris River. There I received instructions from the High Command of the war against the locusts in Aleppo, which was headed by a German professor, brought from Germany for this purpose.

According to the instructions, I was to travel at once to Shatt al-Arab (the joining together the Euphrates and the Tigris which flows into the Persian Gulf near the city of Basra) because the locusts had already reached there. I left instructions for the official in charge of the war against the locusts in Baghdad and headed south for Shatt al-Arab — a broad river, with much river travel upon it, and with forests of palm trees and broad expanses of pasture for sheep, horses and camels on both banks. I did not stay there for very long, because I was weary from the journey. The weather was oppressive, because of the heavy heat, and, most importantly, I did not yet enquire into my duties and preferred to return north, to continue writing my report on the massacre of the Armenians and other subjects which were of interest to Nili."[38]

I returned to Baghdad and from there sent a telegram to Constantinople to Rabbi Chaim Nachum, the Chief Rabbi of Turkey, in which I reported to him the special case of Mrs. Biram, the Jewess who had ended up in the Shumar tribe. I gave him my address in Dir a(l)-Zor, in case additional details about this affair should be needed.

After two weeks [in Baghdad], I went west to the Euphrates in a hurry to return to Dir a(l)-Zor. In the mail which awaited me there I found the reply of Rabbi Chaim Nachum from Constantinople, requesting that I not intervene any further in the case of Mrs. Biram, because she was connected with the massacre of the Armenians which was a military secret. Similarly, I received a letter from my cousin Tzila who was studying at the time in Berlin, in response to a letter which I had sent her by German military post describing all that had happened to the Armenian people. She returned the letter to me with a request that I not write anymore about these matters and to be careful of the German military post since my letters were liable to be opened by the military censor. She also wrote me that in the Zionist newspaper, *Der Yiddishe Rundschau*, from July 1916, my name had been mentioned as recipient of the Iron Cross for my battle against the locusts.

In Dir a(l)-Zor, I stayed with the pharmacist, Adatto, who had five Armenian wives whom he had married in order to save their lives. He told me that in the military hospital there were more than 30 young Armenian women working, saved from death in this manner by the Jewish doctor, Bechor.

During one of my visits in the port, where the barges which transported Turkish soldiers from the north to the Baghdad front would dock, I met, among the soldiers and officers who disembarked to rest on the beach, a friend from military school, a Jew from Constantinople by the name of Buchbut. I received permission from the commander to host him for the night in my house, on the condition that he would return to camp the following morning. He spent the whole day with me and slept in my house as well.

Buchbut told me that he was sick of the army and had tried, several times, to desert without success. I advised him not to do it in this remote city, because he would easily be captured in the desert and perhaps even killed if he were thought to be an Armenian.

He rose early the next morning; I provided him with food and cigarettes, and he told me that he was returning to camp. But at ten o'clock I received an order to appear before the military commander of the city who asked me as to the whereabouts of Officer Buchbut, for whom I had signed a guarantee and taken to be a guest in my house. It turned out that he had not gone back to camp, and his unit was about to sail east that very noon. I told the commander the truth: that Buchbut had left my quarters early that morning in order to return to camp, and since then I have neither seen nor heard from him, to this day.

I should point out that during the course of my entire sojourn in Mesopotamia, I was not able to partake of the fish from Euphrates and Khabur Rivers, which I dearly loved, when I remembered that these same fish had fed upon the bodies of the massacred Armenians, among them children and infants. Similarly, I could not have any contacts with the beautiful Armenian young women who were offered to me by the pharmacist, Adatto, and by Dr. Bechor.

Upon arriving in Dir a(l)-Zor I was instructed by the High Command of the war against the locusts to move to the region of Palmyra, or Tadmor, where the locusts had spread.

After a month's stay in Palmyra, Belkind returned to Dir a(l)-Zor where he was ordered to return to Aleppo, having been appointed as the adjutant to the German professor, expert in matters of locusts, who held the rank of general. Belkind did not remain in Aleppo for long.

> I wanted to go home to finish the reports on the massacre of the Armenians and the other matters which were of interest to Nili.[39]

> While I was still in Damascus [on his way back from Mesopotamia] I was visited by Yosef Lishansky, who had come for certain purposes, together with Yitzchak Rosenberg, secretary of "Hashomer." I then gave Yosef my report on the massacre of the Armenians and all of the details of my journey in Mesopotamia and in Aleppo. He requested that I, having returned to Damascus, gather all of the material in the hands of the Nili people there, Nachum Vilboshevitz and Yekutiel Baharav, and furthermore, that I try also to get to Afula, to meet with Dr. Neiman who had provided Nili with a report of all the rail movement in that place.

> When we got back to the laboratory in Atlit, I remained with Sarah. She told me that my report on the Armenian massacre, which she had passed on to Egypt, had made a great impression.

As stated, Belkind mentions the report several times, but our efforts to find this document were futile.[40]

Nili's Leader: Aaron Aaronsohn

Aaron Aaronsohn was concerned with the Armenian question until the day of his death, on May 15, 1919. In the following pages we will attempt to examine Aaronsohn's attitude to this issue during the years 1915-16, until his arrival in London on October 23, 1916.

During his stay in Copenhagen and London during the months of October-November 1916, Aaron Aaronsohn wrote several important documents in which he expressed his opinion and developed a comprehensive position on the Armenian question.

In the years 1917-19, Aaron Aaronsohn would be involved in the contacts and plans for the future of the Zionist undertaking and in issues regarding the future of the Armenians throughout the world following the war—two subjects which in Aaronsohn's view were tied together. The years 1915 and early 1916 were a time of rumors, testimony, reports. It is reasonable to assume that the reports of the Armenian massacre, as yet unverified, reached Aaron Aaronsohn during the course of 1915, although no written evidence to that effect has been found. As mentioned, Avshalom Feinberg reported to Henrietta Szold (in October 1915) and to Lieutenant Woolley (in November 1915) about the massacre which the Turks were committing against the Armenians.

Eitan Belkind indicates in his memoirs, *So It Was*, written sixty years later, that after the Jews were expelled from Jaffa at the end of March 1915 [not to be confused with the expulsion of the Jews from Tel Aviv in 1917] he was present at a meeting between Avshalom Feinberg (who had seen the expulsion) and Aaron Aaronsohn. Avshalom demanded that they revolt against the Turks "because the Yishuv stands on the brink of annihilation. He remarked that the expulsion of the Jews was implemented, in his opinion, at the advice of the Germans, just as the slaughter of the Armenians, which had then begun, had been implemented at their advice."[41]

In December, Sarah Aaronsohn arrived in Palestine, and she also described what she had seen with her own eyes. It can be assumed that what Avshalom knew and reported was known also to Aaron Aaronsohn.[42]

Aaron Aaronsohn's diary from 1915 is sketchy and has not yet been published. In his diary during that year he records only short periods (March 28 to April 30, November 2-4, and November 22 to December 31, 1915). Thus we cannot know from his diary whether Aaron heard or knew about the massacre of the Armenians in the period prior to November 1915, inasmuch as there is a hiatus from the end of April.

In his memorandum to the British, "Pro Armenia," from November 1916 (see Appendix A), Aaron relates that in November-December 1915 reports reached him about the massacre of the Armenians from Germans residing in Haifa, who returned from travels in Europe and Constantinople and told him of the sights they had seen at firsthand on the way. It should be emphasized that the information which appears in the diary seems accurate, detailed and reliable. Aaron's skill as a scientist and researcher trained in reporting his research and the activities of the laboratory in Atlit, came to the fore in his writing, together with poetic, philosophical, ethical, and emotional comments concerning the events he saw.

An investigation of various details in his diary proves their credibility. It should also be remembered that Aaron and those close to him decided in the course of that year to aid the British. The gathering of information was also intended to further their intelligence activities for the British.

In his journal entry for November 23, 1915, Aaron describes at length his journey from Haifa to Tiberias, and from there to Rosh Pina ("all in the same day, by horseback, at what was considered to be top speed," in his words). He recounts in detail the trip and the places he passed, and describes the extensive road works that were in progress at the time at the order of Jamal Pasha, for purposes of the war. He relates the plans for the construction of a strategic route from Jerusalem to Damascus, and of the paving of roads from Nazareth to Afula, and from Nazareth to Tiberias, which were completed in very short order. Aaron is not willing to guarantee their quality. He also points out that "it is clear that for the demand of those roads, they brutally oppressed the poor citizen." He expands on the question of German-Turkish relations, and reveals a little about his sources of information:

> The money for paving the roads can come only from the hands of Germany, and it is worth noting that not a single German is involved in paving these roads....Something has changed since then, a year has passed. Last year nothing would have been done without the Germans. And the latter were amassing a fortune through their would-be self sacrifice in the service of their precious ally. This year it seems as if there is a tendency to forego their services. Once again, the hand of Jamal Pasha can be seen, because he is not particularly enamored of the Germans. An alliance does not always require love, does it? And indeed the German residents in Palestine are gritting their teeth. Thanks to my blond hair and my German accent, which are irrefutable proof of a *Deutsch Freundlich*—a friend of the Germans—[a cynical tone appears again and again] the Germans have not spared me their complaints and grumblings. They have spilled so much to me! And when a German begins to spill his soul, there is no limit to what he begins to tell about his Turkish ally. It may be overly cautious to listen without reacting.

Later that same day, upon his arrival in Tiberias, he says, "When I entered Grossman's [the Hotel Grossman in Tiberias] I came upon little Hermann (Kurt). What a gossip! A veritable torrent. He is constantly terrified of spies, and sees them everywhere. I tease him and remind him how ridiculous people made themselves in London and Paris by seeing spies in every corner. I hope we will not become like them."

After he makes fun of Kurt Hermann's fear of spies, Aaron Aaronsohn writes in his diary:

> Kurt Hermann says, in the name of young Preuss from Haifa who has just returned from the German army, that a mass slaughter has been conducted

against the Armenians, in Turkey. And Hermann adds: 'They deserve it, a band of pigs like them. Those Armenians, haven't they stooped as low as to poison the flour, and three thousand Turkish soldiers died from eating Armenian bread. The Armenian girls seduced entire platoons of the Turkish army into dangerous passes from which not a man could flee. All of this has been planned in advance by the Russians. The Armenians live with the Russians under the same roof.'

And also in Preuss' name, he recounts that thousands of Armenians have been gathered in Aleppo, where epidemics have ravaged them, while the authorities do not lift a finger, and do not even bury the corpses, in the hope that thus more will die. And what he says, by the way, Kurt Soldier-Boy, about our government: 'Pay attention to what will yet occur.' He already sees himself slaughtered. He, his wife, and all the Germans. You don't believe it? Well he relies on Major Pur.[43] The latter recounted to him the words of a Turkish officer: the number of Armenians before the war was two and a half million. After it, there will not be more than half a million left.

Indeed, a charming perspective, how fortunate that I do not believe in it. But it is impossible to put commonsense back into Kurt who is, after all, like an ordinary gramophone, which spins around on itself, in contradiction upon contradiction, what his ears pick up from the Germans.

In another comment, from January 12, 1916, Aaronsohn describes his trip from Kuneitra to Damascus for a meeting with Jamal Pasha:

We leave Kuneitra at exactly six o'clock. For one hour the road is excellent and then becomes muddy and difficult. It takes us three and a quarter hours to reach Sasa. On the way, there are groups of Armenians working on the road. We see only men here, but after Sasa we see hundreds of Armenian women and girls working along the way. These latter are marvelous. I can easily understand that such strong young women will find buyers for 3 or even 6 *majidas* each, so it is said everywhere, although it has not been proved, or even close to it, that such stories are true.[44]

We still find uncertainty, at least concerning one fact that will later arouse so much attention: the commerce in women and little girls. The next day, on January 13, he meets in Damascus ("a wonderful surprise") Samuel Edelmann, who had been appointed that very day to be the U.S. Consul in Damascus. He had served previously in the U.S. Consulate in Jerusalem and in Aleppo, and after Damascus was stationed in Geneva.

He went to the Consulate (of the United States) and I accompanied him there. In Aleppo he had frequent occasion to see His Highness Jamal Pasha. From his comments, I learn that he had confrontations with the noble Max Von Oppenheim, the "Apostate."

He was in Urfa at the time of the massacre [of the Armenians]; he said it was the most despicable of crimes. Jamal Pasha allegedly proved to him, with documents in hand, that the Armenians were enlisted in the service of the Russians, in order to create a rebellion in the country. He is convinced that the authorities were justified in evacuating the entire region, and he confirms that from the border and all the way to Aleppo they have not left a single Armenian. But the means they used, in order to be rid of them, were horrifying beyond imagination.[45]

In mid-1916, Aaron decides to leave Eretz Yisrael and attempt to reach England. Alexander Aaronsohn describes Aaron's journey from Damascus to Constantinople, on July 15, 1916:

> He took the route by which Sarah came. And he sees with his own eyes that she did not exaggerate in her descriptions of the Turkish atrocities against the Armenians. And he understands why Sarah was so pale and why her whole body shook when she recalled what she had seen....Because he also saw, all along the way, children and tender women, Armenians, who were being sold. He too saw corpses of Armenians and dogs feeding on them....His ears too heard every day the terrible cry of thousands and thousands of Armenians dying of hunger and thirst.[46]

In Aaron Aaronsohn's diary, we find a detailed description of the events of the journey, and numerous facts about the route. He describes the awful sights of thirsty, starving refugees and corpses along the roadside which match the descriptions of refugees from the massacre of the Armenians. Even though there is no explicit indication which confirms that these were indeed Armenian refugees, there is no doubt that he was writing about them. Aaronsohn saw "entire families along the roads searching for something to chew."[47] He was horrified: "And at these sights one must harden his heart. Individual mercy is helpless here." Jamal Pasha and his staff passed along the same route, and Aaronsohn adds, "Were their eyes the eyes of men and their hearts the hearts of men, they had to have been shocked by these sights which horrified me." He returns to those sights in his letter to Justice Mack, "The Confession" (see below): "People starving, wandering purposelessly, and tens of corpses piled at the side of the main roads."[48]

"The Confession"—October 1916

After an arduous journey, Aaronsohn reached Constantinople. There he remained for almost a month (July 22-August 17) and afterwards made his way to Germany, where he spent four weeks, and to Denmark for five weeks. On October 23, 1916, he arrived in England.

In Copenhagen, he took advantage of the freedom to write without restriction of censorship. On October 9, he wrote to Judge Julian Mack, one of the Zionist leaders in the United States. His letter gives expression to his stormy emotions together with a carefully reasoned analysis of his actions and an explanation of his decision to establish the espionage network.

> Here you have my confession. Would I have left the country and openly taken service on the English side, it would already have been bad enough. My character, my standing would be impaired. But I did worse. I stood where I was, I organized a whole movement, I became connected with the Intelligence Office, as people who are afraid of words call it. I do not like mincing words. Put it clearly, and I became a Spy, *horresco referens*....I do not feel the need of any man's apology. I stand very firmly before the tribunal of my own conscience."[49]

Aaronsohn attached great significance to his "confession." And, in fact, this is certainly an important document in understanding his path to contact with Britain, and his Zionist worldview during the war. The letter was delivered via his New York friend, Yehuda L. Magnes, and Aaron requested that it be shown to a very small number of intimates in the United States.[50]

In his letter, Aaronsohn clarifies a number of central points that we will examine briefly, since some of them appear in the following excerpt, which has not been published previously:

Turkey

1. The brutality of the Turks and the methodical execution of their brutality: "I have said and said again that everything the Turks have done to us was done systematically and brutally."
2. The Turks are planning to massacre the Jews: "And then came the horrible days of November, 1914, and I was horrified in getting an entirely unsuspected aspect of the Turkish methods....From November 1914 I came to the conclusion that a massacre of the Jews was planned by the government, and I acted in light of this conclusion."
3. Turkey must be torn to pieces: "My experiences with Jamal Pasha, who was certainly one of the three most prominent men of Turkey to-

day, an experience of several months, anchored my belief that Turkey must be entirely torn to pieces."

England

"Britain, and only Britain, can help us"—believed Aaronsohn even before the war. Official Zionism at the time believed that "our future is tied to Turkey and we must work with her hand in hand."

But at that stage he refrained from action: "I have taken upon myself to be silent and maintained neutrality." But, "now everybody, even over-patriotic German Jews who have any knowledge of the Turks and of conditions in Palestine, say we must go with England. I, for one, have decided to do so. And if so, I am obliged to do what seems to me to be most effective." "In the first stage," writes Aaron, "I have moved over —at this point in a spiritual sense—to the 'enemy' side. If I have not yet arrived at practical cooperation with the English, I have taken upon myself before my conscience the job of giving them a hand, to do what ever shall be in my power in order to liberate our country from the Turkish curse."

In the next stage, he explains later on, "I have become a spy, God help us!"

Germany

Aaronsohn writes candidly to Judge Mack:

Since the beginning of the War I have not learned where your sympathies are. Are you pro-British or—excuse me if you feel insulted—pro-German? But you can have no doubt that I am more anti-German than ever, can you? In fact this German war came, all too soon though, as a complete corroboration of my predictions. Did I not see long ago how deep the German poison lay? And did I not, à propos et mal à propos, always warn my American friends and colleagues even against the poisoned German science, a thing so many people have recognized now to have been right and timely?

The combination of the Germans and the Turks is a disaster for the Jews and the Armenians. Several times, Aaronsohn recalls the brutality and methodical actions of the Turks against the Jews in Eretz Yisrael as he writes,

Now as to brutality, the Turks have enough of it of their own stock, but methodical performance was a thing they never had before. That was of foreign origin, and in its anti-Jewish aspects that method was too obviously stamped: 'Made in Germany.' The 'Turkization' as applied to the Armenians and the Jews was nothing but a copy of the method of 'Prussianization' worked out for the Poles in Posnany, etc."[51]

Aaronsohn states, as mentioned, that since November 1914 he has reached the conclusion that a massacre of the Jews has been planned by the government, and acted in light of that understanding.

Still I had no proofs, documentary proofs, I mean.

A month ago in Berlin I got written evidence from official circles that I was right in my conviction, and had not gone wrong in my appreciation of the new capacities the Turks had acquired, or developed under German education.[52]

In older days people used to try a new medicine on the dog and watch the result. Here we had the same experience: German Kultur tried on the Turks, and the beautiful results. German education was the right vehicle to bring out a new aspect of what the Turk was capable; thanks should be given to the Germans.

Armenia

Aaronsohn reminds Judge Mack of "something which you may have forgotten since then"—an event which occurred in late 1912 or in the spring of 1913, in connection with a lecture Aaronsohn was to present in New York, together with other famous scientists, at the United States Department of Agriculture:

You gave us a good breakfast at which and after which we talked over Oriental problems. I unpacked my views on a free Armenian State in the near future. I cannot remember on what ground I came to the conclusion that such a State might be established within 12 years—'ausgerechnet!' I could not foresee, of course, that 800,000 of this poor Nation might be massacred within one year.

The Letter to Jacobson

Another important document which has won little attention in attempts to understand Aaronsohn's activities during the war is his letter to Victor Jacobson. The letter was sent to Copenhagen from London on October 30, 1916, a week after Aaronsohn arrived and three weeks after his letter to Judge Mack.[53] Victor (Avigdor) Jacobson was the political representative of the Zionist Organization in Constantinople during the years 1908-1915, and afterwards managed the office of the Zionist Organization in Copenhagen from 1916 to 1919.

Lichtheim, who worked with Jacobson and afterwards replaced him, relates,

> Jacobson, who left Constantinople in late April, 1915, was not able to return because Talât [Pasha, Minister of the Interior] did not want him around. As a Russian citizen he was considered a foreign enemy, and the German authorities, who had permitted him to travel to and from Constantinople several times, announced that they were unable to accept responsibility for his safety on Turkish soil. He therefore spent the coming years between Copenhagen and Berlin, where his presence in the negotiations with the Foreign Ministry was extremely helpful.[54]

In contrast to his reserved attitude toward many of the leaders and activists in the Zionist Movement, Aaronsohn displays friendship, sympathy, and admiration for Jacobson. He reveals to him his pro-British activity, sharply and candidly examining the two opposing orientations: his own pro-British orientation—its chances and achievements, versus Jacobson's pro-Turkish/German orientation, which was similar to that of the mainstream of the Zionist leadership at the time.

The detailed letter attests to Aaronsohn's writing talents and to his broad intellectual horizons. We present only a few brief excerpts from the letter which are relevant to our subject. The letter begins thus:

> Very Dear Friend,
>
> The last time we met [in Germany, it would seem] it was premature for me to lay before you my plans. I waited for you for a full month in Copenhagen, and bad luck prevented you from arriving. You are, I think, too clever for me to fool you completely. You surely questioned whether my desire to reach a neutral country was, as I said, a goal in itself or rather a means to an end... in order to reach a non-neutral nation. I am finally there, thank Heaven, and here I am now in London, and that is what matters. You know me well enough to realize that the goal is not one of personal benefit.
>
> How could I decide upon such a step? You, who are familiar with affairs in Eretz Yisrael and in Turkey only via the reports you receive from Tahon

and Ruppin, filtered by the naive Lichtheim, via the Embassy [the German Embassy], do not know what is going on there at all.[55]

I know that with the appointment of your friend Richard Kühlmann,[56] you will become even more the optimist regarding the political successes which Zionism has achieved in Constantinople. A mistake, my very dear friend, a mistake with grave ramifications.

For those of us who are well familiar with Turkey, for those of us who have seen the Turk lift his mask—*"made in Germany"*—and seen in his face the bloody and horrible portrait of Ghengis Khan and his bands, for those of us who have trembled for the future of our women and sisters and a fate worse than death, for us, the decision which has been made is irreversible. We shall destroy the hornets' nest because we know that no possible effort can turn it into a hive of honeybees....And now, to extract its full measure, Turkey sought to commit a massacre against us. I have known this for sure for quite some time. Since you read Lepsius' secret pamphlet [about the Turks' massacre of the Armenians, see below] you also know beyond a doubt. It does not matter that the massacres were not committed. I view the Turks as guilty and treat their intentions the same as their actions. The Turks have committed against us crimes which are destroying the past and closing off the future.[57] The sooner we break away from Turkey, we will better fulfill our destiny vis-à-vis humanity.

"Pro Armenia"

At the beginning of November 1916, Aaronsohn was in London, waiting for permits, agreements, and coordination between the various departments of the War Office, the Foreign Office, the Intelligence services and other agencies in London and Egypt, which would allow him to travel to Egypt to establish intelligence contacts with the laboratory in Atlit. Aaron was frustrated and impatient. He feared for the fate of his people in Atlit and bemoaned the loss of valuable time. In his diary from those days we find numerous evidence of this.

London, November 11, 1916

The good weather continues, there is no rain and I take advantage of the situation to take long walks around London. In addition to the physical exercise, this also helps me to lighten my mind, for if I were to think too much about the situation I might go mad. How slowly the decisions are made. It will soon be a month since I left Berlin, and basically, nothing tangible has yet been done in order to provide assistance to the people in Atlit.

The newspapers announce that the Turkish law, from October 14, has gone into effect and everyone is being taken for military service. Will Avsha's [Avshalom Feinberg] words as they were told to me, turn out to be prophetic? 'You will come and probably not find a single person in the nest.'[58]

Aaron finally departs London on November 24, 1916, and reaches Port Said on December 12, 1916. In the meantime, he works in the War Office with Major Walter Harold Gribbon, the Secretary for Turkish Affairs in the General Command who had spent considerable time in Constantinople and was familiar with the Ottoman Empire. The cooperation between them was fruitful. Gribbon instructed him to write various reports and memoranda (perhaps as part of a process of examination and acceptance into Intelligence, and a desire to take his measure). On November 5, Aaron delivered a memorandum for the Foreign Office to Gribbon, on the subject, "Why It Is Urgent To Renew the Contact Between Atlit and Egypt."[59]

A week later, on November 13:

At four o'clock to Gribbon who is busy and cannot receive me until 4:30. There is still nothing new [on the question of arrangements for his trip to Egypt]. "Tomorrow, without doubt"—he consoles me. He asks that I prepare for him a report on the acts of brutality against the Armenians, and a different report on the administration of Jamal Pasha."[60]

The next day, on November 14: "I spent the day writing *Pro Armenia*. This has been good for my leg which, by the way, has improved." [In London, Aaron was in the habit "of doing my daily walk of 20 kilometers."] He continues writing the following day, Wednesday, November 15: "Since the morning, I have been writing about the Armenian problem." Thus on Thursday, November 16: "During the morning hours I write the memorandum: 'Pro Armenia.'"

Indeed, the document presented to the British War Office is dated November 16, 1916. It is noteworthy that Aaron was asked to write, according to his diary, a report to the War Office "about the acts of brutality against the Armenians." He gave the report a title that also testifies to its character. It is not just a comprehensive intelligence report of twenty pages, which presents facts and details, as we shall see, but also, and perhaps primarily, a personal statement, humane and moral, from the point of view of a Jew. Aaron's spirit and personality infuse the report.

The British did not preserve the original title of the report. As edited by them, the report is entitled "Turkish Treatment of Armenians." It discusses questions of who knew, what part the Turkish population played in the annihilation, how the Great Powers reacted, etc.

We have two reports written by Aaron Aaronsohn in November 1916, both dealing with the Armenian massacre. One is entitled "Pro Armenia," dated November 16, 1916, and intended for the British War Office. The other, intended also for the War Office, dated simply November 1916, is entitled "On the Armenian Massacre." They are two different documents.

The second document deals mainly with the theft of Armenian property by the Turks, and the severe damage to the faltering Ottoman Empire following the Armenian massacre. The Turks are incapable of economic or agricultural management, or of organizing the civil service without the Armenians who had provided the brains and hands for the Turkish government.

The organized theft of Armenian property and its redistribution to influential Turks, without compensation to the Armenians, is called "internal colonization." According to Aaron, it was implemented by the Turks but first proposed by the Germans and replicated the method of "internal colonization" in Posnan, which was intended to block the Polish advance. Aaron remarks that information about this which reached the outside world through the German press was blocked by the German and Turkish authorities. The manuscript of this report is preserved in the Aaronsohn Archives in Zichron Yaakov. We do not know if it was delivered to the British.

Another of Aaron's reports to the British, about the administration of Jamal Pasha, which apparently contains references to the Armenians massacre as well, has not been found.[61]

Aaronsohn's reports were passed by the War Office to the Foreign Office and to the Intelligence Services, and also sent to the British Military Command in Cairo. They were highly respected by the British.[62]

We also have at least two British reports based on Aaron's work, "Pro Armenia," which is, in our estimate, the most comprehensive and important report and which was edited by the British and retitled "Turkish Treatment of Armenians."[63] The document was also passed on from the War Office to prominent figures in the British Foreign Office where it aroused interest.

An additional British document is entitled, "On the Internal, Economic, Political and Military Situation in Turkey, Syria and Palestine." In this detailed thirty-one-page document, there is a brief paragraph in the political section dealing with Turkey entitled, "The Armenians and the Pan-Turanic Movement,"[64] referring, among other things, to the Lepsius Report. The British document presents the informant as "an inhabitant of Athlit, Mount Carmel."[65]

The specific British report on the Armenian issue, "Turkish Treatment of Armenians," is based, as mentioned, on "Pro Armenia," presented by them as "an addendum to the report of an inhabitant of Athlit, Mount Carmel, Syria."[66]

The British Deletions from "Pro Armenia"

The British abridged and edited "Pro Armenia." They deleted a significant portion of the personal treatment and the moral criticism. The British document is matter-of-fact and official. Of twenty typed pages, eight remained. It should be emphasized that the British valued Aaron's reports, and in particular "Pro Armenia," which served as the basis for their own report. At the beginning of their report they indicate,

> The writer, when speaking of the treatment meted out to the Armenians by the Turks since the beginning of the war, fears that he will be accused of exaggeration. He has kept this fear in view when describing atrocities committed by the Turks. The writer has not been in Armenia proper but has lived in Syria since the war began, and has visited Konia and Constantinople, and has many acquaintances, including Germans.[67]

The report was passed, together with a short letter from the head of military intelligence, to the Deputy Foreign Secretary, and classified "secret." From the cover page we learn that the document was sent to the "News Department."

The cover page also teaches us something about the number of people who read it and noted their comments and impressions. The comments of the head of military intelligence, attached to the report, describe Aaronsohn as one of those Zionists who consider nationalism more important than religion, and limit themselves, at this stage, to working to obtain freedom of settlement in Eretz Yisrael.[68] In an intelligence comment about Aaron's report, the head of British espionage notes, *inter alia,* that "the facts which the author [Aaron Aaronsohn] presents concerning the Armenians are heartrending." Later on he relates to Aaron's estimate that the destruction was systematic throughout the interior of the country.[69]

The final British report was edited, undoubtedly, by Gribbon, and possibly by others before him, in the War and Espionage Offices. The editing is felt in deletions of two subjects: (1) the responsibility and culpability of the Germans in the Armenian massacre; (2) the fear that the fate of the Jews may be that of the Armenians.[70] It is important to remember that these were Aaron's two main points in his attitude toward the Armenian massacre and the fate of the Jews during the period of the First World War.

German Culpability

The British deleted Aaron's accusations of German failure to stop the barbaric treatment of the Armenians, as well as his fairly detailed treatment of the Lepsius report (see below).

Aaron is extremely critical of the Germans, and comments that the German mentality arouses wonder. "The Armenian question was a safe question to tackle with official Germans and the writer failed on no occasion to start on it, so he had the opportunity to have the minds of hundred stories proving the cruelty of the Turks, the useless and shameless barbarity, and so on." Aaronsohn is also shocked by the German exploitation of the Armenians' distress:

> Every clean-minded man would shrink at the idea of making any profit from a situation like that the Armenians were in. Not so the Germans. They made bargains. It would be unfair to say they robbed the Armenians, but these poor souls being compelled to consideration—the Germans took advantage of conditions and bought carpets, jewelry, trinkets at a tenth part of their real value. Germany will be the richest country in carpets.

Aaron sees the imperialistic political reasons for the German approach to the Armenian question. The Germans thought that if it was worthwhile to attempt colonization of areas in East Africa and other places, it was criminal to leave Anatolia which was so blessed in its geography, climate, agricultural and natural resources. Seventy-five years earlier, Moltke had pointed out that this land was the region for future colonization by the Germans. More and more Germans were pointing this out recently. Aaronsohn sums up:

Looking at it from this light, would any one who knows something of Germans and the long and something crooked way they can go for the realization of their high ambitions which are in fact nothing less than divine missions, would any such man hesitate to say that wiping out of those countries the thriftiest element there was, could not have displeased, not even hurt German politics? And would not the Germans themselves, when better fed and in more boisterous spirits than today, said: a crime? That is arguable, but good, farsighted German real-politik, is it not?

The Armenian massacres are the carefully planned acts of the Turks, and the Germans will certainly be made forever to share the odium of these acts.

The British deleted all of these sections when they edited Aaron's report, as well as the sections dealing with the Lepsius report which we will examine later on.

In Line For Destruction—Jews and Other Minorities

The British also deleted Aaronsohn's conclusion that the next in line for destruction in Turkey were the other national and religious minorities: the Jews and the Christians. This conclusion is the starting point for Aaronsohn and his comrades in their decision to cooperate with the British.

Aaron mentions this several times in "Pro Armenia," once in the context of the Lepsius report and again when describing the case of a young Armenian bride, daughter of a respected family in Constantinople. Her husband, a physician, was murdered by the Turks in front of her eyes, three months after their wedding. For several months, the bride grieved and preserved her dignity in the face of her Turkish tormentors. Little by little she was forced to sell the beautiful carpets and other possessions...all of the mementos from her former happy married life. "The last time the writer was in Constantinople she was a notorious prostitute having exclusively Turks as her patrons."

From this specific case, he concludes,

The writer took the liberty to report this case because to him this is not a special, individual case. This ought to be looked upon as the illustration of what is to happen to all the races and all the nations living under the deadening Turkish rule.

It has been often, but probably not sufficiently said that the Turk has never been any more than an invader in the countries he was ruling. The Turk never settled down to anything like real conservative Government. He lived as a camping barbarous invader and as such he treated the countries and the races he conquered for a while.

If this war is really fought in order to free the world, then the poor nations and races under the Turkish despotism, be they Armenians, Greeks, Jews or Arabs, must be delivered. Otherwise their decadence must follow sooner or later, just as was sure to come the downfall of the Armenian girl cited above.

This detailed story is mentioned in the British report in two lines. It tells of a young woman, from a good family, recently married, whose husband was murdered in front of her. She was forced into her present situation (prostitution) only after a struggle of several months to live chastely. All of the accompanying musings and conclusions were deleted.

Aaron Aaronsohn writes in his report: "The wholesale massacre of the Jews ordered by the Roman General Titus is the only record in History to be paralleled with the wholesale massacre of the Armenians. And now, just as then, here, just like there, it was a Government scheme."

"Pro Armenia" contains additional descriptions and Aaron's personal testimony, such as a description of the hunt of the Armenians by the Turkish police in Constantinople, brutal arrests in broad daylight, in public parks, at large gatherings of people, where they would gather up their prey.

Aaron pays special attention to the disappearance of a gentleman of about forty-five and his three-year-old son while they were walking in the park at about five p.m.: "The writer has been witness to one such case which will stay for years in his memory." He recounts the gentleman's arrest by the police and adds, "The distressed look of the poor man with the small boy clinging in his arms is indescribable, and the whole scene was so quickly and noiselessly performed that practically no one besides the writer noticed the fact. Of such a captive one never hears any more, he disappears for ever."

He deals in his report with questions of principle, which any discussion of genocide is obliged to treat, such as Armenian collaborators, who turned other Armenians into the Turkish police in Constantinople. Another question that he raises is the following:

It might be asked: what part of the population or of the organized public services was carrying out those wholesale destructions of Armenian life and property. The reply is that no class of the Mohammedan population, rich or poor, high or low, young or old, men or women kept away from murdering and robbing, which of course does not mean to say that every individual Mohammedan is to be blamed, without exceptions. A few noteworthy exceptions were reported, cases of individual help tendered by old Turks are known, but they were very rare, isolated and always rebuffed by the Authorities, military and civil.

These passages, too, were deleted from the British report.

Aaron Aaronsohn on the Lepsius Report

The Protestant German pastor, Johannes Lepsius, who worked on behalf of the Armenians during the earlier massacres of 1896, protested the widespread acts of destruction which were committed during 1915-16, and tried to organize circles of sympathizers in Germany and the United States. (It is interesting to note that Lepsius submitted a memorandum entitled "Armenians and Jews in Exile" to the Zionist Congress in 1897, proposing cooperation between the two national movements. The memorandum has not been found.) His impressive figure, helpless and despairing in the face of his failure, appears in the monumental work of Franz Werfel, *The Forty Days of Musa Dagh*, in the chapter "Interlude of the Gods." The chapter, which is one of the high points of the book, describes Lepsius's meeting with Enver Pasha, Minister of War, "the war god," based on notes of the conversation between them.[71]

Werfel writes admiringly of Lepsius, "the guardian angel, sent by God to defend the Armenian people," with whom Werfel himself identifies. Through the Protestant pastor Lepsius, Werfel the Jew asks himself questions which are also being thrown at him by others: "do Armenians really matter to me?" "These Armenians mattered a great deal to him—even more, if he dared vigorously to examine his heart—more perhaps than even his own countrymen, mad and sinful as that no doubt may be."[72] The huge eyes of the Armenians stare at Lepsius, and strengthen his sense that "he had felt himself especially sent to these unfortunates," "they were his task on earth," eyes such as these belong only to creatures who must drink the poisoned chalice to its dregs. Those same enormous Armenian eyes touched Werfel during his trip to Damascus in 1929. It was those eyes which gave Werfel himself, so he stated, the "final impulse to snatch from the Hades of all that was, this incomprehensive destiny of the Armenian nation."

In his reports of the Armenian massacre to the British in November 1916, Aaronsohn mentions the report of Lepsius, who was head of German missionary activities in the Middle East until 1917. In Aaronsohn's report, "On the Internal, Economic, Political and Military Situation in Turkey, Syria and Palestine," from November 4, 1916, there is also a discussion of "The Armenians and the Pan-Turanic Movement," and of Dr. Lepsius's pamphlet.[73] The report states, *inter alia*: "The writer [Aaron Aaronsohn] saw a "secret" book which was distributed privately and written by Dr. Lepsius, head of the German missionary movement, with an introductory letter written by Bethmann-Hollweg, Chancellor of Germany when the war began. The letter includes a promise by Bethmann-Hollweg to do his utmost in order to prevent a recurrence of atrocities, and his denial that the Germans had any connection to them."

Aaron further remarks, "Lepsius proves that these massacres are part of the permanent policy of the central Turkish Government. Massacres of Jews and Christians were to follow."[74] In the original, more detailed report on the Armenian question, "Pro Armenia," dated November 16, 1916, there is a more thorough treatment of the Lepsius report, not without reservations:

> Officiously the Germans put the whole blame of the Armenian massacres on the Turkish Government and want to shake from themselves any burden of participation or responsibility in the Crime. A good deal of propaganda work has been in this respect, the most important piece of work to the knowledge of the writer, being the painstaking document full of American and German statements privately printed and circulated as strictly Confidential by Dr. Lepsius, head of the German Missionary works. It may be granted that Dr. Lepsius is fairly sincere in his indignation to see malevolent people charging the Germans with participation in the massacres of 650,000 Christians by the hands of the Heathen. He brings good proof of the Massacres being planned quite carefully by the Central Government in Constantinople. He goes even further and discloses that the Armenian massacres were only a *coup d'essai* (though a *coup de maitre*) and were the so called civilized World to accept it with not too loud displeasure, the Greeks, the other Christians and the Jews would have followed.

> But just like all the most honest and sincere German productions, Dr. Lepsius's work has to be taken *cum grano salis*. He fully admits the Turkish cruelty, the Turkish deep-laid plot, he supplements proof and witnesses to the facts, that far we may follow him. His whitewashing of the German Government may be argued. It would probably be unfair to suspect Dr. Lepsius having written his apologia by order, but like all law-abiding Germans he submitted his apologia to the Authorities; Dr. Bethmann-Hollweg

has allowed one of his letters to be published in the "Introduction," a letter in which he assures of doing "in the future" his Christian duty by straining all means to prevent a repetition of the disgraceful massacres, etc....Therefore the document takes a holy, official character which makes it dubious. If the German Government had reasons to approve (without approving) of massacres, they have probably not found fit to take Dr. Lepsius into their Confidence.

Aaronsohn claims that the German Government made use of the Lepsius report for its own propaganda purposes. It should be noted that as early as 1919 Lepsius published an important work, which deals with the Germans and the Armenians in the years 1914-18. The book presents 444 documents, including numerous reports from German consuls in various cities of the Ottoman Empire—Adana, Aleppo, Erzerum, and other cities where Armenians were massacred. It appears that Lepsius enjoyed the support of the German authorities in the preparation of the book that shows the "pretty face" of the Germans.

Aaron Aaronsohn writes that he spoke with tens of Germans: officers, physicians, and others, who were in the heart of the region of the massacres and this is what he found:

All and every German was individually horrified at what he has witnessed. Trained with a superstitious respect of property, order, etc... a German cannot be expected to look in cold blood placidly at the robbery, massacres, etc....To say therefore that the Germans were leading the massacres, or even taking directly a hand in them, as it has often been repeated, is doing them a wrong or at least advancing things which can never be proved, whereas the Germans will always be able to prove by testimonials, diaries, protocols, etc... that in each their soul revolted.

But slaves to discipline, having given every individual thought or movement the Germans who were ordered to duty in the massacre-area, saw the outrage, felt indignant, but made no move to stop it. That is certainly, from a higher moral ground, participation even if not direct.

Aaronsohn ends his report: "The Armenian massacres are the carefully planned act of the Turks, and the Germans will certainly be made for ever to share the odium of this act." It should be remembered that the British deleted these passages when editing Aaronsohn's report.

Lepsius's report, which first appeared in Germany in 1916, was entitled "A Report on the Armenian Situation in Turkey."[75] It was written out of the author's conflict between German patriotism and his duty of conscience and humanity as a Christian, in light of "the danger of destruction of the most ancient people in Christendom."

In the introduction, Lepsius wrote to "my dear friends in the [German] Mission: our political and military interests obligate us. Turkey is our ally, and has greatly aided us in the war. Our camaraderie of arms places upon us a duty, but it should not prevent us from fulfilling our duties to humanity. If we must remain silent in public, our conscience will not, nonetheless, cease to speak."

Therefore, the report is classified "top secret," "handwritten," and "all uses and publication by the press are forbidden, in whole or in part." Lepsius points out that, "the censorship cannot permit in wartime publication of events in Turkey."

The purpose of the report, according to its author, is solely to arouse awareness of the need to extend aid and assistance in order to save women and children, now living in the deserts of Mesopotamia, after some of their brethren were murdered and others forcibly converted to Islam. The necessary and feasible aid now is Christian-humanitarian, and there is no reference to political or military issues. "Among all of the Christian peoples, we the Germans, are best placed to fulfill the [Good] Samaritan duty to these poor people. For other peoples who may wish to assist, the channels are blocked." The report is uncritical of the German government and it is reasonable to assume that it was published in its would-be secret form (20,000 copies) with the agreement of the German government.

Lepsius mentions in his introduction that "the German Imperial Government, which is aware of the facts regarding the fate of the Armenians, has done all it could do to prevent this devastation." The introduction presents, as mentioned earlier, the reply of the Chancellor, Dr. Bethmann-Hollweg, to requests he received from German Christians. The reply contains the Chancellor's promise that "the German Government will, in the future as in the past, fill its moral obligations to use its influence, lest Christian peoples be destroyed because of their faith." "The German Christians may depend on me that I will do everything in my power." "Under no circumstances," emphasizes Lepsius, "should our political interests be harmed as a result of a lack of credibility concerning Turkey [in the report]." Thus it is clear that the point of view of Lepsius, a German Christian, regarding the role of the Germans, their responsibility and their culpability for the Armenian massacre, is fundamentally different from that of Aaron Aaronsohn, a Jew, a Zionist, and an inhabitant of Palestine, and different from the perspective of Ambassador Morgenthau, an American Jew.

The Lepsius Report: The Fate of the Jews

Aaronsohn makes use of the 1916 Lepsius report on several occasions in order to bolster his claims that the Turks intend to do to the Jews what they have done to the Armenians. He makes reference to this, as we have seen, in his letter to Victor Jacobson and in his reports to the British which discuss the Armenian massacre and the Lepsius report. In 1919, Lepsius published an expanded version of the 1916 report and included testimony and additional sources, such as his notes of his meeting with Enver Pasha in August 1915.

In the report, which Lepsius himself wrote, the fate of the Jews is mentioned several times, in three different contexts:

1. In Lepsius's opinion, there is no doubt that the massacre of the Armenians was committed by the central government in Constantinople and at its orders. On the other hand, in the German press which had no reliable information, there was frequent repetition of the claim that the massacre of the Armenians "are comparable to the persecution of the Jews in the Middle Ages."[76]
2. In the German press and in Turkey there was frequent reference to the important role of Armenian commerce in the Ottoman Empire. Thus, there was a tendency to view their alleged domination of Turkish commerce as a cause of the hostility toward them. Lepsius rejects these "facts" and says that the only basis for this assertion, which seems so obvious as to need no proof, is an alleged Middle East saying which is applied, depending upon the circumstances, to the Armenians, to the Jews, and to the Lebanese.[77]
3. Lepsius quotes from statements of members of the Young Turks Committee, who often publicly declared that "the foreigners must disappear from Turkey. First the Armenians, then the Greeks, then the Jews, and finally the Europeans." The Moslem is not obliged to prove the guilt of an Armenian, and regarding Christians, one must be rid of them for the good of the country.[78]

Lepsius, the Christian, concerns himself primarily with the fate of the Armenians. He refers to the Jews in various contexts but does not explicitly conclude that the fate of the Jews is liable to be similar to that of the Armenians. At the same time, one may infer such a conclusion from reading the report. Aaron, in any event, did, or at least viewed the report as an important source to strengthen his assessments that the Turks might try to destroy the Jews as well.

At the end of Werfel's chapter on Lepsius's meeting with Enver Pasha, there is a literary reconstruction of his conversation with the second most powerful man in Turkey at the time, the Minister of the Interior, Talât Pasha. Enver tells Talât about his conversation with Lepsius: "Yes, the German. He tried to threaten a bit in the Reichstag." Talât, while he signs the telegrams ordering the destruction of the Armenians in the regions of Aleppo, Alexandretta, Antiocha and the coast, responds, "These Germans are scared only of the stain of complicity."

It is exactly this sensitive point which concerns Aaron. His fundamentally critical attitude and his condemnation of the Germans is unambiguous. In 1916, he blames the Germans for their role in the massacre of the Armenians and charges them with responsibility and complicity in this atrocity.

In contrast, Lepsius, at least in his "secret report," does not attack his government, does not criticize its lack of intervention, does not break Germany's conspiracy of silence (at best) in the massacre. He chooses to act on behalf of the Armenians without fighting against his government's official position which is, at the least, hypocritical. Lepsius prefers to work "through official channels," together with the German government. Aaron surmises that perhaps he even operated, in retrospect, as its agent.

We should remember that contemporary assessments (including that of the American Ambassador in Constantinople, Henry Morgenthau Sr., who was extremely active on behalf of the Armenians) indicated that the only ones who could stop the Turkish massacre of the Armenians were the German authorities. And they did not lift a finger.

Another point to remember is that compared to Lepsius or the Britishers Toynbee and Bryce who were, at the time, composing a "Blue Book" about the Turkish massacre of the Armenians, Aaron Aaronsohn's situation was different. Lepsius, the German, and Bryce and Toynbee, the Englishmen, protested the massacres and did not stay on the sidelines. They are among those few who stand between the murderer and the victim and give aid to the victim. But they themselves and the members of their group are not in jeopardy.

Aaronsohn, who raised a moral protest against the massacre, is not in their position. In his view, he, too, together with his family and people, may become victim of a Turkish massacre—"the next in line." This fear arouses in him existential anxiety and is an additional motive for his action.

Notes

1. And he adds, "Everyone here [in Paris] is amazed at the clarity with which I predicted all of this, during the height of the euphoric days of the Constitution. Someone even asked me if I had given them a plan so they would act precisely as I wished?" Paris, October 14, 1907. Aharon Amir, ed., *Avshalom (Papers and Letters of the Late Avshalom Feinberg* (Haifa: Sikmona, 1977).

2. Avshalom goes on in the letter to deal with the ramifications of the new reality of the Jewish People. The biggest, most fateful question for him is whether the Jewish people will choose the right path. "Enough wanderings, go home children. Enough dancing at other people's weddings. Enough sacrificing our people's children to Moloch and all the other bloodthirsty idolatries. Enough of giving our blood to the European vampire." Because "the people which does not turn its suffering toward the sublime, and its heart to a lofty purpose will never find salvation. It shall die its death with no hope of redemption."

3. *Avshalom*, pp. 364-65.

4. See Eliezer Livneh, *Aaron Aaronsohn: His Life and Times* (Jerusalem: The Bialik Institute, 1979), pp. 209-10. (Henceforth: *Life and Times.*)

5. When Sarah Aaronsohn returned, Avshalom was already deeply involved in an additional attempt to reach Egypt, this time over land. On December 12, 1915, he headed south from Gaza to El-Arish. His attempt was unsuccessful: he was captured, charged with espionage, imprisoned, and finally released through bribery on January 10, 1916. In yet another attempt to reach the British in Egypt, in January 1917, he was killed.

6. *Avshalom*, p. 252. It is possible that he wished to hide his sense of helplessness from the English lieutenant.

7. Ibid., p. 367.

8. Ibid., p. 293. It is worth pointing out that there were those, at that time and afterwards, who thought that it was the Germans who had a moderating influence on the Turks. We will discuss this briefly later.

9. Ibid., pp. 367-68.

10. Ibid., p. 333.

11. The workers' circles in the Yishuv naturally could not praise "British imperialism," due to their socialist worldview. This may be one of the explanations for the pro-Turkish stance of these circles during the war, certainly during its early years.

12. The report to Henrietta Szold (written originally in French) is in the Archives of the Aaronsohn House.

13. Avshalom points out that 750,000 Jews are now fighting on the various fronts: "their blood is spilled anonymously, in order to improve life in Russia or to obtain freedom for the Poles who will use it in order to torture us. Will we agree that the blood of our victims be of no value and that we remain in our wretchedness?"

14. Nili Archives, Aara A.1/5. In a short book that Alexander Aaronsohn wrote in 1942, *Sarah: The Flame of Nili*, the first chapter is entitled, "The Cry of the Armenians," and contains an excerpt from the document written by Alexander in 1915. See Alexander Aaronsohn, *Sarah: The Flame of Nili*, Karni, 1965, pp. 11-12. (Henceforth: *Sarah: Flame of the Nili*.)

15. Eliezer Livneh, Yosef Nedava, Yoram Efrati, eds., *Nili: A History of Political Daring* (Jerusalem and Tel Aviv: Shocken, 1980), p. 244. (Henceforth: *The History of Political Daring*.) This new, revised edition was edited by Yoram Efrati. Aaron Aaronsohn's letter to his brother, Alexander, October 28, 1916, is in the Nili's Archives, Aara. A.1/5.

16. Ibid., pp. 244-45.

17. *Sarah: The Flame of Nile*, pp. 26-27.

18. *A History of Political Daring*, p. 245; *Sarah: The Flame of Nili*, pp. 26-27.

19. Ibid.

20. Alexander Aaronsohn, *With the Turks in Palestine* (Boston and New York: Houghton Mifflin Company, 1916), p. 36. The book is based on articles that appeared previously in the *Atlantic Monthly*. During the same period, additional articles appeared in the magazine on the destruction of the Armenians.

21. Ibid., pp. 41-42.

22. Ibid., p. 85.

23. See *A History of Political Daring*, pp. 95-96.

24. *The Diary of Aaron Aaronsohn*, Aaronsohn House. This period of his diary is not included in his published journals.

25. The above excerpt appears almost in its entirety in *A History of Political Daring*, p. 95. The last sentence, which does not appear there, is of great importance.

26. See *His Life and Times*, pp. 206, 298.

27. See the following sections of the chapter.

28. See Gershon Gera's, *A House In Tel Aviv* (Tel Aviv: Ministry of Defense, 1990) (in Hebrew). Also see the diary itself which is preserved in the Hagana Archives in Tel Aviv.

29. Levi Yitzchak Schneerson had literary ambitions even in his youth and wrote poetry and essays in Russian. His spiritual and linguistic affinity for the Russian culture continued even after he settled in Eretz Yisrael. Like other spiritually minded young people of his day, he also kept a journal. His diary comprises, in effect, a collection of essays and musings, sometimes a dialogue with himself, which were written originally in Russian. Levi Yitzchak Schneerson was born in Russia in 1888. In 1904, he settled in Eretz Yisrael with his father, a wealthy man and one of the first modern Zionists in Russia, on an estate in Hadera. In 1906, Levi Yitzchak returned to Russia in order to continue his studies. During that time, he became involved in anarchist activity and was eventually forced to flee Russia. In 1910, at the age of 22, he returned to Eretz Yisrael. The rest of his family—his mother and sister—arrived a year later.

30. It should be noted that this was precisely one of the (later) methods employed by the members of Nili in their contacts with the British.

31. Lyova Yitzchak Schneerson, *From the Diaries of a Nili Member (Haifa:* Renaissance, 1967, p. 14 (in Hebrew).

32. *Sarah: The Flame of Nili*, pp. 111-15.

33. Ibid., pp. 88, 103.

34. A similar version is found in Yehuda Yaari-Polskin's work, *The Nili* (vol. 4: Sarah) (Tel Aviv: Masada, 1940), pp. 142-43. "I alone did the job and dug their grave. The grave is already open for them. Tomorrow the day of redemption will come. Certainly it will come. And you shall fall into the pit I have dug for you. And why have I done it? Because I saw with my own eyes how you spilled the blood of the Armenians, with my own eyes I saw how you rounded up the wretched and the defenseless into a camp between the railroad tracks, and sent the trains to run them over!—Trample, trample my flesh!"

35. According to *A History of Political Daring* (1980), p. 309, in the chapter entitled "The Sacrifice [of Isaac]." In the earlier edition of the book (1961), p. 273, it is stated that Sarah's words during her torture were recorded by various people who heard her, and they are preserved in the Aaronsohn House Archives. To the best of our knowledge, there is no detailed testimony of this.

36. See Moshe Neiman, *From Petach Tikva to the Valley of Gloom, Memoirs of a Man of Nili*, Jerusalem, 1964, pp. 55-56. Also see the testimony of Divsha Erlich, *A History of Political Daring*, pp. 345-49.

37. See Eitan Belkind, *So It Was* (Tel Aviv: Ministry of Defense Publishers, 1977), pp. 115-25 (in Hebrew). (Henceforth: *So It Was.*)

38. The report which Belkind mentions has not been found.

39. See the previous note.

40. Also in an appendix of the book, *Nili: A History of Political Daring*, which contains short biographical sketches of the members of Nili, it is stated that Belkind "sent a detailed report about the slaughter of the Armenians which was passed on to Egypt." See *A History of Political Daring*, p. 442.

41. *So It Was*, pp. 77-79.

42. Eliezer Livneh writes that "Sarah was consumed by horror and anger by the events of the Armenian Holocaust. The reports about it reached Palestine even before this. Aaron Aaronsohn relied upon them in the reports he sent abroad, and they were part of his political considerations. But hearsay is not the same as seeing." *His Life and Times*, p. 206.

43. Major Pur, a German officer who was commander of a camp of 800 soldiers of the engineering corps, of whom it is said, writes Aaron in his diary, "that his actions will not be pleasant for the enemy, let him come and fear." Aaron adds, "This Major Pur is a terrible fellow. On November 3 last, he had executed, in a ritual attended by all of his men, two deserters, so that they 'may see and be in dread.'"

44. *Aaronsohn Diaries*, January 12, 1916, p. 27.

45. Ibid., p. 29, January 13, 1916.

46. *Sarah: The Flame of Nili*, pp. 38-39.

47. *Aaronsohn Diaries*, July 15-22, 1916, pp. 51-69. In his diary, Aaron describes his trip from Beirut to Damascus on July 13, including a description of terrible sights of hunger and want, and "entire families along the roads searching for something to chew."

48. *A History of Political Daring*, Appendices, p. 425.

49. Ibid., pp. 431-32.

50. Ibid., pp. 433-34.

51. The reference here is apparently related to the internal German colonization in Poznan, which was undertaken in order to block the Polish advance.

52. We cannot know what Aaron meant by this sentence. The explanation that Aaronsohn viewed this as alleged official proof of the active participation of the Germans in the massacre of the Armenians has no basis.

53. Nili Archives, container 18, file 2316.

54. Richard Lichtheim, *Shaar Hayishuv* (Jerusalem: The Zionist Library, 1954), p. 374.

55. Ibid., p. 321. Lichtheim recalls that the Zionist delegation in Constantinople was given permission by the German government, after negotiation, to use its telegraphic code and its diplomatic courier services.

56. Kühlmann served in the German Embassy in Constantinople as senior attache. In early 1915, he was appointed Legate in the Hague. At the end of 1916, he was appointed Ambassador in Constantinople. In August 1917, he became Secretary of State in the Foreign Ministry. He hoped to bring peace in the form of a treaty between Germany and its adversaries, but "his wish was shattered by the opposition of the military, and in 1918 he was removed from his office." Lichtheim, *Shaar Hayishuv*, p. 412, and pp. 374, 376.

57. Aaronsohn sees positively the fact that Turkey treated the Jews fairly and that the 400 years of life together with them passed without a single massacre. However, he points out, "We have chewed our cud enough over this issue. Moreover, the Jewish intellect was killed by Turkey: the Turks managed to kill everything that was noble in the Jews: the racial aristocracy, the intellectual aristocracy, the financial aristocracy: the Abarbanels, the Ibn-Ezras, the Nakoses, etc."

58. *Aaronsohn Diaries*, p. 125. See also the description of his depressed mood prior to his departure from London on November 24, 1916, and his (subjective) sense of failure. Ibid., pp. 135-36.

59. Aaron writes in his diary, "A short superficial article which does not satisfy me at all, but I have great hope that it may serve as an opening in the matter." Ibid., p. 121.

60. Ibid., p. 126. It should be emphasized that the report had an important analytical dimension and raised piercing, substantive questions that must preoccupy anyone who is concerned with genocide.

61. *Aaronsohn Diaries*, p. 132, and *His Life and Times*, p. 223.

62. See *Aaronsohn Diaries*, November 17, 1916, and footnotes, pp. 130-31.

63. Document 242528, December 1, in file 221220, collection F.O. 3712783. The same report appears again as document 253852, F.O. 3712781.
64. F.O. 3712783, 221220. It seems that it is to this document which Aaron refers in his diary on November 21, 1916: "At 5 to Gribbon, and he reads me the report which he wrote based on my testimony and notes. He has gathered it all very well into 21 pages."
65. In document F.O. 371/2783, 236593, which is an intelligence assessment by the head of the military intelligence service, the W.T.I.D., to the Deputy Foreign Minister (November 23, 1916) about "the report of an inhabitant of Atlit" and its author, there is detailed treatment of Aaron's personality and character traits, his sources of information, and to the report he wrote. Aaron Aaronsohn is respected because he was "very fairly correct in his estimates and information and if anything, he appears to err in understating rather than in exaggerating matters." Later on, "The report itself as a whole may be taken as very correct." It is noteworthy that at this stage the British still did not entirely trust Aaron and his motives. In summing up his evaluation, the head of Intelligence writes that the informant [Aaron] speaks well and freely, and he is very correct in his assessments. But "of course we do not know the object of his visit to this country but he might be just as observant of things here as he has been in Turkey and a purveyor of information of the conditions in England, if he could get back to Turkey." In other words, the British are still suspicious of Aaron Aaronsohn. The report is nine pages in length.
66. Addendum to "Report of an inhabitant of Atlit, Mount Carmel, Syria."
67. Ibid.
68. In a comment on the report, F.O. 371/2783, 221220, November 3, 1916, the head of military intelligence points out to the Foreign Secretary: The informant belongs to a special Zionist group. The Zionists may be classified into three differing streams: (1) The Zionists who wish to promote the unification between all the Jews in the world, and by joint effort to improve their situation in those countries where they still operate under negation of their rights; (2) The Zionists who view religion as more important than nationalism and wish to acquire the holy sites and to resettle the Jewish People in Palestine, as an independent sovereign state; (3) The Zionists who consider nationalism more important than religion and, at this time, limit themselves to efforts to obtain freedom to settle in Palestine. The informant belongs to the last category.
In other comments regarding Aaronsohn, he is presented as "a keen supporter of Zionism" and as "very exact in his words." (*Aaronsohn Diaries*, pp. 130-31). Harold Nicholson entered his comment: We can scarcely publish this but it confirms or extends the propaganda material which we have already amassed." Sir Lancelot Oliphant writes, "Horrifying report"; Sir Ronald Graham and Lord Reading confirm by their signatures. S.G. passes the report to Lord Bryce: "He might possibly like to see the paper, if he should be thinking of any supplement to the full White Paper on the Armenian atrocities." Lord Cecil also receives the document and confirms its receipt. The report was also given to Mark Sykes.

69. F.O. 371,2783, 236593.
70. See *Aaronsohn Diaries,* pp. 128-29 (footnotes), and *A History of Political Daring,* p. 118 (footnote 7).
71. Franz Werfel, *The Forty Days of Musa Dagh* (New York: The Modern Library, 1934), pp. 123-51. Although the description is literary, it doubtless expresses the spirit of the events. Lepsius included the minutes of his meeting with Enver Pasha in August 1915, in an expanded 1919 edition of the report that was published in 1916.
72. Ibid., pp. 124-25.
73. See F.O. 3712783, 21220. The report of the British War Office was distributed to a small number of people in the War and Foreign Offices.
74. "Massacres of Jews and Christians were to Follow."
75. Johannes Lepsius, *Bericht uber die Lage des Armenischem Volkes in der Turkei Tempelverlag*, Potsdam, 1916.
76. The Lepsius Report, p. 177, the French edition: Johannes Lepsius, *Rapport secret sur les massacres d'Armenie (1915-1916)* (Paris: Payot, 1987), p. 177. This edition is based on a microfilm of the first French edition, which was published by the same publisher in 1918.
77. Ibid., pp. 272-75.
78. Ibid., pp. 256-57.

Mt. Ararat under Turkish control is the symbol of Armenia.

Child survivors of the uprising in Musa-Dagh in transit to Egypt.

Horrific scenes from the massacre.

Sarah Aaronsohn (1890-1917), member
of Nili, eyewitness to Turkish actions
against the Armenians.

Aaron Aaronsohn (1876-1919), agricultural scientist and member of the Nili
group.

Itamar Ben Avi (1882-1943), editor of
Hatzvi and author of the controversial
article, "We."

Avshalom Feinberg (1889-1917),
member of Nili.

Mark Sykes, initiator of the Jewish-Arab-Armenian alliance.

Franz Werfel, author of *The Forty Days of the Musa Dagh.*

Henry Morgenthau, U.S. ambassador to Constantinople (1913-1916) who gave considerable support to the Armenians.

Photographs of Armenian refugees taken by Armin Wegner, Red Cross worker and medical corps officer in the German Army during World War I. He was decorated as a Righteous Gentile by Yad Vashem for his struggle against the Nazi regime.

Pro Armenia

To sit down in peaceful London and write about the Armenian massacres is a very hard task; no man unless he be a Kipling or a Masefield should try it. The massacres were carried out on such a wholesale scale, with such refinements of atrocity and carried on for such a length of time in such a systematical way — the only work in which the Turks seem to be able to be systematical, that no matter how much one tries to chastise ones style, no matter how moderate one tries to be one is still liable to be considered as indulging in exaggerations.

The writer has not been in Armenia proper and has not seen, therefore, the worst acts of atrocity. But what he has seen, actually seen in Syria, in Konia and in Constantinople, what he learned from the agents he had sent out to parts of the Turkish Empire where the massacres were carried out on large scale enough to fill volumes and make the hair stand on edge.

The writer is trying here to bring to paper, in a very incomplete way some of the things he has seen or learned from the most trustworthy persons, just to serve as illustrations of what was going on in the outskirts of the area of the massacres.

Several Germans established as farmers in Palestine and who were either on military duty in Germany or for contracting enterprises in and around Constantinople, returned home, i.e. to Haifa during the months of Nov. — Dec. 1915. The writer made it his business to travel frequently on the railroad line between Damascus and Tiberias in order to get in touch with those Germans whom he personally knew, and through them with the other Germans travelling on the line and he had in this way first hand reports of what these Germans have actually seen on their way. All reports concorded to say that thousands of human

Armenians demonstrate in Jerusalem (April 24) in memory of the Armenian genocide.

5

A Jewish-Arab-Armenian Alliance

Aaron Aaronsohn and Mark Sykes, 1917-1919

On November 24, 1916, after a month's stay in London, Aaronsohn left England on his way to Alexandria, and from there to Cairo. He remained in Egypt until September 11, 1917. He would return to London on October 1, 1917, during the tense, frenetic days preceding the Balfour Declaration, more than ten months after he had set out on his journey.

Aaron left London with a heavy heart: "Despite my serenity, my nerves are too strained." He regrets the waste of four precious months in Constantinople, Berlin, Copenhagen, and now London. "And what, in fact, have I accomplished? Nothing. I must recognize and admit that from a diplomatic perspective it has been an utter failure. I did not realize in time that Sykes is all-powerful, or he is, together with Fitzmaurice."[1] He writes again about his gloomy mood on November 24:

> If I had gone off on a private hunt of my own, I would have sent them to the devil. But this issue is not about us, our wishes, or ourselves. This is a matter of a mission and one must rid oneself of pessimism and begin everything all over again....Indeed, I could have met in London with Sokolow's group, etc., but I preferred to remain in full shade and *incognito*.

And later on the same day, he said: "Would at least that our people remain alive and free."

Aaron was correct in his estimate of Sykes' importance and centrality in advancing the Zionist cause, but tended, so it seems, to underestimate the importance of his own actions during his month in London. During that month he made a vivid impression on Sykes and others, thus opening a door in the London War Office to Zionist representatives.[2] Sykes maintained a close friendship with Aaron when the latter was in Egypt during 1917, and afterwards, when Aaron was in London at the end of 1917. In fact, their friendship continued until Sykes' death at the time of the Paris peace talks, on February 16, 1919, three months before Aaron was killed. Aaron writes in his diary on the day of Sykes' death:

> Malcolm brings us sad news. Mark Sykes is dead. He was in bed for two days with influenza; just now, he has expired at about 5 o'clock. A great loss! In Chaim's [Weizmann] company, we go to the Lotey Hotel to visit the remains of our friend. Wilson is prostrated with weeping. Lady Sykes receives us and thanks us. It is a terrible situation for this unfortunate woman, alone, in a hotel room, without relations or friends.[3]

It is symbolic that Aaron is informed of Sykes' death by Malcolm, the Armenian representative in London. For the Zionists and the Armenians, Sykes' death was truly a great loss. With his passing they had lost the most important pillar of the cooperation between the English, the Zionists, and the Armenians, which worked to create an Arab-Jewish-Armenian alliance under British auspices.

Sykes played a central role in shaping the British government's Middle East policy during the First World War. It later became known that he had played a key role during 1917 in the steps that led to the Balfour Declaration. He was a close friend of the Zionists (and of the Arabs), greatly admired Weizmann and Aaronsohn, and tried to reconcile between Aaronsohn and the official Zionist leadership in London. Sykes was lost to the Zionists after the Balfour Declaration had already been made and after England had conquered Palestine. The Armenians, on the other hand, were left after Sykes' death with no tangible achievement.

The idea of a Jewish-Arab-Armenian alliance under British auspices had little chance for success from its inception. The third—Arab—leg of the triangle was unsympathetic to the idea and even opposed it, as we shall see below. The death of Sykes, the prominent British figure that pushed for the alliance, ended any chance of its realization.

Underlying the idea of the alliance were British strategic political considerations regarding Britain's postwar status. Nonetheless, moral ideals and principles also played an important part in the concept. Original, strategic, political thinking, suffused with sensitivity and moral values, was characteristic of both Aaron and Sykes. Both were intellectuals in the deepest sense of the word, with broad, creative vision.

Because of a combination of realistic and ideological considerations, Aaron Aaronsohn supported Britain enthusiastically. He was chary of the Turks and Germans and attached great importance to an agreement with the Arabs. Because of political and moral considerations he also supported the Armenians. Sykes, because of strategic political reasons and moral principles, greatly feared a victorious German-Turkish alliance and supported the Arabs, the Zionists, and the Armenians. In the early stages of the war, both men already believed that the battle and victory over Turkey must be waged northward from Egypt and Palestine. This, they believed, would create a better chance for quick and easy victory than an attack from the north.

As mentioned, Aaronsohn had been troubled for quite some time by the "Armenian experience," and from the possibility of its recurrence vis-à-vis the Jews. In November, 1916, he delivered his memoranda, including those dealing with the Armenian massacre, to the British. The memoranda reached Sykes, among others. Aaronsohn and Sykes were in agreement about the "Armenian problem" and its solution. Both men supported postwar Armenian sovereignty. Furthermore, both believed that the future balance of power in the Middle East needed to be based on an Arab-Jewish-Armenian alliance.

In his comprehensive and important biography, *Aaron Aaronsohn, The Man and His Times,* Eliezer Livneh claims that Aaronsohn's support for the establishment of an Armenian state in eastern Asia Minor "was strengthened by the Armenian holocaust in the years 1914-17, but the motivating impulse was political."[4] In a different article, "In the Shadow of the Armenian Holocaust," Livneh argues that Aaronsohn "saw a Zionist need for the establishment of an Armenian state."[5] In Livneh's opinion, "Aaronsohn was interested in a local political factor, an intermediary between the Jews and the Arabs, especially when the two peoples would attain their independence. He viewed the Armenians as this factor. As early as November 1916, he planted his idea in Sykes' heart."[6]

We have no evidence that it was Aaronsohn who influenced Sykes. It is not clear at what point exactly Aaron began to support the idea of an alliance, and whether it was not, in fact, Sykes who influenced him or, indeed, whether the influence was mutual. In any case, in 1917, Sykes and Aaronsohn together enthusiastically supported the idea of a Jewish-Arab-Armenian alliance. It should be remembered that by the end of 1916, at the latest, Sykes had established close contact with Malcolm and other Armenians. Sykes already displayed active interest in the Armenian question by the spring of 1916.[7] At the beginning of 1917, he engaged in dialogue with Malcolm about the creation of an Armenian national state. According to his plan, Russia was to be the shield of defense for a united Armenia.[8]

James Malcolm was the son of a well-known Armenian family that had settled many years before in Persia. Educated in England, he became a British subject, and after leaving Oxford entered business in the City of London. He was chosen to be one of the members of the Armenian National Delegation which was created in early 1912 under the auspices of the Armenian Catholicos. Inasmuch as the seat of the delegation, headed by Nubar Pasha, was in Paris, Malcolm became its senior representative in London. Malcolm was active in a number of spheres, had extensive personal contacts and a wide circle of acquaintances. He had close relations with Sykes and with Weizmann and Sokolow. The relations between Malcolm and Aaronsohn were, it seems, very close. In 1917, both Sykes and Aaronsohn supported the idea of an alliance. Aaron was more outspoken about the idea than any other Zionist leader of the period. Weizmann and Sokolow, who were also working with the British at the time, tended toward the idea, but probably did so because Sykes pushed them to it. They also recognized Sykes' importance to the Zionist cause during 1917.

When Sykes came to Egypt as head of the British political delegation in April 1917, he and Aaronsohn met frequently. On April 27, 1917, they had a meeting in Cairo. Aaron writes in his diary, "9:15 with Sir Mark Sykes. Finally! We turn at once to the intimate issues. He promises me that in speaking to me as a Jewish patriot he will reveal very secret matters, some of which are not known even to the Foreign Office."[9]

Sykes tells him that after Aaron's departure from London he had turned to Dr. Gaster (Gaster was an important Zionist activist, but had no official authority to speak in the name of the Zionist Movement. From 1887 he held the position of "Hacham," the Chief Rabbi of Sephardic Jewry in England). After learning of Gaster's true status, or according to Aaron, after Sykes "realized the fact that Gaster exaggerates his own value, and that his selfishness destroys him," Sykes turned to Weizmann and Sokolow through the Armenian, Malcolm. He liked the two."[10]

Sykes and Aaronsohn were discussing the idea of an alliance at the time and it appears from Aaron's diary that it was acceptable to both of them. Sykes relates to the events of the war and is frustrated by the lack of British progress in conquering Palestine and the slow advance of British forces from Gaza to Palestine. A decision must be made, he says, "either we move forward in force with the sacrifices necessary, or we continue this game of I shove you and you shove me, in which case we should immediately cut off all discussion with the Arabs, the Zionists, etc."

Sykes fears political activity—contact with the Arabs and the Jews—if it is not accompanied by military progress. British political activity without military progress may, in his opinion, expose the Arabs and the Zionists to grave harm by the Turks, on the pretext of contact with the enemy and treason. He raises another problem: "The Russian problem. If Kerensky is triumphant and Russia gives up Constantinople, this means that the Armenians, the Arabs, the Jews, etc., will remain under the Turkish boot. It is necessary, therefore, that precisely from here come the call to Kerensky and his party, praising and congratulating them for their battle, not for territory, but for the liberation of other oppressed peoples: Armenians, Jews, Arabs, etc."[11]

They met again the next day, Saturday, April 28, to discuss several matters. Sykes told Aaronsohn, according to Aaronsohn's diary for that date, that he and Picot were working on the fundamentals of an agreement. He also related, with regard to our subject, that "he explained to Arab leaders that if they arouse the silent enmity of the Jews, then even France, England, and Germany together will not be able to overcome it. By its passive power alone, such enmity is capable of preventing Arab independence, which in his eyes represents important potential power." According to Sykes, writes Aaronsohn, the Arab leaders chose to ensure the support of the Jews and of England and "they believe that it is preferable not to antagonize the Jews. Sir Mark believes that by uniting the interests of the Armenians, the Jews and the Arabs, it will be possible to create something of enormity in the East, something like a Buffer State, etc."

Sykes' archives reveal additional bases for his views and activities regarding the Armenians, the Jews, and a connection between them. A fear that the Turks would not be satisfied with the massacre of the Armenians and would harm additional minorities under their rule, arose several times in the course of the First World War among the Jews and, as we shall see below, was discussed in the British Cabinet. Ambassador Henry Morgenthau, Sr., also expressed a fear—as early as April 1915—that the actions against the Armenians would later be directed against the Zionists.

In a meeting of the British Cabinet on December 16, 1915, Sykes expressed his concern that the Christians in Syria would be exterminated like the Armenians. Sykes added,

> I am sure it is a mistake to imagine that hitting Turks urges them to kill Christians. It is going away that produces the massacres. They did not touch the Armenians until the Russians were fairly back in the Caucasus: and I can give a reason for this. Massacres are generally carried out by notables and mobs, and if the notables and the mobs think that there is any prospect of Christian soldiers appearing within three or four months, while there is still evidence of their crime, they hesitate to commit it for fear of retaliation.[12]

At this point, the concern is for the Christians in Syria. Later on it would extend to the Jews in Palestine. We do not know if Sykes was aware of Aaron's concerns at the end of 1916. It appears that he read only the edited version of Aaron's report, which did not include the passages relating to Aaron's fear of the extermination of the Jews in Palestine. They may, however, have discussed it between them.

In April 1917, we find ourselves at the height of preparations for the Balfour Declaration, and in the advanced stages of the war. We have the protocol of another meeting in the office of the British Prime Minister, Lloyd George, on April 3, 1917. The discussion relates to the instructions to be given to Sir Mark Sykes, head of the political delegation to the British Army Command in Egypt, on the eve of Sykes' departure for Egypt (and prior to his meeting with Aaron in Egypt cited above).[13] The discussion deals with developments in the Middle East, including preparations for the British conquest of Palestine and decisions regarding the termination of the war. It should be remembered that the discussion was held after the signing of the Sykes-Picot Agreement between the British and the French in May 1916. That agreement was not yet known to the Zionist leadership which was in contact with Sykes.

At the meeting, the Prime Minister suggested that "the Jews might be able to render us more assistance than the Arabs." In his opinion it was important not to prejudice the Zionist movement and the possibility of its development under British auspices.

Sykes, while agreeing that every possible assistance should be obtained from the Jews, said that it was important not to stir up any movement behind the Turkish lines which might lead to a Turkish massacre of the Jews.[14] In his opinion, the Arabs probably realized that there was no prospect of their being allowed any control over Palestine. The Jews, although originally pro-Turkish, were tending, he thought, to become much less anti-Arab. There was, he felt, in fact a distinct rapprochement. It may be that Sykes based his comments on his conversations with Aaronsohn, and with Weizmann and Sokolow (who were pro-British and sought compromise and agreement with the Arabs). Lord Curzon remarked at the meeting that when he visited Palestine the Jews were a minority in that country. Sykes, in response, pointed out that since then a number of Jewish colonies had been established in Palestine.

In a telegram that Sykes sent from Egypt to London on April 24, 1917, he analyses the military options available to the armed forces.[15] In his estimation, they must choose between two alternatives:

Alternative A: the Egyptian force may find itself not strong enough to gain more than local successes in its immediate front.

Alternative B: the Egyptian force may be reinforced sufficiently to enable it to continue its advance. In event of Alternative A being followed it will be necessary to drop all Zionist projects and all schemes involving negotiation with settled rural and urban Arab elements in Syria, whether Christian or Muslim. Any other policy will expose our adherents to greater rigours of oppression than heretofore and will make us morally responsible for the increase of their misery. Zionists in London and U.S.A. should be warned of this through N. Sokolow. The Press should be warned that Zionist newspaper articles can only endanger lives and property of Palestinian Jews.

Sykes, whose support for a British military advance north toward Palestine was unambiguous, adds,

However, though we may drop Zionism and rural and urban Arab movement this will be no guarantee that the Turks will not take advantage of a stationary attitude on our part [i.e., Alternative A] to treat both settled Arabs and Jews as they treated the Armenians, viz., destruction by systematic deportation and starvation, and it is to be noted that matters have now gone so far that we shall in any case have to endure the enmity of having caused these misfortunes to befall these people by encouraging Zionism in London and Paris and fostering the Arab and Syrian movement.

Sykes adds that political action which is not based on parallel military action can only exacerbate the situation which is bad in any case.

On the other hand, Sykes believed that if Alternative B was adopted the current policy could be continued, namely the exploitation of all the friendly connections of the allies with the Christians, the Jews, and the Muslims in every place where they existed.

Sykes and Aaron worked together in cooperation and trust, and what Sykes said to his British colleagues in London was what he said to Aaron as well. The two were in agreement about the danger to the Jews of Palestine, and about the necessity of a quick British military advance. The concern for the fate of the Jews in Palestine became extreme with the deportations from Tel Aviv in April 1917. We remember that Aaronsohn worked, with the aid and support of Sykes, to limit the damage caused by this grave incident, by arousing world public opinion.

The Second Half of 1917—Towards the Balfour Declaration

In the latter half of 1917, the situation at the war front tended to favor the Entente Powers. On questions regarding a postwar world order, Sykes voiced innovative opinions and approaches which matched the spirit of the era. At the same time he struggled against other more conservative trends in British foreign policy, which were represented mostly by Lord Curzon. Sykes attached great importance to an agreement, although it would involve concessions, between the Entente Powers, particularly between England and France, with regard to the postwar period: "I have tried to work on war lines and not prewar lines viz: Nationality, Cooperation, and Alliance, instead of imperialism, isolated action and special individual war aims."[16] Sykes described himself, according to Aaron, saying, "I'm a Tory, a progressive Tory, I hope."

When the possibility arises, in May 1917, of a separate peace with Turkey, Sykes opposes it. His opposition clarifies his principles: "[I]t would seem imperative to consult not only France, Italy and America, but also the King of the Hejaz, representative Armenians and Nationalist [i.e., Zionist] Jews, to whom we and the other Entente Powers have obligations and whose fate is bound up with the principle of nationality, the antidote to Prussian military domination." Later in the same memorandum, Sykes warns that Turkey's past record in granting autonomy is discouraging. In 1895, Turkey pledged itself to grant autonomy to Macedonia and Armenia, and despite pressure refused to carry out its commitment. "Both areas became charnel houses with periodic disorders, revolts, massacres, leading up to the Balkan war and the present world conflict.... Were we now to back the Turk against the Arab, Armenian, Nationalist Jews, Bulgarians (Gumurgin), and Greece (Mitylene and Lemnos) we should undoubtedly be putting our money on the wrong horse and sowing the seed of bloodshed for future generations."[17]

Both Sykes and Aaronsohn sincerely viewed the liberation of oppressed peoples as one of the aims of the war. With respect to some of the leadership of the Entente Powers, it would later become clear that these were baseless declarations and certainly not goals or aims.

On August 14, 1917, Sykes presented the British War Cabinet with a memorandum entitled, "Memorandum on the Asia-Minor Agreement."[18] The paper discusses the guidelines of an agreement between England and France regarding the territories of the Ottoman Empire after the war. Sykes emphasizes the necessity for Jewish-Arab-Armenian cooperation. He tries to convince the Cabinet to support this approach even if France displays reservations or opposition, inasmuch as such policy represents the real interest of both countries. He points out: "When the [Sykes-Picot] agreement was originally drawn up I think it was then in consonance with the spirit of the time that certain concessions were made to the idea of nationality and autonomy, but an avenue was left open to annexation. The idea of annexation really must be dismissed, it is contrary to the spirit of the time." Sykes goes on to say that England and France will find it difficult to confront Turkey and Germany in a struggle over the future of the region if they adhere to the outdated imperialistic agreements which oppose the idea of nationalism. Both Sykes and Aaronsohn fear the German-Turkish alliance. Sykes ends his memorandum saying, "I want to see a permanent Anglo-French Entente allied to the Jews, Arabs and Armenians which will render pan-islamism innocuous and protect India and Africa from the Turco-German combine, which I believe may well survive the Hohenzollerns."[19]

In his opinion, if France rejects the direction of the proposed policy as a joint policy of the two countries, then England must make clear that she will work toward this direction alone. England must state, among other things, "That we cannot prevent the Zionists, Armenians, and Arabs being hostile to the idea of annexation and that if a European Conference is held the French cannot expect us to support them in a policy which we do not pursue ourselves....That we know that the Armenians and Jews will begin a vigorous agitation in America which will be supported by the Arabs." It is clear to him "that it is certainly our duty to get these people righted, and that it will be in our interest to get them righted on lines compatible with our economic and political interests."

Sykes proposes pro-Zionist, pro-Arab, and pro-Armenian solutions which are not mutually exclusive but rather complementary, and are compatible with the political, economic and strategic interests of England and France.[20]

It should be remembered that the presumption, that Britain would more easily obtain Palestine if it were perceived as a nation which had supported a solution of the Jewish question in the spirit of Zionism, was reinforced in 1917 when both Russia, after the October Revolution, and the United States, under the leadership of Woodrow Wilson, took a position opposing territorial annexations (i.e., imperialism) and supporting the right of national self-determination.

During the course of 1917, Weizmann and Sokolow cooperated with the Armenians (see below) to encourage Sykes in his tireless efforts for a Jewish-Arab-Armenian alliance prior to the Balfour Declaration, and after it, publicly.

Sykes saw great advantages in such an alliance. He was very apprehensive of conflict between Jews and Arabs and thought that an independent Armenia could help to mitigate it. Speaking at a rally in Manchester in early December in support of the Balfour Declaration, Sykes said that it was essential for the implementation of the plan that it be based on a Jewish-Arab-Armenian alliance. Armenian independence was vital to the success of a Jewish Palestine. The Jews of Palestine needed a stable and progressive Armenian state which would stand between them and any potential aggressor.[21] Sykes points out that the Arabs, despite their primitive situation at the time, would become a major factor in the East due to their past, their natural increase, their unifying language, their fertile countries, and their petroleum. He asks the Jews to see matters through Arab eyes, to understand Arab fears of Jewish domination. In the Jewish-Arab context, the Armenians may serve as a buffer state, just as a Jewish-Arab-Armenian alliance tied to England and France may, in Sykes' opinion, serve as a buffer between the Germans and Turks and Africa and Asia. Sykes ends with a note of caution, a sort of prophecy for the future: "Good will and co-operation are necessary from the outset in order to save both Jews and Arabs from a final disaster....Hostility between the two peoples will bring such terrible tragedy that it is obligatory to sound a warning."

Aaron Aaronsohn wholeheartedly supported the establishment of an Armenian state in Asia Minor, both for moral reasons and because he thought that the Armenians, as a local political factor, could serve as an intermediary between the Jews and the Arabs, particularly when the latter obtained independence.

Aaron remained in Egypt and worked for the British until September 13, 1917, when he left Port Said on his way to London. When his ship docked in Malta he met, by chance, with his brother, Alexander, who was on his way to Egypt to take Aaron's place. Aaron's diary is silent from September 11 to November 16, but we know that he spent ten days in Paris (September 21-30), where he met with Baron Edmond de Rothschild, Wermser, Meyerson, Sir Mark Sykes, and others.

He remained in London from October 1 until November 15, conducting discussions with the British War Office and the Foreign Office, and meeting with Sir Ronald Graham and Sir Mark Sykes, among others. This time, unlike his previous visit to London at the end of 1916, he did not keep his presence secret from the Zionist leaders and met with Weizmann, Sokolow, Jabotinsky, and others.

Eliezer Livneh argues that Aaron made contact with Armenian leaders in London and Paris—James Malcolm, Boghos Nubar Pasha, and Ahronian—by the end of 1916.[22] We have no evidence that he indeed met with Armenian leaders at that time. The entries in his diary during that period are sketchy, as mentioned. Yet the possibility that Aaronsohn met with them seems most reasonable. When notes of meetings with Armenian leaders appear later in his diary, it seems from the wording and the description of relations between them that these are not the first meetings between them. As noted, there had been contact between Weizmann and Sokolow and Sykes from January 1917, and the person who introduced them was none other than the Armenian representative in London, James Malcolm. Through him they met with additional Armenian leaders.

This was a period of intense activity before and after the Balfour Declaration. We shall examine the Jewish-Arab-Armenian connection and the political contacts of Weizmann and Sokolow with the Armenian leadership in the next section. Here we will discuss only those contacts in which Aaron Aaronsohn was involved. The British and the Zionists held discussions "about the best ways to gain maximum political benefit from the new situation which has been created by the declaration of support by His Majesty's Government for Jewish aspirations in Palestine." Aaron took an active part in discussions, alongside Weizmann and Sokolow who were the official Zionist leaders in England. Sykes participated in some of the discussions and was familiar with all of the details. The plan was for Sokolow, Chlenov, and Jabotinsky (additional Zionist leaders) to go immediately to Russia to enlist public opinion. "Mr. Aaronsohn has gone to America where his expertise on the situation in Palestine will be of valuable benefit."[23]

Not all of the Zionist leaders in London were enthusiastic about the "alien" Aaronsohn and his mission to America. Sykes persuaded Aaron to make the trip and he appears to have convinced Weizmann to support it. Aaron enjoyed Weizmann's respect and sympathy, due to his close relations with the British and with Sykes in particular. Aaron also had greater esteem for Weizmann than for the other members of the official Zionist leadership in London.

On Friday, November 16, 1917, Aaron resumed writing in his diary:

> After a conversation with the territorialist, Zangwill ("a genius, a very sharp fellow but incurably lazy who gives the impression of someone who will become an old loafer"), I rush to Sykes. He is occupied with the Arab officers he is sending to Egypt. I ask him, do you want me to go to Eretz Yisrael or do you still insist that I go to America? To America. Do you want me to leave tomorrow or in eight days' time? Tomorrow. Well then, all right. The preparations begin.

Aaron met twice more with Sykes that day, and twice with Weizmann. Members of the Zionist group in London tried to limit the scope of Aaronsohn's activity in the United States. Aaron relates, "I amuse myself by opening Weizmann and Sokolow's letter ["the letter of instructions," he terms it, "the guidelines," according to Tolkowsky's *A Political Diary*], and discover that the section in which it says that it is 'desirable to refrain from speeches and interviews' has been inserted into the body of the letter, despite Weizmann's promise to me that he would order it to be removed." Aaronsohn is angry at Weizmann's lack of candor: "This saddens me. I tell Sykes of my anger. Sykes writes a draft of a telegram from Balfour to the English legation in Washington in which he says that they are now reaping the fruit of my efforts on the Palestinian front, etc. We part as friends."[24]

Weizmann was worried about Sokolow and Chlenov's opposition to Aaronsohn's mission: "I anticipate problems in the Political Committee because their opinion has not been asked. Ahad Haam is very upset about this."[25]

Aaronsohn's tasks were to influence public opinion in favor of the Entente Powers, to strengthen Zionist efforts in the United States, to maintain ongoing contact between the Zionist Organizations in England and the United States, to work toward cooperation with Armenian and Syrian organizations. These draft guidelines were apparently written by Sykes himself.

Aaron left London on November 17 and reached New York on December 1, 1917. While en route, the Nili Affair exploded and upon his arrival in New York he received the news of his sister Sarah's death in a telegram from his brother Shmuel, six weeks after the tragic event had occurred. He writes in his diary: "The complete sacrifice! I knew that the worst of tragedies might befall us. But there is no fear to compare to the arrival of the evil decree, to the certainty that it has come and there can no longer be any hope. Poor father, my poor Sarah. Her loss is without doubt the most brutal blow."[26] Discovery of the Nili spy ring rekindled, we remember, the fear of a recurrence of the Armenian experience, both among the British and the Jews in Palestine.

After consultations in the War Office and the Foreign Office, the British decided to release a report to Reuters saying that Germans and Turks were brutalizing the Jews in Palestine. Jamal Pasha had stated that he would turn the country into a second Armenia. In one newspaper, the item appeared under the headline: "Horrifying Brutalities — Germans and Turks Creating a Second Armenia."[27]

Aaron remained in the U.S. until January 31, 1918. In March, he was in Europe, and from there went to Egypt and afterwards to Palestine (arriving in Tel Aviv on April 5, 1918). Shortly thereafter he returned to London and Paris, and in September went back to the United States. He was back in London on November 19, 1918. His diary for those months is sketchy. We do not know if he had any contact during that period with the Armenians in London and Paris.

From the beginning of November, 1918, the contact between Aaronsohn and the Armenians became intensive and close. These were the days prior to the peace conference and the fate of the Armenians hung in the balance. Aaron's diary reveals details about the chain of affairs which led to the French and English abandonment of the Armenians. The Americans also made little effort to help the Armenians.

It is not clear whether Aaron's efforts to aid and advise the Armenians were his decision alone. The Armenians' attitude toward him was one of trust and intimacy. There is no doubt that the British and the

Zionists knew of his activity and while it appears that the Zionist leaders, Weizmann and Sokolow, supported it, it is unclear whether he operated at their behest.[28] Aaron's position in the Zionist delegation was exceptional; he had both admirers and not a few opponents and enemies. It appears to be Aaron Aaronsohn who drew up the map which the Zionist delegation presented at the Paris Peace Conference, and he had great influence over Weizmann. They were in agreement about the Arab question and supported efforts at reconciliation. But Aaron could not get along with the establishment, "the machine"— the power fights, the status, and the pettiness. He was less than discrete in his unflattering description of Sokolow, nor did he believe that Weizmann displayed the necessary leadership. In these conditions, he sought to quit: "Enough of going on in this false situation, like a mistress whom one loves in bed but won't be seen with in public."[29]

As for the British, Aaron worked to prevent the abandonment of the Armenians by the allies, i.e., against the direction in which matters were developing at the initiative of the French and with the assent of the British. We should remember that Aaron operated in Paris, traveling between Paris and London as a member of the British Government delegation, with a British diplomatic passport, and was admired for his work.[30] Nevertheless, Aaron Aaronsohn did not function as an obedient clerk but rather as someone who wanted to influence policy. At the same time, he was aware of the complexity of matters. He notified Sokolow of his intention "to go myself to London tomorrow. This will be of service to the Armenians while proving to our friends, the English, that we are not put off by difficulties when their interests are at stake [the reference here is to the French intentions regarding the Armenian matter]. They agree with me that the matter may serve us."[31]

Sykes, who supported the Armenians and the Zionists, was away from Europe at the time, in the Middle East. He arrived in Paris on January 26, 1919, and Aaron wrote in his diary on February 4, 1919: "It seems that Sykes is trying to obtain the rule in Eretz Yisrael" — a possibility which had been raised before.[32] In any event, Sykes' influence on British policy during the Peace Conference was limited. His position was now weaker than during the early years of the war. On February 16, 1919, he unexpectedly died.

Immediately upon arrival in Paris from the U.S. in November 1918, Aaron made contact with the Armenians. He brought them up-to-date on the efforts of Barton, Mott (the Secretary of the Y.M.C.A.),

Morgenthau, and others in the United States. He reported to them on the tendency not to weaken Turkey too much after the war. He was apprehensive about the renewed activity of Barton, an overseas missionary leader who was influential in various American circles and had attempted to use his influence in late 1917 to prevent an American declaration of war against Turkey. Morgenthau had also been involved in this effort. Aaron feared that "Barton and his followers hoped to supply the Armenians with food and clothing, but it is doubtful whether they had an interest in the liberation of the Armenians."[33] In other words, his fear was that the Armenian situation would be treated as a humanitarian refugee problem, and its nationalist dimension would be ignored. Aaron wrote, "Who here is the deceiver? And who is being deceived?"[34] Aaron and the Armenians weighed various courses of action regarding Barton's delegation to Turkey. The next day they decided that clear statements needed to be extracted from Barton and that he would be accompanied by British commissioners on his trip to Armenia.

An examination of the diaries reveals a grave picture concerning the Armenians: the French were willing to give the Armenians very little. The French were essentially pushing the Armenians aside, while offering them what Aaron termed "real self-extermination instead of self determination."[35] The British tended to agree, or at any rate not to oppose the French action. In light of this situation, the Armenians had an additional problem: "The Armenians are lacking, in truth, much more than we, people and particularly unity and solidarity," Aaron noted in his diary.[36] The Armenian representation at the Paris Peace Conference was divided between representatives of the small Armenian Republic, which had been established in the Caucasus in May 1918, and the Armenian National Delegation in Paris which was headed by Nubar Pasha, and had good connections in London.

An additional example of the problematic Armenian situation: in the beginning of December 1918, Aaron came to London, in order, among other things, to help the Armenians prepare for the "summit" meeting between Clemenceau and Lloyd George at which the Armenian question was to be discussed. He reported to Gribbon, the Deputy in charge of military intelligence affairs, on the French demands regarding the Armenian affair: "Gribbon is pleased that he has learned of so many things and that I took the initiative to rush over here. However, he does not trust the Armenians. They are, as far as he is concerned, 'whiners' and 'liars.' He can always depend, he says, on the facts he is given by

Weizmann or by me and we are never weepy. It is different with the Armenians."[37] At another point Aaron relates, "Gribbon tells me awful things about the Armenians. He advises us to be cautious in our need for them."[38] Aaron does not expand on what these "awful things" are.

It is possible that the British attitude toward the Armenians was meant to justify British policy. The Armenians tended to depend on them: Sykes was close to them and the Bryce-Toynbee report was published under British government auspices. That report was, we recall, one of the most important pieces of war-time testimony about the Armenian massacre. British policy appears to have changed direction at the end of 1918 and in early 1919. The English did not trust the Armenian leadership, refused to get involved with it, and did not view the Armenian question as a "British interest."

At this point, in the winter of 1918-1919, the British were interested in extending their spheres of postwar influence. The arrangement with the French, known as the Sykes-Picot Agreement, meant that the southern regions which were under Turkish rule would come under British rule after the war. The northern regions under Turkish rule would come under some sort of French influence. Thus began a conflict between Armenian aspirations and French interests, just as the Syrian Arabs had their conflict with the French.

The Armenians, primarily the Armenian National Delegation headed by Nubar Pasha, wanted, at the very least, the area of Cilicia on the Mediterranean coast, which contained the largest concentration of Armenian refugees. The French wanted to keep the area, which the Sykes-Picot Agreement had assigned them, for themselves. In the end, they delivered it to the Turkish Republic.

The Armenians received evasive answers on two crucial issues in which they hoped for British support:

1. Support for a declaration of Armenian independence—a declaration of independence by the Armenian National Delegation in Paris, signed by its president, Boghos Nubar Pasha on November 30, 1918, was sent to Foreign Minister Balfour. The British Foreign Office confirmed, in vague, polite terms, receipt of the Armenians' declaration of independence, said Nubar Pasha to Aaron.[39]
2. Representation at the Peace Conference—the Armenians approached the French and the English with a request for representation at the Peace Conference. "Malcolm," writes Aaron in his diary, "is certain that the French opposed this."[40]

Shortly before the cease-fire, the Armenians asked to be considered a belligerent entity against the Turks due to their participation in General Allenby's forces and their support on the Russian front. They comprised an Armenian version of the "Jewish Regiments," which the Armenians hoped would strengthen their case after the war.

Malcolm asked Boghos Nubar Pasha to repeat the request "just as the Zionists have, representation of the Armenians in the committees meeting on matters concerning the Middle East." The Armenians approached both the French and the English about the issue. The British Foreign Office replied, "His Majesty's Government is in contact with its allies with regard to all national representation in the Peace Conference." The French responded that "it is preferable that such problems [recognition of the Armenians as a belligerent, and the future of Armenia in general] be postponed to the conference of the Allied ministers in Paris, where the request for representation and the future of Armenia will be discussed." Lord Bryce, who turned to his colleague Balfour in this matter, received a similar response.[41]

On December 2, 1918, Aaron relates a conversation with Gribbon about implementation of the Sykes-Picot Agreement. "Gribbon cannot give us the latest 'pamphlet' which contains England's requests, but he tells me details regarding the Sinai Desert, Eretz Yisrael, Transjordan, Lebanon, and Armenia. Armenia will spread from Diarbekir north and will also include Cilicia as well as Alexandretta and Trebizond." Aaron emphasized, "Turkey remains! This is scandalous!"[42] It should be noted that in contrast to what Gribbon told Aaron, included in the French demands was all of Cilicia.

It is possible that the French demands in Armenia were a bartering point in questions of disagreement between the French and the English over Syria and Lebanon.[43] France, in fact, aspired to a protectorate over Armenia from the Mediterranean to the Black Sea, without having to make concessions in Syria. The French offered the Armenians two bad options: a French protectorate over the six Armenian provinces, and over Cilicia, from the Mediterranean to the Black Sea. If the Armenians wanted complete independence, they would be left only with the three provinces of Trebizond on the coast of the Black Sea, with the possibility of unification with the Armenian Republic in the Caucasus. In his diary, Aaron cynically defined this: "They forego the crumbs!" On the other hand, if the Armenians were to truly agree to a French protectorate, they would be given the six provinces, including Cilicia.

These were severe conditions: Armenian sovereignty would be very limited. France was unwilling to limit the period of "assistance," and to determine the number of years it would last. Aaron termed this, we remember, "self-extermination" rather than "self-determination."[44]

The Armenians were torn; should they declare Armenian independence thus presenting the world with a *fait accompli*? In the end, after consulting with Aaron, the Armenian National Delegation in Paris, headed by Nubar Pasha, decided to declare independence because "the opinions of Gotte [from the French Foreign Ministry] about arrangements for Armenia are so troubling." Moreover, "the Armenian National Delegation found that this was the only available way to act in light of the recent developments."[45] The English, as stated, offered no help to the Armenians when the French closed off their options.

The person who advised and assisted the Armenians as best he could was Aaron. He proposed a formula which was acceptable to Nubar Pasha, the preeminent Armenian personality in Europe: The declaration of independence would not state that the Armenians inhabiting the six provinces would link up with their brothers in the Caucasian Republic. "I draw his attention [of Nubar Pasha] to how dangerous this could be and may draw away from them the support of those who oppose or mistrust that same Republic. I developed a formula which says that when circumstances permit, the various sections of the Armenian nation will unite in order to establish and create a unified Armenia, which it will not be possible to partition, etc."[46]

Aaron also offered Nubar Pasha assistance with communications between Paris and London, with Malcolm, the Armenian representative in London, circumventing the censorship. "The 'cloakroom' has not been put at their disposal. I suggest that he put into my report everything which may be of interest to Malcolm."[47] Aaron proposed to Nubar Pasha that "He prepare his letters (since they have no way of informing their representatives in London of developments), and although I cannot make any promises, he may expect that I will find him a courier. He immediately asked me if I myself will be the courier."[48]

And, in fact, Aaron decided to go to London the next day since such a trip would be, among other things, "of service to the Armenians." He took along Nubar Pasha's papers, including, it appears, the declaration of Armenian independence. Aaron knew that "in my position as a member of the British Government delegation it is not seemly that I serve as a courier for the Armenians. But it is my privilege and duty to transmit information without delay to my government and to my Zionist leader, Weizmann, who is to meet tomorrow at four p.m. with Balfour. I will go with him and put before him the Armenian matter, presenting as confirmation Boghos' [Nubar Pasha] documents." Weizmann was familiar with the details and Aaronsohn met with him at least twice that day. He noted in his diary: "We meet again with Weizmann about the 'conspiracy' and part after midnight."[49]

Another matter which Aaronsohn (and Weizmann and Sokolow) and the Armenians tried to move forward was the idea of a Jewish-Arab-Armenian alliance. On December 15, 1918, Malcolm told Aaronsohn that he had met several days earlier with Faysal. Malcolm explained to Faysal that:

> The Armenians and the Arabs will receive such extensive territories that for a period of the next two hundred years there can be no danger that the space will be too small. They can, therefore, make mutual concessions to each other on the question of boundaries. This is not the case for the Jews, who will receive minimal territory, such that even a few kilometers are of enormous importance. And that the Arab and Armenian interest is that their neighbor be a strong and prosperous Jewish nation. Faysal must therefore be liberal in the border arrangements with the Jewish nation. According to Malcolm, Faysal tended toward this.[50]

The two also discussed the wording of "our agreement"—Armenian, Arab, and Jewish—and planned a meeting with Sokolow two days hence, together with an expert in international law. "In this manner, when Faysal arrives, we will be able to hold a meeting to sign protocols, before the grumblers receive word of our doings.[51] The Syrians who will have been left on their own will rush toward us." Aaron added, "In our agreements, we will take into account exchange of representatives. This will worry the Syrians even more, since they will not want to remain outside of the movement."[52]

Aaronsohn hoped, at least for a while, for results from the contacts with Faysal. He relates in his diary, on December 5, 1918, that "the French in Marseilles cheered Faysal and condemned the Zionists. Faysal did not interrupt the speakers in the hall and when they finished, he declared that he and the Zionists were moving forward hand-in-hand, and that differences of opinion which might arise 'between cousins' would be worked out 'within the family.' Oh the expression of the French faces!"[53]

Three weeks later, on December 24, 1918, he wrote, "The dinner for Faysal and the alliance with him were very successful."[54] Aaron hoped at the time to reach agreement with the Armenians and the Hashemite dynasty, thus isolating the Syrian nationalists and forcing them to recognize Zionism.

To the extent that Aaron's diaries are evidence of his activities, it appears that he neglected Armenian affairs during the first months of 1919 and concentrated his efforts on direct Zionist political activity. Perhaps he was being cautious following Gribbon's comments condemning the Armenians, or perhaps he felt that without Sykes the chances for Armenian success with the British were slight. The diary is sketchy during this period and does not offer much detail on these issues. In any case, the diary ends on February 21, 1919, several days after Sykes' untimely death.

In summation, it should be noted that Aaron sincerely believed in a Jewish-Arab-Armenian alliance. He was in favor of independence for the Jews, for the Arabs, and for the Armenians. In his view, the visions of independence of the three nations were not contradictory but complementary.

In an essay entitled "General Allenby In Palestine," which appeared in *Asia Magazine* under the pseudonym, Adolph Baroni, Aaron analyses the attitude of the British toward the Turks and the Armenians.[55] The article is harshly critical of British lack of understanding of the German threat in Turkey. "Of all the Allies, Great Britain was seemingly in the best position to watch and to read Germany's machinations in Western Asia. Of all the Allies, Great Britain has seemed to be the last and the slowest one to grasp the dangers of the situation and to take effective measures in order to avert them."

In his opinion, the decision not to open a front in Palestine or in Sinai during the early stages of the war—in 1915—needlessly extended the war and unnecessarily increased the number of its casualties. Now, having lost Turkey, Germany had lost one of the most important factors which had made the war profitable, despite the price. Aaron chose a quote from Vladimir Jabotinsky's book, *Turkey and the War*, to open his essay: "The root of the present plague is in Asia Minor and the first and last aim of the War is the Solution of the Eastern question."

But Jabotinsky and Aaronsohn did not agree about the solution to the Eastern question. Jabotinsky was unsympatheitc toward the Armenian problem and he attached no real importance to compromise with the Arabs. Aaronsohn, on the other hand, suggested that Turkey must be dismantled for the sake of the Armenians, the Greeks, the Arabs, and the Jews, for the sake of all of the nationalities under its rule, and for the sake of the Turks themselves. This was their only chance to progress and become respectable members in the family of nations. He ends:

> But no one who knows their glorious past and their actual endeavors can doubt that the Armenians in a free Armenia, the Arabs in a free Arabia, and the Jews in a free Palestine, will not and cannot apply their ambitions to develop and produce for themselves and to live national complacent lives. They will help towards making Asia Minor again a flourishing center of culture and thus contribute towards making a better world.

It should be emphasized that Aaron was not a "Monday morning quarterback," in his criticism of the British decision about an eastern front in Palestine, nor in his demands with respect to Turkey and Germany, nor in his vision for the Armenians, Arabs, and Jews. He voiced his arguments, as we have seen, in the early stages of the war. He was a combination of idealism and realism which, regretfully, failed in the end.

Internal Armenian documents are also a source of information about Aaronsohn's activities on behalf of the Armenians.

During his two trips to America on behalf of Zionist ventures, Aaronsohn also assisted the Armenians. It should be remembered that in 1918 the Armenian cause was in jeopardy. The United States was essentially opposed to an independent Armenia in Turkey proper. American policy reflected the influence of Morgenthau, Elkus, and the missionaries over President Wilson. The former were sensitive to the Armenian problem but supported an "integrated Turkey," the result of which was a lack of support for Armenian independence or sovereignty.

The information Aaron brought from America was very important in this context. In the correspondence between Malcolm and Nubar Pasha, Aaronsohn is described warmly: "A friend," "I hope in the next few days the Zionist emissary will come to Paris, almost especially to see you [Nubar Pasha]."[56] Malcolm was cautious in mentioning Aaronsohn's name, knowing that other people might read the letters: "I have already mentioned his name to you in Paris, and he will bring a letter from someone in America whom both you and I well know." The "someone" was Felix Frankfurter, a pro-Zionist American Jewish leader who wrote to Nubar Pasha about Aaronsohn: "My very close friend who will tell you how things are in America. I recommend his judgment and his disinterested devotion to your cause in warmest terms."[57] In another letter from Malcolm to Nubar Pasha, Aaron is termed "the gentleman from America" and Malcolm states that "the information that my friend brought from America is most important."[58]

Aaron was in Europe several times during November and December 1918, and appears to have maintained close contact with Nubar Pasha in Paris and with Malcolm in London.

On the eve of Aaron's second trip to America, Malcolm wrote to Nubar Pasha that Aaronsohn was going to America "to see what he can do in the direction which we all desire. You can speak to him quite frankly."[59]

At the time of Aaron's first trip to America, in early 1918, Malcolm wrote to Sevasly, one of the important Armenian activists in the United States, about Aaron: "He is one of the Zionist leaders who is working with us, and he has great sympathy with our cause. He is very clever and in a quiet way has a great deal of influence and he could be of assistance to you. I therefore suggest that you should cultivate his friendship. He is a man to whom you can speak frankly."[60]

After Aaron's return from his first trip to the United States, Malcolm presents Aaron in his letters of recommendation to Nubar Pasha as an "influential Zionist, who will doubtless be able to throw some light on the situation."[61] In another letter, Malcolm writes about Aaron: "A well-known Jewish leader" who will be happy to meet with you. "Like our other Zionist friends, he is intensely pro-Armenian, and you can speak with him with absolute frankness."[62] This time the trust and candor are complete and unreserved.

Aaron Aaronsohn was killed on March 15, 1919—only three months after Sykes' death—when his plane crashed into the English Channel. He was forty-three years old at the time. If we wish to look for symbolism, it is significant that Malcolm had planned to fly with Aaronsohn, but postponed his trip.[63]

The Armenian journal, *Ararat*, which appeared in London, published excerpts from an obituary that appeared in the *Times* of London, on May 20, 1919, after Aaron's death. The article points out Aaronsohn's valuable work in agricultural research, in the espionage ring, and in the Zionist movement. The editor noted that Aaronsohn's death is a grave loss not only for the Zionists; he was also a friend of the Armenians, who had proved his friendship more than once.[64]

Sykes, NubarPasha, Malcolm, Weizmann, Sokolow, 1917-1919

Compared with the expanded and accelerated Zionist activity in London preceding the Balfour Declaration, previous efforts and contacts were merely preliminary attempts. The starting point for this development was a meeting of Zionist leaders in Great Britain with Mark Sykes, on February 7. The meeting established, for the first time, guidelines for the political activity which culminated in the Balfour Declaration. The central figure in the activity was Mark Sykes. When a new government was formed in London in December 1916, with Lloyd George as Prime Minister and Arthur Balfour as his Foreign Secretary, Mark Sykes was appointed as Assistant Secretary of the War Cabinet, and the Palestinian question was put in his hands.

Sykes had, in March 1916, rejected previous Foreign Secretary Grey's proposal to issue a pro-Zionist statement because he believed that Britain ought to base its policy on cooperation with the Arabs and to refrain from bringing the Zionists into the picture. He had changed his position at the end of that year, apparently influenced by Herbert Samuel, who became the first British High Commissioner of Palestine. From the beginning of 1917, Sykes worked to coordinate between the three national movements—the Arab, the Armenian, and the Jewish—and saw no contradiction between his pro-Arabism and his pro-Zionism.[65]

As we remember, Aaron Aaronsohn and Sykes knew and admired each other from the time of Aaron's sojourn in London in late 1916. "Sykes investigated with much gravity the tenor of my nationalism within Judaism," wrote Aaronsohn in his diary at the end of October 1916.[66] Weizmann was presented to Sykes, on January 28, 1917, by James Aratoun Malcolm, the representative of the Armenian National Delegation in London, who was in contact with Sykes and had discussed with him, *inter alia,* the idea of Arab-Armenian-Zionist cooperation. Norman Rose, Weizmann's biographer, describes the meeting:

Circumstances could not have been more propitious for the Zionists when, in January 1917, Sykes sought out more representative leaders of Zionism than [Chief Rabbi] Gaster. He consulted James Malcolm, a British subject of Armenian descent, and a well-known spokesman for Armenian nationalism, yet another of Sykes' pet causes. Sykes, his imagination on fire, was already weaving the tapestry of a born-again Middle East constructed on the revived nationalisms of Judaea, Armenia and Arabia, and beholden to Britain. His Armenian contact man, Malcolm, one of those fly-by-night characters of history, led him to the leaders of the third dimension of his master plan, to Weizmann and Sokolow."[67]

Malcolm first met Weizmann in January 1917. On February 4, 1917, Weizmann wrote to Sokolow: "Tomorrow, I want you to meet without fail a certain Mr. Malcolm, a friend and assistant of Sykes. I have made an appointment for tomorrow, Monday, between 5:30 and 6. I'll be at your place at 5, and we shall go to this club. *Very important.*"[68]

James Malcolm (1868-1952) believed that Armenian and Jewish aspirations for independence in the Middle East were linked, since both were contingent upon the downfall of Turkey and the protection of British interests. Malcolm was working on a solution for the Armenian problem, the Arab problem, and the Jewish problem, and on cooperation between the parties. Sykes and Malcolm were in agreement about a Zionist-Arab-Armenian arrangement, and one of the foundations of Sykes' position was that Britain's Middle East policy must be based on the realization of national aspirations of the three movements working together in harmony. In the very first meeting between Malcolm and Weizmann, the Armenian question occupied a prominent place.[69]

Weizmann met again with Malcolm during the month of March 1917, and at his instruction, Tolkowsky—who was a member of the Zionist delegation in London and Weizmann's close assistant at the time—asked Malcolm "to send him information about the Armenian problem." Tolkowsky, according to his diary, received from Malcolm books, a magazine and a list of additional books dealing with the Armenian problem.[70]

On March 31, 1917, Sokolow went to Paris with Malcolm. The idea of Sokolow's trip to France was first raised by Sykes, and was discussed at meetings which Sokolow held in London with Picot, Sykes' French counterpart, in February and March of 1917. Sykes hoped to obtain French support for Zionism. Sokolow was to present the Zionist demands in Palestine to the French Government. According to Sykes' plan, Weizmann would join him after he left Egypt in early April at the head of the political delegation attached to the British Expeditionary Forces. However, Weizmann's trip did not come to pass because of a slowdown of the campaign on the western front.[71]

Sokolow remained in Paris with Malcolm until April 20 at which time Malcolm returned to London. Sokolow continued on to Rome where he was to be received by the Italian Foreign Ministry and the Vatican.[72]

We should bear in mind that Sykes and Picot worked in coordination. In May 1916, they had signed a secret agreement which bears their names, about which Sykes was unable, possibly also unwilling, to tell the Zionists and the Arabs. The agreement shaped the postwar boundaries of the Middle East and determined the future spheres of influence of England, France, and Russia. Sykes worked, despite the disagreement of many in the British Government, for a British policy coordinated with the French. Sykes and Picot met frequently in March and April 1917, and Sykes participated in some of the meetings between Malcolm, Sokolow, and Picot in Paris in early April. Sykes also met, of course, with Malcolm and Sokolow alone, including on the very day, April 9, that Sykes and Picot left for Egypt.

Sokolow's meetings in Paris were fruitful. The French Government decided to support the Zionist plan in Palestine, in coordination with Great Britain. It was almost surely Malcolm who brought the letters from Paris in which Sokolow reported to Weizmann about the promise he had received from the French for support of the right of the Jewish people to a national homeland and autonomy. Upon returning to London, Malcolm met several times with Weizmann and reported to him on the discussions in Paris. Malcolm's contacts, both with Weizmann and Sokolow, were close and strong. Malcolm even presented Weizmann with a copy of his report on the trip to Paris with Sokolow.[73]

In Sokolow's meetings with Picot and other representatives of the French Foreign Ministry regarding Zionism, Malcolm played an active part and assisted Sokolow in his dealings with the French. In some respects, he was a liaison and tutor for them about Zionism. He met alone with Picot twice, once for a long interview and a second time when Picot asked Malcolm to come to his home half an hour before Sokolow in order to give him certain information in private and in secret.[74]

Malcolm believed that if the question of British suzerainty over Palestine were not removed from the table, the French Foreign Ministry might indefinitely postpone a satisfactory decision. He therefore thought that the Zionists should not demand formal British suzerainty over Palestine. Since Picot was due to depart shortly, Malcolm told him, in their meeting on April 2, even before Picot had met with Sokolow, that the Jews were willing to leave the question of suzerainty to the British and French governments.

Sykes, the Englishman, and Picot, the Frenchman, represented, each in his respective country, an approach which viewed cooperation between the Allies, particularly France and England, in shaping the postwar character of the Middle East, as crucial. Both believed that it was worth making mutual concessions in order to achieve this aim. In a consultation between Sykes, Sokolow, and Malcolm on April 5, the latter explained the position of the French Government on the matter of suzerainty and pointed out the danger of an indefinite postponement, if the question continued to be raised. They decided unanimously to remove the issue of suzerainty from the agenda, i.e., not to determine explicitly that the sovereignty in Palestine would be British, and to leave the matter up to the decision of the British and French governments (even though the British position on the issue was firm). It should be remembered that time was running short. Within a few days Picot would leave for the East, and the matter might be delayed for a long time— time which was precious to the Zionists.

In the meeting with Picot and Malcolm, Sokolow adopted a position to which they agreed: The Jews were compared to a child who must decide whether he loves his father or his mother more. It would be hard for them to say whether they preferred the English or the French as the sovereign power and therefore the two governments must resolve the issue between them.

Another issue on which Malcolm and Sokolow were active in Paris was the subject of cooperation between the Zionists and the Armenians, and cooperation between the Zionists, the Armenians, and the Arabs in keeping with the idea of a tripartite alliance.

Jewish-Armenian cooperation proceeded smoothly. Malcolm and Sokolow met a number of times with Nubar Pasha, head of the Armenian National Delegation and one of the most important Armenian political figures—if not the most important—at the time. They paid a call on him on April 10, and joined him for breakfast three days later, when they met other prominent Armenians for a discussion about cooperation.[75] "A very friendly and satisfying talk; they promise to help," reported Malcolm. Nubar Pasha said at the meeting that the Armenian press in Russia and elsewhere had always been supportive of the claims of the Jews. On April 15, Sokolow, Malcolm, and Nubar Pasha met again, to continue their conversation about cooperation, which both the French and British governments favored. The Baron de Rothschild, with whom Sokolow had also met in Paris, also endorsed the idea.

The third leg of the triangle, the Arabs, remained difficult and problematic, and continued to be one of the main stumbling blocks in the proposed alliance, for the entire period. Malcolm wrote in his report that on April 18 he had discovered the source of the fierce Syrian opposition to both the Armenian and Zionist plans. The Syrians claimed that part of Cilicia, including Alexandretta, and part of Palestine, including Jerusalem, must be part of the Syrian state, under French suzerainty. On April 19, Malcolm found a contact between Sokolow and the Syrians. The contact was Sebag Bey, from the Bank of Paris and Holland, one of the Syrian leaders in Paris. After some discussion, Sebag Bey agreed that the Syrians and the Jews, the Armenians and the Arabs, needed to work together wisely. Malcolm established a connection between Sebag Bey and Nubar Pasha as well. Sokolow was scheduled, after his return from Italy, to meet again with Nubar Pasha and Sebag Bey, together with additional Syrian leaders.[76]

Another goal of Sokolow's visits was to change the attitude of French Jewry toward Zionism. In the first meeting between Sokolow and Picot in Paris on April 5, the latter stated that the Zionist claims were reasonable and could be acceptable to the French Government but added that the opposition of French Jewry must be neutralized or removed, so that French government support could be more easily justified. He suggested that several representatives of French Jewry lend their support to the "claims," in order to bolster his own position. Sokolow dedicated much effort to this and met with representatives of the Jewish community. Nubar Pasha was acquainted with one of these Jews, S. Reinarch, who had publicized his anti-Zionist positions in the press, and promised to speak with him.[77]

Malcolm made comments and presented conclusions from the report. "These are the major factors to be considered in France: the French Government, French Jewry, the French press, and the Syrians in Paris who have great influence on the financial elite and on the press." He adds,

> For the first time in history, the French Government is now a real supporter. The French Jews are still an uncertain entity, and they should be given attention. The Zionist Organization in France must be strengthened or rebuilt. The Syrians will be attended to satisfactorily now that the source of their power has been discovered. But the press may turn out to be the most dangerous element if it believes that it has found ammunition in the opposition of the French Jews. The Zionists must prepare to deal with this element at any time.

The relevant factors in England, in Malcolm's opinion, were the British Government and certain circles within the British Jewish community. He was apparently referring to the "Joint Committee" which was hostile to Zionism. Malcolm felt that the Zionist "claims" should be formally presented to the British Government, signed by as many prominent Zionist leaders as possible. Sokolow's trip to Paris was the result of a decision of two Zionist leaders, Weizmann and Sokolow himself, in partnership with two external figures, Malcolm and Sykes, who actually initiated and pushed for the trip. The rest of the Zionist leadership in England was not directly involved and part of it was even critical. Tolkowsky relates that Weizmann gave him one of two copies of the report that he had received from Malcolm.[78]

A letter, which Sokolow sent from his hotel in Paris to Weizmann in London on April 21, 1917, reveals interesting details of his relationship with Malcolm, Nubar Pasha, and the other Armenians.[79] Sokolow wrote to Weizmann that he had reservations about "M's" [Malcolm] participation but "they imposed him on us." The boss [Sykes] thought he had influence with the bosses in Paris, as well as many connections. After being with him for three weeks, wrote Sokolow, there was no need to fear Malcolm, "He is a businessman and a visionary, an Armenian patriot who identifies with the distress of the Zionists and of the Jews in general; he is highly intelligent." Malcolm wanted to go with Sokolow to see "the old man," Rothschild, but Sokolow thought it would be better not to. Sokolow asked Weizmann to maintain good relations with Malcolm in London, to accept his cooperation where it was feasible, but not to involve him too deeply in their work. Sokolow praised Nubar Pasha: "He is a very wise man, sympathetic, greatly appreciated and esteemed....He has high standing in Egypt and is *persona gratissima* here. If the Armenian project is implemented, he will receive the crown, even if he does not want it." Sokolow added that the acquaintance with Nubar Pasha could be beneficial beyond the Armenian context. He, too, wanted to meet "the old man" but Sokolow managed to extricate himself from this delicate situation.

Referring to Malcolm's idea of an Armenian-Arab-Jewish alliance, Sokolow wrote, "I think that with regard to the Armenians, this is a fantasy. As for the Arabs, it is difficult to talk with them, though necessary. We have no conflicts with the Armenians, so there are no points of friction with them. One might think the Armenians would help us talk to the Arabs. Now is not the time to indulge in such speculations. M [Malcolm] insisted that we set up a [tripartite] committee. I delicately evaded this issue."

The close contact between the Armenians and Weizmann, Sokolow, and their associates continued throughout 1917-18. Various sources enable us to delineate the outlines of the connection. Shmuel Tolkowsky's diary serves as an important source of information in documenting the relations. Tolkowsky, Weizmann's secretary, was well-read about the Armenian problem, and, at Malcolm's request, assisted in the copyediting of a book dealing with Armenia and the war. He attended a lecture about Armenia, its past and future, to which Weizmann had also been invited but could not attend. Tolkowsky apparently went as an official representative: "It was agreed that I would attend." The lecturer was Arnold Toynbee and the chair of the evening was Viscount Bryce. Bryce and Toynbee, we recall, were the authors of the "Blue Book," a comprehensive report about the massacre of the Armenians in 1915-16, which included much eyewitness testimony. Tolkowsky later wrote an article, in coordination with Weizmann, about the Armenian question from the perspective of the Zionist Movement.

Cooperation between the Armenians and the Zionists in 1917 revolved around another practical matter: the Morgenthau mission to the Middle East in June 1917, to explore the possibility of a separate peace between Turkey and the Allies. The initiative for a separate settlement came from the U.S. State Department, at a meeting between Secretary of State Robert Lansing and Henry Morgenthau, Sr., former U.S. ambassador to Turkey. Morgenthau expressed his willingness to go to Switzerland to open negotiation with Turkish plenipotentiaries. British Foreign Secretary Balfour gave his consent, and the U.S. State Department proposed that French and British representatives meet with Morgenthau in Gibraltar. The plan caused much concern among the Armenians and the Zionists who believed that a separate peace with Turkey would harm their post war national aspirations.

Malcolm, who was well connected, told Weizmann of the plan. On June 10, 1917 he arranged a meeting for Weizmann with Eric Ormsby-Gore, Sykes' replacement in Egypt.[16] According to Tolkowsky, Ormsby-Gore allayed their fears saying that "the whole matter was unimportant and there was no place for concern." That same day, Weizmann met with the Armenian Committee in London, which was "very worried by the new strategy."[81] The Zionists and the Armenians feared that a separate peace with Turkey would mean, from Turkey's perspective, "no loss of territories."

Ormsby-Gore stated that both Weizmann and Malcolm "were very much excited and very angry and both stated that we were not only [the British] playing with fire in approaching the Turks at this juncture, but also imperiling the interests of the British Empire and the causes which they have more especially at heart."[82] Weizmann was open in his denunciation of Morgenthau who was, he said, notoriously pro-German and was serving the interests of an international ring of Jewish financiers from Hamburg, Berlin, Vienna, Paris, and New York. According to Weizmann, this international ring was violently hostile both to Great Britain and to Zionism.[83] Weizmann also opposed the trip of M.P. Aubrey Herbert as Britain's representative at the meeting, since he was notoriously pro-Turkish, anti-Armenian, and anti-Zionist. His mission would be a grave betrayal, contrary to the promises which Weizmann had allegedly received from responsible ministers in the country. Weizmann proposed that he himself attend the meeting with Morgenthau. The suggestion that Weizmann go to meet with Morgenthau was viewed favorably by Balfour.

Weizmann also made an effort to ensure that the representatives of the British Foreign Office at the meeting with Morgenthau would not be pro-Turkish. His candidate was Sykes: "It seems to me that the only man by whom the British Government could be adequately represented and who thoroughly knows the question and also enjoys the full confidence of the Arabs, Jews and Armenians, is Sir Mark Sykes—the man who had this particular question in his hands for the last three years....One would feel absolutely safe with Sir Mark Sykes in Gibraltar, and I am not saying this only from the Jewish point of view, but from the British."[84] Weizmann rightly knew that he could depend on Sykes who vigorously opposed a separate peace.

In a memorandum submitted to the War Cabinet, Sykes wrote, "Before entering on pourparlers, it would seem imperative to consult not only France, Italy and America, but also the King of Hejaz, representative Armenians and Nationalist (i.e., Zionist) Jews, to whom we and the other Entente Powers have obligations and whose fate is bound up with the principle of nationality, the antidote to Prussian military domination."[85]

On June 23, 1917, the journal of the Zionist Organization in London, *Palestine*, published an article entitled "A Separate Peace With Turkey."[86] Peace would be possible only under four conditions: liberation of the straits; Palestine and Syria must be freed; Mesopotamia must be resettled and the Arabs must be allowed to revive their greatness there; Armenia must be liberated. Under these conditions, no one would oppose a separate peace with Turkey. "But imagine the situation if a separate peace were made and Palestine left under Turkey. You would create a new Armenia with Jews in the position so long occupied by the Armenians as victims of Turkish incompetence and spite. Palestine would then be a most important border province of Turkey, and any expression of nationalism would be brutally quashed."

In another article published a week later, *Palestine* writes that the test of a separate peace with Turkey is the granting of the unencumbered development of the three peoples—the Arabs, the Armenians, and the Jews.

> One cannot oppose a separate peace with Turkey, or with any other power, on the condition that such a peace would not be a child of imperialism but of democracy. In the case of Turkey, the tests are simple. A separate peace with Turkey, like any peace regarding Turkey, must ensure the national future of the Armenians, the Arabs and the Jews....The real test of any projected separate peace with Turkey is what it will do for Armenians, Arabs and Jews.[87]

The American delegation left for the Middle East. In order to conceal the true purpose of his mission, it was stated that Morgenthau had been sent to deal with the situation of the Jews in Palestine, and to work for improvement of the situation of the Jewish villages. Weizmann described his meeting with Morgenthau and the British and French representatives:

> I ventured to submit that from what I know of the views of the British Government, it appears to me that the British Government would not consider a peace with Turkey unless it were satisfied that Armenia, Mesopotamia, Syria and Palestine are to be detached from the present Turkish Empire. Neither Mr. Morgenthau nor his advisers nor M. Weyl thought that such conditions would be acceptable at present to the Turks.[88]

Morgenthau ultimately dropped the scheme and canceled his planned trip to Egypt or Switzerland to work for a separate peace. He went to Paris and expressed his willingness to aid the Foreign Ministries of England and France as a liaison with the President of the United States. But the activity of Morgenthau, Edelmann, and Barton continued to distress the Zionists and the Armenians throughout the war. The Armenians especially feared Morgenthau's influence over President Wilson because of the former's support of an "integral Turkey," and his opposition to an independent Armenian state. Morgenthau had also made his anti-Zionist position known publicly.

It should not be forgotten that Morgenthau greatly assisted the Armenians and the Zionists in the early years of the war. His help was extremely important and considered by some to have been crucial. Yet Morgenthau, who worked tirelessly to obtain humanitarian and philanthropic aid for the Armenians, did not support their national aspirations for sovereignty. The man who had been their greatest, almost sole friend in the political frameworks which could help them when the war began, became a danger which imperiled their hopes as the war drew to a close.

A Jewish-Arab-Armenian Committee

The question of establishment of an Arab-Jewish-Armenian committee arose as early as April 1917, during Sokolow's trip to Paris with Malcolm. Sokolow was ambivalent about cooperation between the three national movements and related to it somewhat disparagingly. The issue was brought up again during the visit of Weizmann and Sokolow in Paris in July of that year. Upon their return from Paris, at the end of July, Weizmann and Sokolow reported to the Political Committee in London on their discussion with the Armenian leader, Boghos Nubar Pasha, about the idea of establishing an Armenian-Arab-Jewish committee. "They reached agreement with Nubar Pasha about the establishment of an Armenian-Arab-Jewish committee for the purposes of agreement and understanding between the three peoples. This committee would sit in London and a representative of the King of Hejaz would participate in it."[89]

The fate of that committee has not been fully researched but from the material at hand it appears that it never really began to work and certainly achieved no concrete results. The committee, an initiative of Sykes in February 1917, was established in London in late 1917. At the beginning of 1918, its members were Chaim Weizmann for the Zionist Organization and James Malcolm for the Armenian National Delegation. They were both the senior London representatives of their respective peoples. The Arab representation included individuals appointed by the Syrian and Arab Committee in London and it was clearly the weakest leg of the triangle. Nonetheless, Weizmann made efforts to engage them in dialogue.

In April 1917, Weizmann wrote to Felix Frankfurter in Washington:

The second point is the formation of a close union between us and the committees which direct the Armenian and the Arab movements. There seems to be difficulty in establishing contact with the right sort of Arabs and the only people who are really interested and with whom it is desirable to reach an understanding are Hejaz' people, but they are so far away and one would probably have to go to Egypt to meet them."[90]

The tripartite committee was created, as mentioned, at Sykes' urging. The Armenians were enthusiastically supportive and hoped to derive benefit from cooperation with the Zionists. The Zionists supported the committee for two reasons. First, because it was Sykes' initiative and his vision. Second, Weizmann and his colleagues understood that it was very important for the future of the Zionist endeavor that they attempt to reach agreement with the Arabs. On this question, too, Weizmann and Aaronsohn agreed with Sykes, from their own Zionist perspective.

The British documents relating to Sykes reveal the great importance he attached to Arab-Jewish-Armenian cooperation and his slightly naive belief that such an undertaking could succeed. Sykes sent telegrams to Sir Gilbert Clayton in Cairo dealing with the tripartite cooperation, subsequent to the Balfour Declaration. Clayton was the head of British intelligence services in Cairo, and was, in effect, responsible for the British military and civilian intelligence as well as the Egyptian military intelligence. He was thus in a central position to shape the Arab policy of the British government. Sykes and Clayton were close and Sykes reported to Clayton that the Armenians had sent the Zionists a letter of congratulations following the Balfour Declaration, to be publicized at the appropriate time. The Zionists were ready to give their help to the matter of Arab and Armenian independence, and would possibly send a telegram to that effect to Egypt.[91] On the other hand, Sykes warned against Turkish activity and the Pan-Turkish trend which sought to sow disunity and discord between the Arabs and the Jews, and among the Arabs themselves.

Sykes therefore asked Clayton to convene the Arab Committee in Cairo at once, and to make clear to its members the vital need for the good will of the Jews and the Armenians. "Point out," he wrote, "that with Jewish cooperation they have advocates in every country in the world and with Armenian help they have a strong grip in the imagination of British and American Democracy; without cooperation of these two elements, there is, I think, no prospect of their gaining their full desiderata."

Sykes proposed that a joint committee be established in London to be comprised of Weizmann for the Zionists, Malcolm for the Armenians, and Nagib Hani for the Christian Syrians and an unnamed representative of the Muslim Arabs. The committee would work for the benefit of oppressed peoples in the non-Anatolian Turkish provinces in Asia. It was very desirable, Sykes added, that the two Arabs receive official backing from Cairo and from Mecca. Two days later, on November 16, Sykes sent another telegram to Clayton with a letter attached for the members of the Arab Committee in Cairo, on the same issue.[92]

He reported to Clayton that matters were progressing swiftly in London. The Zionists and the Armenians had agreed and it was crucial that the Arabs join in. Sykes recommended that, in addition to Nagib Hani, two additional Arab representatives be added to the joint committee. They were currently working at the School for Oriental Studies and would wait for a reply on the matter.[93] It would be desirable to gain support for their participation from the Arab Committee in Cairo or from the King of the Hejaz, or both if possible. The committee was defined as a "joint committee for the defense of Arab, Armenian and Jewish national interests" and its purpose was to work for harmony between the parties and for their mutual cause.

Sykes wrote to Clayton: "I would argue that this is really the biggest opportunity the Arabs have yet had of getting strong support for their cause. The committee will convene only under my chairmanship or the chairmanship of Ormsby-Gore. [Major Ormsby-Gore was introduced to Zionist leaders by Aaron Aaronsohn. He was called back from Cairo to London, and from the spring of 1917 was at the center of affairs in his position as personal assistant to Lord Milner, member of the War Cabinet and Sykes' replacement in the Secretariat of the War Cabinet.] The committee will maintain contact with you regarding the situation in Europe and the United States, and will be a channel for propaganda which the Committee in Cairo or the King in Hejaz choose to send through you to me." He attached a letter to the members of the Arab Committee in Cairo noting the fact that almost half of the Arab provinces were already no longer under Turkish rule, and that the liberation of the remaining provinces was now only a matter of time. Along with the importance of the Arab Corps he pointed out the importance of political activity in the changing international circumstances, and warned of the danger of disunity in the Arab world. He cautioned that unless "the greatest wisdom and foresight is shown, that nothing will be easier than for the whole Arab movement to collapse." Sykes went on:

> Having said this, I now desire to lay before you my most earnest advice on the present situation. The British Government has recognized Zionism. Zionism is the greatest motive force in Jewry—Jewry is scattered through the world. If Zionism and Arab nationalism join forces, I am convinced that the liberation of the Arabs is certain. If, on the other hand, Zionism and Arab nationalism is opposed, the situation will become not only complicated but impossible to control."

Sykes pointed out that the Zionists, partly as a result of his action, were now willing to cooperate in liberating Syria and other territories under Turkish rule. The Zionists and the Armenians were already cooperating fully.

Sykes understated the meaning of the Zionist aspirations: "The only thing the Zionists seek is the right of settlement in Palestine and to live their national life in their villages. I urge you to accept the policy of Arab-Armenian-Zionist Entente. [Sykes used the term "Zionist" in his letter]. If such an Entente becomes a public fact, then your national movement becomes recognized in every country in the world." Sykes asked that Nagib Hani and two additional people be appointed as representatives to the Committee.[94]

Sykes and Clayton continued to confer on the subject of the tripartite committee in December 1917. Clayton was more skeptical than Sykes with regard to the possibilities for success of an Arab-Jewish-Armenian entente, despite attempts which were being made in Cairo and, according to him, in Mecca.[95] Clayton, in effect, pours cold water on Sykes' dream:

> I do not, however, expect much success as, in spite of all arguments, Mecca dislikes Jews and Armenians and wishes to have nothing to do with them, while Arabs of Syria and Palestine fear repetition of the story of Jacob and Esau. In any case, an Arab-Jewish-Armenian combination is so foreign to any previous experience and to existing sentiment that we must proceed with great caution. Violent propaganda will accentuate feelings which it is desired to allay.

Clayton also drew attention to the discord and lack of authority of the Arab representatives. Sykes would not, however, give up on his vision and wrote back to Clayton the next day: "Patience, enthusiasm and determination surmount obstacles and make circumstances. Dimness of future can only be overcome by vision." When referring to the discord in the Arab world, Sykes pointed out the successful establishment of the Arab Committee in London, and the hope for similar committees in Paris and New York. "All of the national movements need to overcome similar difficulties, which only the energy of people from outside can surmount."

On December 15, 1917, after the British conquest of Jerusalem, Clayton sent Sykes a longer letter from Cairo reflecting the excitement at the unfolding events. Clayton also refers to Sykes' proposal for an Arab-Jewish-Armenian entente:

> I quite see your arguments regarding an Arab-Jew-Armenian combine and the advantages that would accrue if it could be brought off. We will try it, but it must be done very cautiously and, honestly, I see no great chance of any real success. It is an attempt to change in a few weeks the traditional sentiment of centuries. The Arab cares nothing whatsoever about the Armenian one way or the other—as regards the Jew, the Bedouin despises him and will never do anything else, while the sedentary Arab hates the Jew, and fears his superior commercial and economic ability."[96]

Clayton said that declarations by Jews like Sokolow and Weizmann would change nothing. He saw no chance of a Jewish-Arab-Armenian agreement except through gradual and cautious action. He again cited the fears and suspicions of the Arabs and repeated his warning that vigorous activity could elicit a hostile reaction toward the Allies and their cause. And he added a handwritten note to Sykes: "Do not think from the above that we are not trying to act on the lines you suggest, but I wish to point out clearly the dangers and difficulties which exist here."

The Balfour Declaration and Its Aftermath: "Arabia for the Arabs, Armenia for the Armenians, and Judaea for the Jews"

The Balfour Declaration, which was sent to Lord Rothschild on November 2, 1917, evoked tremendous enthusiasm among Jews around the world, although there were, of course, some who were less enthusiastic. Several mass rallies were held in England to celebrate the Declaration. A rally of thanksgiving, organized by the English Zionist Federation and chaired by Lord Rothschild, was held on December 2 in the London Opera House. The British Government was represented by

Deputy Foreign Secretary, Lord Robert Cecil, who echoed Mark Sykes' ideas but possibly went beyond his official brief when he summed up his government's intentions in one sentence which was loudly cheered at the time and has been frequently quoted since: "We welcome among us not only the thousands of Jews whom I see but also the representatives of the Arabian and Armenian peoples who are struggling too in this great battle for their freedom. Our wish is that Arabian countries shall be for the Arabs, Armenia for the Armenians, and Judaea for the Jews."[97]

The Balfour Declaration was indeed welcomed by the Armenian representatives in London and Paris who sent their congratulations to the Zionists in London. In their reply, the Zionists emphasized the circumstances common to both peoples—the suffering and the hope for national freedom—and expressed their hope that "a new chapter of freedom and independence both for the Armenians and the Jews will begin."[98] Nubar Pasha, head of the Armenian National Delegation, sent to Lord Rothschild, chair of the gathering at the Opera House, sincerest congratulations of the Armenians who joined in the joy on the occasion of the Balfour Declaration.[99] Nubar Pasha expressed his hope that on this day of victory of those struggling for the liberation of oppressed peoples, the Armenian aspirations would be realized and at the same time the Jewish people would reestablish its nationalism and fulfill its historic aspirations in the land of its forefathers. Nubar Pasha sent another letter to Weizmann and Sokolow after the Zionist rally at the Opera House on December 2. He recalled Cecil's words and their great importance, saying "This is indeed a historic date." In their reply, Weizmann and Sokolow wrote, "Like you, we think our aspirations which are so closely linked to yours will be achieved at the same time." They pointed out that after the "demonstration" in London, there was another rally in Manchester where the idea of a Jewish-Armenian-Arab alliance "was raised in the same way and with the same clarity."[100]

Those attending the rally in London included, apart from the Jews and Zionist leaders, Robert Cecil, Mark Sykes, Ormsby-Gore, a Christian Syrian representative and a representative of the Armenian Committee in London, Mosditchian. Greetings from Nubar Pasha, head of the Armenian National Delegation in Paris, were read. The recurrent theme of the rally, mentioned at length by most of the speakers, was the need for Jews, Arabs, and Armenians to help one another and to move forward in harmony. Sokolow, the main Zionist speaker, said,

Relations between Jews and Arabs have hitherto been scanty and spasmodic, largely owing to mutual ignorance and indifference. There were no relations whatever between the two nations as such because the oppressive power did not recognize either of them, and whenever points of connection began to develop they were destroyed by intrigue to the detriment of both nationalities. We believe that the present-hour crisis and the opening of a large perspective for epoch-making developments offers a fruitful opportunity for a broad basis of permanent cordial relations between the two peoples who are inspired by a common purpose. We mean a real *entente cordiale* between Jews, Arabs and Armenians, such an *entente cordiale* having already been accepted in principle by leading representatives of these three nations. From such a beginning we look forward with confidence to a future of intellectual, social and economic cooperation; we are one with the Arabs and Armenians today in the determination to secure for each of us the free choice of our own destinies. We look with fraternal love at the creation of the Arab kingdom reestablishing Semitic nationality in its glory and freedom, and our heartiest wishes go out to the noble, hardly-tried Armenian nationality for the realization of their national hopes in their old Armenia. Our roots were united in the past, our destinies will be bound together in the future.[101]

The Times of London was of the opinion that "the presence and the words of influential representatives of the Arab and the Armenian peoples, and their assurances of agreement and cooperation with the Jews alone would have sufficed to make the meeting memorable."[102]

Weizmann, in a letter reporting on the rally to Jacobus H. Kann in the Hague, cited Cecil's remarks and added, "The Zionist Organization attached great importance to harmonious work in future with Arabs and Armenians."[103] At this stage, the Zionist leadership, or at least Weizmann and Sokolow, attached great importance to the idea of tripartite cooperation. It is also worth noting the words of Mark Sykes, the moving spirit behind the idea of a Jewish-Arab-Armenian alliance, at the Manchester rally on December 9, 1917. Having consolidated the Zionist leg of the triangle, Sykes sought to calm the Arabs and promise the Armenians that the struggle on their behalf would continue. In his view, the success of each leg of the triangle was contingent upon the success of the other two, and the fate of the Jews and the Arabs were inextricably linked to their joint success or disaster.

According to Reuters News Agency, Sykes stressed that the success of the Zionist program was conditional on its reliance upon a Jewish-Armenian-Arab alliance.[104] Sykes called on the Zionists to allay Arab fears of economic competition and displacement, and not to forget in the heat of political activity that Jerusalem was holy to the three religions. The Armenians, he stated, were one of the oppressed peoples and until they were able to realize their national aspirations, there would be no assurance for the Jews that tyranny against the Armenians would not strike at them as well. He had been told, he said, that the Turks had behaved tolerantly toward the Jews, but this was because the Jews in Turkey did not constitute a political element and were not part of the agrarian population. With the appearance of Zionism, when the Jews too had become landowners, their status vis-à-vis the Turks was the same as the status of the Bulgars, the Serbs, the Greeks, the Armenians, and the Arabs. If the Armenians were not liberated there would be no security for the Jews. Against a potential aggressor, the Jews needed an enlightened Armenian state.

Sykes alluded to the Turkish claim which had been made numerous times during that period: "We (the Turks) love the Jews and hate the Zionists." The significance of Sykes' words has not faded, almost eighty years after they were uttered: The Arab national revival which was just beginning would embrace millions in the decades to come. The destiny of the Jews was to be closely linked in competition with the Arabs, or, alternatively, in cooperation and good will with them. If not, disaster would strike both Jew and Arab. Sykes therefore cautioned the Jews to examine matters through Arab eyes and to understand their concerns (according to the Reuters' report, there were cries from the audience, We shall! We Shall!). Reuters reported that Sykes' remarks about the Armenians and the Jews were enthusiastically received by the Zionist leadership. All of the speakers, including Sokolow and Weizmann, stressed the need for a united front against their common aggressor.

Weizmann brought Sykes' remarks at the Manchester rally to the attention of Jacques Mosseri, president of the Zionist Organization in Egypt, son of a prominent family of bankers and an activist in the Jewish community. Weizmann emphasized: "Insist upon you and your friends doing your utmost to assure Arabs our sympathy, mutual interests, and cooperation. Try to introduce our declaration of sympathy to Arabs and Armenians to Arabic Press and get in touch with Arab leaders. Remove misunderstandings. *This work is most essential for the success of our cause*" [emphasis mine].[105]

Thus we see that relations between the Zionists in London and the Armenian delegations in Paris and London were friendly and close at the end of 1917. Their cooperation included assistance, advice, and information of various sorts. Tschlenow, who was slated to go to Russia in December 1917, took with him packages and letters from Nubar Pasha for the Armenians in Russia. Malcolm attended a private party at the Ritz Hotel in London where Jewish activists involved in the Balfour Declaration celebrated their achievement. Malcolm also attended an intimate dinner party for eight, which Weizmann and Sokolow hosted on November 14, in honor of several friends who had helped to attain the Balfour Declaration.

Weizmann and Sokolow suggested to Nubar Pasha that he meet in Paris with Captain Emery and Sir George Clark, British representatives in the Allied Council in Versailles: "they are great friends of your cause and ours."[106] These are just several examples of the tenor of the relationship.

Palestine, the journal of the Zionist Movement in England, *Ararat*, the Armenian journal in London and *La Voix de l'Armenie* in Paris all published articles of mutual support and sympathy. In private congratulatory letters, Armenians openly expressed their good wishes to the Zionists on the occasion of the latter's success. The decision of the Armenian Committee in London to congratulate the Zionists officially in England and other countries was publicized in *Palestine*:

> The Council of the Armenian United Association of London, having read in the Press that the British Government had now formally expressed its sympathy with the project for the reconstitution of Palestine as the National Home of the Jewish People, at their meeting held on November 10, 1917, at the offices of the Association, resolved: To record their unalloyed gratification and to convey their cordial congratulations and sincere and neighbourly greetings to the President, Dr. Ch. Weizmann, Committee, and members of the Zionist Federation of Great Britain, and through them to all other Zionist leaders and Zionist organizations, and especially those in the United States, Russia, France, Italy, Poland, and Roumania, upon the recognition of that Jewish nationality and their righteous and inalienable claim to the historic soil and country of their ancestry."

The journal emphasized that the good wishes of the Armenians would be welcomed by every person of political imagination, and, of course, by every Jew. *Palestine* published another article, entitled "Armenian, Arab and Jew," and commented:

> Between the Armenian and the Jew there are notable points of community. The persistence of Armenian nationality through long generations of op-

pression is one; the fellowship of suffering is another; a certain harmonising of East and West is a third. The survival of the Armenian nation is a political miracle only second in wonder to that of the Jews. If the Jews have preserved their national quality in exile from their land, the Armenians have maintained the life and the hope of theirs under the heel of a foreign tyrant and sundered from the kindred West by a surrounding ocean of different and often hostile elements. Only a high moral fortitude and a rare spiritual virtue could sustain a nation under such circumstances. Of all the peoples who have suffered in this war none has passed through such torments as those of the Armenians. The Jews have known what it is to see brother armed against brother, to see their dwelling places trampled under the heel of contending armies, and their lives made a plaything by a tyrannical Government. But at least they have been spared the final extreme of misery—to be the victims of a systematic organised conspiracy by a Government aiming at the blotting out of a whole race. That has been the unhappy lot of the Armenians.

One may doubt whether even now it is commonly understood how terrible have been the massacres of the Armenians during the war. The Tartars slaughtered when they invaded Asia Minor, but they slaughtered their enemies. It was left to their spiritual children, the Young Turks, to carry their logic further, and to rest strategy and statesmanship upon the slaughter of their own subjects. The clique who hold Turkey in their power decided that it was politically expedient and profitable to individuals to extirpate the Armenians, and they have carried out their policy about as rigorously as such policies can be executed. It is an indelible stain upon the Germans that they did nothing to stop these atrocities, that some of them even collaborated in them. They will learn that this was a great blunder as well as a great crime.

The Allied policy in Turkey has been defined as the redemption and revival of the oppressed nationalities. Three nationalities have now been given by the Allies their charter of liberty and nationhood—Jews, Arabs, and Armenians. These three peoples comprise the conscious nationalities of Turkey in Asia, and it is they who must be the architects of the new Middle East. Not all are at precisely the same stage of political and social evolution, but because they have a common task they cannot too soon learn to think of it as such. There is no occasion or warrant for rivalry between them. The sphere of each is clearly defined, and none can desire to imitate and transplant from Europe to the Middle East the vulgar ambition to dominate and expand generally which has brought these present miseries upon the world. We would urge, therefore, the leaders of the Jewish, the Armenian, and the Arab national movements to get into the habit of thinking of all three nations as co-workers in a noble work of civilisation in which each has his allotted task.[107]

The Armenians and the Zionists emphasized their similar fate in the past and the suffering both peoples had endured. "In the past, we had the same suffering as the Jewish People," wrote Nubar Pasha in his letter of congratulations to the Zionist Federation in London on November 13.[108] But they also stressed their common future and the fact that the destiny of both oppressed peoples was contingent upon an Allied victory.

The Armenians were sincerely happy about the Zionist victory. Their success "strengthens our hope that the victory of those fighting for the liberation of the oppressed peoples will bring the realization of the Armenian hope, at the same time as the Jewish People achieves the establishment of its nationality, and the realization of its historic demands for the land of its forefathers."[109]

The Armenians mistakenly assumed that the Zionist victory would bring them closer to the achievement of their own aims. They were encouraged when they saw that devoted and persistent efforts could indeed bear fruit. The Zionists also hoped for the success of the Armenians, but the difference was that the Zionists had already made significant progress in achieving their goals while the realization of the Armenian hopes became more distant with every passing day.

Regular contacts between the Zionists—especially Weizmann and Sokolow—in London and the Armenian delegations in London and Paris continued throughout 1918 and early 1919. The full story of these relations, which included consultations, meetings, and mutual assistance, has yet to be told.[110]

Following the Balfour Declaration, Zionist activity in London focused on translating the success of the Declaration into further achievements at the upcoming Peace Conference. Internal discussions of the Zionist leadership in London dealt, among other issues, with the Armenian question and particularly with a comparison between the two peoples and their demands to the Peace Conference. In the winter of 1917-18, it was assumed that the Armenians would obtain some form of sovereignty.

At a meeting of the political committee on November 6, 1917, Weizmann argued vigorously about the Zionist political orientation with his opponent, Tschlenow: "You base everything on an appearance at the Peace Congress. This seems to me most naive. I am, perhaps, more pessimistic than you. If England does not conquer Palestine, you will come to the [Peace] Congress but I do not believe you will find a sympathetic ear. Look at the Armenians. They have hundreds of thousands of victims, and [the Congress] will have to listen to them. We will appeal to humanitarian emotions and achieve nothing."[111]

At another meeting, on November 16, 1917, convened to clarify matters and resolve differences, Tschlenow and Ahad Haam related to the Zionist demands, comparing them to the demands of the Armenians.[112] Tschlenow argued,

> I am convinced that our demands must be more extreme than they were three years ago. Perhaps we should demand a Jewish State like the English dominions. For half a million people, the Armenians are demanding an independent state, simply a protectorate.[113] Perhaps we should behave like them. In any event, it must be clearly stated that the goal is the establishment of a Jewish State in Palestine, although there is need for a period of transition before independence, similar to the dominions. The official language must be Hebrew, from the very beginning; the administration must be in the hands of the Jews, with several local exceptions; the currency, postal stamps, etc., must be Jewish. We must immediately demand, in unambiguous terms, establishment of an independent colony (and we will be given this), or a transitional state for 20-25 years, which will have all of the trappings of a Jewish State, and its administration will have a Jewish character. They will give it to us; they will give us the same rights that they will give to the Armenians.[114]

Ahad Haam, on the other hand, claimed:

> I am party to all of Dr. Tschlenow's concerns, but I draw from them different conclusions. The Arab problem existed three years ago as well, and Egypt was always the center of Arab propaganda. Syria also existed before. In any case, it appears that the attitude of the French toward Syria has chilled a bit. This has become known to us, and the conclusion is not that we must demand an independent state but quite the opposite (since we are still only a very small minority in the productive factors in Palestine). I have never envisioned a state for a people which does not live in it. The Armenians have lived there for thousands of years and the land belongs to them. If the Arabs are so strong in Palestine, we and the English must take this into account. One cannot demand a Jewish currency or a Jewish governor in cities where the majority of inhabitants are Arab. We will be ridiculed if we present such demands.[115]

Although the contacts with the Armenians continued in 1918, not everyone was pleased with the situation. On February 11, 1918, Tolkowsky wrote in his diary:

> In the evening we went to see Ahad Haam. I told him that I had taken upon myself to write an article for the Armenians, and asked him if I might show it to him before publication. He would not hear of it, and he wants nothing

to do with the Armenians. 'This match seems inappropriate to me,' and we have no reason to join forces with the Armenians, since the Russians have declared an end to the state of belligerency with Turkey, and the Turks are about to reimpose their rule over Armenia with no opposition. There is no foundation for this Armenian-Arabic-Jewish alliance, except perhaps for the Arabs in Palestine with whom we must live in peace. Apart from this, the entire alliance is an artificial issue created by the Foreign Office which wants to use us as an instrument to achieve goals which are incomprehensible to me. Therefore, I do not wish to be involved in this.[116]

Weizmann, on the other hand, had adopted Sykes' line and insisted on the political and moral importance of Jewish-Arab-Armenian independence, at least as a strategy for presenting Zionist policy and support for it in the United States. The combination of political and moral considerations which is so prominent in Sykes' thinking appears as a guideline in Weizmann's letter to Louis D. Brandeis on January 14, 1918.[117] Weizmann vigorously attacked the political, economic, and ideological forces which, for various reasons, supported Turkey ("Your Morgenthaus, Elkusses and Edelmanns belong to the same species," he wrote.)[118] "All of those groups would naturally prefer a weak Turkey, integrated Turkey, but weak, instead of a strong Armenia, Arabia and Palestine," he continued and termed them a peculiar "Internationale" which opposed the very ideals for which the war had been fought. Weizmann was particularly bitter about the hypocrisy of Germany and its aspiration to establish a German *weltherrschaft*. He added,

The Germans well know that a Jewish Palestine initiated by Great Britain and supported by America, a Palestine which stands in friendly contact with a free Armenia and an independent Arabia means a death blow to the combination of Islamo-Prussian-Turanian domination in the East. This is why Germany is so very much perturbed about the British Declaration given to us; this is why Germany has 'mobilised' all her sudden 'sympathies' for us, has made Czernin and Talât speak sweet words to us.

Weizmann cited the movements and trends whose principles were opposed to the fundamental principles upon which the Allied Entente was based, and which America had entered the war to defend.

The above mentioned movements must necessarily lead to an integral Turkey which may find new strength in the nationalities of the Caucasus, Ural and Central Asia and which under the tutelage of their German masters may become a power which will crush out of existence Palestine, Armenia, Arabia, and spread its deadening influence across to India. It may become a modern Ghengis Khanate with Krupps guns and poisonous gases, wireless telegraphy and U-boats. It is a danger to Europe and America alike.

Weizmann concluded his letter:

For it must be abundantly clear that there is a complete coincidence of American-British-Judean interests as against Prusso-Turkish interests....It is also clear that the creation of a Jewish Palestine and the liberation of Armenia and Arabia is in the interests not only of the British Empire, but of British, American democracies, in fact of all genuine democracies. These three nations will form a powerful barrier against which the waves of the German-Turanian ambitions will break; a wall which would prevent the spread of German might over the world.

In personal correspondence with Jewish and Zionist friends as well, Weizmann adopted Sykes' political strategy and moral assessments, at least at this stage.

The Armenian Question from the Zionist Point of View

As mentioned above, Shmuel Tolkowsky had been asked to write an article for the Armenian journal, *Ararat*, which was published in London. Tolkowsky relates in his diary on February 16, 1918, that he has written the article. Several days later he received a thank you note for his interesting and valuable contribution to *Ararat*.[119] The article reflects not only Tolkowsky's personal opinion, but also the stance of the Zionist leadership in London. Ahad Haam did not want to read it, apparently because he had reservations about the Zionists' relationship with the Armenians, but it is probable that Sokolow and Weizmann read it and that it reflects the "official" position of the Zionist Organization in London. The article, entitled "The Armenian Question From the Zionist Point of View," is relevant to our subject and appears, in its entirety, in Appendix B.[120]

The article was written in the spirit of Weizmann's remarks (see above). The subsequent edition of *Ararat*, May 1918, published Weizmann's comments at the Governor's residence in Jerusalem before an audience which included the Armenian Bishop of Cairo representing the Patriarch and the Armenian community, Arab notables, and others, on the occasion of the arrival in Jerusalem of the delegation of the Commission of Deputies. Weizmann's remarks, on April 27, 1918, were intended to allay Arab concerns and fears of the Zionists. The headline of the article in *Ararat* was "Arabs, Jews and Armenians."[121] Weizmann spoke warmly about the Arabs' aspirations, about their past and about Arab-Jewish cooperation, which had found its most noble expression during the Golden Age in Spain. He envisioned the creation of a new society in Palestine, based on the vision of the biblical prophets, which would be a source of knowledge and idealism for the benefit of humanity.

In his speech, Weizmann also dedicated some of his remarks to the Armenians, the alliance, and the common destiny of the Jews, the Arabs and the Armenians, in the spirit of Sykes' dream.

To the north the Armenian nation, which at the present is paying the bloodiest toll in blood to the cruel enemy, will rise triumphantly to claim justice and the right to live in peace on the soil which is being drenched with the blood of its best sons.

To this nation, our heart goes out and we feel that these three nations—Arabs, Jews and Armenians—who have suffered most in the world have perhaps of all nations the highest claim to a life of freedom and peaceful development. Destiny has chosen these three nations to guard the classic gates into the ancient world against the Turanian hordes [i.e., the Turks] which, armed with the deadliest of modern and destructive weapons, are being organized by their task-masters [i.e., the Germans].

We Jews are already feeling the effects of the new menace; the Armenian massacres in the Caucasus and the fresh Jewish massacres in Turkestan should serve as a warning sign to all of us. They should teach the Arab, Jew and Armenian to stand united in order to resist by all and every means in our power the forces of darkness and oppression, which now threaten to overwhelm the civilised world. If this guard of freedom stands united, Palestine may look forward to a future as great as its past. It will become the connecting link between East and West, interpreting the one to the other, and harmonising their different, but not opposing, conceptions of life. We Zionists ask therefore for an opportunity for free, natural development in Palestine and in justice that demand cannot be refused.

Sykes' death in February 1919 was, as Aaron Aaronsohn wrote in his diary, a great loss to both the Armenians and the Zionists. They had lost a defender and an advocate for the oppressed nationalities. As time went by it became clear that matters were becoming increasingly difficult for the Armenians. France, England, and the United States, each for its own reasons, dropped the Armenian cause. The victorious powers did not fulfill the commitments they had made publicly. The Zionists, on the other hand, achieved much.

Although Sykes had lost some of his power and ability to shape British policy during 1918, he did not neglect his friendship with the Armenians and the Jews. In a secret letter to Nubar Pasha in March 1918, Sykes wrote that the situation was not encouraging and that they were living in dark times.[122]

In his opinion, there were two objectives confronting the Armenians: firstly, to save as many Armenians as possible from extermination, and secondly, to never give up the idea of an independent Armenian state. In order to save as many Armenians as possible from annihilation, he proposed that they investigate the possibility of paying the Kurds and other tribes in the Armenian regions to protect or ease the flight of Armenians. Another possibility was to continue to put pressure on the Vatican. The third option—and the most interesting in our context— was the possibility that Zionist organizations would exert some influence, if they could be persuaded to give public expression to the issue. From this it can be inferred that Sykes believed that other countries, including the Entente Powers — England, France ,and the U.S.—would not save them.

As for keeping the dream of an Armenian state alive, Sykes thought it was very important to refute the claim that the Armenians were now a minority in their own provinces, and therefore not entitled to independence. The crime of turning a majority into a minority by physical annihilation must never be sanctioned; it were as granting the murderers a divine right to profit from their crimes. Sykes opposed the possibility—which ultimately came to pass—of the biblical injunction: "Shall ye murder and yet inherit?!"

His dream of a Jewish-Arab-Armenian alliance was never realized. Armenia obtained its independence and separate sovereignty for a very brief period, 1918-1920, only to become, thereafter, the Armenian SSR within the bounds of the Soviet Union. Most of the territory of historic Armenia remained under Turkish rule. Nor were Jewish-Arab relations built on agreement and cooperation. It appears that Sykes' warning— that non-cooperation would bring disaster upon both the Jews and the Arabs—has come to pass.

David Fromkin, in his important and comprehensive book, *A Peace to End All Peace* (1989), deals with the fall of the Ottoman Empire and the creation of a new Middle East. In summing up the historic events,

Fromkin writes that the story of the Ottoman Empire came to an end in 1922. The agreement of 1922, which was ratified in a peace treaty with the Allies in Lausanne a year later, brought an end to the Ottoman Empire and divided the Middle East between Turkey, France, and England. In Fromkin's opinion, "it embodied much of the program of the postwar Middle East that the British Government had formulated (mostly through the agency of Sir Mark Sykes) between 1915 and 1917."[123] Fromkin emphasizes, again and again, Sykes' importance in formulating British Middle East policy. The claim that much of what Sykes had proposed during the war became the basis for the Middle East which emerged after the war may be accurate with regard to the Arabs and the Zionists, each in their own way, but it is groundless with regard to the Armenians. The hope that an anti-German front, based on an Arab-Jewish-Armenian alliance, would develop in the Middle East was also not realized, as was seen during the course of the Second World War.

In July 1917, Sykes wrote to Balfour: "I have tried to work on war lines and not pre-war lines *vis*: Nationality, Cooperation, and Alliance, instead of imperialism, isolated action and special individual war aims."[124] "France and Britain must recognize the fact that they are Allies, now and after the war. Each one of them must recognise that the other is a better neighbor than Turkey or Germany," wrote Sykes in July 1917 in another memorandum. Cooperation based on mutual concessions—the concept which guided Sykes—was weakened, and considerations of the particularistic interests of each of the parties came to the fore. "The importance of the moral dimension," "the ideals for which the better forces are struggling—liberation of the oppressed peoples and preservation of the peace"—lost their centrality. Sykes cautioned against a "narrow imperialistic approach"; "if France and England move sincerely toward the Arab nationalism, when France suppresses its financial aspirations and Britain its imperialistic aspirations, it will then be possible to create a defense shield, an Arab-Jewish-Armenian buffer between Persia-Egypt-India and the Turkish-German combination."[125]

Fromkin states, "By the time the war came to an end, British society was generally inclined to reject the idealistic case for imperialism (that it would extend the benefits of advanced civilization to a backward region) as quixotic, and the practical case for it (that it would be of benefit to Britain to expand her empire) as untrue....From the British point of view, the settlement of 1922 had become largely out of date by the time it was effected."[126]

The strategy adopted by Weizmann and Sokolow during the years 1917-19 was one of cooperation with the Armenian delegation in Paris, and dialogue with Armenian representatives. They did so, first and foremost, because they were aware that it was important to Sykes, whose support was crucial to their own cause.

It is evident that they believed, as he did, that the future of Zionist hopes and the future of all oppressed peoples was heavily dependent upon the victory of the Entente Powers. The moral ethos championed by representatives of the Entente Powers was frequently no more than a slogan—certainly with regard to the Armenian question. Sykes, on the other hand, was a sincere and authentic exponent of this ethos and his influence over the Zionist leaders was profound. Considerations of *realpolitik*, which proved in retrospect to be correct, impelled them to rely on Britain. They also understood, correctly from the perspective of Zionist interests, that under the auspices of British rule they would be joining forces with partners who insisted that politics must be moral and that British interests would best be served if England assisted the oppressed peoples instead of working against them or ignoring them.

It is important to note that the Armenians regarded Aaronsohn, Weizmann, Sokolow, and the Zionists who acted on their behalf in London as true friends. Even in their internal correspondence they spoke of them warmly and with appreciation. The Armenians also believed that the Zionists held the key to considerable power and influence which could aid them in their struggle.

Notes

1. *Aaronsohn Diaries*, pp. 135-36. In his diary from November 11, 1916, several days previous, Aaron writes, "It appears that Sykes is the go-between for the War Office and the Foreign Office." Colonel G.H. Fitzmaurice was present at one of the discussions between Aaron and Sykes. They talked about Zionist matters and the landing of the British forces on the beaches of Eretz Yisrael, which Fitzmaurice supported. Ibid., October 30, 1916, pp. 120-21.
2. See on this matter: Leonard Stein, *The Balfour Declaration* (New York: Simon and Schuster, 1961), pp. 289-95. (Henceforth: Stein.)
3. *Aaronsohn Diaries*, p. 503.
4. *The Man and His Times*, p. 292.
5. Eliezer Livneh, "In the Shadow of the Armenian Holocaust," *Hauma*, vol. 3, no.(10)2, September 1964, p. 366.
6. *The Man and His Times*, p. 292.

7.   Quotes by Aaron Aaronsohn, *Diaries*, pp. 251-52.

8.   See note 7.

9.   See note 7.

10. The meeting between Sykes, Weizmann, and Sokolow was held at the end of January 1917. Afterwards, on February 7, Sykes met with a wider forum of Zionist representatives in England in a meeting which was to be decisive for the Balfour Declaration. It should be emphasized that it was Malcolm who introduced Sykes to Weizmann and Sokolow. There is no doubt that Sykes and Malcolm had met previously, but the exact date is unknown.

11. Their conversation on April 27, 1917. *Aaronsohn Diaries*, pp. 251-52.

12. The Sledmere Papers, War Committee meeting held at 10 Downing Street on December 16, 1915 on the Arab Question.

13. The Sledmere Papers, protocol of the meeting at 10 Downing Street on April 3, 1917, to discuss instructions to Lieutenant Colonel Sir Mark Sykes, head of the political delegation to the High Command of the Egyptian Expeditionary Force (E.E.F.), in the Sykes' Archives.

14. This may be an allusion to Aaron Aaronsohn's organization.

15. Draft telegram, April 24, 1917, to Sir Ronald Graham.

16. The Sledmere Papers, a private letter from Sir Mark Sykes to Sir Eric Drummond, July 20, 1917. Sykes asks Drummond to bring the letter to the attention of Foreign Minister Balfour.

17. The Sledmere Papers, a Memorandum from Sir M. Sykes to War Cabinet. The document is undated but appears to have been sent in May 1917.

18. The Sledmere Papers, Memorandum on the Asia-Minor Agreements by Sir Mark Sykes, August 18, 1917.

19. His proposals are similar in spirit to the resolutions of the Labour Party and indeed Sykes says that "The Labour Conference's resolutions are a very good formula."

20. General G. A. Clayton, in a telegram to Sykes on November 28, 1917, says he is not optimistic about Sykes' plans because of difficulties on the Arab side. He remarks that the only consolation is that George Picot, the French representative, agrees with Sykes' views. See *The Man and His Times*, p. 294.

21. Ibid., p. 295. The following passages are taken mostly from the Sledmere Archives.

22. Eliezer Livneh, "In the Shadow of the Armenian Holocaust," *Hauma*, vol. 3, no. (10)2, September 1964, p. 366.

23. From a letter from Sir Ronald Graham to Lord Harding, Deputy Foreign Minister, November 3, 1917. See *Aaronsohn Diaries*, pp. 352-53, editorial note quoting from British documents. Balfour brought these matters before the War Cabinet.

24. *Aaronsohn Diaries*, pp. 355-56. A telegram of this nature to the British ambassador in Washington indeed exists. The diary reveals the reservations of Sokolow, Chlenov, and Ahad Haam toward Aaronsohn, as well

as Sykes' involvement in the activities. The information in the diary is reliable and is confirmed by information which appears in the diary of Shmuel Tolkowsky, *A Political Diary: London 1915-1916* (Jerusalem: The Zionist Library, 1991), p. 223. (Henceforth: Tolkowsky.)

25. Tolkowsky, pp. 221-22. And, in fact, at the meeting of the Political Committee on November 23, 1917, Ahad Haam complained that "several days ago an emissary was sent to America on a very important mission—one of the most important problems which have arisen since the establishment of this committee" without a bit of notification to the committee. Ibid., p. 223.

26. *Aaronsohn Diaries*, pp. 359-60. Some of the information in Shmuel Aaronsohn's telegram to his brother was incorrect. Sarah had indeed committed suicide, but their father was not dead, and Naaman Belkind was also still alive, imprisoned in Damascus.

27. Ibid., notes 13, 13a, quoting from British documents.

28. See, for example, *Aaronsohn Diaries*, pp. 434, 436.

29. Ibid., February 16, 1919, p. 503.

30. See, for example, ibid., December 28, 1918, p. 461. "Major Gribbon and Captain McInod are satisfied with my work in Paris, which Webster reported to them in a flattering report."

31. Ibid., p. 436.

32. Ibid., p. 502.

33. From a report by Aaronsohn appended to a letter by Weizmann which was sent to Sir Ira Crowe in the British Foreign Office. See F.O. 371/3415, document 194778. Appears in *Aaronsohn Diaries*, pp. 428-29.

34. Ibid., November 26, 1918, p. 427.

35. Ibid., November 29, 1918, p. 433.

36. Ibid., November 27, 1918, p. 429.

37. Ibid., December 2, 1918, p. 437.

38. Ibid., January 18, 1919, p. 482.

39. Ibid., December 14, 1918, p. 449.

40. Ibid., January 19, 1919, p. 483.

41. Ibid., p. 483, note citing British Foreign Office references.

42. Ibid., p. 437.

43. Ibid., p. 433, citations from British Foreign Office documents.

44. Ibid., November 29, 1918, p. 433. In the original: "une vraie 'self-extermination' et non 'self-determination.'

45. Citation from Malcolm's letter to British Foreign Secretary Balfour. See *Aaronsohn Diaries*, p. 436, notes.

46. Ibid., November 29, 1918, p. 434.

47. Ibid., p. 428.

48. Ibid., p. 439.

49. Ibid., December 1, 1918, p. 436.

50. Ibid., December 15, 1918, p. 450.

51. The reference may be to Ahad Haam, who expressed reservations about cooperation with the Armenians.

52. Ibid., p. 450.
53. Ibid., p. 439.
54. Ibid., p. 459. But in a different entry he expresses concern about Faysal's instability.
55. Adolph Baroni, "General Allenby In Palestine," *Asia Magazine*, November 1918, pp. 896-906.
56. Malcolm to Nubar Pasha, November 20, 1918, Nubar Pasha Archives in Paris. The other documents cited in the remainder of this chapter are also in this archive.
57. Felix Frankfurter to Nubar Pasha, November 2, 1918, Nubar Pasha Archives in Paris.
58. Malcolm to Nubar Pasha, November 21, 1918. Malcolm writes that after receipt of such comprehensive information, a protest must be lodged against the monstrous proposals of Barton, Morgenthau, and their group.
59. Malcolm to Nubar Pasha, September 5, 1918.
60. Malcolm to Sevasly, January 15, 1918, Nubar Pasha Archives in Paris.
61. Malcolm to Nubar Pasha, January 31, 1918.
62. Malcolm to Nubar Pasha, February 26, 1918.
63. *A History of Political Daring*, p. 361.
64. *Ararat*, no. 65, May 1919.
65. See Tolkowsky's introduction pp. 12-13, written by Deborah Barzilay-Yaeger; Stein, pp. 210, 278-80; David Fromkin, *A Peace To End All Peace* (New York: Avon Books, 1989), pp. 290-92. Both Stein and Fromkin emphasize Sykes' importance in shaping British policy in the region.
66. *Aaronsohn Diaries*, October 27, 1916, p. 119. Sykes took an interest "but is not close to the views of Gaster or of L. Wolff."
67. Norman Rose, *Chaim Weizmann: A Biography* (London: Weidenfeld and Nicolson, 1986), p. 166.
68. *The Letters and Papers of Chaim Weizman,* vol. 7, series A (London: Oxford University Press; Jerusalem: Israel University Press, 1975), letter 305 to Sokolow, February 4, 1917. (Henceforth: *Weizmann Letters.*)
69. Stein, pp. 366-67.
70. According to Tolkowsky's diary, pp. 36, 37, 371, et al.
71. In Malcolm's report on his trip he notes, "March 30, in view of the imminent trip of Sir Mark Sykes and Mr. Picot to the East, Sir Mark, Mr. Sokolow, Dr. Weizmann and Mr. Malcolm met at 9 Buckingham Gate. It was decided that Mr. Sokolow and Mr. Malcolm would leave for Paris as soon as possible."
72. Malcolm relates in his report that Sokolow wanted him to accompany him to Rome, but Malcolm did not think he could be of use in Rome.
73. "Precis Report of the Special Mission of Mr. N. Sokolow and Mr. J.A. Malcolm to Paris re: Zionist Demands for a Jewish Home in Palestine." The main portions of the report appear in Tolkowsky's diary, pp. 48-52. The complete report is in the Zionist Archives A/226/30/1 (The Samuel Landman Archive), and contains important material relevant to our subject.

74. Malcolm also met on April 11, after Picot's trip to Egypt, on prior coordination, with Mr. Gotte, an official attache in the French Foreign Ministry who was standing in during Picot's absence, for a long general discussion about Zionism and Palestine. See Malcolm's report.

75. Among them were Hovhannes Khan, former Persian ambassador to Berlin, and Mr. Varantin, who was acquainted with Weizmann.

76. Other Syrian leaders in Paris were Dr. Samney and Mr. Shukky Ghanem, from *Le Matin*. They were, it appears, the heads of the "Central Syrian Committee," which had been organized by Syrians residing in Paris for the purpose of working toward the liberation of Syria from French control. The Committee was officially established on May 2, 1917.

77. On April 14, Sokolow met with Jewish representatives, including Reinarch, and reported—according to Malcolm—the results: "A long debate, several sharp exchanges with Bogard and Reinarch, but the result seems to be satisfactory." The next day Sokolow lunched with Reinarch.

78. Tolkowsky's diary, p. 56. It appears that several additional people read it. We read in Tolkowsky's diary: "Boris [Boris Dov Goldberg] also tells me that after reading Malcolm's report on the mission in Paris, Ahad Haam was very angry that the English Government had deceived us— so it appears to him—by concealing from us the matter of an arrangement between England and France. According to Boris, he (Ahad Haam) was very critical; Boris repeats his own criticism on this issue, working without the committee. He says that Sokolow should not have gone to Paris without discussing the matter in the committee. I again explained to him the difficulties involved in working with the committee (Gaster, etc.)."

79. Zionist Archives, A18/512. Sokolow wrote to Weizmann that he wanted him to read his assessment before Malcolm returned and reported to him.

80. According to Ormsby-Gore's report from June 10, 1917, it was Malcolm who disclosed the plan but refused to reveal his source of information.

81. Tolkowsky's diary, p. 127.

82. Ormsby-Gore report.

83. Note Weizmann's sharp language with regard to Morgenthau. Weizmann also argued that Morgenthau wanted to support Talât Pasha, his personal friend, against the pro-German, Enver Pasha, even after the meeting with Morgenthau. *Weizmann Letters*, July 6, 1917.

84. Weizmann to Charles P. Scott, June 26, 1917, *Weizmann Letters*, vol. 7, letter 443. Weizmann also mentions the tension between international financial interests and movements based on nationalist ideals. For additional details on Weizmann and Malcolm's activity and its influence on the cancellation of the attempt to make a separate peace, see Stein, pp. 295-97; Jehuda Reinharz, *Chaim Weizmann: The Making of a Statesman* (New York: Oxford University Press, 1993), pp. 153-66.

85. The Sledmere Papers, "A Memorandum from Sir M. Sykes to War Cabinet."

86. "A Separate Peace With Turkey," *Palestine*, June 23, 1917.
87. "The Revision of War Aims," *Palestine*, June 30, 1917.
88. Weizmann to Sir Ronald Graham, July 6, 1917, *Weizmann Letters*, vol. 7, letter 453.
89. Tolkowsky's diary, August 7, 1917.
90. Frankfurter took part in the American delegation headed by Morgenthau which held discussions in Gibraltar on the possibility of a separate peace with Turkey. *Weizmann Letters*, vol. 7, letter 479, August 17, 1917.
91. Telegram dated November 14, 1917, Documents at St. Antony's College, Oxford, No. 85.
92. Documents from St. Antony's College, Oxford, November 16, 1917, No. 86.
93. Sykes mentioned the names of Said Noutnify and Moustafa Renfoy.
94. Sykes this time suggested the names of Lt. Ismail Ablo Hkkawai and Lt. Abodin Huskoymi.
95. Telegram to Sykes, December 12, 1917. It appears that not all of the correspondence is available.
96. The Sledmere Papers, No. 95.
97. Stein, p. 565.
98. Zionist Archives, Z4/186.
99. Telegram from Nubar Pasha, December 7, 1917, Zionist Archives, Z4/106/85; Z4/196; Z4/106/25.
100. Weizmann and Sokolow to Nubar Pasha, December 20, 1917, Zionist Archives, Z4/106/2.5.
101. The journal of the Zionist Organization in Great Britain published the speech separately under the title, "Jew, Arab and Armenian," *Palestine*, vol. 2, no. 18, December 8, 1917.
102. David Fromkin, p. 299. Fromkin relies in this matter on documents of St. Antony's College, Oxford.
103. *Weizmann Letters*, vol. 8, letter 21, December 6, 1917.
104. Reuters' report of Sykes' speech at the Manchester rally, December 6, 1917, sent to Cairo December 10, 1917. The Sledmere Papers.
105. *Weizmann Letters*, vol. 8, letter 22, December 11, 1917.
106. Sokolow and Weizmann to Nubar Pasha, November 27, 1917, Nubar Pasha Archives, Paris.
107. "Armenian, Arab and Jew," *Palestine*, vol. 2, no. 16, November 24, 1917.
108. Nubar Pasha also sent personal letters of congratulation separately to Weizmann and Sokolow on November 14, 1917.
109. From greetings sent by Nubar Pasha on November 27 to the Zionist Assembly which took place on December 2, 1917. The letter was received by Weizmann, Sokolow, and Lord Rothschild.
110. See, *inter alia*, Sokolow's letter to Malcolm on March 19, 1919, Zionist Archives, A/226/30/1. The Armenian delegation in Paris and London sent letter of condolence on the death of Tschlenow in December 1918. Sokolow spoke at a meeting with the Armenians in May 1918. On his trip to Russia, Sokolow carried letters from Nubar Pasha to Armenian

leaders there. Zionist Archives, A18/28, Z4/186, and A18/32 (Sokolow Archive). This was in addition to the correspondence relating to the Balfour Declaration.

111. Tolkowsky, p. 205.
112. Tolkowsky and others attended the meeting.
113. In October 1916, after learning of the Sykes-Picot Agreement by which parts of the Armenian provinces were to be ceded to Russia, the Armenian National Delegation obtained a promise from France that Cilicia and three Armenian provinces would be under French rule, similar to the arrangement in Tunisia and Algeria, and that they would enjoy broad autonomy. After the Russian Revolution in February/March and Russian declarations opposing territorial annexation, the Delegation reverted to its original program and demanded the establishment of a neutral, autonomous Armenia comprising Cilicia and the six Armenian provinces, under the collective protection of the Great Powers. This demand was based on an assumption that the Peace Conference would grant to one of the Great Powers a mandate over Armenia until this was ready for independence.
114. Tolkowsky, p. 217.
115. Ibid., p. 218.
116. Ibid., p. 269.
117. *Weizmann Letters*, vol. 8, letter 63, January 14, 1918.
118. Morgenthau was, as mentioned, the U.S. Ambassador in Constantinople during the years 1913-16. Abraham Elkus was the U.S. Ambassador there in 1916-17. Samuel Edelmann served in the U.S. Consular Service in Constantinople, in Jerusalem, Aleppo, Damascus, and Geneva (1909-19). All three aided the Armenians during the war, and although they were not Zionists, they were very helpful to the Jewish community in Palestine during that period.
119. Tolkowsky Archive, A/248.
120. S. Tolkowsky, "The Armenian Question from the Zionist Point of View," *Ararat*, No. 57, April 1918, pp. 346-47.
121. *Ararat*, No. 58, May 1918, pp. 417-20.
122. Mark Sykes to Nubar Pasha, March 20, 1918. Nubar Pasha Archives, Paris. Sykes added that Malcolm had probably told him about their conversations in London.
123. Fromkin, pp. 170, 562.
124. Personal letter to Sir Eric Drummond, July 20, 1917, which Sykes asked be delivered to Balfour.
125. All of the quotes are from a memorandum written by Sykes on July 18, 1917, St. Antony's College, Document 66. One can find numerous remarks in a similar spirit by Sykes.
126. Fromkin, pp. 561-62.

6

Silent Muses—The Armenian Massacre as Seen in the Literature of the Jewish Yishuv in Eretz Yisrael

In numerous ways and from varied directions, literature serves as an imperfect mirror of life in its broadest sense. Literature represents reality in an art form; it is a manner of relating, and of constructing action. In this sense, literature is also an artistic form of a documentary. One can, therefore, use literature to examine the attitude of the Jewish community in Eretz Yisrael toward the massacre of the Armenians. We shall do so in two ways: first, by investigating the reactions in the Jewish community in Eretz Yisrael to Franz Werfel's *The Forty Days of Musa Dagh*. This epic work, which tells the story of the annihilation of the Armenian People and the most heroic chapter in its history, first appeared in 1933 and was translated into Hebrew a year later. Secondly, we explore the manner in which the Armenian tragedy was treated in original literary works.

Although we searched exhaustively, aided by researchers and critics of the literature of Eretz Yisrael, our efforts bore little fruit. Only two writers, Aaron Reuveni and Shmuel Bass, deal with the Armenian genocide in any significant fashion in their literary work.

Aaron Reuveni wrote his comprehensive trilogy, *Unto Jerusalem,* during the years 1916-20. He began work on the first volume, *In the Beginning of Confusion*, in the winter of 1916, and completed it in August 1918. The book was written at the height of the First World War, "days of emergency," as he put it. In the summer of 1919, he completed the second volume, *The Last Ships,* and in the summer of 1920, he

271

finished the third and final volume, *Devastation.*[1] Shmuel Bass completed *Ara* in 1928. Both works were published before the appearance of Werfel's book, *The Forty Days of Musa Dagh*, which was apt, perhaps, to fire the literary imagination.

These two works differ in quality. Later criticism views *Unto Jerusalem* as one of the important works of the literature of Eretz Yisrael, although at the time it was unenthusiastically received by its readers. But while Reuveni won later acclaim, it appears that Bass' body of work in general, and *Ara* in particular, have been forgotten to this day.

Another difference between them is the place of the Armenian tragedy in the work. In Reuveni's trilogy, a broad, sweeping novel from the time of the First World War ("a novel about the period," "a meta-period novel," according to Yigael Schwartz), the subject of the Armenians appears as only one aspect of this expansive novel. Nonetheless, the Armenian question occupies a significant, albeit not central, place in the work.

The Armenian question stands, in fact, at the center of Reuveni's short story, "In The Wagon," which will be examined below. It is almost certain that "In The Wagon," which was published in 1928, was excerpted from the trilogy in its original form.[2] In contrast, the Armenian tragedy stands at the center of Bass' *Ara*, in the figure of the Armenian girl, Ara.[3]

Moreover, from both of these literary works we understand, directly and indirectly, that the Armenian tragedy was known in Eretz Yisrael very close to the time of its occurrence. Although it wins significant mention in *Devastation*, the third volume of the trilogy, it occupies a place in the second volume, and the earlier Armenian massacre (in 1894-96) is also mentioned—as raising questions concerning the war-torn present—in the first part of the trilogy. Shmuel Bass apparently wrote his novel during the 1920s, but from reading the work it becomes abundantly clear that he had heard about the disaster during the last days of the war, before the English had completed their conquest of Palestine.

The present chapter is different in character from the other parts of this volume and deals mostly with a presentation of excerpts of these literary works which are relevant to our discussion. Essentially, this is a presentation of the books as a source of documentation and literary testimony rather than an analysis of literature. I hope also to bring these works, particularly the forgotten *Ara*, to the attention of my readers.

Aaron Reuveni: *Unto Jerusalem*, "Into the Wagon"

In the early 1920s, Aaron Reuveni (Shimshelevitch, the brother of the future president of Israel, Yizhak Ben Zvi), published three novels which together form a trilogy: *In the Beginning of Confusion* (1920); *The Last Ships* (1923); and *Devastation*, (1925). All three were reprinted as a collection in the 1950s, under the title *Unto Jerusalem*. Sections of the trilogy were reprinted, separately and in collection, during the 1960s and 1980s. The trilogy, a sweeping story of the life of Jerusalem during the First World War, has been rediscovered by the Israeli reader. With rare talent and great power, the author describes the interior world of individuals as it blends with the broader world, the activities, events, and emotions of the multifaceted spiritual, cultural, and social milieu of Jerusalem during that gloomy and tumultuous period.

Reuveni writes in the introduction to the book, "All of the characters and events in this novel are fiction, but the fiction is composed of bricks taken from life at that time. If there are even the slightest similarities between events in the story and events which have occurred, they are to be found partly by coincidence and partly in the nature of the materials from which this composition has been constructed."

Literary critics and commentators have identified some of the main characters in the novel as figures who became, over time, leaders and prominent personalities in the Yishuv: Yizhak Ben Zvi, second president of the State of Israel, appears in the figure of Chaim Ram; David Ben-Gurion, several times prime minister of the State of Israel and the predominant public figure in its early history, is Givoni; and Yaakov Zerubavel, one of the leaders of the workers' movement, is Ben Mattitiyahu. Reuveni knew them personally from his public literary and journalistic activity after he settled in Palestine in 1909. (We shall examine the attitudes of Ben Gurion and Ben Zvi to the Armenian massacre in the later chapter, "The Indifferent.")

A central character in the trilogy and the hero (anti-hero?) of the third volume, *Devastation*, is Meyer Ponek who, after numerous wanderings, vacillation, and physical and spiritual agonizing, finally decides to enlist in the Turkish army. Meyer Ponek is deeply involved in the lives of his fellows and in the affairs of his time, but attempts to fight against the stream of events, and to distinguish himself from the mass of which he is a part, emotionally and morally. In the Turkish army he ends up performing military chores assigned to a Jewish contractor.

The contractor would get drunk with the army commanders, fawn upon them and supply them with young boys. Toward those who could be of no use to him, he was vulgar and brutal, speaking with his whip and fists and working them without mercy.

Meyer could not understand this....And the drunken contractor, with his bloodshot eyes, could not understand him either. In the end, he was transferred to a different work brigade, to the Turks, where he felt more comfortable. At least he did not have to see Jews with faces like the dead, whose hands and legs trembled and whose strength was being steadily drained by carting soil....One day a German commander happened by and noticed him. Why him? Because he was tall, fair-haired, and of striking visage. The German asked who he was and what he was doing and took him with him. Ponek lay in the German military hospital for six weeks and recovered. Afterwards, he was assigned to the sappers' brigade.[4]

The climax and the conclusion of the novel is Ponek's final night. He leaves the German military camp and goes off to his death. On the brink of madness he chooses to take his own life:

He was tall and painfully thin. He moved heavily and wearily. His rough boots left deep tracks in the smooth sand. His clothes were those of a German soldier. Not the child of the desert. Alien!

After plodding on for two or three hours, he lay down on a sandy hill, barren as all the others around... in the desert, in the Mountains of Moab beyond the Dead Sea. On this very hill, only minutes before, clustered four jackals howling to their heart's content. The man did not howl, and contentment was distant from his heart.

The weight of sorrow which had built up around him for many months, ever since he had become a military man, again flooded his soul, filling it with darkness and black as the desert night. In his imagination he saw the small sappers' encampment from which he had come, and the tent of Sergeant Hirt. He imagined them sitting around and getting drunk as they did every night.

For more than three months he had wandered with them in the desert. They would dig wells in search of water for the army which would pass that way. And the deeper they went into the wasteland, the deeper became the wasteland in his heart, the less he believed he would ever see home again, and the less he wished to return. The people, too, in whose company he traveled and for whom he had not the slightest feeling of affection, were a burden on his spirit which grew day by day. How would he come to them, those people in the city with whom he truly belonged?... Not just to dwell together?...Estherke....He had received two letters from her and had not replied. He had not wanted to reply. Had taken pen in hand—and could not....What is this web of a miserable life? The web still sticks to him, reeking, but its center was torn. There is no going back, one cannot go back... All of these grumbling, groaning Germans and Turks and Arabs, who never cease to think of their release....Release?

Aha?... Yes, release! For they are as they have been, and he is different!... They are like the wagon which has broken down, wobbling and squeaking, about to collapse at any moment, yet, continues to roll on, and on.

Have his sufferings been worse than others'? Indeed he has seldom been beaten and has not been tortured, and worked only briefly in "Amalia." And yet those who remained back there would, as long as a breath of life was left, continue to grasp at this wretched life. While he, who had been saved from that purgatory, would let go of the rope. Saved?... Ha, ha!

In any case, he had seen things... seen sickly deserters, condemned to death; seen how they were put to death by shooting—and seen them afterwards; seen those who had been viciously beaten when they ached and suffered and slowly died; seen the Armenian doctor who had poisoned forty ill soldiers, seen him as he died; seen Jewish boys, pale, tortured city kids, who were playthings for the lust of the army officers and commanders; seen sick people rolling around without help, rotting alive, covered with lice and filth; seen people who wandered like shadows, who could not adjust, who could not understand how they had gotten here, whose souls had turned into a jumble of fear, anger, stubbornness and despair, and who had been tortured for the sport of it; seen a man stumble and fall, laying like the dead. The army commander had ordered that he be buried—and they buried him...but he was not yet dead, he was breathing while they buried him alive...seen masses of people who went where they had been told to go, did what they had been ordered to do, chewed what they had been given to eat and slept where they had been laid. They were angry and bitter, these masses—and as obedient and impervious as a herd of cattle.

Their hearts were filled with bitterness and fury, and above all—fear. When one or two or ten people were selected among them, placed where all could see, and their brethren given orders to shoot them, they were shot. And afterwards the rest gathered even closer together, stayed silent and even more obedient.... These armed masses, who work so hard and are fed so little, who get little sleep, so utterly oppressed, he saw every day until he could no longer bear it...and could no longer run away....He should have fled at once. Now all of this was part of him, in his bones. And one cannot flee from oneself.

When had it begun? Perhaps in the office of the "Kolorassi," on the terrace, when he saw the few tyrannizing the many, a tyranny base by its nature and awful in its degradation, capable of crushing a man like an insect, without effort or responsibility, with the wink of an eye. And the man is so wretched, so worthless, so downtrodden that the very possibility of being crushed has broken him! It built up in him...even more...until it overflowed!

Ponek lies sprawled on the sand, his head down and his forehead resting on his fists, reconstructing the road from Jerusalem back to the camp in the desert, and remembers the news he had learned in Jerusalem.

Around him all was silent. Suddenly the air was pierced by the howl of the jackals. "As if they have found out!" He was amused by the thought. "How do they know?" he asked himself mirthlessly and felt his hair stand on end and a thread of cold terror crawl in his heart. He lifted his head and looked around. What is that hiding over there behind those mounds? He leaped suddenly to his feet, rifle in hand and finger on the trigger—stood up to his full height and looked ahead.

"Ho, ho, ho!" a great laugh burst from his mouth and quickly stopped. "What is this?" he asked himself in amazement. "They say that when the moment approaches, the mind goes mad...but I am not mad! No I am not crazy!'

Why indeed had he decided on this? It was no longer clear to him. Surely there must be a point—but what could it be? He could be laying in his tent sleeping peacefully right now. But what?...Tent?...peaceful sleep?...and to-morrow?... No, I've had enough!...This time there will be an end to it....An end!" He cried in a mad fury.

He sat down for a moment and his whole body trembled. Afterwards he again lay on the sand and covered his face with his hands. His heart was empty of feeling or fear. And he no longer had need to look around him.

With eyes closed he envisioned the camp, the hordes of soldiers who had become a herd of cattle, and those few who could not adjust and were consumed like dry grass. And he himself—with whom did he belong? He had done his work, behaved courteously, and kept his feelings to himself . But in his heart he had not adjusted. His soul was a wasteland which filled his very being....The desert had invaded him. All of the living springs had dried up, been overrun with sand and thorns. There was no going back. He had already known this then, when he had left home.

He had once entered the military hospital. The Armenian doctor lay there, sick with typhoid fever. He was dying. His face, pale and shiny in the dim light, looked like glass. His head rested heavily on the pillow. His eyes were sunken into their sockets. His belly was swollen like a barrel. He was too weak to move. Only his eyes moved: eyes that saw everything and understood, preserving the last shred of life. Those eyes called him and he came closer. They laughed at him, demanding that he come even closer, closer. Yes, they laughed, he was not mistaken about this. Even now he could see them — those laughing dying eyes and the whispering voice like a wisp of breath: "Listen please...Jew! Listen...I shall tell you, tonight I will die...I knew this...I poisoned forty soldiers...Turks...sick with typhoid...forty...I counted them...a Turk stole my wife...and my children...they killed my father...they killed my brother...I poisoned forty...I counted...good." Did he say more? His voice was gone. Only his eyes moved in their sockets lucidly and laughed and laughed.

They are laughing...they call him...he is coming...yes, he is coming...right away! Right away!!...they have called him all month.

And he has killed only one—the black Haj—and he is not sorry....The memory has not even entered his mind during this whole period, has not interrupted his sleep....How he had grabbed him by the throat!...and pressed, and pressed...and afterwards had shoved him with his foot—off the road, the bastard!...What? You have come to see too?...Silence, dog!...Black slave!...Stealer of babies!...The doctor, take him away from here, and if not —I will change my mind!...I will return to camp!

Ponek sits and stares before him with the eyes of madness. He has removed his cap and straightened his chopped off hair. He has calmed down a bit. Only his breathing still roils in his chest.

"The devil knows!" he says in irritation. "A man could truly lose his mind like this."

Everything pent up in him for so many days, everything that had infected his soul and lay in wait for it, now came to him, burst through the flaccid screen of normal thought and flooded his mind. In a flash the black night became an abyss and the abyss swallowed the gloomy sky and the dark earth, the dim light of the stars and the twists of his shadowy spirit. It was dark and he dove down and down into the dark abyss.

The jackals waited patiently. They saw the man get up again. He stood on his feet, leaning on his rifle. What would he do? Now he shoved the iron barrel of his rifle into his mouth. Would he eat the metal? Strange doings! Now he took the rifle out of his mouth, sat down on the ground, and untied his shoes. He got up again, one foot bare, and again placed the gun barrel in his mouth. His bare foot then touched the rifle butt. Thunder and lightning. The man fell.

In his fantasies-memories before Ponek kills himself, the Jewish-Turkish-Armenian triangle (with the German in the background) is one of the central visions, together with his wife, Estherke, and his unborn child. The sight does not leave Meyer Ponek alone: it troubles him, annoys him, maddens him. The Armenian doctor and the Jew, Ponek, are accomplices. The Armenian is dying; only his eyes move; the eyes of the dying man laugh; and his voice—like a wisp of breath—tells his secret to Ponek the Jew, and only to him ("Jew! Listen!...I will tell you.")

Ponek's friends, Branchuk the writer, and Anzelmus Mayer the bank clerk, are saddened by the report that reaches Jerusalem by roundabout ways some time later, and wonder about the cause of his death. The explanation—depression and melancholy—is surely correct but explains nothing. Ponek is the only character in the novel who reflects upon the sorrows of the Armenians and identifies with them.

The Armenian tragedy is also briefly mentioned several times in the first volume of the novel *In the Beginning of Confusion*, which describes the early period of the war.

Aaron Zifrovitch, an accountant, the bookkeeper of the newspaper, *Haderech*, "a thirty-five-year-old bachelor, a shy dreamer and sophisticated skeptic rolled into one"—the figure of the *luftmensch*—argues with his friends, the editors. From charges against his friends he suddenly switches to an attack on the general situation:

All of the politics of the settlement in Eretz Yisrael has been nothing more than insanity....Madness!...Built on a volcano....There can be no possibility of a secure and healthy life in Turkey. The 'Bund' [an anti-Zionist Jewish socialist workers' movement] was right in insisting all along that Eretz Yisrael was nothing more than a province of Asiatic Turkey. Are you aware that the Turks are capable of annihilating us, of sweeping us off the face of the earth with the brush of a hand, the way one sweeps a bunch of ants off of a table, so that not a trace of our meagre community remains? Do you remember the riots against the Armenians eighteen years ago? Three hundred thousand souls were destroyed during those riots![5]

Branchuk heard his words and feeling, and smiled to himself in satisfaction. He allowed a broad smile to spread to his lips that evening when he went to see Chaim Ram. "Do you still remember," he said as he stood talking with some of the editorial staff, "the discussions we had before the Capitulations were revoked—how he defended Turkey? Without Turkey we have no hope for the future! And today... ha, ha, ha...his arguments today were the complete opposite of his arguments then: it is no less than insanity or madness to build the Yishuv on a volcano."[6]

The reports of the Armenian massacre appear in the novel again, in the beginning of the second volume, *The Last Ships*. Anzelmus Mayer, the fastidious clerk of the Viennese Bank, tells Gedalia Branchuk, the self-centered writer who occupies himself in constructing and wrecking conceptual models and in an attempt to write a novel, about the news he has received:

> He had suddenly learned about the hanging of prominent Arabs in Beirut, by order of Jamal Pasha; about the new massacre of the Armenians by the Turks; about Jamal Pasha's comment, thrown lightly at one of the Jewish mediators and repeated by him on several occasions, to the effect that the very same thing could happen to the Jews of Eretz Yisrael as well; about the danger of Arab attacks on the Jewish villages; about the informant who had informed on the newspaper, *The Way*.

> This stream of news aroused in Branchuk a sense of isolation, as though only now he had realized how cut off he was from the world. Were it not for the reports brought to him by this new, chance acquaintance, he would have known nothing. But the restless Mayer did not allow him to lapse into bitter reflection.[7]

The long passage from Ponek's musings before his suicide is important in understanding the process of banalization, of transforming the individual into part of a herd, of the degeneration, stupidity, and indifference which characterize times of war and acts of mass murder. With his scant resources, Ponek attempts to distinguish himself from the herd, to be different, and when he can find no other way, he is left only with the option of suicide.

The Armenian doctor—who not by coincidence calls the Jew to share his secret—also attempts to struggle. More precisely, after all possibility of struggle is gone, he finds slight consolation in vengeance. From the human perspective, Ponek and the Armenian doctor symbolize despair and the end of the road.

"In the Wagon"

In 1928, Aaron Reuveni published a collection of short stories, including "In the Wagon," which tells the story of a night journey in a wagon traveling from Jerusalem to Jaffa during the First World War.[8] The story may have been intended as part of the trilogy, *Unto Jerusalem*, in its original version. In the wagon rides, without a permit and properly authorized papers, Menachem Shapiro, a typesetter in a printing house. He is afraid to remain in the city lest he be called up for military work and, according to rumor, shirkers are in danger of being hanged. A year earlier, Shapiro had managed to avoid military labor by paying a ransom. He has embarked upon this journey in order to save himself and worries that his attempt to escape may fail.

With him in the wagon are three yeshiva students, well dressed in winter attire and new boots. They are also traveling illegally. In order to avoid inspection of the passengers of all wagons entering and leaving Jerusalem, Shapiro and the students have joined the wagon outside the city. At first, suspicious of informers, they remain silent. Later, Shapiro overhears their conversation about banknotes and financial certificates, and "wonders about these people, traders in financial certificates who lower the rate of government bonds and build themselves at the expense of society," "What types! Like the trespassers we knew of in Russia."

At Bab al-Wad, at the foot of the Judean Mountains, they are joined by two more passengers, soldiers in the Turkish army. One is a Turkish "shawish" (shawish in Arabic or chawoosh in Turkish, a military rank of a sergeant), and the other is a local Arab, from a village along the route, who manages to trick his commander during the journey and to desert from service in the Turkish army. In the course of the night's journey, the wagon owner engages the Turk in conversation who tells him enthusiastically:

So, I had good times....We were once in Gherasun—there's a town like that... have you ever heard the name Trebizond? Well, before Trebizond sits Treblus, and before Treblus, Gherasun, and before Gherasun, Ordu; they're all on the coast....And last year was when it happened, after we got rid of the Armenians, and Gherasun was already clean of them....No more Armenians, as if a big broom had swept them all away...and here I am walking along their streets, peeking into their abandoned houses—maybe there was something left, maybe some little object of value....Rags and tatters there were, everywhere....Walk along poking around, and all my effort for nought—the Muslim neighbors, may the devil take them, them and their fathers—had been there before me....So I continue to walk along angrily, wandering in and out emptyhanded....And in one of the houses I come upon an old Armenian, with a long white beard and a pale bloodless face; he stands in front of me shaking all over....I was startled myself when I saw him suddenly like that... I said, maybe there are some more of his brothers hiding around here, got to be careful....I looked, checked into every possible hiding place in that house—and not a soul....I walked over to the old fellow and grabbed his beard and shook him like this until his rotten teeth clattered in his mouth and then I shouted:

How do you dare to remain in our city, you miserable cur?

And then he pulls out a paper and shows me, signed with a stamp of the Kaymakam, and the paper says that because of his advanced age and weakness, the bearer of this letter has been permitted to remain in the city on the condition that he not leave his house.

This is a forgery! I shouted at him. For that alone you deserve to die!

And I take out my dagger and put it up to his gullet, under his beard.

The old man trembles and his lips are white.

Money....He says to me.

Hand it over!

I let go of him, and the old man put into my hands fifteen gold liras.

And more! I said, and put the dagger to his neck again.

The old man stands shaking and silent. I can see he has no more.

Have you got a wife? I ask.

No, he replies.

And a daughter?

No....Everyone has gone from here.

I search the house, in every corner, and I don't find a soul. It seems the old man was speaking the truth. So I turn to him and say to him: and what shall I do with you, grandad? And that forged note of yours.

And he says: take me to the Kaymakam.

Come along then!

We walk along the beach, he in front and I behind him, like a policeman and a prisoner. We don't meet a soul along the way. I chose that lonely path on purpose. And the beach is all rocky, high straight rocks like a parapet and the sea is deep in that place—an abyss!

My old man hurries along, walking with the speed of an awakening—hoping for salvation from the Kaymakam....Of course, the fellow is greedy, and maybe the old man's good friend was too—and when we arrive the old man will get his liras back, and I—a couple of blows about the legs. Aye, old man—I say to myself—do you take me for a fool? Ali Shawish is no fool, Ali Shawish sees what will happen....Ali Shawish knows what he has to do.

Stop there, granddad! I tell him, and with the push of my fist in his side— drrrr...like a stone he rolled off the cliff and into the water, fell and was gone.

Noah, who had listened intently to the Shawish's story, sat back a bit, his face turned to the storyteller and in his eyes of look of incomprehension: well, and then? he asked at last.

What 'and then,' replied the Shawish, he fell in and that's it. I told you, the water was deep in that place—a real chasm.

The wagon continued on its journey, and Shapiro imagined to himself the two of them, the Shawish and the old Armenian man, at the water's edge, at the top of the high rocky cliff. The former stands behind the old man—a sudden shove and the old man flips into the air, falls headfirst—and 'like a stone' plunges into the water....And it is as if a thin stream of cold has passed and chilled the typesetter's back....A scoundrel next to him, and behind him... more scoundrels—'Jewish scoundrels.' Their hands are not stained with blood—they have only destroyed their city and their people will perish in hunger....A Gentile scoundrel, a real one, a murderer...and those yeshiva students....Who is better? Shapiro chuckles bitterly and answers himself: each according to his ability.

The second army man, who had also been sitting next to the wagon owner since they had left Bab al-Wad, with his head resting on the metal rod which enclosed the driver's seat, awoke from his nap at the end of the Shawish's story, and interrupted the silence with a question: Ali Shawish, and what was the end of the Armenians?

Wiped them all out, was the laconic reply. And, as if to make himself clear, he repeated them in Turkish: Armenileri hap kesdiler!

He was aware of the impression his story had made on the other passengers, and took strange pleasure in it.

What do you mean?

Thus...slaughtered them...inhabitants, we would take all of them out to the city square....We treated them like a flock of sheep, thousands, tens of thousands... and the outskirts of the city we would separate them: the men to one side and the women to the other. We would kill the men afterwards by shooting, and the women and girls—we knew what to do with them....Then, later on, we would sell them to Kurds or in the Muslim villages....You, peasant brain that you are—you don't know the taste of those days. Aye, what a wonderful time it was for us!

But his listener was already distracted from the Armenians and turned, saying: Ali Shawish, let me go from Ramla to my home, to El Hadid, a little village not far from Lod....Just for a few days, I ask.

The powerful description, taken from the end of the trilogy, *Unto Jerusalem*, and the passage from "In the Wagon" are perhaps the only significant literary expressions—apart from the novel, *Ara*, which will be discussed below—of the complexity of the Jewish-Armenian connection. To the best of my knowledge, there is no additional testimony in the literature of Eretz Yisrael, nor in modern Israeli literature, to the tragedy of the Armenians.

Reuveni was a nonconformist who detested the "establishment" of the Yishuv, both literary and ideological-political. In 1920, after the publication of several sharply critical articles, he quit the "Poalei Zion" political party, to which he had belonged since settling in Eretz Yisrael in 1909, at the age of twenty-three. He was also contemptuous of the literary establishment of the late 1920s and 1930s and refused to join either of the major literary circles which battled between them over positions of literary power and influence. Therefore, the trilogy, which had been coldly received when it was first published, was widely acclaimed when it was reprinted forty years later, receiving literary accolades "the like of which only a few books in the history of modern Hebrew literature have won."[9]

Clearly the "boycott of silence" and the "intentional neglect" of Reuveni have no connection to the Armenian issue. But one ought to wonder why everyone ignored the issue while a marginal figure who refused to follow the mainstream was the one to react?

Shmuel Bass: *Ara*

A unique and forgotten literary work, which may not have been widely known even when it first appeared, is the novella, *Ara*, written by the poet and author, Shmuel Bass, and published in 1929. [10] Shmuel Bass (1899-1949) was a Russian-born Hebrew poet and critic. In 1906, he moved with his parents to Eretz Yisrael and his lyric poetry is closely tied to the landscapes and milieu of Eretz Yisrael. His book, *Nachal Kedumim* (Ancient Stream), contains poems about biblical subjects. He worked as a teacher and published poems, stories, and children's stories as well as essays of literary criticism. He also worked as a translator of foreign literature into Hebrew.

The book is dedicated to the volunteers of the Jewish Regiments in the British Army on their tenth anniversary, 1918-1928. At the center of the book stands Ara, a young Armenian survivor of the massacre. The narrator, Sheffy, who speaks in the first and third persons intermittently, falls in love with Ara. The 160 pages of the book weave the story of the Armenians and their tragedy with the destiny of Ara and her family. Through Ara's story, the reader is exposed to the Armenian tragedy. The descriptions reveal identification with the Armenians, their suffering, and their pain. The connection of a son of a people which has known suffering and empathizes with the adversity of another persecuted people appears numerous times in the story.

The book almost certainly contains autobiographical elements from the life of Shmuel Bass who was a soldier in the Jewish Regiments. At the end of the war, Sheffy is transferred from his camp on Mount Carmel to a camp of Armenian refugees near the gulf of Haifa, "on one side the trickling Kishon Creek and on the other, the beach." Guarding the Armenian refugee camp is an English detachment, a corporal and three soldiers. "Our job was to supervise the camp."

As he wanders around, patrolling the camp, he is invited to take shelter from the rain in the tent of an Armenian refugee family. There are three inhabitants in the tent: the head of the family, a tall elderly Armenian who is a leader of the refugees in the camp.

> The old man's virtuous face, his white beard, the graceful nobility of his movements, remind me of my own grandfather, in whose lap I would sit as a small boy listening to legends of the destruction [of the Temple]. This precious grandfather (I do not know why he has suddenly become precious to me), speaks little and sighs often. His hairy arms find no rest and his black robe shakes with the trembling of his body from the horrifying memories which seize him. It seems that this grandfather also has many stories of the destruction, but it is difficult to relate. The destruction was only yesterday and has not yet become legend.

The old man's daughter, Ara, "with the large serene eyes of a Madonna, a supple young figure, has the scent of Spring." He is attracted to Ara, "this magical figure," at first sight. There is another person in the tent, Ara's aunt. Sheffy takes an interest in the fate of the Armenians from his first day in the camp:

In the evening I left my tent to look around. From the English guard whom we are replacing I received this fragmentary information: these refugees are but a handful of the thousands of nomads who have found shelter with the English government. They were expelled from Armenia by the Turks. After riots, torture and long exile, they were saved by the English in Musul. More than this the English soldier does not know nor wish to know. I could not be satisfied with this information and I drew closer to see these wretched people who were gathered in small groups and sat like prisoners. I see among them old people, women and children. There are few young persons among them. Most of them mutilated, they apparently escaped by a miracle. The others must have remained at the border of their country, the living and the dead.

Occasionally I stop alongside one of them, while I distribute food, engage in conversation and become acquainted. Exhaustion is stamped on their poor faces! Their fate is not distant from ours. Who knows what tomorrow will bring? What will happen to them? Will they again see their devastated nests and their homeland? They know nothing. There are fathers here who have left their sons behind. Women who have lost their husbands. Orphans who fled with strangers from the devastation and have lost their way forever—for many months they wander from camp to camp; they have traversed all of Asia Minor on foot, hungry and thirsty. It is hard to walk among them and find happy faces. It seems that you are an insult to the sorrow etched in their faces. Only the infants are free of cares. The sound of their play is heard all day. Ragged, barefoot and half-starved, childhood demands its due—to play. I am the only one who attends most of the day to what goes on around, and all of the Armenians in the camp are my friends. I come to the children to play and to the elderly to listen. How I love the games of the children! These brave mountain people—their games too are games of bravery; they know how to throw stones, to shoot with bow and arrow, to fight with swords, and marksmanship.

Sheffy and Ara slowly become friends, and meet secretly to converse. They fall in love and have an occasional rendezvous. Their relationship, which is a important element in the book, is beyond the purview of our discussion. Their relationship ends when Ara goes off to nurse her father in hospital in Haifa where she meets an English-Jewish painter who assumes she is a Jew. Afterwards, her father decides to go to Lebanon and to marry her off to "the respectable Tetussian, his acquaintance and compatriot."

Like a storm, the word spread among the Armenian refugees that the elderly Arian was leaving. He was the intercessor for the camp. Only he took care of affairs, and even the commander held him in great respect. Now their situation would be much more difficult. They would have no one who could connect them with their brothers in their various places of exile. Only he, the goodhearted old man, could carry their burden. He would write their letters, inform the Armenian associations of their situation, and comfort them in their bitter destiny.

Who will care about us now that he has gone—groaned a crippled Armenian, his eyes filled with tears.

The promise to transfer me to a safe place, what will become of it, without him—wept another. The women wrung their hands and wailed. Even the children became serious.

Sheffy's longing and emotions for Ara did not end with her departure. Nor did his sympathy and friendship for the Armenian refugees fade.

It was an autumn evening. The weary sun sank slowly toward the sea. Sheffy wandered aimlessly past one of the tents and the melody of a violin reached his ears. He entered and found a blind Armenian sitting on a mat, playing the violin, surrounded by women and children. Healthy children, in rags and tatters, holding wooden bows, gathered round the tent opening. When he approached, they invited him to sit at the head of the gathering but he thanked them and remained standing. The old man continued his melody. It seemed at first to Sheffy as if he were hearing the ancient melodies like "by the rivers of Babylon." He was suddenly hot and a tremor of wonder passed through his body. The melodies were very wild, and the echo of suffering of a lost, persecuted people rose from the simple, powerful notes. The blind man's son, a handsome lad, accompanied him in song, reading the Armenian lyrics written in Turkish from a torn old notebook. The women stood frozen like marble statues. Only the light of the sunset briefly illumined the tortured faces. The sun grew dimmer and even the sound of the melody waned only to burst out again with renewed intensity. The violin played the insistent tones of the army commander, cries for vengeance, trumpet calls, and a battle cry. The air trembled with hidden threads which reached out from this tent, from the blind Armenian's violin, far off to his abandoned homeland—and vengeance echoed in the wind.

Sheffy meets the blind old man twice more, and then the blind man tells him his story and the story of Ara and her family:

"For God's sake, tell a bit of what has happened to you," beseeched Sheffy. "Our destinies are similar, your people's and mine, and I always take great interest in your situation, yes, I know how terrible it is!"

"Thank God we have arrived here," sighed the blind man and began his tale. There, far off, the massacre continues while the entire world stands aside and goes about its business. What does it care?" He then began to tell of the events which had brought him to this place.

"Does my lord know that I too had eyes which could see, that I enjoyed the glory of the world like other men, for I am not blind from birth. Ah, the atrocities which followed the rebellion! It is they which stole the light from my eyes, they!"

His hand tightened into a fist, his arms shook, and the weak old man rocked like a strong wind. Trembling, Sheffy moved the candle closer to his face. It was the face of a wretched, agonized man who had nothing left but his ability to tell the story. And the materials for his story were abundant. "It was not easy for them to steal everything from us. Every one of us fought desperately. Will my lord please move the candle closer to me," he asked. He raised his garment and exposed his chest. Spear marks covered his chest. More than one bullet was stuck in his ribs. "Oh, the last events in Van! Only they have remained in my memory in all their clarity. Everything before that, in the first days, seems so far away. The rebellion was what sealed our fate. My lord has surely heard of these events. At the time, they aroused interest even beyond the borders of our poor country. It was during the time of our revolution. I was one of the first revolutionaries in Van. After several days, the revolutionary associations were discovered, my comrades were captured after successful espionage, and sent to prison. I too was sent to prison, in Stambul. With great effort I managed to escape from there and return to Van. We renewed our activities with even greater intensity. We built fortifications in a suburb outside of the city walls. The Turks were ready for any rebellion and attacked us with heavy, incessant fire. But we held out against them for many days with heroic persistence. We too had weapons. With our own hands we prepared the arrows. Our women and daughters gave all of their jewelry to the association to make bullets. Old and young, we stood on guard. 'To live a life of freedom or to die a death of dignity' was our oath. But in the end we were overpowered by the enemy. The atrocities were not long in following. They massacred us without mercy, and if not for the Russians and the Armenian volunteers, not a soul would have survived. When they reached the city, the Turks fled from Van. For a brief moment we were left in peace. But the terrible massacres began in the other cities. Oh, it was terrible, terrible! In the days of Abd al-Hamid our lives were better than now!"

The blind man stopped, coughing. His face was contorted in pain. He began to rise, but sat down again with his feet folded under him. The rain grew stronger, but they were unaware of it. He resumed his tale of their wanderings. Truly horrifying! The Turks gleefully robbed and murdered. Every Turk permitted himself to enter a house and take whatever he wished. In the villages they would attack, in broad daylight, the granaries and set them afire. The Armenian masses held back as long as their dear ones were not touched. In Moush, the inhabitants did not rise up until the soldiers came and raped the women and daughters in front of their fathers and brothers. Only then were they unable to restrain themselves any longer. In a flash a terrible rebellion broke out in the city. A furious battle with spears and bayonets took place in the streets. And the results were bitter. All of the surrounding villages were burned together with their Armenian inhabitants....In the streets of Bitlis the Turkish soldiers roamed happily shooting every passerby. During the three days of the rebellion, some thirty thousand Armenians were killed and some three hundred villages were erased from the face of the earth. "Armenia without Armenians" was the Government's slogan.

The blind man talked on and on without pause. It seemed as if he had waited for this moment during all of the days since he had first been exiled. Sheffy sat close to him, trembling all over at the sound of the narrator's voice which would sometimes become drawn out and shaky. In the darkness of the night around them, one could feel an awful sense of abandonment. The world slept peacefully. And against the continuous beat of the rain, in the deep of the night, sat the two, Jew and Armenian, sharing the sorrow of a lost people. One fate. "You too have known the taste of murders such as these"—the blind man would say—"You too can tell of horrors." And the pictures were most terrible when the blind man came to the chapter of the expulsion, the stations along the endless road. "We were sent to Urfa," he said. "We passed Harput. The Kurds heard that we were on our way and they came with their women to beat us. The bastards! The women helped their husbands to stab us with spears and knives. Then our daughters were slaughtered in front of our eyes and they had been brutally tortured....Oh, better my eyes had not seen these things! Indeed it is also a curse from God to see these sights, to be alive and to be considered a dead man!"

The blind man could not go on. The sound of his words rang in his ears and brought the tortures alive again. He began to speak incoherently. As though the thread had suddenly been cut: "Oh the roads, the roads! At every crossroads we stood hoping that they would leave us in peace. But no! They knew how to brutalize us beyond comparison. When we reached the place, we were cut off from one another, fathers from sons, women from their husbands, without mercy. Fathers would send a farewell letter from prison to their families signed in their own blood. In Diyarbakir more than two thousand people were slaughtered in the prison in a single day. Our priests were beaten and dragged through the streets, to be cursed and ridiculed by the Muslims. The prisons which would fill up in the morning would be emptied out in the evening into the Euphrates. Between Urfa and Diyarbakir the corpses of our brothers and sisters were our ferries. Broken bodies floated on the water with no one to gather them up."

Only those who converted to their religion, the "true" one, survived. In another place six Armenian families wanted to convert to Islam and were tortured: "No less than a hundred at once."

In Harput and other places the Armenian women were not received into Islam, unless they married "believers." Many of the Armenian women threw themselves into the Euphrates and the Tigris rather than convert to Islam. I have heard that my lord has frequently visited with the worthy old man, our Arian [Ara's father]. If he only knew the fate of his poor family! His wife, too, is a saint." The blind man stopped in the middle of his words, and crossed himself. Suddenly he covered his face with his hands. Sheffy jumped up, surprised, filled with wonder and concern. "Yes, yes, this is what interests me so! Please tell me, tell about Ara's mother!" He asked.

The blind man sat silently for several minutes, hesitant to continue his story. The fate of their leader, Arian, was like a sacred secret in his eyes. Only after numerous entreaties, he stuttered, unwillingly: "Sir, I would betray my soul and the souls of my brothers were I to awaken the precious and saintly soul from her repose, may God forgive me! Yes, poor Ara's mother was truly a saint. You know, as I have told you, that Armenian women had the right to convert to Islam if they married a Muslim. Arian's wife was the most beautiful woman in the entire district. She was still young, the daughter of an ancient and very respected Armenian family. Her name was known throughout the region. She was Arian's second wife. (From his first wife he had three sons, and this wife bore him his only daughter, Ara). The Turkish Wali proposed to her, several days before the terrible massacre, that she convert to Islam and marry him. Thus she would save her own life and the lives of all of the Armenians in the district. Fate was in her hands. The villages around were already in flames. And now it was the turn of the district's town. The entire community discussed it. The lives of thousands of people could be wiped out. And now a little crack of salvation had opened. After many consultations, the secret national association decided that Ara's mother must sacrifice her religion, to all appearances, until the fury had passed. They hoped that in the meantime they would prepare the ground for a new rebellion which would succeed. Oh how fate has laughed at us! This Arian, who had lived all his life in wealth and respectability in his estate in Van (in Stambul too, on the banks of the Bosphorus, he had a summer home and citrus groves), who would travel to Europe each year to meet with statesmen about our cause, whose every fiber was dedicated to helping our national associations, would be the one who must give what was most sacred to him, to them, those accursed ones!

But there is nothing a man will not do as long as he has faith in his heart. He could not betray his faith in the hope of liberation. And so he sacrificed everything one day.

His three sons were sent to the Caucasian front. His only daughter, Ara, was not at home, having been sent at the outbreak of the rebellion with a German officer, a friend of the family, over the border. And now his wife was to be taken from him before his very eyes. Poor Arian was left alone. After a heartbreaking parting from her husband, Ara's mother prayed, together with the whole community, and the following day went to the Wali. On the first night she was with him she tried to assassinate him. When his lust overcame him, she plied him with poisoned wine. But black and bitter fate! The Wali was miraculously saved from death and she paid for the attempt with her life.

The next day she was burned on a cross....Good Lord! How beautiful and solemn she was in her final moments! Ah, sainted Mary! Her black hair blew in the breeze, her eyes blazed with a sacred fire, and a laugh of forgiveness touched her lips as she softly made her final prayer. We were brought to the great square to witness the sight. They brought us there with whips. They stood the women and children in the front row to watch, each standing as though on burning coals. Every bloodshot eye was turned to the empty heavens, is there still a God?

Vengeance fermented in the depths. The Wali knew that his act would not pass quietly. The following day he ordered the terrible massacre, the likes of which had never been seen. The district town was emptied of Armenians within a few hours.

The slave procession began. We crossed all of Asia Minor on foot. The weak were thrown into the rivers. And the sound of the women's weeping silenced the cannons' roar."

The blind man's teeth chattered. His body began to shake with cold. "Awful, awful! The mouth wearies from the telling! The old man, Arian, so good and modest, who had never let a bad word pass his lips, stood afterwards on the bank of the Euphrates, before the entire Armenian community, his fists upraised to heaven, a bitter curse on his lips. He pleaded that he might die. All along the way he moaned: Ara! Ara! My only one! My soul! How awful! His poor sons did not know a thing, and could not even avenge their mother and their homeland! Afterwards we heard horrible rumors from the Caucasian front, that the Armenian soldiers had been sent to the front line to draw the fire of the enemy guns! Not a trace was left of them, of all these troops. What brutal fate! More than once Arian tried to take his own life, but the image of his only daughter stopped him. He yet hoped to be reunited with her. She was the last remnant of her mother who had been sacrificed as a saint on the altar of this doomed people."

The passages quoted, as well as others, bring alive the deep identification of the author with the fate of the Armenians and their suffering.

His empathy doubtless stems from his sense of a common destiny: "[S]at the two, Jew and Armenian, sharing the sorrow of a lost people. One fate." His identification with the suffering Armenian people brings Sheffy at the end of the story to an outburst of humanity, a desire "to hear the beat of all of the hearts," not to be preoccupied entirely with the sorrows of the individual but to return to the whole. Unlike the mood of despair in *Unto Jerusalem*, *Ara* ends on a note of optimistic and active humanism.

In a series of essays that Shmuel Bass published in 1932 in the Hebrew daily, *Ha'aretz,* appears his article, "Young Armenia." He writes of a meeting with an Armenian on the deck of a ship sailing from France to Egypt. The Armenian, a poet and sculptor who lives in Egypt, longs for his Armenian homeland and for Mount Ararat, "from which I draw strength and confidence in my people's future." In his shipboard meeting with the Armenian, Bass also expresses his identification with the suffering and pain of the Armenians: "In vain I seek the flag of liberated Armenia," says the Armenian.

In 1930, in the literary journal, *Hed*, the reviewer, Chaim Weiner, praises *Ara*: "The book infuses the reader with a delicate spirit, soft and lyrical and filled with yearning. The reader cannot put the book down until the end, and is sorry to part from the book upon finishing it." He also lauds the fact that "in the book we discover the 'hidden light' in the soul of every man, and contemporary man in general. We can only hope that Bass will continue to show us more and more of this light." [11]

And the same time, the writer wonders that the life of the Jewish Regiments are not described at all in the book, and that about "the soldiers of the Brigade themselves absolutely nothing is told." He also expresses amazement: "But it is incomprehensible how his strange, almost Platonic love, for Ara, the Armenian girl, is completely unaffected by that same 'new framework' [the Jewish Regiments]. The unique phenomenon whereby a man who goes off to dedicate his life to the ideal of rebirth of his people and land, is so attracted to a foreign girl that his love fills his entire being to the point that he forgets the entire world, requires wider artistic illumination and a more satisfying psychological explanation." Is there not something here which is seemingly "very removed from the [Jewish] ideal of redemption," wonders the critic.

His wonder recalls the wonder which was expressed at Werfel's "preoccupation" with the tragedies of others, as we shall see next.

Notes

1. Yigael Schwartz, *Vivre Pour Vivre* (Aaron Reuveni, Monograph) (Jerusalem: Ben Zvi Institute and Magnes, 1993), pp. 159-61. (Henceforth: *Vivre Pour Vivre.*)
2. Ibid., p. 99.
3. Interestingly, I am told by my Armenian colleagues, with some surprise, that Ara is an Armenian male name.
4. The following excerpts are taken, slightly abridged, from Aaron Reuveni, *Unto Jerusalem* (Jerusalem: Keter, 1987), pp. 396-406. (Henceforth: *Unto Jerusalem.*) The excerpts which appear without quotation marks are also abridged from the original.
5. The reference is to the massacres of the Armenians which took place between 1894 and 1896, in which, according to some estimates, 300,000 Armenians were killed. According to other estimates, the number of victims was much smaller.
6. *Unto Jerusalem*, p.106.
7. Ibid., p. 130.
8. A. Reuveni, *Stories*, vol. 1 (Jerusalem and Tel Aviv: Achiezer, 1928), pp. 143-74. The following passages are quoted from this edition.
9. See "A Novel of an Era: Epilogue," by Yigael Schwartz, for the new edition of *Unto Jerusalem* (Jerusalem: Keter, 1987), p. 420. See also Yigael Schwartz, "The Work of Reuveni in the Eyes of the Critics," *Aaron Reuveni, A Selection of Critical Essays on His Writing* (Tel Aviv: Hakibbutz Hameuchad, 1992). See also Yigael Schwartz, *Vivre Pour Vivre* (mentioned above). It is interesting to note that in neither of these comprehensive books is there any mention of Reuveni's Armenian scenes.
10. Shmuel Bass, *Ara* (Jerusalem and Tel Aviv: Tarbut, 1929).
11. Chaim Weiner, "Ara," *Hed*, winter 1930.

7

The Forty Days of Musa Dagh:
Symbol and Parable

Franz Werfel's saga, *The Forty Days of Musa Dagh*, tells the story of the inhabitants of the Armenian villages at the foot of Musa Dagh (Mount Moses) in the Cilicia district during the First World War. Gabriel Bagradian, an Armenian expatriate who has lived in France for twenty years, brings his family on a personal visit to Turkey at the eve of the First World War. Political events and the outbreak of war compel him to make fateful decisions. He organizes the villagers in a rebellion against the Turks. The story of the uprising is interwoven with Gabriel's personal story.

When writing the book, Werfel relied on journalistic accounts, official documents, and oral testimony. But the book is fundamentally a literary work based on the story of the uprising at Musa Dagh, one of the isolated incidents of Armenian rebellion against the Turks. The book was widely acclaimed when it was published, was translated into many languages, dramatized and made into a feature film. Beyond its importance in presenting the historical event of the Armenian genocide and in bringing it to the awareness of the international public, the book is a great work because of the questions it raises and the powerful way in which it does so.

Werfel's book shocked millions throughout the world and influenced many young people who grew up in Eretz Yisrael in the 1930s. For many Jewish youth in Europe, "Musa Dagh" became a symbol, a model, and an example, especially during the dark days of the Second World War. Jews in particular have lauded Werfel's book and have sometimes emphasized the author's Jewishness claiming that "only a Jew could have written this work."

Werfel, it should be noted, completed the book in 1932 after two visits to the Middle East (including Palestine), and was horrified by the Armenian massacre and by the refugees and orphans of the massacre whom he saw in Damascus.[1] When the book first appeared in 1933, Hitler had already come to power and *The Forty Days of Musa Dagh* was burned together with other important literary works.

The reader of this extraordinary historical novel will find it difficult to believe that the book was written before the Holocaust. The book, unquestionably, raises problematic issues, associations and reminders, and questions of Jewish identity that troubled Werfel himself. The assimilated Armenian (Jew) who comes to lead his people in its time of distress, Mount Moses-Musa Dagh, Massada-Musa Dagh, are only some of the symbols and allusions which are woven into the book.

Questions like the meaning of life and death, the purpose and reason for struggle and war, the individual and society, responsibility and leadership, and others are imminent in the Jewish experience of the Holocaust and appear in all of their power and intensity in throughout Werfel's book.

Franz Werfel, a noted writer and poet, was born in 1890 in Prague and published his first poem at the age of eighteen in a Viennese newspaper. In 1911, his first collection of poetry was published in Berlin. During the First World War, he served in the German Army and fought on the Russian front. After the war he settled in Vienna, and during the 1920s traveled extensively. After the Anschluss in 1938, Werfel was forced to flee to France and from there reached the United States where he died in 1945. In addition to his poetry, Werfel wrote several Expressionist plays and was popularly received during his lifetime in Europe, but he is remembered primarily as a novelist and as the author of *The Forty Days of Musa Dagh*. Werfel belongs to a large group of Jewish authors and artists who wrote in German and were active in Central Europe at the turn of the century. This group, much of which was preoccupied by questions of Jewish identity, played a central and dominant role in the flowering of German culture in those years. This "German-Jewish symbiosis" came to a tragic end with the rise of the Nazis to power.

Werfel's book was translated into Hebrew by Joseph Lichtenbaum and published by Steibel in 1934.[2] It aroused strong reactions and criticism, only part of which we will examine. It is important to emphasize that the following study is in no way exhaustive.

The writer, Dov Kimchi, whose books and especially his novel, *The House of David*, have won new audiences, wrote an article in 1933 about *Musa Dagh*, before the book appeared in Hebrew, based on excerpts which were published in the Viennese *Neue Freie Presse*. Kimchi praised Werfel saying: "Werfel's scope this time is broad and humane, and the tragic destiny of that unfortunate people was indeed a great tragedy and it is fitting that a poetic soul plunge into it, elucidating its eternal humanity."[3]

In Kimchi's opinion, beyond its historical and factual background, the crux of the book was its fundamental idea:

> A people ravaged by 'sacred' suffering on the biblical pinnacle of tragedy, unparalleled in the twentieth century; would not this people become sanctified and uplifted to new life which must necessarily follow in the wake of the torment as a reward for its suffering? Or would it be like all sufferers, tortured and weak, whose agonies do not shock the planet nor turn the individual or the people into Chosen Ones?

> This is a typical Jewish question which the Jewish poet has transposed to a different dimension, seeking answers among the Gentiles, since he will not seek them here, among his own people.[4]

After describing the "Great Assembly," one of the most dramatic passages in the book in which the refugees finally decide to ascend the mountain and there to fight, Kimchi writes,

> But what reverberates in the text is not at all 'typically Armenian.' Many of these great passages, the immense cry for life, could have been uttered by other heroes, closer to the Jewish poet Werfel, who also ascended a high, steep mountain for a last attempt at life and looked down from the heights of an eternal ideal to the depths of the Jordan Rift and the Dead Sea, where powerful Roman armies assembled with weapons of death and catapults. Looked down in scorn from the heights of the ideal at the heroes assembled below and then slew themselves in proof of the great eternal truth that "all flesh is dust....And the word of our God will reign forever."

> But, as stated, Werfel chose the Armenians to express the theme of human tragedy, although there is a human tragedy that is closer to him. But since man cannot escape himself, we Hebrew readers—for whom the problems which Werfel presents are our daily bread, the essence of our existence—read into his book on the Armenians our very own tragedy as Jews.

> And that is what is most precious to us in these pages.

Kimchi connected Werfel's book to Massada, thus expressing the contemporary experience of Eretz Yisrael, which nurtured the story of Massada as a heroic myth. He then raised another issue which would reappear in his various references to Gabriel Bagradian, the non-Armenian Armenian, the assimilated leader of the rebellion, and to Franz Werfel himself: "The prodigal son who returns to the bosom of his people." Furthermore, wrote Kimchi, "You listen to our pained voice, the voice of the Jew—if indeed it disappears in the tragedy of others— for only the Jew can know the full meaning of exile."[5]

A literary review by R. Zeligman, published in *Hapoel Hatzair* in August 1934, mildly criticizes the literary weaknesses he finds in the book, but "apart from this, the story is so heart-wrenching, and the author has invested so much love and pathos in his work, that we cannot dwell on these weaknesses and we scarcely notice them." The reviewer summed up thus:

> The book is very interesting for the educated reader in general, but the Jewish reader will find it of special interest. The fate of this Armenian tribe recalls, in several important details, the fate of the people of Israel, and not surprisingly the Jewish reader will discover several familiar motifs, so well known to him from the life and history of his people. Thus, for example, the Jewish reader knows that the Armenians are persecuted and suffer because of their race. Thus Gabriel Bagradian says to his French wife: 'No, this you cannot understand, Juliet; no one who has not been despised because of his racial origin can understand this.' Or, for example, something of this sort is written: 'The eyes of the Armenians are almost always enormous, eyes horrified by a thousand years of shocking visions.' The ordinary Jewish reader will also be surprised to hear that the whole Armenian people is suffused with a desire for education and knowledge.
>
> This book which is valuable in and of itself for its content, has enhanced value for the Jewish reader because of these motifs.[6]

The similar fate and the Jews and Armenians as victims were a prominent theme in the literary reviews of Werfel's book, together with the recurring question, "Why does a Jew write about the fate of another people and not about the fate of his own people?" These elements were especially prominent in an article written by Moshe Beilinson, one of the outstanding leaders of the workers' movement in Eretz Yisrael. The article, entitled "A Glorious Monument to Israeli Alienation," appeared in *Davar* in early 1936.[7] Beilinson took exception to the term "Armenian fate" and claimed that "this term is unjustified." He wrote,

I confess to a peculiar feeling when I took this book in hand, and I was already aware of its reputation, and the role it has played and will ever play in extolling the heroic struggle of the Armenian people, in creating a poetic monument to their suffering and agony, in nobly avenging their destruction. And what is this peculiar feeling? A mixture of envy and irritation— envy of one unfortunate that another unfortunate has some reward, and irritation that a fellow-Jew erected the monument to a foreign people. Have we not suffered? Have we not been persecuted? Has not the sword of destruction been laid on our heads countless times? Have we not struggled against our cruel fate? And now, when a great poet arises from our midst, known around the world and at the height of his powers, not of us does he write.

The book opens: 'The picture of misery of the refugee children, wretched and starving, who worked in the carpet factory (in Damascus), was the decisive push to rescue from the depths of history the incomprehensible fate of the Armenian people.' Were the author's eyes afflicted by blindness? Had he traveled the face of the earth and never encountered a 'picture of misery' of 'wretched' children other than the Armenian refugees in Damascus? Has he descended to the depths of history and found no 'incomprehensible fate' save that of the Armenian people? Indeed this is assimilation, ready to serve others.

And possibly: an unsavory feeling, a feeling of despondency and misery, completely overwhelming, which can not be shared with another. I confess, there was such a feeling.

As I read on, the feeling dissipated not only because this is a great and powerful book, a book for the generations, which no unsavory feeling can resist. More importantly, with every new page another feeling took the place of envy and dispelled the irritation. What if the book glorifies the heroic struggle of the Armenian people in the eyes of strangers and inspires sympathy for the sorrow of this people? This is no more than a shell, for in truth this is a Jewish book, not only because it was written by a Jew but in a less abstract sense, simpler and more concrete, the author speaks of us, of our fate, of our struggle.

The concept of an 'Armenian fate' as Franz Werfel perceives it, as he repeats again and again, in his universal, almost metaphysical view, is unjustified. Terrible persecutions have befallen this unfortunate people—in Turkey and in Russia—but this was no more than the fate of a national minority under an oppressor's heel. No historical hatred followed the Armenians wherever they went. No unbridgeable abyss separated them from the nations. They were not an accursed monster, neither in the eyes of the Christians nor in the eyes of the Muslims. No blood libel hung over their heads. The children of the world did not suckle hatred for them at their mother's breast, nor were they condemned to a life of wandering from one land to another, from one country to another. They have not tasted the bitterness of exile. They have lived on their land even when it was torn between foreign powers. They enjoyed their own culture. They were rooted in their own soil. Their blood was spilled by attackers but this 'fate', suffused with Werfel's tragic-heroic poesy, is not the fate of the Armenians but the fate of Israel. Those 'eyes,' the eyes of despair beyond history, which Werfel describes are not Armenian eyes. They are Israelite eyes. This lad who stands suddenly in the middle of the road and asks his comrade: 'Why in fact are we Armenians?' Asks the question of the Israelite lad in this disjointed generation. And the old man who asserts that 'to be an Armenian is avoidable' is stating an Israelite truth. This intercessor, a German priest, pure of soul, innocent and wise, unhappy, unfortunate, covered in sweat, whose senses have been jaded by impotent emotion, who scurries between the rulers of his people that they might prevent the disaster, is none other than a 'righteous gentile'.[8]

Beilinson transformed the concept of an "Armenian fate," which he felt was unjustified, into a concept of the "fate of Israel." The sad eyes of the Armenian refugee children by which Werfel was so touched, are "Israelite eyes," according to Beilinson. It should also be pointed out that he talks of "Israelite eyes" and the "fate of Israel," not Jewish eyes or a Jewish fate.

Beilinson goes further:

Indeed, it is a book which is entirely Armenian, in which the Jews are not mentioned at all, in which a Christian spirit pervades and the quotations at the beginning of each chapter are taken from the New Testament, which extols the heroic struggle of the Armenian people. It is received by the world as a lamentation and a glorification of the sufferings of the Armenians. But it is not so. Whether the poet consciously sought to do so or not, he has written an Israelite book. Moreover, a Zionist book. Nonetheless, it is also a book of Israelite assimilation, not merely a book written by an assimilated Jew but a book of alienation.[9]

Gabriel Bagradian is, according to Beilinson, a Herzl-like figure with Theodor Herzl's destiny. The character of the assimilationist is justified, says Beilinson in the Jewish context but "there is no justification, in the Armenian reality, for the character of the assimilationist who returns to his people in their hour of peril." Beilinson examines the motif of "Israelite alienation"—essentially assimilation—and draws a parallel between Herzl and Gabriel, who alone of all the people of Musa

Dagh remains on the mount of rebellion. Gabriel, despite all of his efforts and sacrifices, is unable to rejoin his people:

> And who is to say if even at the end Gabriel was not a Herzlian figure. Herzl lived with us only during the first 'forty days' of our rebellion and uprising. Musa Dagh is the Mount of Moses, Mount Nevo. Indeed, 'to each man his Nevo.' And this is the 'Nevo' of the man who returns to his people and remains a stranger to it.[10]

In the introduction to the article in the *Dovrut* anthology, there is, in addition to excerpts from the article itself, an addition apparently written by the editors. The addition deals with "our demand from the Jew and the Zionist." After mentioning the demands of work, immersion in the Hebrew language and culture, the addendum concludes: "In short, the movement demands of the Jew and the Zionist his life, his heart and his entire soul. One cannot accuse it [the Zionist movement] of exaggeration or cruelty. The nature of the movement requires this severity, this enormous demand."[11]

A discussion of Werfel's attitude toward Judaism and his Jewishness is beyond the scope of our discussion. Meyer Weisgal, who was closely acquainted with Werfel in the 1930s, writes in his autobiography that in *Musa Dagh,* "Werfel expressed through the Armenians his awareness of the Jewish tragedy (he told me that the Armenians are his surrogate for the Jews), but he never consciously reconciled himself with his Jewishness."[12]

Many Jews, and certainly many Zionists, perceived Werfel as an assimilated Jew although they did not always understand the deeper meaning of his argument. The reaction to his book in Eretz Yisrael in the 1930s was, in this respect, ambivalent: "Why did he write about the suffering of the Christian Armenians instead of the suffering of his own people?" and on the other hand, the statement that "only a Jew could have written a work like this."

Werfel visited Palestine twice, in 1929 and in 1930. He considered himself an anti-Zionist at the time, although his views changed in the 1940s. Nevertheless, his visits were not simply the result of tourism or a Christian religious sentiment but also, perhaps, a desire to investigate the condition of the "new Jew" in Eretz Yisrael.[13] Werfel confessed his attraction to certain elements of Christian faith but he vigorously rejected any possibility of conversion while the Jews were suffering and persecuted. It appears that in the 1940s Werfel considered writing a novel dealing with the Holocaust but died in 1945, before the project came to fruition.

In any case, *Musa Dagh* had enormous impact on the consciousness of many young people in Eretz Yisrael and the Diaspora in the 1930s and 1940s. Reading the book was for many of them a formative experience.

Haifa 1942: "We want to turn Mount Carmel into the 'Musa Dagh' of Palestinian Jewry"

1942 was a time of deep apprehension for the Jewish community in Palestine, which feared the possibility of a Nazi military invasion of Palestine. The Jewish community in Palestine and its leadership were divided in their view of what needed to be done. Together with thoughts of surrender, defeatism, and helplessness, there were calls for courage, determination, and battle.

One proposal was a plan to concentrate all of the Palestinian Jewish defense forces around Mount Carmel and from there to fight the Nazi invader. Known variously as the "Northern Program," "The Carmel Plan," "The Massada Plan," and even as "The Musa Dagh Plan," the program was developed by the leadership of the Jewish defense forces.

Haviv Canaan's book, *Two Hundred Days of Fear*, relates the testimony of Meir Batz, one of the founders of the Haganah and Palmach Jewish defense militias, who was asked to take a central role in organizing the plan. Batz was asked if he had read *The Forty Days of Musa Dagh*. When he replied that he had, he was told, "We want to turn Mount Carmel into the Musa Dagh of Palestinian Jewry. Our comrades are looking in the mountains for suitable places for defense and sortie. We may turn the Carmel into Massada." That evening he went out to reconnoiter. Batz related, "I will never forget that patrol. We marched from Ahuza along the Carmel ridge. The moon smiled down on us with its round face. I imagined to myself the Jewish Musa Dagh which was to ensure the future of the Yishuv, and guarantee its honor."[14] Batz added, "We put our faith in the power of endurance of the Jewish 'Musa Dagh' and we were determined to hold out for at least three or four months."[15] Some viewed "Musa Dagh as a better example than Tobruk. Musa Dagh was conceived and planned by a man. The matter is crucial and therefore must be feasible."[16]

Another reference to the names and symbolism that the plan aroused appeared in a letter from Yisrael Galili, one of the leaders of the Haganah, to his wife, Tzipporah, on March 24, 1942:

> I returned from my trip to Ashdoti [Davidka Nimri] with Yitzhak S. [Sadeh]. On the way, we reexamined and elaborated on the idea of Haifa-Tobruk. Or perhaps Haifa-Massada-Musa Dagh? In any case the idea is exciting. It has elements of preparation for political action and imagination to rely on. There are mitigating topographical aspects. Britain has a political and military interest in holding on to Haifa. The idea is able to excite and assemble a large Hebrew fighting force. Its political and symbolic-historic significance has great value and glory for the battle of the Jews [together] with the British for the defense of Haifa. A fortified island in the case of invasion. It will not be easy to reject such a proposal.
>
> The idea is worth fighting for politically in London and America, to enlist allies. We shall supply the human material, which will give its life in battle for the land. From our allies we will demand the huge fortifications necessary, the equipment (especially artillery equipment) and naval support.[17]

The associations aroused in Eretz Yisrael surrounding the battle against a German invasion were of Massada, Tobruk, and Musa Dagh. In the Jewish ghettos in Nazi Europe, we shall see that the example of Musa Dagh was cited more often than Massada. Partial investigation of the subject reveals that for Jewish youth in the ghettos, Massada, as a symbol of suicide, was less relevant than Musa Dagh, which symbolized struggle and battle, which might have a chance and a faint hope for salvation.

The Bialystock Ghetto, 1943: "The only thing left is to see the ghetto as our Musa Dagh"

The Jewish underground organizations, which operated in the ghettos during the Nazi occupation of Europe, debated intensely the purpose and meaning of their struggle, the meaning of their lives and death in the harsh reality to which they were subject. From their shocking and fascinating discussions, which highlighted moral and existential Jewish dilemmas, we are left with several records written at the time. One of these is the minutes of a general meeting of Kibbutz "Tel Hai, a group of Jewish activist youth in Bialystock, on February 27, 1943.

The minutes of the meeting were buried in Bialystock and recovered after the war. They were published under the title, *Pages from the Fire.*

During the discussion, which constitutes an important document for our understanding of the dilemmas faced by the organizations of the Jewish ghetto underground, an argument developed over the question of whether to remain in the ghetto or to escape to the forests. Three positions were elucidated in the argument: (1) To remain in the ghetto and to revolt against the Germans ("counter-action") at any price; (2) Rescue; (3) Preference for escape to the forests, and should that prove impossible, armed resistance.

Herschel Rosenthal was the main advocate of the call for "counter-action" and remaining in the ghetto. He said, *inter alia*, "Our fate is sealed. We are therefore left with only one possibility: organizing collective resistance in the ghetto at any price; to view the ghetto as our 'Musa Dagh,' and to add a chapter of honor to the history of Jewish Bialystock and of our movement."[18]

In this deeply moving human document we find the diary of Mordechai Tenebaum, commander of the Bialystock Jewish underground. On February 19, 1943, Tenebaum wrote about an additional argument about whether to remain in the ghetto or to escape to the forests. He describes a meeting to examine the position of one of the youth organizations, some of whose members were in favor of leaving the ghetto. In Tenebaum's eyes, leaving the ghetto was "national betrayal." He writes,

> Our approach is to fulfill the national mission within the ghetto (and not to abandon the elderly!), and if you survive then arm yourself and go out to the forests. For now, search for connections (in both directions) and establish a route, but first and foremost, arm yourself, get hold of weapons.
>
> Opposing me was the argument that 'it is better to be a live dog than a dead lion.' They mentioned that at 'Musa Dagh' the older people wanted to continue fighting on their very doorsteps while the young people wanted to leave, etc. They wanted Aryan documents. In the end, after further clarification, they all agreed with my position.[19]

In a note to this passage, the editors of *Pages from the Fire* point out that "because of the similarity between the fate of the two peoples, the Armenians and the Jews, *Musa Dagh* was extremely popular among ghetto youth."[20]

In a letter to Bronka Klevansky, the Jewish Resistance contact on the Aryan side, on May 25, 1943, Mordechai Tenebaum wrote, "*Musa Dagh* is all the rage with us. If you read it, you will remember it for the rest of your life. Written by Franz Werfel."[21] Bronka Klevansky later said that she had read the book in Polish, or perhaps even in German. She thought that Tenebaum had read the book before the war, and during the time in the ghetto, he and others apparently recommended it.[22]

Among the activists of other youth movements Werfel's book was also highly regarded. Chaika Grossman, one of the leading figures in the leadership of the "Hashomer Hatzair," the Socialist-Zionist youth movement in Bialystock, and a leader of the Jewish underground in Poland, said that the books which were popular among Jewish activists at the time were those whose content and themes were relevant to the reality of the period. "They educated themselves and strengthened themselves. Destiny helped them and their mission encouraged them to be both strong and humane. That is what the movement taught them. That is what they learned from the fine books they read. In those days they read *Musa Dagh*. The book was passed from hand to hand."[23]

Inka Wajbort used almost the same exact words in her memoirs when describing the book's impact on the fifteen- and sixteen-year-old members of "Hashomer Hatzair" in Sosnovitz, after they read it in the summer of 1941:

> The book passed from hand to hand....It completely captivated me. For four full days I was engrossed in the book and could not tear myself away....I myself was at Musa Dagh; I was under siege. I was one of the Armenians doomed to death. If I lifted my eyes from the book, it was only to hear the cry—Mama, how could this be? The world knew and kept silent. It could not be that children in other countries at the same time went to school, women adorned themselves, men went about their business, as if nothing had happened....And there, a people was annihilated.

> Mother knew nothing about Musa Dagh. And that also seemed horrible to me. I was totally shocked by the tragedy and when I finished reading the book and went out to the yard for the first time—it was a summer day, drenched in the afternoon sunlight—I was suddenly overcome by a feeling of joy at my very existence. I was grateful to the Creator for the sunlight and the blue sky, for the vision of two little girls with braided hair jumping rope as they laughingly counted their hops, for the fact that the world still stood.

> Then I did not deal in comparisons. Then, in the summer of 1941 I did not yet sense that a new Musa Dagh was imminent. That happened later.

In May, 1942, before the deportations from the Sosnovitz region, Mordechai Anilevitch, commander of the Jewish Underground in the

Warsaw Ghetto, came to the ghetto and reported to the older comrades of his movement about what had already transpired in other regions of Poland, where a significant part of the Jews had already been exterminated. "And so, again Musa Dagh? And again the world keeps silent?"[24]

And in almost the same words we have testimony from the Kovno Ghetto. Samuel Gringaus, general secretary and later deputy head of the Labor Office in the Kovno Ghetto, recalled that following the *Aktion* of February 18, 1942, Kovno Ghetto was full of the best books. "It was an odd situation," he said, "that much reading was done in the ghetto, and not only in quiet times. I have seen people in the bunkers during the *Aktionen* reading books whole days. A book such as Franz Werfel's *The Forty Days of Musa Dagh* was passed from hand to hand."[25]

Additional contemporary testimony of the period is found in Yitzhak Katznelson's *Vittle Diary*. Katznelson was a poet and an author, teacher and educator, and a prominent mourner of the Holocaust who moved when the war broke out from Lodz to Warsaw. He published his writings in the underground press of the Zionist youth movements. During the January 1943 ghetto uprising, he was in Warsaw with the fighters of the "Dror" unit.

In May 1943, he was transferred as a Honduran national to the French detention camp in Vittle where he wrote his final works, including *Vittle Diary*. He was murdered at Auschwitz in May 1944, at the age of sixty. The Museum of the Holocaust and the Uprising at Kibbutz Lochamei Hagettaot in Israel are named after him.

Mourning the murder of the Jews he asks, on August 20, 1943, "Who will avenge us against this bestial and loathsome people?" To his younger brother he wrote in his heart's blood:

> Where are you? Will we never ever see each other again? The Turkish Army (not the people, only the army) was incited by the Germans, filled then with same spirit of destruction against all peoples as today—although they did not direct their venom solely against the People of Israel then—and the Germans are to blame for the Armenian blood spilled by the Turks, even if a German priest did go to the Turkish authorities to plead for mercy for the Armenians. In that whole verminous nation not a single priest is to be found who will ask those cursed people: "Why do you murder the People of Israel? What do you need all this blood for? The Turks fought side by side with the Germans and smelled their neighbor's blood. The Turk killed the Armenians, a rival people with whom they wanted to settle accounts— more than a million people. The Armenian people found someone to share in their suffering, to mourn for them, to redeem their blood, in the form of

an author of Jewish descent, Werfel the Jew, whose people, Werfel's people, have no argument with that renegade nation of criminals. Who will weep for Werfel's people — a people without a land, without claims or complaints, a quiet, meek, poor people, abandoned and dispersed among the nations — when six million or more are killed, when it is annihilated together with its children and old people? The Werfels will mourn every people but their own....The pseudo-Jews who have survived in these disastrous times will learn nothing from the loss of their people: they did not see its beauty in its life and will not recognize its sanctity in its death, for their hearts and conscience have deserted them. Who will mourn for us? Who will erect a memorial for us? Who will tell others the story of this great people, a nation of Levites, the children of prophets, the forebears of their own God in lands which consumed them, every last one of them, leaving not a child, not an unborn babe, more than six million in a matter of days. Who will write the Jewish Musa Dagh? When the Armenians were killed, they were mourned by a Jewish book but when the Jewish People was killed who will mourn for it? Who will weep for it?[26]

Yitzhak Katznelson's writings were brought to print by Yitzhak Zuckerman and Shlomo Even-Shushan. In a biographical note about Franz Werfel, apparently written by Zuckerman, we read: "His noted book about the Armenian massacre, *The Forty Days of Musa Dagh*, was widely read by youth in the ghettos."[27]

Zvika Dror recalled the impact of *Musa Dagh* on Yitzhak Zuckerman (Antek), who was one of the leaders of the Warsaw ghetto uprising, saying that, "Yitzhak [Zuckerman] was a sort of 'tutor' to me on the Holocaust in conversations, recommendations of what to read, etc."[28] "When he wanted to enlighten us he said that it was impossible to understand the Warsaw ghetto uprising without reading Franz Werfel's *The Forty Days of Musa Dagh*. He added, 'This Jew understood the Armenian soul better than he understood the Jewish soul.'"[29]

Dov Ben Ephraim (Lutek), one of the leaders of the Jewish underground in Tchenstokhova, recalled how he was sent to the Konyestopol forest "for the purpose of organizing Musa Dagh there."[30]

One can learn about the great significance of Musa Dagh in the ghettos from additional testimonies from the same period and from a later testimony about the war period. For example, a member of the staff of Janusz Korczak's orphanage in the Warsaw Ghetto said that in one of their meetings in the summer of 1941, they discussed Franz Werfel's book. When they began to discuss the doctor who abandoned the children in order to save himself (in Werfel's book it was a pastor who later rejoined the children), Korzcak said, in the summer of 1941, that he would under no circumstances be parted from his children, and indeed, he kept his word later in the war.[31]

Furthermore, the chronicler of the Warsaw Ghetto, Emmanuel Ringelblum, wrote in his journal on June 25, 1942:

> What are people reading? This is a subject of general interest; after the war, it will intrigue the world. What, the world will ask, did people think of on Musa Dagh or in the Warsaw Ghetto people who knew for a certainty that death would no more skip them than it had over the other large Jewish communities and the small towns. Let it be said that though we have been sentenced to death and know it, we have not lost our human traits; our minds are as active as they were before the war.[32]

Three days before (June 22, 1942), he wrote, "a rumor has recently been circulating in Warsaw that the Jews have only forty days to live, which reminds us of *The Forty Days of Musa Dagh*."

The book was also influential in the Western European underground. Members of the Dutch underground read the book in German. "It was a 'textbook' for us. It opened our eyes and spelled out for us what might happen, although we did not know what in fact would occur."[33]

The examples cited above indicate the importance and significance that Jewish youth movements attributed to *The Forty Days of Musa Dagh*, probably before the Second World War and certainly during it. The book was an example, a reference, and to some extent a model to be admired and imitated.

The book was probably read in Yiddish (we know of two Yiddish versions), in Polish, and in German. In a study which appeared in 1997, after the publication of my book in Hebrew, *Hunger for the Printed World: Books and Libraries in the Jewish Ghettoes of Nazi-Occupied Europe*, we find that the most widely read books were *The Forty Days of Musa Dagh* and *War and Peace* by Leo Tolstoy among adults, and *The Heart* by Edmond de Amicis among younger readers. The author, David Shavit, documented possible explanations taken from testimonies of people who lived through the period.[34]

A youngster living in Kovno Ghetto explained why *The Forty Days of Musa Dagh* was in such great demand, as follows:

> Minnie and I, meanwhile, were attending most of the concerts and reading [the available] books. One of the books was *The Forty Days of Musa Dagh*, by Franz Werfel, which made an indelible impression on us. The bloody, ruthless massacre of over a million Armenians by the Turks in 1915, in full

view of the entire world, reminded us of our fate. The Armenians were starved to death, shot, drowned, tortured to exhaustion. We compared their fate with ours, the indifference of the world to their plight, and the complete abandonment of the poor people into the hands of a barbarous, tyrannical regime. Our analysis of the book indicated that if the world did not come to the rescue of the Armenians, who were Christians after all, how could we, Jews, expect help? No doubt Hitler knew all about those massacres and the criminal neglect by the free world, and was convinced that he could proceed with impunity against the helpless Jews.[35]

Arcadius Kahan, describing an undramatic day in the life of an ordinary person, a worker in the Warsaw Ghetto, wrote thus:

> After the meeting [of the house committee], the person in charge of book circulation hands over to the woman a package wrapped in a paper and whispers: 'You've got to return it in three days; twenty people are waiting their turn, this is the real thing.' A glance into the package convinces the woman that it is the real thing, *Forty Days of Musa Dagh*, the novel by Franz Werfel about the Turkish massacre of the Armenians. This is the most popular novel among the Adults in the ghetto. They'll read it aloud this evening, if there is electricity.

> There is light in the room and still time before the police hour. The father opens the book and begins to read aloud....The neighbor girl pulls out a book of her own, and while the grown-ups listen to the gruesome details of the massacres the girl plugs her ears with her fingers and takes flight into the romantic world of de Amicis' *The Heart*. It is a tale of the life and struggle of Italian children in the nineteenth century.[36]

There is, in my opinion, a considerable attraction and interest in the thesis that Werfel was actually dealing, in *Musa Dagh*, with Jewish issues and that through the protagonist, Gabriel Bagradian, he was describing his own conflicts and his struggle with his own identity. Gabriel, like Werfel, was alienated from his people. He arrived for a visit in Anatolia after "twenty three years of Europe, Paris! Years of complete assimilation." In Paris, "He had been allowed to live as scholar, a *bel esprit*, an archeologist, a historian of art, a philosopher, and in addition had been allotted a yearly income which made him a free, even a very well-to-do man." "At present, he was more French than ever, Armenian still, but only in a name—academically."[37]

There is no doubt that much Jewish symbolism appears in the narrative. Musa Dagh is Mount Moses; the battle on the mountain continued, according to Werfel, for forty days; the Flood lasted for forty days; Moses ascended the mountain for forty days, etc. In reality, according to the documents which Werfel used, the battle continued for twenty-four days, while other documents speak of thirty-six days. Yet other sources say the story of the rebellion lasted for fifty-three days.[38]

There are also clear analogies between Gabriel, who died on the summit of Musa Dagh while French ships miraculously saved his people, and Moses, who was buried on Mount Nevo and never reached the Promised Land. There are those who see a parallel between Gabriel's visit to his homeland, for which he felt no affinity, and Werfel's visit to Eretz Yisrael. These are, of course, only a few of the symbols.

Nonetheless, it seems that the magnetism of Musa Dagh, which became a symbol for the Jewish underground's resistance fighters, resulted from the powerful text that ignited a spark in so many people in Europe of the 1930s. For members of Jewish youth groups in Europe of the 1930s and the wartime ghettos—especially for those in the underground—the book contained additional elements. Apart from the identification of one victim with another, there was tangible fear that the fate of the Jews would continue to deteriorate. During the period of the ghetto, the reality of the ultimate victim became clearer and clearer, at least to the members of the underground. There was, nonetheless, a notion of dignity and self-respect. An admiration for the victim who struggles, rebels, strives for freedom, and maintains his dignity even after his fate is sealed. Even the dilemma so widely posed in the context of the Holocaust—"going like sheep to the slaughter"—appears numerous times in *Musa Dagh*. "I know how I wish to die—not like a defenceless sheep... not in the filth of a concentration camp." "But, even if no such fortune is in store for us, there would still be plenty of time for dying. And then at least we shall not need to despise ourselves as defenceless sheep."[39] In this sense, reading of the book fortified the spirit of its readers, future underground fighters, as Mordechai Tenebaum and other underground leaders have suggested.

Yet the meaning ascribed to the book may have been different in the undergrounds in Eastern Europe and Western Europe. It appears that the emphasis in Eastern Europe, because of the very different circumstances (and perhaps because of a difference in mentality) was: "The question is how we will die!... [And the preferable answer was] Not like a defenceless sheep." (Quote from the pastor, Ter Haigasun, in the chapter, "The Great Assembly.")

In Holland, on the other hand, and possibly in additional places, the meaning of Musa Dagh was that of the chance of salvation. The struggle against the Germans and victory over them would mean survival. They identified more closely with the question of the assimilated Armenian who became the leader of the resistance, Gabriel Bagradian, when he cuts off the priest: "Why death?"[40]

The book raises moral questions and expresses humanist values to which the members of the Jewish youth movements were sensitive, as well as existential uncertainties which were relevant to them. For the members of the Jewish underground, the story of the defense of Musa Dagh was a parable, a model and a source of inspiration. They equated their own fate with that of the Armenians. In both cases, the persecutor's purpose was the uprooting, the exile, and the physical annihilation of entire communities, and in both cases resistance embodied the idea of an honorable death as a nation, or a chance to be saved as individuals.[41] Musa Dagh was relevant because it was a penetrating treatment of the most existential and moral questions facing young Jews in those terrible years.

Notes

1. Werfel's biographer, Peter Stephan Jungk, argues that Werfel was mistaken when he added a note at the beginning of his book: "The miserable sight of some maimed and famished-looking refugee children, working in a carpet factory, gave me the final impulse to snatch from the Hades of all that was, this incomprehensive destiny of the Armenian nation." In Jungk's opinion, the visit was in the early part of 1930 and not in 1929. See Peter Stephan Jungk, *Franz Werfel: Une Vie de Prague a Hollywood* (Paris: Albin Michel, 1990), p. 339. (Henceforth: Jungk.)
2. A new edition of the book, translated by Zvi Arad, was published by Am Oved in 1979. Comparison of the two Hebrew translations—before and after the Holocaust—provides an interesting subject for research.
3. Dov Kimchi, *Massot Ketanot* (Jerusalem: Reuven Maas, 1938), p. 226. (Hebrew)
4. Ibid., p. 228.
5. Ibid., p. 230.
6. R. Zeligman, "The Forty Days of Musa Dagh," *Hapoel Hatzair*, Issue No. 41, August 1934.
7. Moshe Beilinson, "A Glorious Monument to Israeli Alienation," *Davar*, January 22, 1936. The article was also published in the anthology, *Dovrut: For Reading Clubs and Study Groups, A, Beilinson Selections* (Ein Harod: Hakibbutz Hameuchad Publishers, 1936). (Henceforth: *Dovrut.*)

8. *Dovrut*, pp. 91-92.
9. Ibid., pp. 93-94.
10. Ibid., p. 95.
11. Ibid., p. 96.
12. Meyer Weisgal, *So Far, An Autobiography* (Jerusalem: Maariv Library, 1971), p. 93. (Hebrew)
13. See Jungk, p. 25, p. 264 et al. We are in possession of unpublished correspondence between Weisgal and Werfel which deals explicitly with the question of Werfel's Jewishness, his attitude toward Zionism, and Werfel's rejection of potential assimilation, ostensibly because of Jewish suffering in the face of Christian anti-Semitism. Central Zionist Archives, Z5/702.
14. Haviv Canaan, *Two Hundred Days of Fear*, Mol-Art Publishers, undated, pp. 244-45. Yehoshua (Josh) Palmon was engaged at the time in training units of undercover soldiers, intended to be used behind enemy lines in the event of an invasion by Rommel. According to Canaan, Palmon and his colleagues thought that if the Germans invaded the country, the Jews of Palestine would be condemned to the same fate as the Armenians in the Ottoman Empire in World War I, i.e., horrific mass slaughter. Ibid., p. 253.
15. Uri Brenner, *Facing the Threat of a German Invasion of Palestine: 1940-1942*, Yad Tabenkin, Research Series, No. 3, 1981, pp. 154-55. Brenner relies on Canaan and the radio program, "Musa Dagh on the Carmel," broadcast by Israel Broadcasting Authority, June 3, 1971. See also Yoav Gelber, *Massada: The Defense of Palestine in World War II*, Bar Ilan University, 1990.
16. Emmanuel Markovsky-Mor, according to the Haganah Historical Archive, Galili Files, No. 8.
17. Haganah Historical Archive, Galili Files, letters to Tzipporah, *Facing the Threat*, p. 63.
18. Mordechai Tenebaum-Tamaroff, *Pages from the Fire: Dappim Min Hadleka*, (revised and expanded edition), Yad Vashem, Beit Lohamei Hagettaot, 1984, p. 79 (Hebrew). Herschel was one of the central figures in organizing the Bialystock underground, and Tenebaum's closest friend. He was killed in the August 1943 uprising at the age of twenty-four. Ibid., p. 283 (annotated index of names).
19. Ibid., p. 50.
20. Ibid., p. 238. The editors, Bronka Klevansky and Zvi Shener, from their own personal experience during the period, were intimately familiar with the prevailing mood among the youth movements in the ghetto.
21. Ibid., p. 138.
22. Author's conversation with Bronka Klevansky, July 1, 1990.
23. Chaika Grossman, *The People of the Underground* (second edition) (Tel Aviv: Sifriat Poalim, 1965), p. 125; Levy Aryeh Sarid, "The Fighting Jewish Underground in Bialystock," *Moreshet*, No. 55, October 1993, p. 68. Grossman refers to another book about Fascist methods which relates the story of the German anti-Fascist underground, whose members' fighting

spirit was broken by the Gestapo's "educational" methods: "Breaking the fighters' ethos, their character and their faith in their comrades. They would talk about it at meetings, attempting to draw conclusions regarding a life of action."

24. Inka Wajbort, *Together and Alone in the Face of the Terror*, (Tel Aviv: Moreshet, 1992), pp. 33-34. (Hebrew)
25. Samuel Gringaus, "Dos Kultur-lebn in Kovner," in *Lite*, Mendel Sudarski et al., eds. (New York: Jewish-Lithuanian Cultural Society, 1951), p. 1955.
26. Yitzhak Katznelson, *Last Works, 1940-1944*, new, expanded edition, Hakibbutz Hameuchad, Beit Lochamei Hagettaot named after Yitzhak Katznelson, 1956, p. 211.
27. Ibid., p. 259.
28. Letter to the author, June 28, 1990.
29. Zvika Dror, "Life with Kushmar: In the Presence of Yitzhak Zuckerman," *Davar*, June 8, 1990. Zvika Dror conducted interviews and edited the volume, *Dapei Edut*, ["Pages of Testimony: 96 Members of Kibbutz Lochamei Hagettaot Tell Their Story"] (Tel Aviv: Hakibbutz Hameuchad, 1984).
30. Dov Ben Ephraim oral Testimony, Jerusalem: The Center for Oral History of the Institute for Contemporary Judaism, Hebrew University. The author wishes to thank Dr. Ariel Horowitz for directing him to this source.
31. Yizhak Perlis, *A Polish Jew: The Life and Work of Janusz Korzcak* (Tel Aviv: Hakibbutz Hameuchad, 1986), p. 160. (Hebrew)
32. Emmanuel Ringelblum, *Notes from Warsaw Ghetto: The Journal of Emmanuel Ringelblum*, edited and translated by Jacob Sloan (New York: McGraw-Hill, 1958), pp. 298-99.
33. Author's conversation (November 22, 1994) with Yigael Benyamin, member of the Dutch underground, who is completing his doctoral dissertation on the subject.
34. David Shavit, *Hunger for the Printed World*, McFarland, 1997. Notes 25, 35, and 36 in this chapter are taken from this book.
35. William W. Mishell, *Kaddish for Kovno: Life and Death in a Lithuanian Ghetto 1941-1945* (Chicago: Chicago Review Press, 1988), p. 141.
36. Arcadius Kahan, "A Day in the Ghetto," in *Essays in Jewish and Social History*, edited by Roger Weiss (Chicago: University of Chicago Press, 1986), pp. 180, 182-83.
37. *Musa Dagh* (New York: The Modern Library, 1934), pp. 5-6.
38. Jungk, p. 176. According to the testimony of one of the leaders of the rebellion, published in the American weekly *The Outlook*, on December 1, 1915, the self-defense continued for fifty-three days.
39. *Musa Dagh*, pp. 205-208.
40. The author's thanks to Yigael Benyamin for pointing out this distinction which is worthy of further confirmation.
41. Raya Cohen-Adler, "The Forty Days of Musa Dagh by Franz Werfel as Investigative Literature," *State, Government and International Relations*, No. 32 (Jerusalem: Hebrew University, spring 1990).

8

The Indifferent

Thus far, we have examined the attitudes of members of the tiny Nili group to the Armenian massacre at the time of its occurrence during the First World War. It should be emphasized that Nili was an exception to the general attitude of the Yishuv toward the Armenian massacre. Equally exceptional was the human, Jewish, and Zionist significance they attached to the events at the time. Other groups, individuals, and public personalities were, for the most part, silent about the massacres apart from an expression of concern lest a similar fate befall the Jews or personal expressions of shock at the mass murders (as we have seen in several chapters of this book).

In the chapter before us, we shall examine the reaction—or more correctly, the lack of reaction—by other segments of the Jewish community in Palestine and of the Zionist movement to the massacre at the time of its occurrence. The findings are based on research that is to some degree eclectic. The Zionist and pre-state Yishuv archives do not deal with the Armenian question *per se*. Neither manual nor computerized catalogues define it as a distinct subject. There may be some archival logic in this, and it is clear that not all of the material relating to the people and movements we shall examine was available to us. Nonetheless, the following chapter was written after an attempt to examine the research literature, memoirs, articles, and private correspondence in the archives. It may shed light on the attitude of people and organizations to the massacre of the Armenians. Consultations with researchers with special expertise in the personalities and organizations discussed did not reveal significant reactions.

With regard to some of the personalities and organizations, the archival material from the period is substantial but incomplete. The assumption that the material relevant to the Armenian question has, from all the material of the period, disappeared does not seem reasonable. Moreover, the Zionist and pre-state Yishuv historiography, which has dealt extensively with some of the personalities in question, does not touch upon the Armenian question. Just as the people themselves refrained from relating to the Armenian genocide, so too has historiography ignored it.

Fear of the Turkish authorities alone does not explain the silence about the Armenian massacre. In varied sources from the period we can find considerable amounts of material which was liable to incite the Turks. Conspiratorial methods, the most of extreme of which was the organizational structure of "Hashomer," provide only a partial explanation. The fact is that there exists substantial evidence of positions and operating methods, which were also in total contradiction to the demands of the Turkish rulers. For example, we find evidence of the refusal of members of "Hashomer" to turn over their weapons to the Turkish authorities, as required. "Hashomer" also refused to obey the directives of the leadership of the Yishuv on this issue. Resulting tensions were so high that Arthur Ruppin and Eliezer Hofein even accused "Hashomer" of treason.[1]

What follows is not a complete reconstruction of the historical picture. Nevertheless, the material available gives us a reasonably faithful account of reality. We have no way of knowing what people said in private, intimate conversation or in secret discussions. If they did in fact talk about the suffering and massacre of the Armenians, their comments are not reflected in the various sources which have survived, nor even in later evidence dealing with that period. The phenomenon of silence on the part of the people who were sensitive to the world and to their fellow man is worthy of comment and demands clarification and explanation.

"Hashomer"

When the First World War began, "Hashomer" was at the height of its power and organization. 1908 to 1913 were years of glory for "Hashomer" and its forerunner "Bar Giora" in the Yishuv. In its philosophy of organization and function during the difficult war years, on both the practical and ideological levels, the Armenian tragedy had no part.[2] There is no doubt, however, that the members of "Hashomer" knew about the mass slaughter of the Armenians during the war. Furthermore, the Armenian tragedy had an impact on some of the future members of "Hashomer" even in the prewar years.

There is evidence that this impact, which grew to become a formative influence on the prewar world view of some "Hashomer" members, and especially strong on the group known as "the mountain Jews," or the "Caucasian Jews." Yehezkel Nisanov, a member of "Hashomer" in the Galilee, was killed in a skirmish with Arabs in 1911. Zvi Becker, his childhood friend, published in *Achdut,* in 1912, a piece entitled, "Recollections of a Comrade on the First Anniversary of Nisanov Death." Becker recalls the period when they lived together in Baku.

In Baku Yehezkel was, at first, a member of the Social Revolutionary Party. But he left it together with five other Jewish members who realized that we are Jewish nationalists and we must join up with the small 'Poalei Zion' Party, which had then begun to organize in Baku. During the first days of his entry into the new society Yehezkel was like a person who had wandered for a long long time and had finally found his way. Yehezkel was immediately willing to go and work there for the three years....Eretz Yisrael became the center of his aspirations. At that time there was the famous pogrom against the Armenians in Baku. I was living with Yehezkel at the time in a rented room in an Armenian's apartment, and we witnessed the entire terrible event. The rifles of the Tatars as well as of the Armenians were aimed at Yehezkel more than once, because both of the belligerent sides considered him an Asiatic. And when peace was restored, I would walk through the streets of the city of death. We would look at the dead and count them by the hundreds. Yehezkel was lost in thought and when I asked him what he was thinking he said: Look, heretofore there was solidarity and friendship between the Armenians and the Tatars... I even grew up among the Tatars....And suddenly....This one lies headless before me and that one without an arm.... What makes us sure that this cannot happen to the Jews as well, and who knows whether we will be able, like the Armenians, to defend ourselves.... And from that day on he began to tell me occasionally that we must not live among strangers and that we should not trust strangers. 'Where are they,' he would argue, 'All those who cried: 'Let all peoples unite!' Where were they hiding during the three days of the pogrom while an entire people was being slaughtered in the streets? Where were the thousands of people who would come to their rallies, and are now nowhere to be found? No, I no longer believe their high-flown speeches....The pretty speeches will count for nothing in times of trouble....What has happened to the Armenians can also happen to the Jews.' Once he came to our association and discovered that his speculation about the possibility of pogroms against the Jews was no longer a mere speculation. They told him about Kishinev, about Homel etc. etc. After he heard that Yehezkel decided, together with other comrades, to go to Eretz Yisrael.[3]

Zvi Nadav, another member of "Hashomer," relates in his memoirs, which appeared in the anthology, *Hashomer*, his adventures—together with other "Hashomer" members—as soldiers in the Turkish army at the end of the war.[4] They were stationed in a military camp in Turkey.

We hoped that by the end of our maneuvers the war would end. The maneuvers were not yet over because we had not yet learned to shoot (although as members of "Hashomer," we knew the military theory from home), and we were told that they would soon be sending us into other brigades on the Transcaucasian front to fight against the Armenians who had rebelled against the Turks. I thought bitterly about the peculiarities of fate.... There was indeed a chance that we, Socialist Jews fighting for the freedom of our people, would be sent to oppress a people persecuted by Russian tsarist government pogroms and the Turkish government no less than the Jews.

I said to myself: as soon as we are put into the army and the mutual responsibility ends—I will desert along the way and join up with the Armenian forces.

We arrived safely in Trebizond. Already along the way Zvi Nisanov made contact with the commander of a brigade of railway workers and managed to attach all of us to that brigade. Some of us remained there in various kinds of service work. Zvi could have easily stayed in Trebizond but answered the request of the comrades and went with us by foot to Erzurum. It was after the end of the massacre of the Armenians. We still found clear evidence of the slaughter. In two districts, Trebizond and Erzurum, which we crossed on foot, we found only ruins and dead bodies scattered around.

Some of us were accepted as mechanics in the railway platoon. Zvi Nisanov, as usual, found a job as an interpreter from Russian to Turkish. One by one the fellows slowly dropped away through various tricks. Feldman (who was a laborer in Petach Tikva) and I were the last to remain, and with the first snow we also escaped on foot.

Testimony about the Armenian massacre, or more precisely about evidence and remains of the massacre, also appear in the memoirs of other members of "Hashomer," although not always in detail. In some cases, the events are not mentioned at all.

In the anthology, *Hashomer*, Z. Ussishkin, for example, recalls his imprisonment in Damascus when the Nili affair broke and Lishanky's execution.[5] After Lishansky's trial and execution, members of "Hashomer" were acquitted of the political charges against them and sent to Erzurum. Ussishkin was sent to Aleppo and Adana. From there he was sent to Urfa where he remained until he deserted the army. After numerous adventures, he managed to return to Aleppo. In Erzurum, Adana, and Urfa, there were widespread massacres of the Armenians. The narrator was there for many days but the massacres and their aftermath are not mentioned at all in his memoirs.

In contrast, other members of "Hashomer" describe what they saw and the deep horror they felt. Yizhak Nadav, for example, describes in his memoirs a journey to Huran (southern Syria) at Kalvarisky's request to purchase wheat for the farmers in the Galilee. According to his record it was just before the winter planting, i.e., the autumn and early winter, the end of 1915. Nadav was interested in going to Huran to see the agricultural land purchased by the Baron de Rothschild in preparation for Jewish settlement there. He informed "Hashomer's" executive committee of the true purpose of his trip and reminded them of "our request from [the Baron] during his visit, and his promise to give us the land and the villages he had purchased in Huran."[6]

Nadav accompanied Kalvarisky to the estate of the emir, Abado Algizari, in Segerat Algiulan. They were received with great honor at the emir's estate and a lamb was slaughtered for their repast.

> The next day we toured the farm, guided by the Emir. The farm was enclosed by a wall built of basalt stone two meters high and three hundred meters long. Inside the yard there was a 'modern' apartment with three large spacious rooms furnished with fine oriental furniture. On the other side of the yard there was a barn and next to it a horse stable. On another side were the granaries. To our surprise we found several families of Armenian refugees who had survived the Turks' massacre. It was one of the most shocking sights I have seen in my entire life, and as Jews we were particularly moved by the sight. Afterwards, I went with the Emir to the granaries where he showed me the wheat and in the presence of his representative gave an order to deliver to me the quantity of wheat which had been sold to Mr. Kalvarisky.

Nadav visited the villages that had been established by the Baron in 1895 and were abandoned several months later. In one of the villages, Gilin, he discovered that the farm buildings were inhabited by Armenian refugees.

> On the day that I visited the place, one of the refugees who was in indescribably desperate straits sold his young daughter to an Arab gendarme for two *majidies* (the price of a lamb in those days) in order to feed the rest of his family. In all of the villages of the Huran and the Golan there were Armenian refugees, mostly old people, women and children—since most of the young men had been murdered by the Turks in Armenia and other places.[7]

Pinchas Schneurson, a leader of "Hashomer," was a member of the group sent from Damascus to Turkey which also included Zvi Nadav and Zeev Ussishkin. From Aleppo they were transferred to Adana. "We found the city—inhabited mostly by Armenians—destroyed and in ruins after the brutal massacre which was conducted against its inhabitants."[8] After numerous events, some of the group, including Zvi Nisanov (Yehezkel Nisanov's brother), Zvi Nadav, Proskorovsky, David Fisch, Yaakov Portugali, and Pinchas Schneurson, were sent to Armenia. Schneurson was sent to Trebizond and from there to Erzurum.

For three full weeks we made our way through desolate villages abandoned by their Armenian inhabitants who had fled for their lives from the fury of the Turks. A little here and a little there, we encountered small Greek settlements, which had not been abandoned. We crossed the pine-covered Armenian mountains. We, the Palestinians, who were used to the bald mountains of Eretz Yisrael, with their sparse shrubbery and scanty woods, breathed deeply in awe of the lush forests. We were hungry. Except for 'kosmok' (rock-hard bread softened in water) we had eaten nothing. The Turkish Army was without clothes or shoes. Many of the soldiers went about barefoot and in rags. From walking in the mountains, our feet were cut up and covered with wounds and blisters. Every morning, before starting out, the wounded would complain to the doctor in order to obtain permission to ride the donkeys which were meant for those who could not walk. But since the number of donkeys was limited, the doctor solved the problem of the wounded with the help of one of the officers in a different way. They held sticks and when someone would ask for permission to ride, they would immediately beat him on the head with the sticks. The poor soldier would run for his life. Thus we passed days and weeks until we reached Erzurum. The city was in total ruin. We met our comrades there—Zvi Nisanov, Zvi Hadar, David Fisch and others. They were working on the rail line. All of Zvi Nisanov's efforts to remain in Erzurum and to work on the railway were to no avail.

After additional hardships, Schneurson and Yaakov Portugali decided to desert from the army. They were assisted by "Sobotniks," members of a Christian sect that observed the Jewish Sabbath. The Sobotniks hid them and afterwards took them to a place near Ardahan.[9]

From there they took us by wagon to Ardahan. In the wagons they were also transporting Armenian children who had been assembled in Ardahan. Their parents had been murdered by the Turks and the young children, after being circumcised according to Muslim law, were transported to Constantinople by order of the authorities. On the way we were stopped by Turkish-Kurdish guards who suspected that Yaakov Portugali was an Armenian masquerading as a Turk. They took us from the wagon in order to take us to the nearby guardhouse. The wagons continued on their way and we remained behind with the guards. We told the Turks that we were Russians and that we wanted to return to our homeland. The guards began to beat us brutally. When my nose and mouth began to bleed the guards left us alone. We managed to rid ourselves of them and hurried to rejoin the wagon but in vain. While we were hurrying along our way, there appeared from a side road a wagon laden with sacks and behind it a convoy of 'Sobotnik' wagons carrying wheat to Batum. The 'Sobotniks' were happy to see us and we continued part of the way with them.

We went out to wander around the streets of Batum in the hope of finding a savior. And indeed we met a Jewish fellow named Horowitz and learned that he was a member of 'Poalei Zion.' Horowitz told us that he was the 'last Mohican' left from all of the organization's members in Batum. He took good care of us and through him we contacted Dr. Katznelson who was in Batum at the time. Through him we made contact with smugglers who promised to take us across the border to Tiplis. We made an attempt to steal across the border and failed. We returned to Batum where we met two Jewish officers of the Turkish Army, graduates of the 'Herzliya' Gymnasium [in Eretz Yisrael]. They offered us refuge in their flat in the house of a wealthy Armenian who had fled from the Turks. After long months of hardships, painful illness, imprisonment and wandering, we greatly enjoyed the rest and care we found in this house.

In his memoirs, Yaakov Portugali described the destruction of the Armenians in the region in two sentences: "Thus we entered an empty settlement. We did not encounter even a dog there. It was a large Armenian village whose inhabitants had been exterminated by the Turks."[10]

At the beginning of the war, Yaakov Kanterovitch volunteered for the Turkish army and worked as a censor in Jerusalem, Beirut, and Damascus. He was imprisoned after the Nili spy ring was uncovered. When he was found innocent of any blame, he was sent to Constantinople, and from there to the Caucasian front. He, too, was in Erzurum and its environs at the time. He relates in his memoirs that he did not directly encounter sights of Turks killing of Armenians, but says of himself, "In addition to the private worries, the Armenian question caused me no little pain and sorrow."[11]

There can be no doubt that the members of "Hashomer" knew of the massacre and even witnessed its aftermath at the end of the war. Moreover, it is reasonable to assume that the organization's members and leadership knew about it much earlier. On December 6, 1914, Manya Shochat was arrested and a warrant was issued for the arrest of Yisrael Shochat, who turned himself in to the authorities in mid-January 1915.

On March 21-22 of that year, the Shochats were deported from the country together with Yehoshua Hankin, Yizhak Ben-Zvi, David Ben Gurion, and other leaders of the Yishuv.

Manya Shochat was tried in Damascus, and the Shochats were deported to Turkey, together with Hankin. The American Ambassador in Constantinople, Henry Morgenthau, Sr., interceded on their behalf and in the end they were not sent to Sivas, on the front line in Anatolia, but rather to Bursa, some eight hours' journey by rail and boat from Constantinople. Ambassador Morgenthau continued to take an interest in their condition there and instructed the American consul to visit them every Sunday and send Morgenthau a report on their condition. "The consul's visits to us," wrote Yisrael Shochat later, "were known to the local authorities and to the high officials in Constantinople. I am certain that thanks to the visits we were saved from persecution and perhaps from death."[12] The Shochats and Hankin were in Bursa for more than two years. It is probable that they witnessed the massacre or its aftermath but they do not mention it at all in their memoirs. It is known that they sent letters from Bursa to members of "Hashomer" in Palestine, and that they were extremely cautious in their correspondence. The letters have apparently not survived and we do not know their content.

The only reference by Yisrael or Manya Shochat to the Armenians that we have found—although we do not claim that this is the only reference—appears, not by coincidence, in the context of "Hashomer's" adversarial organization, Nili. "Very strained relations," writes Yisrael Shochat, "exist between 'Hashomer' and Nili. From the beginning these two organizations reflected completely contradictory views which could never reach a compromise."[13] Shochat expands in detail on the affair of Avshalom Feinberg's mission to Bursa when he brought a proposal from the Nili for cooperation between the two organizations. He concludes,

And indeed what we have feared and surmised has come. The espionage affair has been discovered and the capture of the spies has brought disaster upon us all. The Yishuv stands before total destruction. The bitter fate of the Armenians, the fate of brutal annihilation, was to befall the Jews [in Palestine] were it not for outside pressure which influenced the Turkish authorities to deal leniently with the Jews and to distinguish between the real culprits and the entire Yishuv.

A possible explanation for the silence regarding the Armenian disaster may, perhaps, be found in the words which Shochat himself wrote about his forced exile in Bursa:

1916 and 1917 have passed. The months have turned into years and we are still sitting in Bursa, with our eyes turned in vain toward freedom and action. From the scanty reports in the newspapers we are allowed to receive, from letters we sometimes receive from friends and comrades, we have seen that the war continues unabated around the world. The first to suffer are, as usual, the Jews. Especially great was the suffering of the Jews in Eretz Yisrael: starvation and persecution, decrees and plagues. I was unable to concentrate my thoughts on anything at the time, except to search for a way out of our oppressive and debilitating exile, so that I might again dedicate my strength to our People and our Land.[14]

I wish to emphasize that I do not accuse, but rather seek to find an explanation for the disregard of the tragedy of the Armenians. The explanation may be that the extreme concentration on themselves, the concern over what was happening in Palestine, created, in retrospect, a disregard for the suffering of others. An additional point to be noted is that the members of "Hashomer," like almost all of the members of the workers' movement in Palestine, were pro-Turkish in their orientation. Their pro-Turkish bias grew even stronger after the Young Turk's revolution. Their hope was to obtain, within the framework of the Ottoman Empire, national territorial autonomy. The events of the war—including the horrors of the Armenian massacre, which some of them actually witnessed or at least witnessed its aftermath—did not change their orientation, at least until a very late stage in the war. The change began only in late 1917. There are some who date the change from the latter half of 1917, not before September, when the Twelfth Congress of "Poalei Zion" convened in Palestine.[15] From this perspective there is no doubt that the workers' movement supported the evil, losing side, the German-Turkish alliance. It was the good fortune of the Yishuv that the price of this orientation was not high. It appears that the Armenian genocide did not play a part in the considerations and attitude of the Yishuv.

David Ben Gurion and Yitzhak Ben Zvi

The historiography of the Yishuv and the Zionist Movement deals extensively with the history of David Ben Gurion and Yitzhak Ben-Zvi during the war, with special attention given to their attitude toward Turkey. The question of when they changed their pro-Turkish orientation is also examined occasionally. The question of their attitude toward the Armenian genocide is almost never discussed.

During the period of the First World War, Ben Gurion and Ben-Zvi were essentially "local leaders." Their leadership and influence were felt primarily in the Palestinian workers' movement, "Poalei Zion." They were not considered of the first rank of the leadership of worldwide "Poalei Zion."[16] During the war, their influence expanded to wider circles of the international movement and, to a limited degree, to American Jewry, but they were still far from a position of serious influence among the Jewish leadership or even world Zionism. The interest and importance which historical research attributes to their opinions and actions in those early years is explained by the fact that they later became the leaders of the Zionist movement and the state of Israel. Ben Gurion, in particular, became the pivotal Zionist figure. An examination of their actions at the time can teach us something about their future endeavors. They—especially Ben Gurion—were totally focused on one issue, the Zionist issue, to the exclusion of everything else.

Investigation of the archival sources, research studies, and the numerous monographs dealing with these two figures disclose disregard (surprising?) of the Armenian tragedy. An expert on Ben Gurion told me: "If it were the Arabs who had committed the massacre of the Armenians, Ben Gurion would have related to it."

As we have seen, Ben Gurion and Ben-Zvi were deported from Palestine in March 1915, after they were arrested on February 9. Following a short sojourn in Egypt, they arrived in the United States where they remained for most of the war. Before their deportation, the two worked for Ottomanization and for the establishment of a Jewish Brigade, which would serve as a local Palestinian defense militia during the war. Tens of members of "Poalei Zion," including the writer Y.H. Brenner, volunteered for the Brigade and began military training, until the Turkish authorities ordered it to disband. Jamal Pasha, who was the virtually omnipotent ruler of Palestine, viewed the Zionists, in general, and "Poalei Zion," in particular, as dangerous elements that sought to undermine Turkish authorities.

In a memorandum from Ben Gurion and Ben-Zvi to Jamal Pasha in February 1915, the former rejected the charge that they belonged to a "secret organization opposed to the interests of the Ottoman kingdom." They emphasized, "All of our deeds, thoughts and hopes, just as they are focused on the welfare of the Jews in Palestine, are also focused on the welfare of the Ottoman kingdom in its entirety."[17] Clearly, this does not, by itself, constitute evidence of their positions due to their understandable desire to placate the authorities. But these passages do reflect

Ben Gurion and Ben-Zvi's viewpoint and actions at the beginning of the war, before they were deported.

After their deportation the two spent some time in Cairo before going to the United States. In his memoirs, written in 1969, Ben Gurion states, "We met in Cairo with Trumpeldor. He is organizing here a brigade, which will be sent to the Dardanelles to fight the Turks. Both of us stated our opposition to the idea. In Eretz Yisrael there are tens of thousands of Jews, and this proposal may bring about the destruction of the Yishuv. Trumpeldor did not agree with us. Previously it was Jabotinsky who favored such a brigade and in the meantime he has left here."[18] For the same reason they opposed Pinchas Ruttenberg's plan to organize a Jewish Legion: "Both of us, Ben-Zvi and I, were against any step which might bring about the destruction of the Hebrew Yishuv in Eretz Yisrael."[19] He wrote the same things to his father in his first letter after a long hiatus due to the war.[20]

In the United States, Ben Gurion and Ben-Zvi published articles in the Jewish press. Ben Gurion's first article in the U.S. was entitled, "Toward the Future," and appeared in *Hatoren*, in August 1915. The article was written in a tone of enthusiasm: "In the blood and fire of this awful war burns one great and sacred world right, the right of liberty and national independence in the homeland. Defense of the homeland and national liberty are the soul of the current events of our times."

Later on in the article, Ben Gurion discusses the Ottoman regime, the Arabs and relations with them. He also defines the Zionist aims: "We strive to concentrate, to become part of, and to hold the Land of Israel just as every people is concentrated, is part of and holds on to its land: like the Poles in Poland, like the Bulgars in Bulgaria. We aspire to make the Land of Israel an Israelite country, and the Hebrews to an Israelite people."

In his view, the Land of Israel, like the whole world, "stands at the edge of a new era." The new era of Eretz Yisrael will be, according to Ben Gurion's vision at the time, within the framework of the Ottoman Empire.

"Eretz Yisrael in the Past and in the Present"

Ben Gurion and Ben-Zvi dedicated two whole years to writing a book about Eretz Yisrael. The arguments within the American Jewish community about a Hebrew congress and Eretz Yisrael pushed Ben

Gurion to write such a book. In his letter to his father describing the period of the war, Ben Gurion talked about writing the book.

> From the beginning I thought that I would finish my work in [one] year, but after working for two full years and many months—sixteen hours a day—I realized that I will finish the work over fifteen years. In the course of the work I saw that my original plan needed expansion because I discovered that not only is there no Hebrew volume or book for the Hebrews about their historic homeland, there is not, in all of the languages of the world, not a single comprehensive and thorough volume about our country. At the same time there is not another single country about which so much has been written in so many languages.

> To my sorrow, I could not continue my work and postpone the printing of the book until I had finished my research. On the one hand there were events which pushed me to exchange my book for a sword, and on the other hand my comrades were waiting impatiently for the promised volume.

> Thus, despite my intentions, the first volume of 'Eretz Yisrael' appeared, and was well received by the critics, and the 'Palestine' organization of the pro-Palestinian committee wrote that it was the most authoritative and comprehensive work on Eretz Yisrael in the literature on Palestine in any language. But the book does not satisfy me and this is not *the book* [emphasis in the original] which I had set my heart on.[21]

Ben Gurion relates in his memoirs (1969): "On January 15, 1918, I finished writing my part of the book. Y. Ben-Zvi finished [his part of the book] before me. In February 1918 the printing and binding of the book was completed. The book made a great impression and four thousand copies were sold within several weeks."[22]

The book embodies the pro-Turkish orientation of its authors. This is particularly apparent in the article, "National-Religious Autonomy for Non-Muslim Peoples," written by Ben Gurion.[23] Ben Gurion writes, *inter alia*, that the Turks "did not reach the level of culture of some of the more developed peoples under their dominion, such as the Armenians, the Jews and the Greeks. Turkey was and remains 'a state of nations.'[24] And yet it must be said, to the credit of the Turks that their rulers behaved toward the conquered with a degree of tolerance and generosity which is unparalleled in the history of the Christian peoples of the same period."

Ben Gurion points out that broad national-religious autonomy was granted to the Greeks and shortly thereafter to the Armenians and the

Jews. "These rights have not been infringed upon to this day." There are three recognized "nationalities" in the Ottoman Empire (which enjoy the rights of "millet"): The Greeks, the Armenians, and the Jews. They enjoy the right of self-rule in all national, cultural, and religious affairs. According to Ben Gurion "At the root of these rights is the principle of national autonomy which was developed in recent days by the Austrian thinkers Rudolph Springer and Otto Bauer, and was accepted in 1899 at the Austrian Social-Democratic Conference in Brin."[25]

Ben Gurion does not mention in a single word the massacres of the Armenians at the end of the nineteenth century and the beginning of the present century. Furthermore, it is as if the mass destruction of hundreds of thousands of Armenians at the beginning of the war had never happened. It should be noted that reports of the Armenian massacre were common knowledge in the United States and Europe from the middle of 1915. The events were prominently reported in the press. It is unreasonable to assume that Ben Gurion did not know or hear about them even if, in his words, "I have almost ceased to read even the daily newspapers except as I travel from my house to the library" while he was spending most of his time on writing the book on a province within the Ottoman Empire.

The only place, to the best of my knowledge, in which Ben Gurion mentions the Armenian tragedy during these years is the letter he sent to his father on December 5, 1919, from the 39th Jewish Regiment, after a break in their correspondence during the war.

"As you know, I was deported from the country [Palestine] five years ago by order of Jamal Pasha. I was caught by the authorities because they found my name in the list of delegates to the Zionist Congress and a Zionist in those days was considered a traitor. Jamal Pasha planned from the outset to destroy the entire Hebrew settlement in Eretz Yisrael, exactly as they did to the Armenians in Armenia. But the central government, primarily Talât Bey who was then Vizier for Domestic Affairs, blocked Jamal's plan."[26] There are, of course, erroneous generalizations and incorrect facts in Ben Gurion's letter to his father.

Mention of the Armenians by Ben Gurion and Ben-Zvi in the prewar years was negligible. Their statements deal with the legal status of the Armenians in the Ottoman Empire, their participation in political life, and their highly developed national consciousness. Participation in the political life of the Ottoman Empire in the early years of the second decade of the century was very important in the view of "Poalei Zion" in general, and of Ben Gurion and Ben-Zvi in particular.

For example, in the issue of *Ha'achdut*, the weekly journal of the workers and the masses in Eretz Yisrael, from autumn 1913, there is a front-page article by Avner (Yitzhak Ben-Zvi): "Our National Demands in Turkey." Ben-Zvi relates to the question of nationalities in the multi-national states of Russia, Austria, and Turkey. The nationality question arose in Turkey in the discussions of the "Union and Progress" Party and the Parliament in connection with the question of education of the people, and now, in his estimate, will have to be resolved in one way or another.

> Now is the hour of decision, the hour of good will, all of the peoples have come on in a vigorous demand for their rights. The Bulgars, like the Greeks and the Armenians, do not cease to present the matter in the press, for they are a unique people that have unique demands. And they demand equal rights for their language, their culture, and freedom to conduct their own internal affairs. Active efforts on the part of the Jews is therefore necessary precisely now.

> We are now living in an important political moment. Before us lies a noble and wondrous task, a national mandate tied to the entire Jewish national essence in Turkey, and not only in Turkey....All of the peoples have come out with a declaration of their demands. We must do the same. And it is not enough to declare our demands; we must also enter into discussion with all of the subjugated peoples and with those same Turkish elements who understand the value of national rights and respect them, in order to ask for their help and to offer our assistance.

The national question in the Ottoman Empire was the subject of Ben-Zvi's lecture, "The Political Situation in Turkey," at the Fourth World Convention of the international "Poalei Zion" Party held in 1913.[27] Ben-Zvi dealt with the enormous changes that had taken place in the Ottoman Empire following the Balkan War. "If prior to the war Turkey was a European country—now it is an Asiatic country." The other point, which characterizes Turkey after the war, is the weight and role of the Arab people within the Empire. In his opinion, "The Armenian question takes second place after the question of the Arabs, two questions which have taken the place of earlier ones, the Albanian and Macedonian questions." With regard to the various national movements Ben-Zvi states: "There is no need to state that the most complete movement with the highest level of consciousness is the Armenian movement,

which poses a grave danger to the entire eastern Ottoman [Empire]."
Ben Gurion fills out Ben-Zvi's words and reflects on the activity of
"Poalei Zion" in Turkey. He points out that one cannot find in
Constantinople "organized syndicates, not only among the Arab workers who live in very difficult economic conditions, but also among the
other peoples, except for the Armenians, who have managed to create a
strong association."[28]

Ben Gurion returns to the national question in a series of articles,
which he published in *Haachdut*, beginning in the winter of 1914, under the title "Self Rule in Vilayets [provinces]"—following the new
vilayet law, which had been enacted in Constantinople.

He examines the difficulties and complexities of the national question, especially in a country of nationalities. "But in no place is this
question so acute as in a multicolored striped state such as Turkey, full
as a pomegranate with contradictions and contrasts, nationalities, races,
religions and societies. The national question is the rock of destruction
against which the Ottoman State has shattered several times, and its
leaders devoured in the wake.

> In the old regime the question of the peoples and their struggle against the
> authorities would have ended, at best, with total secession or something
> similar under Ottoman domination, and at worst, in mass slaughter. The
> Balkan War brought down the military force, which the 'Young Turks' tended
> to lean on. The position of the ruling race was shaken and weakened. The
> center of gravity moved from Europe to Asia, where the Arab question
> exists in full force. The question of the Armenians became more acute since
> they were intended to play an important role in the new balance of power
> within the Empire, a role that was greater than their size and weight would
> warrant.

> How will the ruling party resolve the national question? How will it recon-
> cile between [separatist] aspirations for autonomy of the Armenians and
> the Arabs who have become, due to territorial and political changes, the
> masters of the situation—in effect if not in fact—and the aspirations of the
> regime to preserve Turkish dominance and the integrity and solidarity of
> the State? It is difficult to offer a specific answer at this time but it is clear
> that it is no longer possible to go back to the former system.

It is worth mentioning that the position of Ben-Zvi and Ben Gurion
regarding the national demands of the Armenians remained unclear.
They did not express support publicly, which is understandable given
the circumstances. But one can sense between the lines a reservation

about the power and national aspirations of the Armenians that may be harmful to the Ottoman Empire. We should remember that the political orientation of both Ben Gurion and Ben-Zvi concerning the national aspirations of the Jews was based on the survival of the Ottoman Empire and not on its disintegration.[29]

In contradiction to Ben Gurion's statement, Turkey under the 'Young Turks' did not become more progressive: it reverted to its former methods of mass murder, in unprecedented dimensions, of the Armenians. Even after the huge massacre, Ben Gurion did not deal with the Armenian question, as far as we can ascertain, except in the context of fears that the Jews would be neglected and abandoned as were the Armenians. Ben Gurion was a sober pragmatic leader with deep political understanding who was striving to achieve sovereignty for his people.[30]

He mentioned more frequently the massacre of the Assyrians by the Iraqis in 1933. The scope of the massacre was much more limited — "only" some hundreds of the Assyrian community were killed. But this time the murderers were Arabs and not Turks, and therefore, the massacre of the Assyrians was a weighty argument in presenting the Zionist case.[31]

"Poalei Zion" and the Socialist Internationale

The European Socialist movement supported the idea that after the war a sort of federative state of autonomous national units would replace the Ottoman Empire. The idea was that separate national states would not be established. The idea was proposed in the Stockholm Declaration of the Socialist Internationale.[32] The conference was held in September-October 1917, at the initiative of the socialist parties of the neutral states of Holland and Scandinavia.

The invitation to the Labour Party to participate in the conference aroused bitter controversy in Great Britain and Lloyd George's coalition government. The Prime Minister and most of the press viewed the conference as a German instrument.[33]

The world federation of "Poalei Zion" was involved in the activity of the Socialist Internationale that had been established during the war in the framework of the "Dutch-Scandinavian Committee." A delegation of "Poalei Zion" was invited to participate in the conference that convened, as stated, in Stockholm in the fall of 1917.

One of the options suggested by the conference organizers was that "Poalei Zion" would appear as part of what was defined as the "Turkish delegation," i.e., a delegation which would represent the proletariat of Greater Turkey, together with the Armenians, as two subsections of the Turkish bloc.[34]

The Armenian delegation agreed to the proposal and the "Poalei Zion" delegation attended the conference. We have no further information from contemporary sources. We do not know if there were meetings between the two delegations and if there were, what was discussed. The Zionists involved do not mention it, perhaps because they did not attach much importance to the affair. From their perspective, advancing the Zionist cause and realizing the goals of Zionism were the main issues. The Armenian question was marginal.

In contrast, we find a number of references to the Armenian question—although not to the Armenian massacre—in memoranda submitted by "Poalei Zion" to the Internationale during the First World War. It should be noted that the Socialist Internationale effectively ceased to function after the war broke out because the socialist parties found themselves in opposing camps. The emphasis on nationalism overwhelmed class solidarity. Nevertheless, the Dutch and Scandinavian socialist parties, whose governments were neutral, attempted to operate in the international socialist arena during the war years.

In November 1915, the world federation of "Poalei Zion" issued a memorandum in the neutral Hague. The memorandum, written in German, was addressed to the office of the Internationale and was entitled "The Jews and the War." It addressed the Jewish question and its solution, with appended documentation. It was written by Shlomo Kaplansky who was the secretary-general of the world federation of "Poalei Zion" and was based in The Hague.

The memorandum stressed, "The Jewish nation as a nation is not engaged in a war of conquest or in an unavoidable war of defense." "Nonetheless, no other people has suffered as much from the terrible results of the war."[35] The suffering of the Jews during the First World War was widespread, in the countries of Eastern and Central Europe and in the Near East. The memorandum describes the situation of the Jews in Russia, Rumania, Austria, Hungary, Poland, and Palestine. It describes the suffering and "the experiences endured by almost nine of the thirteen millions of the Jewish People."

In the section entitled "The Jewish Tragedy," Kaplansky writes, "In the midst of the world tragedy, which affects all peoples equally, the Jewish tragedy is revealed in unparalleled severity and scope, full of pain and suffering."[36]

The Jewish tragedy is also unique because of other reasons, some of which are common to both the Jews and other peoples:

> The shocking tragedy of the fact that members of the same people, Jews from the two fighting camps, are killing one another. All the brutality and injustice of the war pale when we see that the Jews of Russia and Austria, united not only in ties of nationality but frequently in ties of blood and family, carry weapons against one another. In this we are similar to other peoples—the Poles, the Serbians, the Armenians, and the Ukrainians—to all peoples who are rent by divisions of nation-state.

> The tragedy of the Jewish People is far greater than we can ever remember because the huge number of victims have been sacrificed for no reason, with no historical or national justification whatsoever. Peoples enslaved and divided by theft of their lands, peoples reduced by hundreds of years of oppression to the level of tribes without a history, hope to receive from this decisive battle renewed national life, unified by longed-for independence and free of the domination of their mighty neighbors. Thus do the Poles and the Ukrainians, the Serbs and the Belgians, the Turks and the Armenians, the Lithuanians and the Latvians hope and believe, consoled by their hopes and expectations. Yet we Jews have no such comforting illusion.[37]

The tendency, understandable perhaps, is to stress the fierceness and uniqueness of the Jewish tragedy. The aim was to convince the Socialist Internationale to deal with the Jewish national tragedy in all of its various aspects and to support a Zionist solution in Palestine, as proposed by "Poalei Zion." In this context, it seems, we ought to try to explain the minimal attention given to the disasters of others, in particular the unprecedented, and greatly more enormous, disaster of the Armenians.

Kaplansky actually refers with gratification, as was usual in other Jewish and Zionist circles of the day, to Turkey's treatment of the Jews. "The Jews are used to following Turkey's fate with a sense of gratitude and appreciation. Because Turkey opened its gates hospitably to the Jews who were expelled from Spain, granting them, insofar as the Koran and the previous absolutist regime permitted, equality before the law and even *the special national rights* given to other peoples within the Ottoman Empire"[emphasis in the original].[38] The admiration for

the rights of the Jews in the Ottoman Empire and the welcome given to
the victims of the Expulsion from Spain is consonant with the view of
territorial national autonomy within the framework of the Ottoman
Empire advanced by "Poalei Zion" at the time.

Turkey was perceived by "Poalei Zion" as the agent for realizing a
"federative state of nationalities," or the "territorial national autonomy."
At the least, in the framework of a "personal national autonomy" the
rights of the Jews in Turkey would be based, after certain changes, on
the law of millet.

In another memorandum of "Poalei Zion" from 1917, also written
by Kaplansky, it was stated,

> The law of 'millet' in Turkey (which was nullified during the war with
> regard to the Armenians) should be seen as a completely practical manner,
> although colored by a religious bias, of national self rule. Certainly it could
> not be given adequate expression under the old Ottoman rule. But in fact, it
> protected the various nationalities in the state from a blurring of their na-
> tional face and minimized to a great degree the areas of friction between
> the nationalities.[39]

Nevertheless, states the memorandum, the war resulted in systematic persecution of the Jews in Palestine. At the same time Kaplansky
stresses that "the Turkish Government did not adopt the method of terrible persecutions which we endured in Russia," and applauds the opportunity of Ottomanization which was offered to foreign nationals at the
beginning of the war.[40] "But we will not be satisfied with so little or give
thanks to governments simply because they do not murder and rob us."

The Turks began to "cleanse" the country of its most productive elements and of the educated leadership of the workers' movement. "And
so, if they humiliate the Jews and incite against them unceasingly, if the
army and the Muslim population, agitated by propaganda for a holy
war, see that the Jews are treated as traitors, who can guarantee that
worse things will not happen! Turkey is still adjacent to Russia, and the
country on its border is called Armenia."[41]

This is the only reference in the memorandum of November 1917
relating to the Armenian massacre, rather than to the Armenian national
problem as one of many other problems. The memorandum turns to the
socialist parties in the countries allied with Turkey to ask for their help
in persuading the Turks to allow the settlement of Jews in Palestine.
There is no way to know if they will be able to help but "the govern-

ments of the Great Powers which see themselves as civilized nations [The reference is primarily to Germany] must know that when they allow 'their friends' to do as they wish, they become accomplices in the attacks on justice and liberty." The memorandum also demands that the Jewish workers' movement in Palestine be given the right of a "national section" in the institutions of the Socialist Internationale.

In yet another memorandum of "Poalei Zion," "Forms of National Autonomy," which was written by Kaplansky in German in 1917 at the Hague, in support of the proposed law of self rule for national minorities, it mentions the joint manifesto of the socialists in the Balkan states, the Armenian socialists and the Jewish socialists in Palestine ("Poalei Zion") against the Balkan War as evidence of a significant development in the idea of federative states or a commonwealth of national states (a multinational state), together with the solution of a sovereign national state. In the view of "Poalei Zion," the multinational reality of Russia, Austria, Hungary, and Turkey would encourage such a development. It was therefore necessary to fight for self-rule of the oppressed nationalities that resided within the borders of the multinational states, thus preventing a period of bloody and brutal warfare.[42]

During the negotiations between the "Poalei Zion" delegation and the Dutch-Scandinavian committee, the Jewish-Armenian aspect was raised since both peoples were under Turkish rule. The position of the committee was indecisive, and ambivalent with regard to the future of the Ottoman Empire after the war.[43] Zerubavel, one of the leaders of "Poalei Zion" during those years and a member of the delegation, stated,

It is eminently permissible to intervene in internal Turkish affairs. The issue is not only the Jews, and the attitude toward them is not a coincidence. It is part of an entire system. It is sufficient to know the opinions of Jamal Pasha, the ruler of Syria and Palestine. This is a system of oppressive centralization and coercive negation of the nationality of the Armenians, Arabs and Jews. Social-democracy cannot approve Jamal Pasha's plans for liquidation.

In a memorandum presented by "Poalei Zion" to the Dutch-Scandinavian Socialist Committee, there appears a passage about "the right of self determination of nationalities," which indicates that the meaning of this principle is an "acceptance of the national demands of the Armenian, Ukrainian, and Czechoslovakian delegations."[44] With regard to Palestine, the "Poalei Zion" demands are "to establish Palestine as a special district which will enjoy self rule; to establish administrative uniformity in the country; and to grant national autonomy to the Jewish population in Palestine." On the other hand, the right of every nationality to unity and democratic self-rule includes the reconfiguration of Belgium, Serbia and Chernogoria, Rumania, and the unification and reestablishment of an independent Poland.

The members of the delegation were Borochov, Hazanovitch, and Zerubavel. The memorandum was also signed by Kaplansky and Berl Locker, who arrived later in Stockholm. This was, in effect, the world leadership of "Poalei Zion."

We have found no reference by Ber Borochov, one of the most outstanding figures of the world federation of "Poalei Zion," during all of the years preceding his death in 1917, to the Armenians except for one letter to his parents in 1905. In the letter, he mentions the riots against the Armenians in Baku (which ended with more than a thousand dead and several thousand wounded), in Batum, Shotta, and other places in the Caucasus. Subsequently, there was great fear of a "general" massacre and riots against the Jews, but "everything passes more peacefully than expected."[45] Apart from this lone reference we have found nothing, nor have Borochov's biographers uncovered anything more on this subject.

In the report of the "Poalei Zion" delegation to Palestine in 1920, the Armenians are mentioned only once. The delegation was sent to Palestine to investigate and report to the "Poalei Zion" federation on the condition of the Jewish settlement in Palestine, and to suggest a plan of action in this matter. The decision to send the delegation was made by the Executive Council of the "Poalei Zion" world federation that convened in Stockholm in September 1919. Among the prominent members of the council were Yitzhak Ben-Zvi, David Ben Gurion, Nachman Syrkin, Yizhak Tabenkin, Zalman Rubashov (Shazar), Nahum Repeleks (Nir), Shmuel Yavnieli, and others. The Committee concluded that for the sake of "mass settlement on a cooperative basis a national loan of £80 million would be necessary." The major source, in the committee's opinion, would have to be the Jewish People itself. But—and here we find an interesting sentence—"The countries of Europe must help us with this, since they have considerable interest in resolving the Jewish question. If rightly demanded a national loan for the Armenians, then surely the world must help the Jewish People to build its society as a wise solution for the Jewish problem. In this matter non-Jewish factors also have a serious interest, and they will be obliged to give their assistance."[46]

The members of the workers' movement were people with sensitive social values and their emphasis on universal solidarity was prominent. Their scanty, negligible, usually instrumental, reference—as far as we were able to uncover and examine—to the awful human and national tragedy, the first major genocide of the twentieth century, which befell on the Armenians virtually next to them, raises questions. And if it may be stated, causes disappointment.

The "Activists"—The Graduates of "Herzlia" Gymnasium

The Palestinian reality created three groups of activists who represented three sectors of the Yishuv on the eve of the First World War. Each of the groups represented not only a specific social stratum, but also identified with a specific ideological stream.[47] We have already examined two of the groups: (1) "Hashomer," which represented the workers of the Second Aliyah who arrived in Palestine between 1904 and 1914, and especially the collective organizations that were affiliated with the "Poalei Zion" Party; (2) the "Gidonites," offspring of the farmers in the veteran agricultural villages, who represented in large measure the native-born generation, sons and daughters of the First Aliyah which arrived in Palestine between 1881 and 1903; some of them later found their place in the ranks of Nili, which we have examined at length.

The third group is the "Tel Aviv-Jaffa Group," which represented the young urban generation centered in Tel Aviv. The group had two components: a bunch of young and energetic craftsmen, among them Avraham Krinitsy, Saadia Shoshani, David Swerdlow, and others. They were joined by "graduates of the Herzliya Gymnasium" that included: Eliahu Golomb, Dov Hoz, David Komerov (Bet Halachmi), and Moshe Shertok (Sharett). Some, like Moshe Shertok and Yizhak Cohen, attended the university in Constantinople with the goal of training for political duties within the Turkish Government. The war found some of them in Kibbutz Degania near the Sea of Galilee (Eliahu Golomb, Dov Hoz, and David Komerov), and they were forced to return to their homes in Tel Aviv.

The question of enlistment in the Turkish Army soon became pertinent. Graduates of the Gymnasia were natural candidates for officer rank in the Turkish Army. In light of the question of Ottomanization and the future of relations with the Ottoman authorities, enlistment in the Turkish Army was considered to be in the interests of the Yishuv. Therefore, public pressure was placed on the Gymnasia graduates to volunteer for the army. Eliahu Golomb was vigorously opposed to the idea and managed to avoid enlistment. He had no illusions about what awaited him and his classmates in the Turkish Army. Golomb believed that Jewish youth in Palestine should not expend their energies in that direction. However, Shertok, Hoz, Komerov, and Avraham Shemyon, as well as others, did not agree with him and enlisted. They argued with Golomb that one of the goals of the "Limited Association" which they had established was to integrate into the Ottoman regime and attain positions of power that could help the Zionist enterprise. Toward the end of the war some of the members of the group assumed key positions in organizing Palestinian Jewish volunteers for the British Army. Central in this effort were Golomb, Hoz, and Rachel Yanait (Ben-Zvi).[48]

Not a few young Jewish Palestinians chose or were forced to join the Turkish Army during the war. Among them were, as stated, students from the Herzliya Gymnasium in Tel Aviv and students from the Teachers' Seminary in Jerusalem; both groups underwent officer training. Some of them spent the war in the battle zones of the Ottoman Empire. Some were, without doubt, in the Armenian provinces where the massacres took place—for the most part, after the atrocities were committed. We do not know what impressions and feelings the scenes of brutality left upon them. We looked for testimony in their letters and memoirs, in articles they wrote or which were written about them. Some of them eventually became prominent public figures in the pre-state Yishuv and in the State of Israel. We found almost nothing. They did not tend to react to the terrible tragedy of the Armenians, even if they witnessed it as it unfolded or shortly thereafter.

Among the writings of Eliahu Golomb, who did not serve in the Turkish Army, we found one reference to the Armenians—not to the massacre itself but rather to the lesson to be learned from it. His remarks appear in his speech to a convention of volunteers to the Jewish Regiments, in 1918, in effect the keynote speech of the convention. Golomb began by saying, "Must we engage in some special action in order to enlarge our movement, or is our act of volunteering sufficient in itself? Yesterday a rumor spread of a peace pact between Russia and Germany, according to which Germany forced Russia to return Armenia to Turkey. Can such a report weaken our movement? To the contrary, in my opinion."[49]

Golomb argued: The Armenians had been slaughtered. The Allied Powers had promised them sovereignty and national liberation, and when the time arrived, the Armenians were abandoned. What had happened to the Armenians should, in his opinion, strengthen within the volunteer movement the significance of the sanctification of the land by the blood of its sons, and the evidence of the vitality of the Hebrew People. These factors could prevent what had happened to the Armenians from happening to us—a "declaration by England" [the Balfour Declaration] would not be enough.

It is interesting to note that the writer, Yosef Haim Brenner, related to the Armenians in the context of the Brest-Litovsk Agreement of which Golomb spoke, and its significance for the Jewish community in Palestine. At the beginning of his story, "The Injustice," written in the brief period between the end of the war and Brenner's murder, the following sentence appears: "Armenia returned to Turkey after the peace treaty of Brest-Litovsk, what will become of us?"[50] The meaning of his rhetorical question was: Armenia failed in its hopes for independence. What will become of us, will our fate be the same?

Brenner wrote about the period of the final days of the war when the country was divided, "at the end of that same winter, when you were there, [at the southern territory] with the English, and I was on the other side, with the Turks." And he states, "Here, among the Turks, we are doomed to annihilation."

In the same issue of *Adama*, the journal that Brenner edited, appears, whether by chance or on purpose, together with Brenner's story, "The Injustice," an article by Chaim Rubin entitled "Recollections of the War." Rubin was a soldier in a Turkish platoon sent from Musul to put down the rebellion that had broken out among the Yezidis, pagans who lived in the Sanjer Mountains. The Yezidis were perceived as enemies of the regime—"enemies of Islam, defenders of the Armenians—an unpardonable crime—and allies of the English, etc."

Rubin recalled that the Yezidis feared that the Armenians in their midst would be put to death. "In these mountains the Armenian survivors found refuge from the massacre inflicted upon them by the Turks on the banks of the Euphrates and in Kurdistan" [Note of the editor Brenner]. One of the old Yezidi men related:

Brother, how hard we worked to save them—those poor wretches. I remember: it was a wintry night, the wind was whining in the mountain clefts.
It was so dark we could not even see the mountains. Just the white peak
shone. We learned that a platoon of *gendarmes* had brought large numbers
of Armenian families in order to slaughter them. The fury in the village
grew. We were all of one mind—to hurry, perhaps we could save the refugees, but the storm increased. We could not see the way and the way was
long, a day and a night through the passes. Then this young man jumped up
(pointed to the man with the black braids): I will go, he cried, I know the
way, straight to Baghdad, off to the right to the Euphrates. And he rushed
off at the head of a group of young men to the site of the massacre. Two
days later they returned to us. What a terrible sight. Women and children
bleeding. They took one baby out from under the corpses. Each of us took
several Armenians to his house....Ah, how much effort we put into them
and now to have them put to death. His eyes filled with tears and he fell
silent. The interpreter also wept.

Several hours later, relates Chaim Rubin sadly, the Yezidi villagers
were also murdered. [51]

Among the young activists, David Hacohen stands out in his attitude
toward the Armenian problem in his recollection of the issue in his
memoirs. He was also a pupil at the Herzliya Gymnasium, younger
than the others in the group: Hoz, Shertok, and Golomb. David Hacohen
decided to join the Turkish Army and served in the officers' school at
the height of the war. Hacohen describes the difficult and humiliating
conditions, the physical exertion, the filth, and the hunger in the army:
"Sleep was on the floor of the barracks—the large houses of the Armenians
who had fled, been expelled or murdered, in the vacation town on the banks
of the Marmara, facing the Prince Islands—and your sleeping space was a
strip of sixty centimeters on a rotted, disintegrating blanket."[52] The officers' school was dispersed among the holiday villages along the Asian coast
of the Sea of Marmara. It is reasonable to assume that the Palestinian Jews
who enlisted in the Turkish Army encountered the scenes of the massacre on their way to Istanbul since they traveled by train to Damascus
and Aleppo, and from there via a pass through the Taurus Mountains
and the width of all Anatolia to Istanbul. After finishing the course and
receiving their officer's rank, the young officers were dispersed throughout the country, in the divisions and battalions. Hacohen, a nineteen-
year-old officer, was assigned at eastern Anatolia.

Hacohen recalls that he heard from his Turkish officer friends who
were more experienced than he that some of them had participated in

the battles on this front at the beginning of the war. He hears about the bloody battles, the thousands of dead, and an even greater number of wounded who were left behind, on the breakdown of the entire logistical system. He adds,

> They talked bitterly about the retreat following the unexpected [Russian] conquests, about the loss of large territories and important cities in the area: Trebizond, Erzurum, Van and Mush, which fell to the Russians. They talked about the Armenian population of Turkey, whose homeland was here, which exploited the historic opportunity, rebelled and betrayed the hated Turks, and collaborated with the Russian occupier and their Armenian brothers across the border. I heard details about the rages of the Armenian General Antranik who served in the Russian Army, and referred to his battalions, mostly Armenians, as the 'Christian Army of Vengeance.' These battalions murdered and massacred the Turkish population when Van and Erzurum were conquered. I was not able to verify their stories. At the same time, my Turkish friends did not speak much about their vengeance against the Armenian population which during that very same period was expelled from every place of residence throughout Turkey and mercilessly slaughtered— Hundreds of thousands of them. Only after the outbreak of the revolution in Russia, and its army's defeat on the European fronts, did the Turks recapture everything they had lost at the beginning of the war.

> As mentioned, I did not follow the massacre of the Armenians. It was primarily in 1915, about a year before we enlisted, but the hair-raising stories reached our ears from solitary Armenians whom I encountered during my service. I felt pain for their repressed uprising, for the shame of their women and young girls whose husbands had been murdered and they were forced to become concubines of the Turkish officers. Even among my fellow officers, in the permanent army camps in the cities and towns in Anatolia, where I spent two years of my military service, there were some who took Armenian concubines. As a Jew, and in the absence of any spark of patriotism for the Turkish rule, I identified with every minority that was persecuted.

A moving human, "Armenian," story appears in Hacohen's recollections of the final days of the war. As a Turkish officer in charge of guarding the coast facing the Aegean Sea, he came across an abandoned Armenian baby girl. David Hacohen, a young officer, took care of her for many days and in the end, after much effort, delivered her into the care of a small Greek monastery.[53]

Additional eyewitness testimony is to be found in the report written by Dr. Moshe Kriegel who served as a physician in the Turkish Army during the First World War. The report deals with the murder of the Armenians, which Dr. Kriegel witnessed during the latter half of 1915 and during 1916. The report does not carry a specific date but it appears to have been written in 1917.[54]

Kriegel writes about what he saw in August 1915:

> The entire rail line form Aleppo to Damascus was filled with Armenian deportees who in most cases were transported in crowded cattle cars. Most of them were not from Armenia proper but rather from eastern and central Anatolia. In Baalbek [northern Lebanon] there were at least 3,000 in the ruins of the temple, many of them sick. I myself found many dead where they had been laying for many days without burial. They died from lack of food and medical care.

> Mrs. Zapf, the owner of the hotel in Baalbek by that name, told me that the condition of the Armenians who had passed through that place beforehand was identical. She herself tried to obtain food for them, without success, except for some Christian westerners who lived in the city. The Authorities and the local population did not lift a finger and viewed these people with suspicion and hostility.

Dr. Kriegel spent the winter and spring of 1916 in the Sinai Desert, where he treated Armenian soldiers who had previously served as combat soldiers and were transferred to serve, under difficult conditions, in special labor platoons:

> Most of the Armenian men who had until then served as combat soldiers were sent to the Sinai Desert in platoons to build roads and railway tracks in order to open transportation through the desert. Without clothing, poor supplies or no supplies at all, limited food, without proper sanitary conditions, all this quickly decimated some battalions by 30%. There were days in which tens and even hundreds of men would die in a single day. A typhoid fever epidemic ravaged them. By the end of March there was, in effect, no longer a single labor battalion in the desert.

> An order then arrived from above to Islamize the Armenians. The task was assigned to the local commanders who managed to convert a not inconsiderable number of Armenians, by threats and sometimes bribery. In some stations there were big conversion and circumcision festivities. In the hospital which I administered I myself was forced to conduct these operations on approximately twenty men. Beforehand I was approached by many Armenian intellectuals who were serving as simple soldiers-laborers, who wanted my advice about what they should do after the local commander had threatened them with harsh treatment if they did not convert to Islam. The men who had left families at home were greatly perturbed.

Zeev Jabotinsky

The position of Zeev Jabotinsky on the Armenian question is of particular interest. Jabotinsky—an original thinker, nonconformist, and opponent of the Socialist Zionist establishment—was outspokenly pro-British from the beginning of the war. He was an early supporter of the Jewish Regiments and a frequent traveler in the region. Part of the explanation for the fact that many circles in the Yishuv and the Zionist movement ignored the Armenian massacre is to be found in the pro-Turkish and pro-German political orientation of most of the Zionist leadership. Jabotinsky, however, disagreed with them sharply and publicly. Furthermore, it was assumed that "the holocaust of the Armenian People greatly troubled Zeev Jabotinsky at the time."[55] The facts seem to be different. In all of Jabotinsky's writings, we do not find a single serious reference that indicates a storm of feeling or a sense of identification. Similarly, an examination of the subject with Jabotinsky researchers does not reveal a different picture.

Jabotinsky related to the Armenians even before the war. In articles that he published in 1910, he uses them as an example of a people which had experienced a national reawakening, in contrast to the half million Jews "who have resided for hundreds of years in the Ottoman lands." In the newspaper, *Hamevaser*, published in Constantinople, Jabotinsky preaches a nationalist-Hebrew-Zionist ideology. He presents the example of the renaissance of the Armenian language, which had largely been forgotten by the Armenians in Constantinople and was now, according to him, their only spoken language.[56]

Jabotinsky did, indeed, deal with the Armenian massacre but his treatment was analytical rather than an expression of identification. His approach was instrumental; he drew conclusions regarding the struggle of the Jews. I was unable to find any expression of an additional dimension to his attitude; neither pro-Turkish orientation, nor fear of censorship can explain his silence.

As a means for spreading his oppositional opinions within the Zionist movement, Jabotinsky, together with Meir Grossman, founded a Yiddish newspaper, *Die Tribune*, in neutral Copenhagen. The newspaper began publication in October 1915. On October 15, Jabotinsky published his article, "Activism," which was a scathing criticism of the Zionist movement. "Activism—this is what is lacking in the Zionist movement. The Zionist movement, because of a disease which is not organic but rather the product of a certain educational influence, is liable to miss the unique historical opportunity offered by the war, which may never recur. "[57]

Jabotinsky argued that the Turks were planning a pogrom against the Jewish community in Palestine, but they were forced to refrain because of the assistance given to the Jews by Henry Morgenthau, Sr., the American Ambassador in Constantinople, and because of the activity of the Commission in Alexandria, composed of refugees who had reached Egypt from Palestine. The commission brought the expected threat to the Yishuv to the attention of President Woodrow Wilson and to the European and American public opinion.

Jabotinsky's position was unambiguous: We have no interest in Palestine remaining under Turkish dominion. We can have no hope for Zionism in Palestine under any form of Turkish rule.

> If it should happen that Palestine remains under the Turks, it is of decisive importance to us that we have allies who are feared by Turkey. This is the only mean to strengthening our status in Palestine, or, more precisely, what will be left of our status.

> There can be no guarantee that there be much left of our status in Palestine. I myself believe that Palestine is not Armenia, and that it will not be so easy to annihilate the Yishuv, as the generals of the 'Young Turks' thought in the first weeks of the war. Speaking frankly, I believe that the locust plague [which attacked the country during the war and caused heavy damage] poses a much greater threat since it is not affected by Jewish influence in New York, Berlin, Vienna or Budapest, nor by ambassadors. But the 'Young Turks' are influenced by all of these factors. Nonetheless, there is no guarantee that they will not try to wreak destruction in Palestine. The matter will depend upon the behavior of the Jews there. From the documents we see that the Turks planned a pogrom long before the Jews could complain about their awful behavior.

> I repeat: I consider all the talk of danger to be three-quarters empty chatter. The Turks may be able to instigate something out of anger, but between an attempt and actual results the distance is great. They have tried once, and nothing came of it. And when it occurred, the cowards said it was imperative to call upon President Wilson for aid, because the real persecutions now begin. The truth was completely opposite. After that attempt the period of oppression actually came to an end. And finally, when the legion of stateless Palestinians was established in Alexandria, then too the fears and predictions of doom again came to naught. Even now I consider them three-quarters groundless. But even if there is some basis to them, we must in any event continue on our path, the path of an activist policy.

It should be noted that Jabotinsky's point of departure was that the Jews were not so weak. They had the power, despite their weakness, to deter the Turks. "Palestine is not Armenia." As stated, this was also the argument of Ben Gurion when he referred, several years later, to the Armenian case. The Armenians were neglected and abandoned but it would not be so easy to abandon the Jews.[58]

Jabotinsky concluded from this that because of the relative power of the Yishuv, the Turks would not agree to its further growth since this would be contrary to their interests. He differed on this point from the Labor Zionists.

Jabotinsky returned to this point and to the comparison with the Armenian experience in an another article which was published in 1916 under the title, "Who Is the Enemy," in the newspaper, *Unzer Tribune*, issue no. 13.

> We need Palestine and we want it and the Turks do not want us to have it. The old Turkey did not want this and the new Turkey does not want this either. From their perspective they are perhaps right. The Jewish Yishuv is too strong for their taste, and too influential. When they massacred half of Armenia they were in fact unhampered. However, the minute Jamal Pasha dared to expel several thousand Jews from Palestine there was an immediate uproar in America and even in Germany.[59]

"Turkey and the War"

In 1917, Jabotinsky published his book, *Turkey and the War*, in London. At the beginning of the book the following sentence appears: "The present war, undoubtedly, was largely a war for the control of Asia Minor."

Jabotinsky dedicates a significant portion of the book to the question of the small nationalities. In dealing with the question of whether freedom for the small nationalities was a necessary goal of the war, Jabotinsky says that this issue is tied to another question: whether the absence of such freedom was a cause of the war.[60]

Jabotinsky lists a large number of small nationalities that had been denied their freedom. The list included not only the Armenians in Turkey but also the Chinese, the Poles, the Ukrainians, the Jews, and many other peoples. The Armenians in Russia were not included in the list.

In his opinion, the question of the future territorial division of the Ottoman Empire was the source of conflict between the large states.

Jabotinsky particularly emphasized the Pan-German appetite for territories of the Empire. "There is almost no corner of the Ottoman Empire which has not been mentioned by the Pan-Germans."

Jabotinsky believed that the Turkish *ancien régime* did not attempt to interfere in the national uniqueness of its subjects. It was indifferent to the language that they spoke in school and at home. The 'Young Turks,' on the other hand, did not conceal their aim of imposing their own language on the Arabs, the Albanians, the Armenians, the Greeks, and the Slavs in the Ottoman Empire. "The massacre of the Armenians in Adana [1909] left nothing to desire for one who remembers the 'high standards' of the massacres of 1894-1896, and the Young Turkish government left the official culprits unpunished like the old Turkish."[61]

The Armenian revolutionaries attempted several times to convince the 'Young Turks' that the only system suitable for Constitutional Turkey was the Swiss system, or at the least the Austrian system of provincial self rule and national autonomy. But the 'Young Turks' implemented far more stringent measures. They were aware of the abyss that existed between the various races that hated one another in Macedonia and Armenia. Jabotinsky stressed the fact that the Turks were a minority in the Ottoman Empire (seven million out of twenty-one million; the Arab minority comprised nine million souls). He pointed out the high cultural level of the Armenians in various spheres, higher than the level of the Turkish population. But in the section, "The List of Demands," he did not deal with the Armenian question. He dealt with the Arab-Jewish-Zionist question and the Palestinian issue. He also recalled the suffering of the Galician and Russian Jews in the war zones, and mentioned that Russia sought to rule over all of historic Armenia. But Jabotinsky did not take an explicit stand on the Armenian tragedy, or to the national demands and hopes of the Armenians in this context.

It was Jabotinsky's opinion that the Turks would ultimately remain only in Anatolia. The rest of the territories would be taken from them and divided up. Syria would, he believed, become French. Palestine could only become a part of the British sphere of influence. Jabotinsky indicated that the Zionists were not demanding, at least at present, full independence. They sought a form of "charter" which would include guarantees of self-rule and settlement rights. As stated, there is no reference to the national demands of the Armenians for the postwar era, which would be resolved, he believed, by the division of the Ottoman Empire, except for Anatolia.

And, indeed, the review of Jabotinsky's book, which appeared in March 1918 in the London-based Armenian journal, *Ararat*, was mild.[62] There was agreement and admiration for Jabotinsky's sharp criticism of Turkey, and his treatment of the German imperialistic aspirations. But the reviewer stresses that two decisive events which had occurred after the book was published—the British conquest of Jerusalem and the Soviet revolution—would likely affect the assessments expressed in the book. The events in Palestine strengthened Jabotinsky's conclusions, and the Zionists' hope for their realization. With regard to Armenia, Jabotinsky's attitude was less unambiguous. His remarks about Armenia were now even weightier than they had been in 1917. (The writer's intention is to the fact that following the Soviet revolution and the Turkish military victories on the Russian front, areas of Armenia had been reconquered by the Turks after losing some of them to the Russians at the beginning of the war.) We have not been able to find additional references to the Armenian tragedy in Jabotinsky's writings.

The one reference we found is directly related to the Jewish tragedy —the Holocaust, when it was just beginning. In his book, *The Battle Front of the People of Israel*, written in January-February 1940, in the chapter, "We Are Not On the Map," Jabotinsky writes,

> In this war (so it seems at the time of writing), it is not desired that the Jews should be 'on the map': neither as active allies, nor as fellow-sufferers, nor as the subject-matter of any special Allied demands or war aims.[63]

> So far—this is written early in 1940—of the peoples attacked by Germany the one which has paid the greatest price of all in human suffering has been the Jewish People. No careful observer is likely to question this statement. True, the Czechs have lost—let us hope only temporarily—their independence, and the Poles have lost more than that, but in terms of actual human misery, hunger, torture and death, the Jews head the list, even in Poland.[64]

In his book, Jabotinsky presents examples from the pages of the "Daily Bulletin" of the Jewish Telegraphic Agency (JTA). "To conclude, here is an item which will remind the reader of Enver Pasha's methods of 'liquidating' Armenians as described by Werfel in *The Forty Days of Musa Dagh*." Jabotinsky cites a detailed description of the expulsion of the Jews from Chelm and Hrubilszow across the Russian border, which began on December 1, 1939. "Thus a total of over 1300 Jews from Chelm and Hrubilszow were massacred by the Nazis during the four days' of forced march to the Soviet frontier."[65] Jabotinsky accuses the general press of not printing the details of these terrible acts. "The author has not seen them printed in any of the major British newspapers, at least not in the London press."

Further examination of the writings, speeches, and letters of other figures from the same period reveals a similar picture. There is virtually no reference to the Armenian suffering. When reference is made, it is usually instrumental. A simple human reaction, a shock or identification with the victims, could not be found, at least not in the extensive searches we conducted. There is also no evidence in the writings and documented comments from those years of figures such as Berl Katznelson, Aaron David Gordon, Yosef Haim Brenner (except for the short passage cited above), Yosef Shprinzak, Yizhak Tabenkin, David Remez, and others, not in their writings, nor their diaries and memoirs which we examined. The members of "Hapoel Hatzair" were apparently no different in this than the members of "Poalei Zion." In the journal *Hapoel Hatzair* from November 1914, we read, "A strong and unified Turkey is for us, as for the Armenians, the only basis for national life and national renaissance. Our destiny is tied to their destiny....Young, free-thinking Jewry needs to walk hand in hand in the most active manner with the young, free-thinking Ottomans." We also found no significant reference to the Armenian question in the writing of Joseph Trumpeldor whose views were different from most of the workers' movement—he was pro-British from the beginning of the war. Trumpeldor envisioned the establishment of a Jewish army after the Russian Revolution of 1917: "Not a brigade, a real army of one hundred thousand men or more," which would fight on the Caucasian front, and make its way from there through Armenia and Mesopotamia to Transjordan. Here too, it seems, there is no mention of the Armenians. The goal, the purpose, and the total focus were the Zionist enterprise.

All of the energy was, it appears, invested in the effort to survive. Some feared that the Turks would do to the Yishuv what they had done to the Armenians. Others were concerned that the Arabs would assist the Turks in the destruction, just as the Kurds had assisted them in the destruction of the Armenians. It is possible that in the Labor Movement there was a fear of dealing with the pain of others. Ironically, it was those who had been hurt by the phenomenon of world indifference who recoiled from the trend of universalism and disdained the revolutionary Jews who held universal and perhaps cosmopolitan views. This appears to have resulted in self-absorption and indifference.

Notes

1. See, *inter alia,* Yisrael Shochat, "Mission and Path," *Sefer Hashomer* (Tel Aviv: Dvir, 1957), p. 40. (Henceforth: "Mission and Path."); Hacohen, *The Family of Nations*, vol. A, p. 64 et al.
2. Yaakov Goldstein "The Organization of Hashomer and Its Functioning During the First World War," from *In Siege and Distress, Palestine During the First World War*, ed., Mordechai Eliav (Jerusalem: Yad Yizhak Ben Zvi, 1990), pp. 111-31 (Henceforth: Goldstein.) (See also Yaakov Goldstein, *On the Way to the Goal ("Bar Giora" and "Hashomer" 1907-1935)* (Tel Aviv: Ministry of Defense Publishers, 1994).
3. Zvi Becker, "The Life of Yehezkel Nisanov," from the anthology *Hashomer* (Tel Aviv: Avoda Archives, 1934), pp. 284-97.
4. Ibid., pp. 412-13. His memoirs were also published in his book, *From the Days of Guarding and Defense* (Tel Aviv: Maarahot, 1954), pp. 203-206. The memoirs were written in 1936.
5. Z. Ussishkin, "From Hadera to Hamra," ibid., pp. 216-17.
6. Yizhak Nadav, *Recollections of a "Hashomer" Member* (as told to Avraham Ovadia, edited for publication by Yosef Tibi) (Tel Aviv: Ministry of Defense Publishers, 1986), pp. 96-99.
7. Ibid., p. 99.
8. Pinchas Schneurson, *In the Front Line*, (collected and edited by Shlomo Shaba) (Tel Aviv: Sifriat Poalim, 1978), p. 49.
9. Ibid., p. 55.
10. Yaakov Portugali, *The Portugali Family*, published by the author, 1979, p. 62. It appears that a sentence in which he describes how they wanted to drink water from a well but discovered the corpses of Armenians within was ultimately deleted from the book.
11. Yaakov Kanterovitch, "In the Khan-el-Basha Prison and in Exile," (typewritten recollections), pp. 52, 33, 60-69.
12. See Mission *and Path*, p. 43.
13. Ibid., p. 44.
14. Ibid., p. 43.
15. Goldstein, p. 124, relying on many other researchers. The majority of the members of "Hashomer" belonged to "Poalei Zion." The delicate relationship between the "Hashomer" organization and the "Poalei Zion" party is beyond the purview of this study. For the position of the leaders of "Poalei Zion," David Ben Gurion and Yitzhak Ben-Zvi, see below.
16. See, for example, the discussions of the Fourth International Congress of "Poalei Zion," which was held in Kharkov in August 1913. Furthermore, Yitzhak Ben-Zvi was the more prominent personality of the two at the time: he delivered the keynote speech at the Congress and was elected to the presidium. See also Shabtai Teveth, *David's Envy*, vol. 1 (Tel Aviv: Schocken, 1977), pp. 238-48.
17. Citations from Ben Gurion, *Memoirs, Vol. I*, pp. 69-70.

18. Ibid., p. 75.
19. Ibid., p. 91.
20. *The Letters of David Ben Gurion*, vol. 1, (1904-1919) (Tel Aviv: Am Oved and Tel Aviv University, 1971), pp. 442-44. See also Michael Bar-Zohar, *Ben Gurion*, vol. 1, (Tel Aviv: Am Oved, 1975), pp. 99-100.
21. *Letters*, vol. 1, pp. 444-45, letter no. 267 to his father, section 39, December 5, 1919.
22. *Memoirs*, vol. 1, p. 85.
23. In the introduction to the book, the authors indicate that the six sections of the book were prepared separately and independently, each author writing three sections, but that they then checked the entire book together.
24. The quotation from Ben Gurion and Yitzhak Ben-Zvi, *Eretz Yisrael in the Past and in the Present*, eds., Mordechai Eliav and Yehoshua Ben Arieh (Jerusalem: Yad Yitzhak Ben-Zvi, 1979), pp. 102-103.
25. It should be noted that Yitzhak Ben-Zvi had mentioned this comparison to the Austrian model in his article, "Our National Demands in Turkey," published in *Ha'achdut*, autumn 1913. "Solidarity of peoples on a basis of equal rights of language, cultural and internal affairs—this is the ideal of peaceful life between peoples in the present regime in Turkey. The Social-Democracy in Austria declared this demand fourteen years ago in its convention in the city of Brin."
26. *Letters*, vol. 1, p. 442.
27. See *Ha'achdut*, nos. 44, 45, September 1915.
28. Report on the discussions at the Convention which appeared in *Ha'achdut*, no. 46, October 1913. It should be remembered that both men went to Constantinople from Palestine to study law.
29. An additional article by Ben Gurion appeared in *Ha'achdut* during the war, no. 19, winter 1915, entitled "Civic Preparedness." Ben Gurion writes that Turkey, despite its backwardness, is a constitutional state; its citizens are equal before the law and the Jews have not been persecuted there. The Jews did not know how to take advantage of the rights available to them and, unlike the Armenians, did not take part in political life and did not fill government posts which were open to them. It is now clear how damaging these omissions were. In his opinion, citizenship is the only way to prevent deportation.
30. See above, Introduction, and Ben Gurion, *Memoirs*, vol. 3, pp. 200-201.
31. Ben Gurion, *Memoirs*, vol. 4, p. 15 (His testimony in closed session of the Royal Commission, January 7, 1937), pp. 127, 315.
32. See Yosef Gornei, *The Ambiguous Tie: The British Labor Movement and Its Attitude To Zionism, 1917-1947* (Tel Aviv: Hakibbutz Hameuchad, 1982), pp. 39-40; Matitiahu Mintz, *New Times New Tunes: Ber Borochov, 1914-1917* (Tel Aviv: Am Oved, 1988), pp. 309-19.
33. Gorney, *The Ambiguous Connection*, p. 55.
34. Mintz, pp. 309, 311, 319; and Berl Locker, *From Kitov to Jerusalem* (Jerusalem: The Zionist Library, 1970), pp. 176-77. The Armenian So-

cialist Party, "Dashnaktsutium," was a member of the Socialist
Internationale from 1907 (before the Balkan War in 1912, there was an
additional sub-section in the Turkish bloc, the Saloniki section.) This party
supported an armed struggle for the liberation of Armenia from Turkish
domination.

35. Shlomo Kaplansky, "The Jews in the War," from Shlomo Kaplansky, *Vision and Realization, Selected Writings, Lectures and Speeches* (Tel Aviv: Sifriat Poalim, 1950), p. 142.
36. Ibid., p. 144.
37. Ibid., p. 145.
38. Ibid., p. 169.
39. From a memorandum promoting the proposed law of national self rule, Hague, 1917, written in German by Shlomo Kaplansky, under the auspices of the world federation of "Poalei Zion." See *Vision and Realization*, p. 189. As mentioned, a similar approach was adopted by Ben Gurion and Ben-Zvi who, like Kaplansky, relied on the decisions of the Austrian Social-Democrats at the congress in Brin, 1899, as a appropriate point of reference.
40. The writer has harsh criticism of the assimilated Jewish plutocracy in France and Germany which used every possible means to "warn" Turkey of the alleged harm to its political interests which would result from a concentration of Jews in Palestine. He charges that they had a part in the changed Turkish attitude toward the Yishuv and Turkey's opposition to Zionism during the war. Ibid., pp. 169, 173-76.
41. Ibid., p. 176.
42. Ibid., pp. 181-82.
43. Negotiation between "Poalei Zion" and the Dutch-Scandinavian committee. From the anthology, *Poalei Zion: The Struggle in the International Proletarian Arena, 1907-1927*, Jerusalem, 1954, pp. 40-44.
44. Ibid., pp. 50-51.
45. *Letters of Ber Borochov, 1897-1917*, ed., Matitiahu Mintz (Tel Aviv: Am Oved, 1989), pp. 142-43.
46. *The Poalei Zion Delegation to Palestine*, Part II: The Full Report, ed., Chaim Golan, Yad Tabenkin, 1989, p. 97.
47. See Yigael Elam, *The Jewish Legion in World War I* (Tel Aviv: Maarachot, 1973), pp. 166-67.
48. At the same time, not all of the members of the group enlisted in the Jewish Brigades. David Swerdlow, for example, was a member of "Hapoel Hatzair" and had sharp internal arguments with his party, which opposed volunteering to serve in the Jewish Regiments.
49. Eliahu Golomb, "Speech at the Volunteers' Convention." From *Latent Power*, vol. 1, revised and expanded edition, ed. Yehuda Erez (Tel Aviv: Ayanot, 1944), p. 141.
50. Y.H. Brenner, *Brenner's Complete Works*, vol. 1, (Tel Aviv: Hakibbutz Hameuchad, 1955), p. 459. First published in the journal *Adama*, vol. 2, no. 8.

51. Chaim Rubin, "Recollections of the War," *Adama*, Vol. 2, No. 8.
52. David Hacohen, "Once I Was A Turkish Soldier," *A Time to Tell* (Tel Aviv: Am Oved, 1974), p. 323.
53. Ibid., pp. 324-25.
54. Central Zionist Archives, Z3/66.
55. See, for example, Amos Elon, "Our Holocaust and the Holocaust of Others," *Ha'aretz*, 1978, from Amos Elon, *Certain Panic* (Tel Aviv: Am Oved, 1988), p. 252.
56. Zeev Jabotinsky, "The Hebrew Language—A Spoken Tongue," *Hamevaser*, First Year, no. 18, 1910.
57. Yosef Nedava, ed., *Zeev Jabotinsky: The Man and His Thought* (Tel Aviv: Ministry of Defense Publishers, 1980), pp. 97-108.
58. See the section on Ben Gurion.
59. Zeev Jabotinsky, *Speeches (1905-1926)*.
60. Vladimir Jabotinsky, *Turkey and the War* (London: T. Fisher Unwin, 1917), pp. 25-26.
61. Ibid., p. 79.
62. *Ararat*, No. 56, February-March 1918, pp. 364-66.
63. Zeev Jabotinsky, *The War and the Jew* (New York: The Dial Press, 1942). The first English-language edition of the book was published in July 1940.
64. Ibid., pp. 31-32.
65. Ibid., p. 34.

9

The Attitudes Towards the Armenian Genocide after the Establishment of the State of Israel—A Brief Overview

The Second World War and the Holocaust on the one hand, and the establishment of the State of Israel on the other hand, fundamentally changed things. The Jewish People experienced its great disaster and three years later lived to witness the birth of the Jewish State and Jewish sovereignty. The attitude of the State of Israel towards the Armenians and their tragedy deserves an attentive study. In the absence of such research, we shall merely sketch the lines which seem to us worthy of mention. The following material is mostly based on newspaper reports.

We should first mention that significant and interesting observations about the Armenian genocide were made by Richard Lichtheim. Lichtheim was, as stated previously, the diplomatic representative of the Zionist Organization in Constantinople during the First World War. He was aware of what had been done to the Armenian people at the time of its occurrence. (In his report to the Zionist delegation in Berlin, on March 19, 1916, he reported on the events. There is no doubt that the archives of the Zionist delegation in Constantinople deserve serious study which will examine the treatment, if any, of the Armenian genocide.)

In his memoirs, written in 1948-49, Lichtheim wrote,

The First World War presented a convenient opportunity to 'eliminate' this bothersome problem of the minorities, as we would say today....In the world's modern history this was the first incidence of systematic racial persecution, and was similar to the early actions of Hitler in his policy of extermination of the Jews in the years 1940-1945....In the novel of Franz Werfel, *The Forty Days of Musa Dagh*, you find a faithful description of the events....The brutal persecution of the Armenians aroused anger all over the world but the protests against the slaughter of this Christian people were of no more avail then than were the later protests against Hitler's persecution of the Jews during the Second World War.[1]

After the Holocaust, in his book, *The Crowing of the Rooster*, Abba Achimeir also compared the events: "What the Germans were in the Second World War to the Jews, the Turks were in the First World War to the Armenians. And here the quota was one third of the people, for the Jews as for the Armenians." He mentions the genocide committed by the Americans against the native Indians and additional cases of genocide. He reaches the conclusion: "Historians have paid almost no attention to the dimension of genocide in human history. It seems that in light of 'October' [his term for the Bolshevik Revolution] and Hitler, history needs to be rewritten again, both, from a more pessimistic and a more realistic perspective."[2]

But the State of Israel has consistently refrained from acknowledging the genocide of the Armenian People. Government representatives do not participate in the memorial assemblies held every year on April 24 by the Armenians to commemorate the Armenian genocide. The public debate in the State of Israel about the attitude toward the Armenian genocide has focused on four prominent media events: in 1978 the screening of a film about the Armenian Quarter in Jerusalem was canceled. In 1982, the Israeli Government intervened in plans for an international conference on the subject of the Holocaust and genocide. In 1989, the Israeli Government was apparently involved in preventing the commemoration of the Armenian genocide by the American Congress in dedicating a memorial day in the American calendar. In 1990, the screening of an American television documentary film, "Journey to Armenia," was canceled. In later years, a controversy also developed over teaching about the Armenian genocide and genocide, in general, in Israeli schools.

In 1978, the Israeli Broadcasting Authority decided to produce a documentary film for television about the Armenian community in the Old City of Jerusalem. The Authority contracted with a private company to produce the film as a co-production. The film script was approved and an English language version was planned for distribution abroad.[3] The film included several references to the Armenian massacre during the First World War, primarily the testimony by several survivors of the genocide of 1915 who resided in the Armenian Quarter of Jerusalem's Old City. The film reached the final stages of production but its screening was prevented and the film has never been shown.

Involved in the efforts to prevent the screening of the film were the Turkish officials, their diplomatic mission in Israel, Turkish Jews in Turkey, activists in the Turkish immigrants' society in Israel and the Israeli Foreign Ministry. All of these forces would be involved in the controversies that came later.

As in future controversies, the phenomenon that stands out is the Israeli attitude to "our Holocaust and the Holocaust of others." Amos Elon, in a series of articles in the respected Israeli newspaper, *Ha'aretz*, attacked the "demonstrations of hypocrisy, opportunism and the moral trepidation within the official bureaucracy of the nation, which ceaselessly reminds the world of our Holocaust while the Holocaust of others is a subject worthy only of political exploitation."[4]

About the demand to delete any mention of the events of 1915 from the film, he writes, "They are like a person who suggests deleting from a movie about the suffering of the Jewish People in the modern era all reference to Germany, the Holocaust or even the Kishinev pogrom." With a certain degree of cynicism, Elon apologizes to his readers for returning to this unfortunate, seemingly marginal subject. There are those who see this as a lack of proportion and even vexatiousness: "Israel is a country of one-day scandals, but what can I do, the issue will not go away." Elon is sharply critical of "the cheap opportunism of hypocrisy."

The Holocaust is the central trauma of Israeli society. We remind the world, at every opportunity, of the Holocaust of European Jewry, and warn of the indifference to the slaughter of the Christians in Lebanon (where we have a political interest). We drag every important visitor to Yad Vashem [the official Holocaust Museum and Memorial in Israel], and while he is still in shock we hand him a list of demands and requests for political and economic assistance. We are sincere in our grief over our disaster, and at the very same time instrumentalist in our exploitation of it.

But where is the boundary between the natural chauvinism of exploitation and the cheap opportunism of hypocrisy? What happens when the survivors of one Holocaust make a political deal over the bitter memory of the survivors of another Holocaust? This is the one and only question of importance. This is the question that ought to arouse public interest. This is the question which ought to trouble all of the serious thinkers who fill our world with lamentation and endless pondering about the meaning of the Holocaust in this generation and the next, for us and for others.

All of the great people of conscience, the very image of sorrow, who give speeches at every opportunity and travel abroad to remind the world that they are forbidden to forget—have followed the Armenian affair as though it had taken place on another planet. They were not shocked, they did not open their mouths.[5]

Another "mini-scandal" surrounding an original television creation took place in 1991. The director, Orna Ben-Dor Niv prepared a television docudrama, "Sarah," about Sarah Aaronsohn of Nili. Forty seconds of "stills" of the Armenian massacre were deleted from the film. The murder of the Armenians, we recall, was a central component in understanding the motives of the Nili's activity. Sarah Aaronsohn was deeply shocked by scenes of the massacre that she witnessed at first hand and later described to her comrades.

In 1982, the Israeli Foreign Ministry applied heavy pressure on the organizers of an international conference on the subject of the Holocaust and Genocide in order to prevent the participation of Armenian researchers in the conference. Six of the 150 lectures planned dealt with the Armenian genocide. Alternative proposals were presented to cancel the conference or to hold it in another country. A compromise proposal by which the Armenian genocide would not be given a prominent place on the conference agenda but would be treated as background material (the Armenians would not speak; they would be limited to written presentations) was also rejected by the Foreign Ministry. The conference was held, instead, in Tel Aviv, with the participation of 300 out of an originally expected 600 researchers from the United States, Europe, and Israel. The formal opening, scheduled to be held at Yad Vashem, was moved to Tel Aviv; and Yad Vashem boycotted the conference. Jewish researchers and personalities from Israel and the U. S. canceled their participation in the conference due to pressure from the Foreign Ministry.[6] Nonetheless, the lectures on the Armenian genocide were delivered, and paradoxically, the conference became a rallying point for the battle to advance knowledge of the Armenian genocide and for academic freedom.

There were numerous lectures and discussions about the Holocaust and about the subjects of the Soviet "gulag," Hiroshima, and incidents of mass murder in Australia, but they did not arouse controversy.

Arguments were also raised about abuse of the word "Holocaust," a concept which, according to Yad Vashem, could not be applied to the disasters of other peoples, and over the fear that the conference was liable to blur the Holocaust by the very act of comparing it to the terrible disasters of others.[7]

At the end of September 1989, fifty-four U.S. Senators proposed a bill in the Senate Judiciary Committee as follows: "The 24th of April 1990 will be declared a 'national memorial day in commemoration of 75 years after the Armenian genocide in the years 1915-1923;' the President will be authorized and will be asked to publish a declaration which will call upon the American People to mark this date as a memorial day for the million and a half people of Armenian descent who were victims of genocide committed by the governments of the Ottoman Empire between the years 1915-1923, before the establishment of the Republic of Turkey."[8]

The U.S. House of Representatives had previously rejected two similar attempts, in 1985 and 1987, to determine a memorial day for the Armenian genocide. The Turkish Government warned that American interests might be jeopardized, including permission to maintain American military bases on Turkish territory. Then the Turks accused the "Jewish lobby in Washington" and the Jewish Representatives in Congress of involvement in the legislation of an Armenian memorial day. (Hebrew-language daily, *Maariv*, December 15, 1985). Involved in the latest battle against a memorial day were Jewish business people from Turkey and leaders of the Turkish-Jewish community who tried to create a rift between the Jews and the Armenians.

Various sources—certain circles in the American Jewish community, the U.S. House of Representatives—reported on the involvement of Israeli representatives in the affair. "Jews and Israeli Diplomats Work to Prevent Commemoration of Armenian Holocaust" was the front-page headline in the respected Hebrew newspaper, *Ha'aretz* (October 17, 1989). The official denials of the Israeli Embassy in Washington, the Foreign Ministry, and the Prime Minister's Office (*Maariv*, October 24, 1989) were received with skepticism in Israel and the United States. Although there was a majority in support of determining a memorial day for the Armenian genocide at first, the proposal was ultimately removed from the agenda.

The administration of American President George Bush took steps to defeat the motion. The administration explained that although it was sensitive to the "tragic suffering" of the Armenians, "we are also aware of the close relations and strong friendship with Turkey, and of the varying opinions about the question of how to properly mark the terrible events of that period." A year earlier, when he was running for the Presidency, Bush had promised to support the congressional initiative to commemorate the Armenian victims (*The Jewish Week*, October 27, 1989). At that time Bush claimed that the United States had an obligation to recognize the Armenian genocide if it wanted to prevent such acts from occurring in the future.

The arguments in the Israeli public debate over the involvement of Jews and Israeli representatives in the affair were similar to those raised in the controversy over the cancellation of the screening of the film several months later.

Against the pragmatic considerations tied to Israeli-Turkish relations, moral arguments were presented both in Israel and the United States.

The enormous sensitivity to Jewish involvement in the affair acquired an additional dimension in the relations between Israel and Diaspora Jewry. Jerusalem did not anticipate or understand the sensitivity.

Liberal Jewish organizations in the United States were embarrassed. Two Jewish organizations that wished to remain anonymous stated that the Israeli intervention had embarrassed them inasmuch as American Jewry tended to support the proposal to mark a day of commemoration. "As a people that was the victim of extermination, we feel a sense of identification with the Armenians. But Israel wants to preserve its relations with Turkey to which it attaches exaggerated importance," stated Jewish sources (*Yediot Aharonot*, October 23, 1989). A Reform Jewish Rabbi convened a press conference and accused the Jewish community of "moral paralysis." In his words, a "political stench" emanated from the role played by the Israeli Embassy in the United States in the matter (*Ha'aretz*, October 27, 1989). "As American Jews," he declared, "we do not march to orders from Jerusalem, Istanbul or Washington. We march to the commandments of our book, the Bible, out of sensitivity to justice."

The Union of American Hebrew Congregations passed a resolution at its biennial convention in New Orleans in early November 1989, in support of a Congressional motion to mark an Armenian memorial day, and to teach in its synagogues the facts and lessons of these tragic chapters in modern history.

Turkish Jewry's prominent involvement in the domestic American debate added an additional dimension. The Chief Rabbi of Turkey sent a personal letter to every member of the U.S. Senate saying: "The new initiative greatly troubles our community. We recognize the tragedy which befell both the Turks and the Armenians... but we cannot accept the definition of 'genocide.' The baseless charge harms us just as it harms our Turkish countrymen." The rabbi's reasoning was identical to that of the Turkish authorities. He also praised Turkish treatment of the Jews after the Expulsion from Spain. An additional argument presented was connected to the concern that such action would diminish and relativize the significance of the Holocaust. Turkish diplomats tried at the time to intervene in Jewish circles to prevent the commemoration of the Armenian genocide in the United States Holocaust Memorial Museum in Washington, D.C. "People all over Turkey follow with great concern the plans for the Museum of the Holocaust....It will be a terrible blow if our great friends, the Americans, will etch in marble a baseless analogy between the Turks and the Nazis. We believe that truth would not be served if the significance of the Holocaust were to be understated or diminished" (*Ha'aretz*, October 27, 1989). The Board of Directors of the Holocaust Museum in Washington decided in 1983, and reconfirmed its decision in 1987, to include a mention of the Armenian genocide in the museum to the extent that it was connected to the Holocaust or helped to clarify it. At the same time, it appears that there was, at one stage, an intention to give more prominent place to the Armenian genocide. As expected, the Turkish government objected to the inclusion of references to the Armenian genocide. "According to the official Turkish version, the anti-Armenian genocidal event never happened. The Israeli embassy lobbied on Turkey's behalf in this matter."[9] One of the arguments was that the uniqueness of the Holocaust would be harmed with all of the resulting ramifications.[10]

On April 24, 1994, the first assembly in memoriam of the Armenian genocide was held by the Armenian community in the Holocaust Memorial Museum in Washington, DC. The Armenian community in the United States viewed the event as an achievement even though it appeared that the mention of the Armenian genocide in the museum was more limited than what they had hoped for. It should be recalled that Hitler's words in 1939: "Who today remembers the massacre of the Armenians..." is chiseled in the wall of the permanent exhibition of the Holocaust Memorial Museum in Washington, D.C.

The press reported that the Turkish Foreign Minister met in 1989 with leaders of the Anti-Defamation League and requested their intervention. Officially, American Jews refused to commit themselves to helping: "We have a problem helping the Turks publicly," explained a Jewish leader. "As a people which endured a Holocaust we have a problem opposing a memorial day for another people." But people from the Jewish community worked behind the scenes: American Jews were aware of the interests of the Turkish Jewish community. "A live Jew is more important to us than a dead Armenian," was the way one Jewish leader bluntly put it. In his opinion, "a memorial day for the Armenians will lead to the approval of other memorial days, for the Indians, the Vietnamese and the Irish or for any other people. That will weaken the importance of Holocaust Day here."[11]

Harsh articles appeared in the Israeli press about Israeli involvement in preventing a memorial day for the Armenians. Akiva Eldar wrote in his article in *Ha'aretz* on October 20, 1989, entitled "The Holocaust and Politics": "The politics of [Israeli] weapons' dealers has long since pushed morality aside. It seems that this time morality has lost to wickedness."

An editorial in *Ha'aretz*, entitled "The Holocaust Obliges Toward the Armenians" and published on October 23, 1989, compares the attempts to deny the Holocaust to the intention of the Turkish Government. Israel cannot whitewash the evil implicit in such assistance. "The memory of the Holocaust which befell us commands us to display understanding for the sense of suffering of the Armenian People, and not to be an obstacle in the path of American legislation of its memory."

The journalist Shmuel Shnitzer protested in the Israeli daily, *Maariv*, ("Genocide, First Edition," October 23, 1989):

> We, who struggle against the attempts of shady historians and slick politicians to deny the gas chambers and the genocide of the Jewish People, are natural allies of the Armenians in the war against erasure and denial....If we have minimal decency, if the truth is precious to us even when it is inconvenient to this government or any other, we are obliged to strengthen the American Senate in its initiative to stand up for memory—ours and that of other victims of the evil plot to exterminate a people and then to enlist a thousand reasons to cover up the horror.

Sheila Hattis wrote in *Davar* ("A Rare Commodity Called Honor," October 29, 1989) that the reports of the involvement of Jews and Israeli diplomats in the efforts to prevent establishment of a day of remembrance of the Armenian genocide were "one of the most nauseating reports appearing in the press in recent times....It appears that honor is not a commodity with which we are blessed these days."

Especially harsh was Boaz Evron's article, "No Limit" (*Yediot Aharonot*, October 20, 1989):

> I am willing to bet that if we were neighbors of Nazi Germany and the latter were to take action against a different minority within its borders, and we had good commercial relations with the Germans, we would behave like the worst of them. We would collaborate in the persecution of the minority just like the Poles and the Rumanians. We would close our borders [to the persecuted] just like the Swiss. If we can behave thus with regard to a country that truly does not effect us, such as Turkey, what would we do toward Germany! And there may be another reason: We, who recall the Holocaust every day, are not willing to allow anyone else any part or possession of his own Holocaust. Why it is our main asset today. It is the only thing around which we attempt to unite the Jews. It is the only thing with which we attempt to frighten Israelis against leaving the country. It is the only thing by which we attempt to silence the Gentiles.

The articles and editorials in the press following cancellation of the screening of "Journey to Armenia" in 1990 reveal that there were other factors. The formal reason presented by the Chairman of the Board of Directors and the Managing Director of the Israeli Broadcasting Authority (IBA) was that they had received requests from the Chief Rabbinate of Turkish Jewry, from the Association of Turkish Immigrants in Israel, and from other Turkish-Israeli immigrant groups. They claimed that screening of the documentary could cause damage or even endanger the Jews of Turkey. An additional reason was a fear of harming relations with Turkey, an important Muslim nation, which was at the time the only Muslim state that maintained diplomatic relations with Israel. There was talk of pressure originating in Turkey and the Turkish Jewish business community. Furthermore, it was claimed, a deterioration in relations with Turkey might hamper the exit of Jews from other Muslim countries, apparently Iran and Syria. Officially, every alleged instance of pressure on Israel by the Turkish Government was vigorously denied. An official denial was also made of the alleged intervention of the Israeli Foreign Ministry and Prime Minister's Office.

A member of the IBA Board of Directors who had supported cancellation of the documentary film said, "The film contains propaganda and injury to part of the public, because a Holocaust happened only to the Jewish People." (*Kol Haeir*, June 22, 1990). The Director of the

Prime Minister's Office was quoted: "It is a problem of the Turkish Jews. We are not interested in the Eskimos or the Armenians, only in the Jews." (*Kol Haeir*, June 19, 1990; *Ha'aretz*, June 22, 1990). Member of Knesset Yair Zaban demanded that the Prime Minister rebuke his director for the latter's comments about the Armenians, and termed the comments "sickening." He added: "The very refusal to screen the Armenian film, when accompanied by offensive declarations such as these, helps to create the impression that the present leaders of the State of Israel condemn genocide only when it concerns the Jewish People and result in the fact that many Jews and Israelis in Israel and around the world hide their faces for shame." (*Ha'aretz*, June 26, 1990).

To all those involved, overtly and covertly, in the controversy—Jews, Turks, and Armenians—it was clear that there was special significance to the issue which went beyond the debate over the screening of a film about the Armenian massacre in any other country. The fact that the country in question was of a people which was the victim of the Holocaust, and the unique problematics which resulted, came to the fore. In the course of the debate the history of the Jews in Turkey was also mentioned. The Turkish people had been outstanding in its humane and tolerant treatment of its Jewish minority for 500 years following the Expulsion of the Jews from Spain, "and saved masses of Jews" said a letter (May 24, 1990) to the IBA signed by the heads of three organizations which represented 100,000 Israeli citizens of Turkish descent. There were those who claimed that not only had Turkey refused to turn its Jews over to the Nazis, it had even served as a refuge for persecuted Jews from European countries during the Holocaust.[12]

The Jewish-Turkish immigrant organizations in Israel essentially repeated in their letter the positions of the Turkish Government ever since the genocide: there is controversy over the facts and there are contradicting versions. "We do not negate the right of the Armenian People to remember its victims in its rebellion against the Ottoman rule, but any attempt to compare between the Jewish Holocaust and the Armenian case is misleading in our eyes and detracts from the importance and uniqueness of the Holocaust which befell the Jewish People solely because of racist views."

But the subject of the Holocaust was raised primarily by those who attacked the decision of the Broadcasting Authority. Those writing in the press sometimes used the general concept of "Holocaust" outside of the context of the Holocaust of the Jews in headlines and statements like "The Holocaust of Others" (*Kol Haeir*, April 13, 1990), "The Armenians Also Had a Holocaust" (*Davar*, April 17, 1990), "The Armenian Holocaust Will Not Be Shown on Israeli Television" (*Yediot Aharonot*, April 13, 1990), or "The Movie About the Armenian Holocaust" (*Ha'aretz*, April 27, 1990). There were articles and editorials which emphasized that "there were only two cases of genocide worthy of being called a Holocaust in terms of their demographic effect, the cultural destruction they created, the uprooting of hundreds of thousands of people from their homes, the mass murder and the justification of the obscenity of the event, that of the Jewish People and that of the Armenian People" (Alon Pankes, "The Armenians Also Had a Holocaust, The Forty Days of Meckel" [Aryeh Meckel was the Managing Director of the IBA at the time], *Davar*, April 17, 1990). In another article the journalist wrote: "only two peoples can term their days of mourning in the horrifying concept 'Holocaust': the Jews and the Armenians" (Ephraim Sidon, "What Is Hateful To You Etc.," *Maariv*, April 27, 1990).

The decision not to show the film was interpreted as a "desire to preserve the uniqueness of the Jewish Holocaust and the lack of desire, or inability, to accept the possibility that another people had experienced a Holocaust" (*Kol Haeir*, June 22, 1990). This argument was also put forward in the other controversies. In this context, several articles point out the connection between our treatment of our own Holocaust and the disregard of the Armenian genocide: "It is worth examining and remembering these things at least until the next Holocaust Day, when the leaders of the nation and its educators once again preach the importance of the lesson and the educational message for the entire world in remembering the Holocaust" (*Kol Haeir*, June 22, 1990). These themes repeat in the attacks on the decision not to show the film: "How can Israel, which is so sensitive to the Holocaust, assist in denying the Holocaust of another people?" (*Ha'aretz*, April 20, 1990).

Representatives of the Armenian community in Israel also stressed the fact that the people in question had suffered from a terrible Holocaust. The spokesman of the Armenian community in Jerusalem reacted: "We are aware of the Turkish pressure in every country of the world. It is astounding that England, France, Italy, Scandinavia, and other states are not affected by the Turkish pressure, whereas in Israel, which is so sensitive to genocide and the Holocaust, they surrender to it."

The Armenian Response Committee in Jerusalem reacted even more sharply: "What would happen if the authorities in France or England, for example, were to decide at the last minute to remove from the screen a film about the Holocaust of the Jews and to show in its place a film about bees and bugs." (Instead of the film about the Armenians, the IBA broadcast, with no prior announcement or explanation, a film about the life cycle of bees.) An Armenian student sent a letter to the editor: "Precisely the Jewish People should display special sensitivity to the subject of the Holocaust of the Armenians, to ensure that future generations will not forget, and that the Holocaust will not reoccur." (*Yediot Aharonot*, May 3, 1990). A petition signed by members of Knesset, jurists, historians and writers also called upon the Prime Minister and the management of the IBA to show the film. The petition used the same argument, this time in a positive light and mentioning the uniqueness: "Especially as members of a people which has experienced a Holocaust unparalleled in human history and which battles today against its denial, we are obliged to display special sensitivity to the tragedy of another people." The petition, initiated by Member of Knesset Yair Zaban, is noteworthy. Members of Knesset from the right, center, and left took a stand in favor of screening the film. The petition was signed by prominent intellectuals, historians—among them historians of the Holocaust—and jurists. (There is a change here in the position of some of the historians. As stated, during the controversy over the international conference in 1982 on "Holocaust and Genocide," academics canceled their participation due to political pressure.) The film has not been shown to this very day despite numerous requests and despite several changes of governments and education ministers in Israel since then.

The writers in the debate sometimes create an associative connection, an analogy, or even an identity between the cases, particularly relating to the human dimension, with the victims and the survivors who appear in the film that was canceled:

> An Armenian survivor of Holocaust appears and sounds exactly like a Jewish survivor of Holocaust—emotional, upset, wiping away a tear, broken and weeping, chain smoking. A Holocaust is a Holocaust, even when the number of its dead is one sixth of the dead in our Holocaust. A massacre is a massacre, even if the victims are not Jews....The film is moving. The scenes of horror are familiar to us from other places, as if they had been replicated and moved to Turkey. Miriam Davis, an Armenian survivor who

lives today in the United States, reconstructs the death of her mother and baby brother. We have seen this in so many films which were produced here about the Holocaust and no one ever thought to say that they were badly made, unworthy of being shown. (*Kol Haeir*, June 29, 1990.)

And the next scene, a long row of corpses lying in a wide, open trench. There is a system in this trench, the bodies are parallel to one another. The Association is to Auschwitz, the area behind the crematoria. The film returns from time to time to this allusion, Auschwitz. But "An Armenian Journey" does not manage to create identity between the Jewish and Armenian Holocausts. That is to say, the film does not infringe on the singularity and uniqueness of the Jewish Holocaust. (*Yediot Aharonot*, May 11, 1990.)

The Armenian survivor who endured the events of those days is described thus: "She has white hair, eyeglasses; she is interviewed in the shade of a tree; there is a sound of birds, like the Jewish survivor in [Kibbutz] Yad Mordechai, after 50 years." (Ibid.)

We should add that the view of the Holocaust of the Jews as a factor that obliges the Jews to deal with the tragedies and suffering of others recurs in the public statements of the Government of Israel and its statesmen.

A proposed resolution supported by fifteen members of the Knesset Defense and Foreign Affairs Committee, which was initiated by Member of Knesset Yair Zaban in October 1989, following reports of Israeli involvement in preventing an official day of commemoration of the Armenian genocide in the U.S. (see above), states: "The Defense and Foreign Affairs Committee believes that efforts to preserve the memory of the massacre of the Armenian People during the First World War should be viewed with understanding and support. The Committee believes that any attempt to blur or deny Holocaust or mass murder inflicted on any people is inherently invalid. As members of a people which has known suffering and persecution we understand the suffering of the Armenian People." (*Al Hamishmar*, October 24, 1989.) In that same debate, Member of Knesset Yossi Sarid stated that the Jewish People which had endured a terrible Holocaust was the last who ought to sanction the denial of the Holocaust of another people, no matter what the momentary considerations might be. (*Ha'aretz*, October 19, 1989.) This frame of reference also appears in connection with acts of genocide that occurred in front of our eyes. A Government resolution of May 22, 1994, regarding events in Rwanda stated: "The Government of Israel, shocked by the genocide taking place in Rwanda and the destruction of hundreds of thousands of innocent people. The Jewish People, which has experienced the bitterest event of the Nazi Holocaust, and its state, the State of Israel, cannot be indifferent to the horrors in Rwanda."

Also noteworthy is the fact that there are few Israeli-Hebrew books in our library dealing with the Armenian massacre: few references in original literary works, few books in translation, not a single book of research in Hebrew translation. In effect, there has been no research in Israel on the massacre of the Armenians. On occasion, following events related to official Israeli behavior, critical articles appear, as we have seen, in the press. On the anniversary of the Armenian massacre we sometimes encounter in recent years articles in the newspaper. Almost nothing more. At one time, people at least read *The Forty Days of Musa Dagh.*

This silence, in stark contrast to the abundance and variety of publications in Hebrew or Hebrew translation dealing with the Holocaust which appear each year, raises questions. Young Israelis have only foggy knowledge—if at all—about something that happened to the Armenians, sometime in the past. The same embarrassing ignorance also exists with regard to the genocide of the Gypsies. Only rarely do they know anything beyond that. The many Israelis who travel and vacation in Turkey in recent years do not know that their tour buses are passing by "Musa Dagh." The Turks do not want them to know. Until recently there was no educational curriculum or textbook available to teachers in the various frameworks of the Israeli education system, even if they wanted to deal with the subject. Even in the universities, the Armenian genocide and other acts of genocide are almost never taught as a subject, and only rarely are they mentioned in any context whatsoever.

The consistent refusal of official Israel to mark or commemorate in any way the tragedy that befell the Armenians arouses harsh thoughts. This behavior, apart from being morally problematical, can have disastrous results in shaping the memory of the Holocaust in our national consciousness, and in human consciousness.

Certain signs of change in the official position began to find expression during 1994. Regional and global political changes strengthened relations between Israel and Turkey, but at the same time, the official Israeli disregard of the Armenian genocide may have begun to "thaw."

As a result of an initiative to prepare a special curriculum dealing with genocide in the twentieth century which would, for the first time in Israel, deal also with the destruction of the Armenians, the IBA's prestigious weekly news program, "Yoman Hashavua," broadcast on April 22, 1994, a feature story on the Armenian massacre. Attempts to cancel the broadcast failed. Following the feature story, "Yoman Hashavua" conducted an interview with the Turkish Ambassador in Israel, which restated the official Turkish denials of a massacre and of Turkish responsibility for its implementation. The Ambassador said, *inter alia*, "In wartime, many innocent victims fall in battle, and in war like in war." The feature and the interview aroused considerable reaction and the subject was again brought before the plenum of the Knesset. Members of Knesset attacked the Ambassador's comments. In his response, Deputy Foreign Minister, Dr. Yossi Beilin, said, "We have never accepted the very superficial analysis that this was done in wartime. That is not war. This is definitely massacre, genocide, and we will assist in its commemoration because this is the sort of thing that the world is obliged to remember."

There were those who were angered by the interview with the Turkish ambassador and compared it, erroneously in my estimation, with granting a public stage to Holocaust deniers. The interview with the Turkish ambassador did not lead to a denial of the Armenian genocide but rather to its emphasis by the official voice of Israel. In contrast, a television correspondent argued that "the interview with the Turkish ambassador only caused a dramatic and historic reversal in Israel's attitude toward the genocide of the Armenian People."[13]

Turkey's Ambassador in Israel protested the broadcast of the feature story, which was, in his view, one-sided. He claimed that the only purpose of the story was to support the Armenians and to slander the Turkish people. The Ambassador further argued that the story presented only one version of what he termed "the Armenian tragedy," which was considered by historians to be controversial and about which one could not draw clear conclusions.[14]

Israeli society may be at the beginning of a new stage in defining its identity and shaping its historical consciousness and relationship to the Holocaust. The Holocaust has been an important, meaningful, and central component in the creation of a Jewish-Israeli identity in the formative stages of Israel's society which were also years of struggle and war. In Israel's formative stages and during the period when its existence was not officially recognized by many nations, the Holocaust and the state's wars were central components in Israeli identity. Nurturing consciousness of the Holocaust and remembrance of the Holocaust played an important function at the time. We witness today two simultaneous processes: the march in the path of peace which we have, one hopes, initiated, and the entry of Israeli society to a stage of collective maturity. While these are separate processes, they are delicately intertwined. They may bring about deep and far reaching changes in our private and public identity.

In January 1995, my experimental curriculum, "Sensitivity to the World's Suffering: Genocide in the Twentieth Century," including a substantive section dealing with the extermination of the Gypsies and the Armenian genocide, was removed from high school curriculum. The decision indicates that my comments in the preceding paragraphs were perhaps premature. It appears that Israeli society, for both internal and external reasons, is not yet "ready" to deal with the subject. In early 1996, an alternative curriculum entitled "Minorities in History: The Armenians in the Ottoman Empire" appeared. The previous curriculum was rejected because, *inter alia*, its author "presented a historical story in which the Turks are the only villains in the drama which took place on the Russian border. The curriculum also ignores the penetrating historiographic debates which have long been part of the study of the massacre of the Armenians."[15] The new curriculum offers a "balanced" treatment of the Armenian genocide. For example, with regard to the question of whether the murder of the Armenians in 1915-16 can be termed "genocide," the curriculum replies: "The Armenians claim that it was while the Turks utterly reject such a claim."[15]

The Holocaust will rightly continue to play a major role in Israeli identity in the future. It was a deeply formative and authentic experience, which continues to bubble within the society's psyche and to burst out from the depths of its soul. But, one must hope and act that a suitable and moral balance may be found between the Zionist, Jewish, and universal "lessons" of the Holocaust. In teaching the Holocaust and in granting its memory to future generations, Israel must also develop the fundamental approach which says that the value of human life is universal, whether that one is a Jew, a Gypsy, an Armenian, or an Arab. In order to achieve that maturity, two principles—which may appear contradictory—must be upheld: emphasis on the singularity of the Holocaust, and a sensitivity towards the tragedies of others, primarily, to other instances of genocide which have taken place in human history. These two principles are not contradictory but complementary. This is the desirable synthesis between the particular and the universal, which lends meaning, moral and spiritual power to the memory of the Holocaust and to the just demand that the world will never forget. We should not fear that such a synthesis may relativize the Holocaust or weaken its unique Jewish aspect.

Notes

1. Richard Lichtheim, *Shaar Hayishuv* (Jerusalem: The Zionist Library, 1954), p. 398.
2. Abba Achimeir, "Genocide," from *The Crowing of the Rooster*, Amichai, undated, p. 139 (in Hebrew). The article was written in the early 1950s.
3. For the production of the English-language version, Michael Arlen, an American writer of Armenian descent, was invited to Israel. Arlen, an internationally known writer, is the author of *Passage to Ararat*, which describes his search for his familial and cultural roots and his desire to understand what it means to be an Armenian. The book also appeared in Hebrew (Yediot Aharonot Publishers, 1978).
4. Amos Elon, "Armenia as a Parable: A. Our Holocaust and the Holocaust of Others," *Ha'aretz*, 1978, appeared also in Elon's book, *Looking Back in Consternation* (Tel Aviv: Am Oved, 1988), pp. 250-60.
5. Ibid., pp. 258-59.
6. Among them: Yizhak Arad and Gideon Hausner from Yad Vashem, the Rector of Tel Aviv University at the time, Yoram Dinstein, Emil Fackenheim, Mark Tannenbaum.
7. See Amos Elon, "Their Holocaust," *Ha'aretz*, June 11, 1982, and the response of the Chairman of Yad Vashem, "We and The Armenians," *Ha'aretz*, June 29, 1982.
   See detail on this issue: *The Book of the International Conference on the Holocaust and Genocide, Book One: The Conference Program and Crisis*. International Conference on the Holocaust and Genocide. Tel Aviv, Israel. The book was edited by Yisrael Charny, who convened the conference—the subtitle of which was "Towards Understanding, Intervention and Prevention of Genocide." Charny's view of the chain of events appears in the book and includes the pressures which were applied against the organizers of the conference, and the subsequent cancellation of the participation of a number of central personalities, including Elie Wiesel who was the President of the Organizing Committee, and the Chairman of Yad Vashem. Ibid., pp. 269-316. Charny continues his efforts in the spirit of the initiative for the conference in 1982, in the framework of the Institute on the Holocaust and Genocide in Jerusalem.
8. Yoav Karni, "Battle of the Politicos Over the Armenian Holocaust," *Ha'aretz*, October 27, 1989.

9. Jeshajahu Weinberg and Rina Elieli, *The Holocaust Museum in Washington* (New York: Rizzoli Publications), 1995, p. 164. Jeshajahu Weinberg was the founder and the first director of The Holocaust Museum in Washington. The efforts to prevent the inclusion of references to the Armenian genocide had to be authorized by high officials in both states of Turkey and Israel.

10. In detail, see Edward T. Linenthal, "The Boundaries of Inclusion: Armenians and Gypsies" in *Preserving Memory* (New York: Viking Press, 1995), pp. 228-41, and also Amir Neuman, "The Armenian Pandora's Box," *Davar,* October 29, 1989, and *Maariv,* August 20, 1989.

11. Zadok Yehezkeli, "The Dead Armenian and the Live Jew," *Yediot Aharonot,* October 25, 1989.

12. See the letter from heads of the Turkish immigrant community in Israel, and a letter to the editor of *Yediot Aharonot,* May 20, 1990. There are those who reject these arguments. The historian Bernard Wasserstein argues that the position of the Turkish Government on the Jewish question during the Holocaust was not particularly generous, but not especially murderous. Its position was cynical and narrow like that of most of the neutral countries. In his opinion, Turkey has nothing to be proud of (*Ha'aretz,* January 14, 1994).

13. Yaakov Achimeir, "Am I Indifferent to the Armenians?," *Maariv,* May 1, 1994.

14. A letter of the former Turkish Ambassador to Israel, Unur Gokce, to the Managing Director of Israel Television, Mordechai Kirschenbaum, April 27, 1994.

15. Yossi Elgazi, "The Holocaust in Controversy," *Ha'aretz,* February 23,1996.

10

Conclusion

This study has attempted to examine the attitudes of the Jewish community in Palestine and the Zionist Movement toward the massacre of the Armenians at the time of its occurrence and thereafter. Although this part of the study is ended, the study is by no means completed. As the first of its kind, this research almost certainly does not exhaust the full range of attitudes. During the years in question, some Jews acted in various places in the world on behalf of the Armenians; they expressed support for their struggle or empathized with their suffering. The present research does not deal with them; however, they should be remembered: the Danish thinker, Georg Brandes; the Russian Jewish poet, Osip Mandelstam; Henry Morgenthau, Sr., the American Ambassador in Constantinople from 1913 to 1916, and his replacement, Abraham Elkus, among others. We do not know what motivated them to come to the support of the Armenians. They did not act as Jews, but as human beings. In this context, we question the uniquely Jewish motives, morality, and identity in their stand and their actions. In any event, it appears that a Jewish component existed in them even when they were sometimes to be found on the fringes of the Jewish establishment and on the outskirts of the organized Jewish world.

The study offers an opportunity to explore a particular case of general phenomenon that goes beyond the Armenian genocide and the Jewish attitude, and that is the reaction of the bystander who remains on the sidelines while atrocities take place.

In the same or in similar circumstances, peoples, groups, and movements do not share uniform views, nor do they behave in a uniform manner. To the question that was hidden in the pages of this volume

369

and sometimes peeked out from and between the lines—why does one person react while another does not?—there is no answer. An abundance of emotions, opinions, and differing circumstances shape one's decision, consciously or not, to take action. Persons absorbed in themselves, in their group or their people, have trouble relating to the distress of other individuals, movements, or nationalities. The leaders of the Yishuv and the Zionist Movement were engrossed in a hard battle, existential in many senses, to preserve and advance the nascent Zionist enterprise. During the period of the First World War, there was a struggle for existence, for survival. In this battle, the Zionist Movement succeeded. An almost total absorption in the Jewish cause, in effect the Zionist cause, appears to be one of the main reasons why the leaders of the Yishuv and the Zionist Movement ignored or remained indifferent to the Armenian tragedy. For the most part, their view of the world from a Zionist perspective caused them sometimes, it must be admitted, to take the side of the "Young Turks," the side of the immolator, or to stand on the sidelines. Considerations of *realpolitik* tipped the scales.

Those who related, who reacted, who protested, those who felt a moral and humane, sometimes explicitly Jewish revulsion at the genocide of the Armenians shared two characteristics. The first factor was their descent. Among the reactors, the majority were born in Palestine: Itamar Ben-Avi, "the first Hebrew child;" the native-born members of Nili; the children of the pioneers of the first wave of Jewish immigration to Palestine, the first generation of "sabras," although they were not yet known by this term at that time. They were connected to the land; they spoke Hebrew, Arabic, and French; and they were more critical and less submissive to the Turkish ruler than the new immigrants, mostly Russian-born, who arrived in the second wave of immigration after 1904. Open to Western culture, some had studied in France and were familiar with and influenced by French culture. They displayed more sensitivity and openness to the suffering of the Armenians. Differences of sociology and mentality, and perhaps even an intergenerational struggle over the leadership of the Jewish society in Palestine, led to a confrontation between the "native" Palestinian approach and the "born-in-exile" approach. The second factor put to the fore was their personal, idiosyncratic differences. *The reactors and those who extended a hand of support—Bernard Lazare, Itamar Ben-Avi, Aaron Aaronsohn, Yaakov Rabinovitz, Israel Zangwill, and Aaron Reuveni—were in one way or another exceptional. They did not follow*

convention; they were each of an independent mind, "troublemakers,"
critical in their approach to the Zionist establishment.

We have already noted in the Introduction that acts of genocide can
occur when there is a group of bystanders—the indifferent—between
the immolator and his victim. They are the overwhelming majority who
are not directly involved in the action. The necessary but insufficient
condition for destruction—that other forces do not come between the
murderer and his victim, particularly forces identified with political
and military power—is irrelevant in the sense of simple rescue, in the
case at hand. Morgenthau and Elkus were able to offer tangible assistance, and did so to the best of their ability. The Yishuv was not able
physically to come to the rescue. But our investigation has a moral
significance. In the circumstances of that time, pragmatism and self-
interest were frequently the most significant considerations, and many
of the leaders of the Yishuv and the Zionist Movement were not im-
mune to them.

For the reader who finds it difficult to digest this reality and needs a
comparison with others, we should add that a less-than-comprehensive
examination of the behavior of peoples during the period of the destruction of the Armenians teaches us that indifference and inaction
were the most prevalent stands taken. The examination of their behavior—their indifference—has a practical aspect, in addition to a moral
one. The European Powers were able, in fact, to come to the rescue and
did not do so. They added insult to injury and, after their victory, re-
neged on their explicit and public promises given to the Armenians
during the war.[1]

In recent decades, a number of works have appeared dealing with
the attitude of peoples, including Americans, to the destruction of the
Jews in the Second World War. In 1968, Arthur Morse published his
book, *While Six Million Died*, which appeared in Hebrew in 1972. In
1993, Yad Vashem published the Hebrew edition of David Wyman's
book, *The Abandonment of the Jews: America and the Holocaust, 1941-
1945*.[2] The central issue of the book is the question that continues to
trouble Jews and non-Jews alike for whom the Holocaust is an open
wound, the question that remains unanswered: How was Hitler allowed
to implement his plan in such enormous dimensions? Why was there
no serious effort at rescue?

Wyman concludes with the determination that the true obstacle to
the rescue of the Jews by the United States was the absence of will on

the part of the American establishment to do so. In other words, the American establishment lacked the desire to save Jews.

In her study, *Eichmann in Jerusalem*, Hannah Arendt describes Adolf Eichmann's last minutes before his execution: "[H]e [Eichmann] was summing up the lesson that this long course in human wickedness has taught us—the lesson which could not be verbalized and comprehended—the banality of evil."[3]

Arendt's important, original, and, some would argue, controversial book was rejected by Israeli intellectuals and by the Israeli academic community, which included some of Arendt's close friends. Despite its wide publication throughout the world, her book was not translated into Hebrew. The book has harsh words, some possibly unfounded or incorrect, for the role of the Jews and their retrospective responsibility for their own destruction. But the central claim of the book, which makes it original and important, is the thesis of the "banality of evil," that evil is part of the experience of all human existence. There has never been a meaningful discussion of this claim in Israeli society. For years, Israeli society has preferred, out of its own needs and considerations, to place evil on "a different planet," to stress a dichotomous Manichaean world of good and evil and not to see evil (of which the Nazi's deeds are the height) as a diffuse element, existing on different levels — refusing to acknowledge the prevalence of the "banal evil" within its midst. Only in the last decade have different voices begun to be heard in Israel's public debate.

With all due caution and humility, I suggest that we consider the concept of "the banality of indifference." The picture that becomes increasingly clear regarding the attitude toward acts of genocide (of which, we emphasize, the Holocaust is the most extreme and unique case in this category) is a picture of the banality of indifference.

The reaction of the multitudes, those located in the space between the immolator and the victims, is characterized by indifference, conformity, and opportunism. The Jews, too, in the circumstances of time and place, do not go beyond this banality, with several exceptions.

One of the formative influences on the historical consciousness of a society is the question of what society can and wishes to know about historical occurrence. In Israeli society, there are many people who would prefer not to know about the genocide of the Armenians and the genocide of the Gypsies. In any event, there is no doubt, indeed, that most know nothing about it.

In shaping historical consciousness, beyond the rational dimension, which is given expression in historical research whose task is to reveal historical truth, there are also emotional forces at work, sometimes irrational, both conscious and unconscious. Historical truth, historical research, and historical consciousness are not synonymous. The task of research and education is to try to *influence* the formation of historical consciousness. The researcher and the educator are meant to be among the formative agents, together with the government, the media, and various interest groups in society and communities that wish to influence the historical consciousness of their society.

The attempt in writing this book, which now draws to an end, was that of a researcher to uncover—with as much precision as possible—the historical veracity of events decades after their occurrence. The book seeks also to arouse questions and deliberations about the historical consciousness of the Israeli and the international communities. In Israeli historical consciousness, the Holocaust plays a central role—becoming increasingly stronger over the years. This consciousness stresses the singularity of the Holocaust. It contains, in my opinion, an extreme and almost utter focus on the Jews as victims, and a disregard—consciously or not, intentionally or not—of acts of genocide that have taken place in the twentieth century, among them the murder of the Armenians and the extermination of the Gypsies.

We ought to emphasize the characteristics that make the Holocaust unique while comparing the Holocaust with other instances of genocide. At the same time, in shaping the historical consciousness of Israeli society, we must try to act in such a manner so as not to ignore genocide when it relates to other peoples. Retrieving this missing element—"the lack of presence" in the historical consciousness—will allow us to explore "our" Holocaust in a broader, more comprehensive, and perhaps more correct perspective, in terms of the Jewish experience, in particular, and human experience at large.

Notes

1. The fact that there is almost no research dealing with the question of the attitude of the Great Powers toward the Armenian massacre is significant. See, for example, Akaby Nassibian, *Britain and the Armenian Question 1915-1923* (New York: St. Martin's Press, 1984).
2. The English edition was published by Pantheon Books in 1984.
3. Hannah Arendt, *Eichmann in Jerusalem* (revised and enlarged edition) (New York: Viking Press, 1964), p. 252.

Appendix A

Pro Armenia

Aaron Aaronsohn

Memorandums presented to the War Office London, 16 November 1916.
The original handwritten manuscript is in the Nili Archives in Zichron Yaakov, Israel. This is a verbatim, unedited, and uncorrected transcription of the text.

To sit down in peaceful London and write about the Armenian massacres is a very hard task; no man unless he be a Kypling or a Masefield should try it. The massacres were crried out on such a wholesale scale, with such refinements of atrocity and carried on for such a lenght of time in such a systematical way – the only work in which the Turks seem to be able to be systematocal, that no matter how much one tries to chastise his style, no matter how moderate one tries to be, one is still liable to be considered as indulging is exagerations.

The writer has not been in Armenia proper and has not seen, therefore, the worst acts of atrocity, But what he has seen, actually seen, in Syria, in Konia and in Constantinople, what he has learned from the agents he had sent out to part of the Turkish Empire where these massacres were carried out on large scale is enough to fill volumes and make the hair stand on edge.

The writer is trying here to bring to paper, in a very scrappy way, some of the things he has seen or learned from the mouth of most trustworthy persons, just to serve as illustrations of what was going on only in the outskirts of the area of the massacres.

Several Germans established as farmers in Palestine and who were either on military duty in Germany or for contracting entreprised in and around Consple, returned home, i.e. to Haifa, during the months of Nov., Dec. 1915. The writer made it his business to travel frequently on the railroad line between Damascus and Tiberias in order to got touch with those Germans whom he personally knew, and through them with the other Germans travelling on the line and he had in this way first hand reports of what these Germans have actually seen on their way.

All reports concorded to say that thousands of human bodies were to be seen on both sides of the railroad track from Anatolia to Syria.

A sister of the writer travelled from Constantinople to Haifa in the month of December 1915. She never had systerics before, but since that trip whenever any allusions to Armenians are made in her presence she gets into a fit of hysterics. A few of the things she had actually seen: Hundreds of bodies of men, women and babes on both sides of the track and dogs feeding on these human corpses. Turkish women rummaging in the clothings of the corpses in hope of some hidden treasure,

At one station (in Gulak or Osmanieh, the writer can remember no more where it was) thousands of starving, typhus stricken Armenians were waiting since days for a train to carry them southwards. They were lying on the ground near the main track and on the sidings. When the train arrived the engineer, on seeing Armenians on the rails, purposedly pushed his locomotive in the mass of Armenians and overran and hurt about fifteen of them. He then triumphantly jumped off his engine, rub his hands in Joy and colled out to a friend of his "Did you see how I smashed may-be 50 of these Armenian swines?" (   )

The same witness has seen trains arriving packed with 60–80 Armenians in each goods when, 40 would have over croweded the car, and at the station 10 or 20 dead (of hunger – spot-typhus) . Armenians used to be thrown out of the car and a respective number of alive Armenians packed in state. Useless to say that not even mock measures of disinfection were considered. This special form of typhus being very contagious the result was that not only among Armenians did this disease spread but even in the surrounding Mohamedan villages this spot typhus killed whole families, in certain instances, as the writer was shown later, on his trip; no living human being – or to be correct, one should say no Turk being, which is far from being the same thing – was left. Dozens of totally deserted villages were noted by the writer and the reasons for the desertion given him was always the same: the epidemies following in the tracks of these accursed Aremenians have emptied the land of the righteous or the sons of the Crescent (   ).

The same witness has seen Armenians robbed of all their belongings in the most kindly way in the Amanus. In Hassan Beyly, a village on the Amanus thousands of Armenians were laying outdoors in the cold and the snow waiting for an opportunity to be carried forward. In ordinary times a carriage trip (Yalu) from Hassa Beylu to Salchieh costs about 3 medjidiehs. With the onrush of Armenians the prize of a carriage trip went up as high as 4–5 Turkish pounds and very usually the Armenian used to be searched and robbed of all the money he had, which was taken as "payment for the trip" using no violence, treating him in fact with those kind words (yavrum, kara kuzum, etc..) of which those good humoured and soft hearted Turks have such an inexhaustible and nice sounding stock.

In some of the transfer stations, like Aleppo for instance, where thousands of Armenians used to be piled up for weeks outdoors, starving, awaiting to be carried forwards, epidemics spread rapidly, chiefly spot typhus. In almost all of these cases the dead were not buried for days, the reason being, as cheerfully explained to the writer by a superior turkish officer, to have the epidemics sweeping off more rapidly these accursed Armenians and get rid of them at once and for good.

The writer could give dozens of more instances of same treatement and same spirit of the Turks, but it would add nothing to what we already know, He would only report this more.

When the European and especially the American public opinion was stirred up by the massacres Dj.P. repaired to Consple and insisted that these outrages should be stopped, they were a disgrace to the Y.T. Besides, he needed those industrious people for his public works in Syria and Palestine. It was reported that Tallat and his colleagues were not willing to give up their prey, but the firm attitude of Dj.P saved the lives of over hundred thousands Armenians doomed to massacres; they were, all of them to be sent to Syria. At once Dj.P. was ironically nicknamed the "Armenian Pasha" (   ) in Constantinople. But the poor helpless Armenians felt grateful. Demonstrations being out of question in Constantinople for anybody and still more so for Armenians, the latter arranged for a dumb manifestation, For more than 3 hours a steady flood of about 40.000 Armenians passed before the casual residence of Dj.P. in Consple not a word being uttered but just looking up with grateful eyes to their savious, who stood all the time on the balcony with crossed arms in the Napoleonic attitude he so loves to pose in.

Outside of Consple, in Asia, on his return trip, the extra train of the Satrap Dj.P. was often stopped by Armenian delegation who spontaneously.

Writer makes bold to say that this again was a farce, arranged to fool those simple-minded Occidentals and make at the same time capital for Dj.P.

Having some sense of adion, Dj.P. directed all his salvage-Armenians out of the way places. By this method he shielded the larger centres from sufferings and epidemics, on the other hand he could handle the Armenians as he lived without too many reports leaking through those plagued Neutral-Consul-ridden places.

But here the writer can supply first hand information having been out himself to some of those armenian camps, in Hauran, in Adjloun, south-east of the Dead Sea, etc..

The armenians are forbidden to stay in yowns and villages, to do any work, i.e. to earn any salary. They are actually parked in the desert, where they depend for food and water on Government supplies. Men, women and children have to work at hard labour in fact, making roads, opening quarries and the like. Every working man or womaa gets 4 metalliques 2 d. a day. That is the whole income of the people on that they should live. In ordinary times and in large centres that ridiculous pay would hardly keep a man from starving, still more so out in the desert where the scarce supplies are to be found only in the Government stores run with the most outrageous dishonestly,

Water has very often to be brought to these centres by train, no spring to be met within a radius of 10 miles. That the train in those days of war cannot call regularly at those camps goes without saying, One does not too much injustice to those "clean-fighting" Turks in voicing one's suspicion that too often the water trains do not call having voluntarilly forgotten to do it. At any rate when the water train arrives thousands of starving altered people rush, who with his earth-jar, who with his tin-can towards the stopping place. A fearful melée usually ensues. But in nowadays Turkey order must prevail. The kind hearted-gandarms butt in and with their "courbages" beat right and left, keep the people away from the train in order to avoid accidents, the locomotive stops, the engineer smilingly opens the severral cocks, the water runs out on the sun-baked ground and the thirsty people are kept by dreads of courbages and filled rifles from filling their vessels with the water they are longing for since so long, their recipients are smashed, etc.. Water has been sent to the desert, the mindful Government of the good administrator Dj.P. has done all it can to provide for the thirsty, an unfortunate, accident happened, but this can happen under the best of regines.

The above sketched scenes have been actually witnessed by the writer and the above reported answer is what Dj.P. had to say when informed. It is peculiarly illustrating the whole regime that Dj.P. did not even feel falled upon to inquire who were responsable of this shameless murder by thirst and submit them were it only to a mock-trial.

That under such circumstances death sweeps off a third and a half of the camp population in a few weeks is nothing but natural.

The writers prefers not to write about the promiscuous life in these camps. New groupings take place in those camps. Men who have lost their wives on the long way, women who have lost their husbands group, together, children of whom nobody knows whom they belong to are adopted in these new families and the Turkish "soldatesque" watches all that and brings in its share of immorality, vice and disease.

Small wonder then that a representive of a neutral Government in Consple who proposed to go to Syria in a private quality, promising to make no report, not even to his Gov. but only to satisfy himself as a man to what was going on, that said representative was refused the authorization he applied for.

It might be asked: What part of the population or of the organized public services was carrying out those whole-sale destructions of Armenian life and property. The reply is that no class of the Mohamedan population, rich or poor, high or low, young or old, men or women kept away from murdering and robbing, which of course does not mean to say that every individual Mohamedan is to be blamed, without exceptions. A few noteworthy exceptions were reported, oases of ind help tendered by old Turks are known, but they were very rare, isolated and always rebuffed by the Authorities military and civil. These authorities signalled themselves for brutality and greed whereever Armenians were found, even in the Areas outside of the Massacre-zone. So no one who knows something of the Turk and of the Moslem in general will be surprised to learn that the High dignitaries of State and Church were the first to avail themselves of the extraordinary opportunities the established Armenian white slave market were offering.

Real female slave markets were established in all the human – Pardon; Mohamedan – agglomerations where the Armenians were driven through. The price of a young Armenian girl 12, 14 of age, was varying from 3 medjidiehs to 3 t. Pounds, The writer has seen such sales of girls in Damascus but on a very small scale; he came too late. But reports of girls-sales on very large scale were reported to him by americaa ladies engaged in Missionary Work in Beyrouth and in Damascus, by relatives of his established in Aleppo, where it is estimated that several thousand girls were thus sold by a very trustworthy Frenchwomen (Mme. Soulie) established since years in Konia, besides the hundreds of tales he was told by Armenians with whom the writer has been in direct touch.

Nothing can convey to an Occidental mind the horror and shame of these slave markets. The writer has seen himself a grey bearded Mohamedan mustering with the eyes and fingers of an exert a row of such slaves, putting on his glasses, in order to better see feeling his victims one after the other and picking out a young maybe 13 years old child, for 6 medj. explaining his choice in these horrible words: "Kutshuk ama etli" with a smack of his old perverse tongue.

Untold thousands of Armenian young women were sold in this way to Mohamedan harems (Arabs – whom the allies are now padding on the back in the same headless criminal way as the Germans adopted for the Turks/heroes of the day among allies/, are too greedy speculators to leave such a good opportunity of replenishing their harems without profiting by it). But here one must in fairness point out the liberalism of the modern Mohemedan under the civilizing regim of the cultured young Turks. Though the slave market was, in its essence, intended for the benefit of Moham. Only still, even now – Mohamedan were allowed to moderately profit of the bargain and many a young girl has been saved from her cruel fate by a non-mohamedan buying her, so to say for a few medjidieh.

The Mohamedan intellectual leaders, the hodjas and ulemas, the Kadis and Muftis were not the alowest to avail themselves of the bargains of the white slave markets. But very cunnungly they added to the number of their slaves by making converts for which no hard cash was to be paid. These converts were usually young women – a depreciated merchandise on Mohamedan markets – who by beating and sheer brutality were simply pushed into the harems of the learned men who were supposed to instruct them in the high Ethics of Islam.

In fact conversions were carried out on very large scales. True to the order of the Prophet: Yukatilama non yusalamonna "Kill the infidels or convert them by the sword" the Turks forced whole armenian Communities to embrace Islam. With some of the Communities of the Caucasus where the Armenians weremore than half turcised, where their women are veiled like mohametan women, where they have a mere nominal knowledge of the believes and tachings of Christianity these conversions were quite easy. But surprising as it may sound quite a considerable number of highly educated Armenians of Consple and other Coast towns became Mohemedans, One of them, who had been driven out of Consple, whose wealth (amounting to millions) had been confiscated, returned to Consple a converted Mohamedan. In the presence of the writer he explained that he had done it in order to save from utter ruin thousands of houses, knowing that the failing of his firm would have brought ruin of thousand other small firms of Armenians, Greeks and Jews with whom he was connected. This explanation is given for what it is worth, The fact is that as soon as this converted Armenian was reinstated into his wealth he took up his business and kept very strictly to all the engagements of his firm.

Bent on the destruction of the Armenian race tje Turks well knew that in order to succeed they must ruthlessly kill the valid men from boys to gray beards. And for these real butcheries were organized. The usual way was to organize labor batallions of 400 to 600 such Armenians, disarmed, driven without food or water to some out of the way place under the escort of 20 – 25 turkish soldiers and one or two Chaouiches. These were ordered to keep a close watch on the treacherous deserters and instructed to make use of their rifles if mutiny or desertion were forthcoming. A certain twinkle of the eye from the commanding officer to the chaouiches in giving them those orders was enough to make them realize what was expected of them.

Usually after a day or two the military escort would return, drunk from their blood orgies and report that the whole bataillion mutinied or deserted as the case maybe and in self-defence they were compelled to shoot all the Armenians to a man.

The writer has not witnessed any such case but several were reported him by most trustworthy persons, An Ottoman Bank branch director who had to be transferred from his region in Armenia to Jaffa, on account of his being an Armenian, speaking Turkish and dressing like a Turk and travelling as such, came to a place where he found a crowd of blood-mad soldiers who boasted of their just accomplished dee, butchering of more than 400 Armenians. All the details were given him in the most repulsive way. The next day on his road he came across the heap of dead Armenians. On reaching Aleppo said Armenian made a full report of the case to the American consul.

When writer inquired in Consple of German officers if such stories may be true, these officers admitted that they were entirely and absolutely true.

Nor should it be believed that because we hear no more of wholesale Armenian Massacres, those have been completely stopped. The Turks keep on their task with a steadiness worth of a better cause. The writer has witnessed dozens of heart-rendering cases being carried out in a noiseless, soundless way in Consple proper, most of the inhabitants not realizing what was going on. He came across the first one quite by mere chance and once he had the clue he could watch the whole process,

Orderes have been issued that only Consple – born Armenians should be allowed to remain in Consple. With a surprising real the Consple police force carries since months a chase for Armenians. A house to house search is made usually at the small hours of the night,

Hour of their beds, 8, 12 Arnienians, old men and women, young boys and girls half asleep, half clad are driven together and pace noiselessly through the walks of Chichli to the Taxim framed in by two, rarely 3 policemen. When the writer first came across such a dumb, apparently calm squad he did not realize what it meant. A german officer draw his attention to it, and after that for weeks the writer became noctambule and saw dozens of such squads driven to police headquarters where – from never any more is heard of, they disappear without leaving traces. That is oing on for months and months, carried out zealously by the police in dozens of city quarters every night. The writer has recorded stories of "Kapoudschis" and other old Armenians who succeeded in hiding themselves for 5, 6 months but finally discovered by the police blood hounds and carried off to never be heard of any more. It must be added that quite a number of Armenians are working as spies for the Turks what makes it so easy to find their victims. Nor does the police limit her blood chase for the night hours. In broad day light, in public gardens, in large gatherings they pick up their prey. The writer has been witness to one such case which will stay for years in his memory. A well clad, quite distinguished gentleman of about 45 was walking in an isolated corner of the Taxim Garden in Consple, at about 5 p.m. and has a small boy of about 3 with him. Quietly, politely he was approached by a police, asked a few words, ordered to follow, after some bargaining he was allowed to hire a carriage and the man and the child accompained by the police were off for Police headquarters. The distressed look of the poor man with the small boy clinging in his arms is undescribable, and the whole scene was so quickly and noiselessly performed that practically no one besides the writer noticed the fact, Of such a capture one never hears any more, it disappears for evere

It must be tedious to read about such cruelty but one has recorded so many hundreds maybe thousands of such stories so that it is impossible to keep in the proper limits when once asked of one who knows about it. One feels a kind of outburst and physical need to tall a few of the things one has seen or heard of.

And to conclude writer would beg to be allowed to say a few words as to how these massacres have affected the Armenians, how they have affected the whole Turkish Empire and who are really responsible for this unparalleled blood bath.

The affect of the massacres on the Armenian race has been a crushing one, The figures and statistics will never give an approximation of the real numbers of massacred and destroyed lives. But the most interestedly moderate estimate, the German estimate admits of 650.000 killed and lost up to last summer.

What what has been said above of the conditions of those remaining in camps, ete... it can be concluded that we have to reckon with 200.000 to 300.000 more lives lost before a year.

Even in these days of fierce battles such tremendous numbers of innocents killed and destroyed must call out attention. Morally and Economically the Armenian race in Turkey is totally ruined – the few private fortunes which by clean or unclean ways have been spared destruction make no difference. From one of the most thrifty and most industrious elements of the Turkish Empire if not the most thrifty and most industrious – mind it is a Jew who gives this certificate – the Armenian race is now a race of starving down trodden beggars, The purity of its family life destroyed, its manhood killed, its children boys and girls enslaved in the Turkish private homes for vice and dabauchary, that is to what the Armenian race in Turkey has come to.

The knowledge of writer, hundred of girls of 13, 14 are living on prostitution in Consple. Worst than that, they are maintaining their parents on their trade, the only one left them to make aliving. Amd the same surely applies to hundreds of other places.

Writer knows the case of a young Armenian bride in Consple well bred and of an excellent family whose husband, a physical, was killed by the Turks before the eyes of his wife, 3 months after their wedding, For a few months she mourned and kept a dignified attitude in presence of her Turkish tormentors. Little by little she had to sell her furniture, the beautiful carpets, etc... all the souvenirs of her former happy married life. The last time writer was in Consple she was a notorious prostitute having exclusively Turks as her patrons.

Writer taked the liberty to report this case because to him this is not a special, individual case, this ought to be looked upon as the illustration of what is to happen to all the races and all the nations living under the deadening Turkish rule.

It has been often but probably not sufficiently said that the Turk has never been any more than an invader in the Countries he was ruling. The Turk never settled down to anything like real conservative Government. He lived as a camping barbarous invader and as such he treated the countries and the races he conquered for a while.

If this war is really fought in order to free the world, then the poor nations and races under the Turkish despotism, be they Armenians, Greeks, Jews or Arabs must be delivered, other wise their decadence must follow sooner or later just as was sure to come the downfall of the Armenian girl cited above.

The wholesale massacte of the Jews ordered by the Roman General Titus is the only record in History to be paralleled with the wholesale massacre of the Armenians. And now just as then here just like there it was a Government scheme.

The full and entire responsibility of the Turkish Governmen – whatever and whoever it be – in these massacres makes no doubt. The massacres were planned out by the Central Government in Consple end it is only for that reason that it was possible to carry them out on such a large scale, with such simultaneousness, persverance and method.

It may be doubted if at first the Governmeat wished to give a possibility to be looded through and is quite possible that it is only in the heat of the bloody work they have been carried away, uncovered their cards and forgot all elementary measures of decency. But whatever indignant protests the Government pretends to put up now their full participation in, their instigation of the crime is above any shadow of a doubt.

Their subsequent consistent policy of ruining the whole Armenian Community is supplying fresh of their aims: the dismissal of old, indispensable Armenian servants from all public services, the persistent chase after Armenians in in Consple and elswhere, the sbolition of the religious autonomy of the Armenians church, the destitution of the Katholikos[1] (which sounds like the Christian Protectorate say of Tunis for instance disabling the Sherif of Mecca), but which has nevertheless a tremendous bearing on the Armenian Communal life, all points towards a set purose of the Gevernment, It cannot be the purpose of the writer to go into the historical causes of the Turkish outbursts against the Armenians but there can be but little doubt that among other recent reasons the killing of Armenians was a welcome scheme to Envar Pasha, for one, to avenge himself of the undisputed defeat he has earned on the Caucasus. People inade him directly responsible of foolish interference im military matters above his capacities leading tc the disaster of Ardahan. To shift the whole matter on the treacherous Armenians of whom stories of poisoning wholo regiments, misleading through their handsome women whole army-staffs, etc.. were current talk at the time and helped to stirr the holy wrath of the Faithful.

If the full responsability of the Turkish Government in Armenia massacres is above doubt the share of the Germns in it is a debatable question.

The defence made by the Turkish Government in re Armenian Massacres reminds very much of an old Jewish story which was told once at the German Reichstag. Two Jewish women brought their dispute before the old rabbi about a kettle plaintif could not got back from defendent. To which defendent said; first she knew of no such kettle, second she had returned it long ago and third the kettle was not worth speaking being a broken one.

The Turkish Government claims: First there were no such thinks as Armenian massacres. Second the massacres had in every place only a local and unofficial character, no orders hnving been inssued by the Government and third the Government orders were issued only if self-defence and had the approval of their enlightened Ally the Germans.

To which the innocent Germans retort that they have no share whatever in the scheme and they were mere horrified powerless lookers on.

Officiously the Germans put the whole blame of Armenian massacres on the Turkish government and want to shake from themselves any parcel of participation or responsibility in the Crime. A good deal of propaganda work has been in this respect, the most important piece of work to the knowledge of the writer, being the painstaking document full of American and German statements privately printed and circulated as strictly Confidential by Dr. Lepsius, head of the German Missionary works. It may be granted that Dr. Lepsius is fairly sincere in his indignation to see malevolent people charging the Germans with participation in the massacres of 650.000 Christians by the hands of the Heathen. He brings good proof of the Massacres being planned quite carefully by the Central Government in Consple. He goes even further and discloses that the Armenian massacres were only a "coup d'essai" (though a "coup de maitre") and were the so called civilized World to accept it with not too loud displeasure the Greeks, the other Christians and the Jews would have followed.

But just like all the most honest and sincere German productions Dr. Lepsius' work has to be taken cum grano salis. He fully admits the Turkish cruelty, the Turkish deep laid plot, he supplements proof and witnesses to the facts, that far we may follow him. His whitewashing of the German Governmerit may be argued. It would probably be unfair to suspect Dr. Lapsius having written his apologia by order, but like all law-adiding Germans he submitted his apologia to the Authorities, Dr. Bethmann-Hollweg has allovied one of his letters to be published in the "Intropduction", a letter in which he assures of doing "in the future" his christian duty by straining all means to prevent a repetition of the disgraceful massacres, etc... Therefore the document takes a holy, official character which makes it dubious. If the German Government had reasons to approve (without aproving) of massacres they have probably not found fit to take Dr. Lepsius into their Confidence.

The writer has spoken to dozens of German Officers, physicians, etc... who have been ia the thick of the massacres and that is what he found out. All and every German was individually horrified at what he has witnessed. Trained with a supersitious respect of property, order, etc... a German cannot be expected to look in cold blood placidly at the robbery, massacres, etc... To say therefore that the Germans were leading the massacres, or even taking directly a hand in them, as it has often been repeated, is doing them a wrong or at least advancing things which can never be prooved whereas the Germans will always be able to prove by testimonials, diaries, protocoles, etc.. that in each their soul revolted.

But slaves to discipline, having given every individual thought or movement the Germans who wereordered to duty in the massacre-area, saw the outrage, felt indignant, but made no move to stop it.[2] That is certainly from a higher moral ground participation evea if not direct.

Officially the German Government has not entirely repudiated the recognition at least of the cruel necessity of the massacres. Official inquiries have been made no smaller man than Basserman (see the German magsin Nord and Sud), who may be meaningless as an individual, but whose words carry weight as leader of the National Liberals, have openly and unmistakenly given the Turkish Government absolution for what they done invoquing of course the higher Raison d'Etat. So that German official approval has not been entirely witheled the Turks.

Now one more thing has to be considered. For some time already the Germans realized that if for political reasons it may have been wise to try the colonization of the kilimandjaro or arid, relatively unfertile East Africa and other colonies, which are not a white-man's country, it was on the other hand a crime to leave Anatolia, a thinly people white-man's Country blessed by favorable geographical, climatical, agricultural and mineral conditions. Moltke, more than 75 years ago pointed to that Country as the future colonization ground of the Germans, more and more Germans have pointed out this fact more recently.

Looking at it from this light would any one who knews something of Germans and the long and something crooked way they can go for the realization of their high ambitions which are in fact nothing less than divine missions, would any such man hesitate to say that wiping out of those countries the thriftiest element there was could not have displeased, not even hurt German politics? And would not the Germans themselves when better fed and in more boisterous spirits than to-day said: A crime? That is arguable, but good, far sighted German Real politic, is it not?

The Armenian massacres are the careful planned act of the Turks and the Germans will oerainly be made for ever to share the odium of this act.

Notes

1. The destitution of the Katholikos and the nomination by the Turks of a head of the Armenian Church in Turkey at Jerusalem happened after the writer has severed his connections with the sources of information he had in the country and he is lacking therefore internal information on the matter. But he would be but little surprised to learn that Djemal Pasha has a hand in the sheme. If this supposition were true Dj.P. would have expected a double stroke from this blow; beheading the Armenian Church and creating in Palestine a strong colony of 30, 40.000 thrifty Arm. people with the head of their church amongst them, the beat way in Dj.P.'s mind to oppose

the undesired spread of the Jewish movement in Palestine, to compete which the Turks are no match.

2. The German mentality is always pussling. The Armenian question was a safe question to tackle with official Germans and the writer failed on no occasion to start on it, so he had opportunity to have the minds of hundred stories proving the cruelty of the Turks, the useless and shameless barbary, and so on. But every clean minded man then would shrink at the idea of making any profit from a situation like that the Armenians were in. Not so the Germans. They made bargains. It would be unfair to say they robbed the Armenians, but these poor souls being compelled to consideration – the Germans took advantage of conditions and bought carpets, jewellery, trinkets at a tenth part of their real value. Germany will be the richest country in carpets.

Appendix B

The Armenian Question from the Zionist point of View.

In the midst of the present world upheaval which has divided humanity into two huge armed camps, one consoling feature which is perhaps a harbinger of those better times that will see the true league of nations established is offered by the *entente* which is gradually being shaped between the three old nations of the Middle East : the Armenians the Arabs, and the Jews. to each of them the world owes a debt of gratitude and sympathy ; gratitude for the notable contributions they have made towards the advancement of civilisation, and sympathy for their sufferings during centuries of servitude or exile. At present everything seems to presage that very soon they will arise to a new life and be reinstated in their respective national inheritances ; and it is especially significant that this should happen at the precise moment when the political and social ideals of the whole world are in the melting pot and are being re-crystallised into new and juster forms. The thinking democracies of the Old and New World now understand that whereas it is the militaristic state-organisation of the Germanic Powers that is directly responsible for the outbreak of this war yet that was only the spark which set fire to the powder magazine. The evil consisted of the burning fires of discontent and resentment against age-long injustice and oppression which had become unbearable by the small nationalities whose freedom of development was threatened or even forcibly held down by powerful miltiary States. It is thus not out of pure abstract idealism that most of the great peoples have espoused the cause of small and oppressed nationalities. No, the very magnitude of the war, with all the sufferings it is inflicting on an unprecedented scale on friend, foe and neutral alike, has led the better part of humanity to pledge all its resources to the securing of a peace that will remove, for some generations at least any causes of new armed conflicts. How far that result will be achieved we shall be able to gauge by the amount of National justice which the Powers assembled in the future Peace Conference will succeed in meting out to the Armenian, the Arab and the Jewish nations.

We Zionists look upon the fate of the Armenian people with a deep and sincere sympathy ; we do so as men as Jews and as Zionists. As men our motto is *"Homo sum ; humani nihil a me alienum puto."* As Jews our exile from our ancestral home and our centuries of suffering in all parts of the globe have made us, I would fain say specialists in martyrdom ; out humanitarian feelings have been refined to an incomparable degree, so much so that the sufferings of other people—even alien to us in blood and remote from us in distance—cannot but strike the deeper chords of our soul and weave between us and our fellow-sufferers that deep bond of sympathy which one might call the solidarity of sorrow. And among all those who suffer around us, is there is people whose record of martyrdom is more akin to ours than that of the Armenians? As Zionists we have a peculiar question of principle. Zionism being in its essence nothing else than the Jewish expression of the demand for National justice, it is natural and logical for us to be deeply interested in the struggle for emancipation of any other living nation. And secondly, believing as we do with the great democracies of the world that, as President Wilson said in his speech of February 11th last "this war had its roots in the disregard of the rights of small nations and nationalities which lacked the union and the force to make good their claim to determine their own allegiance and their own forms of political life." We are convinced that the future peace and happiness of that part of the world—the Middle East—of which our own national homeland, Palestine, is only a section, will be best assured when "all well-defined national aspirations shall be accorded the utmost satisfaction that can be accorded them without introducing new or perpetuating old elements of discord and antagonism that would be likely in time to break the peace." In our opinion a free and happy Armenia, a free and happy Arabia, and a free and happy Jewish Palestine, are the three pillars on which will rest the future peace and welfare of the Middle East.

S. TOLKOWSKY
Ararat, April 1918

Index

review, analysis and criticism
of *The Forty Days of Musa
Dagh,* 295-9, 303-305
Wermer, 225
Weyl, M., 245
While Six Million Died, 371
Wiesel, Elie, 19
Wilhelm, Kaiser, 90, 106
Wilson, Woodrow, 46, 47, 224, 235,
245, 341, 390
With Tel Aviv in Exile, 70
With the Turks in Palestine, 174-175
Wolf, Lucien, 115, 117, 118
Woolley, Leonard, 162, 166
World War I, 40, 41, 45, 352, 353, 370
    Armenian loyalties, 40-41
    British interests, 222-223,
    224, 229-231, 240, 241, 260-
    261
    French interests, 223-224,
    229-232, 239, 240, 241, 260-
    261
    Jewish loyalties, 60, 70, 169-
    170, 174, 177, 330
    settlement plans, 222-224,
    233, 239, 243-246, 257
World War II, 351, 352
World Zionist Organization, 108
    Democratic Faction, 108, 110
Wyman, David, 371-372

Yad Vashem, 50, 353, 354, 355, 371
Yaffe, Hillel Dr., 85
Yavnieli, Shmuel, 333
Yerevan, 33, 46, 49
Yezidis, 336-337
    aiding Armenians, 337
    stereotypes, 336
Yiddishe Rundschau, 141
Yishuv, 1, 5, 12, 13, 25, 59-83, 84, 85,
86-88, 101, 126, 131, 159, 162, 163,
164, 168, 176, 313, 314, 320, 321,
323, 334, 335, 340, 341, 342, 370,
371
    Armenian Genocide, 66-73,
    75, 176, 321, 334
    demography, 59, 65
    deportations, 73-83
    economy, 59, 61-62
    expulsion, 64
    history, 59-64

    "Ottomanization," 63, 322,
    331
    social institutions, 60
    World War I, 62-63
Yoman Hashavua, 365
Young Turks, 8, 17, 18, 40, 48, 51, 52,
53, 122, 123, 124, 132, 133, 136,
141, 143, 207, 255, 321, 327, 328,
341, 343, 370, 377
    death sentences *in absentia,*
    52
Young Workers' Movement, 137
Yugoslavia, 3

Zabon, Yair, 360, 362, 363
Zadarbaum, Alexander Halevi, 144
Zangwill, Israel, 27, 226, 370
Zapf, Mrs., 339
Zeligman, R., 296
Zerubavel, Yaakov, 138, 273, 138, 273,
332, 323
Zichron Yaakov, 65, 85, 87, 88, 92, 159,
175, 176, 178, 179, 198, 375
Zionism, 1, 5, 8, 10-12, 24-8, 46, 59-
60, 64-83, 84-86, 91, 92, 101, 106,
108, 110, 112, 114, 119, 120, 139,
141, 159, 171, 174, 193, 213n, 216,
218, 220, 221, 222, 225, 226, 228,
231, 234, 239, 240, 241, 242, 247,
249, 251, 256, 257, 259, 261, 321,
322, 323, 325, 329, 330, 340-341,
343, 344, 345, 351, 369, 370, 371
    Armenian Genocide and, 9-
    12, 373
    Armenian Question and, 389-
    390
    Armenians, criticism of, 144-
    147
    Balfour Declaration and, 225-
    226, 250-251
    credit and finance sources, 61
    France and, 241
    Mark Sykes, impact of loss of,
    216
    perspectives on the Armenian
    genocide, 9-12, 24-8, 67-83,
    101-152
    Turkey and Germany, support
    for, 145, 160, 174, 193, 195,
    221, 324, 328, 330-331, 340, 370
    Young Turks and, 140-141